Es...ion
fro...Press

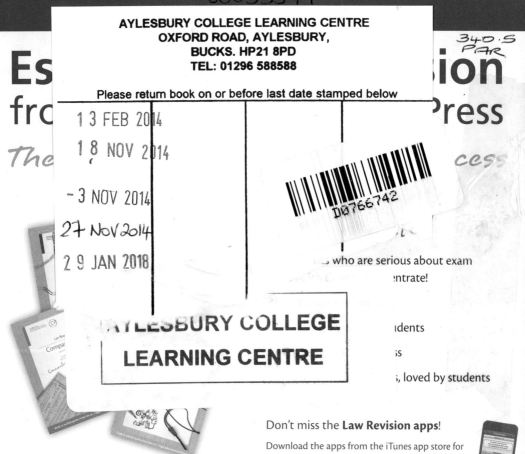

D0766742

...s who are serious about exam
...ntrate!

...dents

...ss

..., loved by **students**

QUESTIONS & ANSWERS

Keeping you afloat through your exams.

- ✓ Typical exam questions
- ✓ Suggested answers
- ✓ Advice on exam technique and
  making your answer stand out

'Nothing else compares to such reliable study-aids
and revision guides.'

Heather Walkden, law student

'Comprehensive, functional, stylishly innovative;
superior to any of its rivals.'

Michael O'Sullivan, law lecturer

Don't miss the **Law Revision apps**!

Download the apps from the iTunes app store for
your iPad, iPhone, or iPod touch. Hundreds of
multiple choice questions with feedback, helping
you to study, learn and revise, anytime, anywhere.

For the full list of revision titles and additional resources visit: www.oxfordtextbooks.co.uk/orc/lawrevision/

Study & revision guides from the no. 1 legal education publisher

INTRODUCTION TO THE ENGLISH LEGAL SYSTEM

2013–2014

MARTIN PARTINGTON

OXFORD
UNIVERSITY PRESS

OXFORD

UNIVERSITY PRESS

Great Clarendon Street, Oxford, OX2 6DP,
United Kingdom

Oxford University Press is a department of the University of Oxford.
It furthers the University's objective of excellence in research, scholarship,
and education by publishing worldwide. Oxford is a registered trade mark of
Oxford University Press in the UK and in certain other countries

© Martin Partington 2013

The moral rights of the author have been asserted

Fifth edition copyright 2010
Sixth edition copyright 2011
Seventh edition copyright 2012

Impression: 1

Public sector information reproduced under Open Government Licence v1.0
(http://www.nationalarchives.gov.uk/doc/open-government-licence/open-government-licence.htm)

Crown Copyright material reproduced with the permission of the
Controller, HMSO (under the terms of the Click Use licence)

British Library Cataloguing in Publication Data
Data available

ISBN 978–0–19–967053–6

Printed in Great Britain by
Ashford Colour Press Ltd, Gosport, Hampshire

QR Code images are used throughout this book. QR Code is a registered trademark
of DENSO WAVE INCORPORATED. You can scan the codes with your
mobile device to launch the relevant webpage. If your mobile device does not have a
QR Code reader try this website for advice: www.mobile-barcodes.com/qr-code-software/.

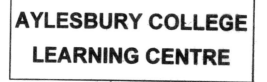

About the author

Martin Partington is now Emeritus Professor of Law and Senior Research Fellow at the University of Bristol.

For over 45 years, he has been a law teacher, researcher and writer on a wide variety of legal subjects (including administrative justice, legal education, and the English legal system), a (part-time) legal practitioner, legal policy adviser, and a law reformer. He taught at the Universities of Bristol, Warwick, the London School of Economics, and Brunel University.

He was associated with a wide range of bodies and institutions including, at different stages in his career, and for different lengths of time: the Hillfields Advice Centre in Coventry; the Legal Action Group; the Training Committee of the Institute of Housing; the Management Committees of Citizens' Advice Bureaux in Coventry, Paddington, and Uxbridge; the Education Committee of the Law Society; the Lord Chancellor's Advisory Committee on Legal Aid; the Independent Tribunal Service for Social Security Appeal Tribunals; the Judicial Studies Board (both the main Board and its Tribunals Committee); the Council on Tribunals; the Civil Justice Council (and its sub-committee on Alternative Dispute Resolution); the Committee of Heads of University Law Schools; the Socio-Legal Studies Association; and the Socio-Legal Research Users' Forum.

For a number of years he was Training Adviser to the then President of Social Security Appeal Tribunals and also sat as a part-time Social Security Tribunals Chairman.

He acted as an expert adviser to the Council of Europe, examining Alternatives to Litigation in Disputes between the Individual and the State. In May 2000, he was appointed expert consultee to the Review of Tribunals, set up by the Lord Chancellor and chaired by Sir Andrew Leggatt. He was a member of the Gaymer Review of Industrial Tribunals, 2002.

From 2001 to 2005, he was a Law Commissioner for England and Wales; he was retained as a Special Consultant to the Commission from 2006 to 2008.

In 2002 he was appointed CBE; in 2006 he was elected as a Bencher of Middle Temple; in 2008 he was appointed QC (Hon).

He is currently an academic adviser to the University of Law; a member of the Executive Board of JUSTICE; and chair of the Board of The Dispute Service, a company under contract with government to provide tenancy deposit protection.

This book draws on his life-time of experience in the law, though it goes without saying that he writes in a personal capacity only.

Preface to the 2013–2014 edition

When I was first asked to write this book, my instructions were that it should: be genuinely introductory; be not too long; be relatively uncluttered by footnotes; be accessible to the more general reader; and, at the same time, offer an approach to thinking about the English legal system and its place in society not found elsewhere. With these requirements in mind, this book has been written especially for those coming new to the study of law. I also hope that others, keen to look behind the magical veil that all too often shrouds the legal system and its actors in mystery, will find the book of interest. It is, in short, intended for all those interested in the phenomenon of law and the important role it plays in the ordering of our society but without any detailed knowledge of it.

Although only a year since I completed the 2012–2013 edition of this book, the pace of change in the legal system has continued unabated. The Coalition government's focus on cuts in public expenditure is having a significant impact on the English legal system. To reflect those changes and to flag up changes in contemplation, I have revised and updated the whole text. Among the most significant changes that may be noted here are:

- uncertainty about the size of the House of Commons and related changes to electoral boundaries (*Chapter 3*);
- abandonment of proposals for reform of the House of Lords (*Chapter 3*);
- debate on the use of referendums in the law-making process (*Chapter 3*);
- latest developments to promote diversity in the judiciary (*Chapters 4 and 9*);
- elections of Police and Crime Commissioners (*Chapters 4 and 5*);
- changes in sentencing policy (*Chapter 5*);
- moves to charge fees to appear before Tribunals (*Chapter 6*);
- introduction of major changes to the family justice system (*Chapter 7*);
- developments in the use of mediation (*Chapter 8*);
- details of proposals for reform of the county court (*Chapter 8*);
- developments in the work of the Legal Services Board in the regulation of the legal professions and others who provide legal services (*Chapter 9*); and
- further proposals for the reform of the costs of litigation (*Chapter 10*).

The aims of the book remain the same—to provide all those coming new to the study of law, whether at A-level, degree level, or postgraduate conversion level, with an overview of the context within which law is made and practised in England and Wales; to encourage readers to start to think more broadly about the role that law plays in society; to provide a text that is as approachable as possible; and, more generally, to create a resource for those teaching citizenship in schools, which can inform and encourage the development of this very significant part of the national curriculum.

The importance of better public understanding of law and legal institutions can hardly be overstated. I hope this book will make a contribution to this better understanding.

The increasing amount of material available on the internet is reflected in the large number of websites listed (with description) in the Online Resource Centre (ORC). Information about new websites that you find interesting but that are not mentioned in the text may be fed back to me through the ORC or as comments on my blog (www.martinpartington.com). Similarly, please let me know of links that no longer work. I have continued to develop Spotlight on the Justice System—my personal blog on new developments in the English legal system, which is also available via the ORC. This now contains a number of podcast interviews with key figures in the English legal system.

I remain grateful to successive generations of students at Bristol, and before then Brunel, to whom I offered instruction in English Legal System and English Legal Methods for their critical responses to what I had to say. I was particularly fortunate that I was able to deliver early versions of the original text as introductory lectures to first year students at the University of Bristol; and to discuss them in an informal 'reading group'. I am also very grateful to current students at Bristol, Exeter, Kent, Warwick, and York to whom I have been able to talk about the book.

At Oxford University Press, my new editor Joanna Williams has ably continued the OUP tradition of tact and courtesy. I thank her and others involved in the production of this book. I would also like to thank Nick Wehmeier for all his work on the Online Resource Centre and the blog.

I am most grateful to the anonymous referees who, as part of OUP procedures, commented on the strengths and weaknesses of the 2012–2013 edition. They often provided me with conflicting advice. Thus, while I may not have fully incorporated their comments, I can assure all those who made comments that they all provoked thought and reflection, and indeed encouragement. I was particularly pleased with the responses from the student panel that OUP now consults. I remain responsible for all errors and omissions.

The book is dedicated to my children Adam and Hannah—my original 'target readership'—and above all to Daphne for her insistence that I retain a sense of balance in my life.

Bristol, 12 November 2012

Guide to the Online Resource Centre

www.oxfordtextbooks.oc.uk/orc/partington13_14/

The Online Resource Centre that accompanies this book provides students and lecturers with ready-to-use teaching and learning materials. These resources are free of charge and are designed to maximize your learning experience.

....

Student resources
....

Author blog with podcasts

Please see overleaf for full details on the author blog.

Multiple-choice questions

The best way to reinforce your understanding of the English legal system is through frequent and cumulative revision. As such, a bank of self-marking multiple-choice questions is provided for each chapter of the text. These include instant feedback on your answers and cross-references to the textbook.

Questions for reflection and discussion

Questions are included for each chapter to test your understanding of the topics covered, and also to help you reflect on the key challenges and debates.

Flashcard glossary

A series of interactive flashcards containing key terms and concepts are provided to test your understanding of legal terminology.

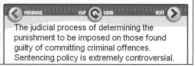

Crosswords

Key legal definitions are presented in an interactive crossword format, allowing you to test your knowledge.

Weblinks

A selection of annotated weblinks allow you to easily research topics of particular interest.

Lecturer resources

Password protected to ensure only lecturers adopting the book can access these resources. Registering is easy: click on the 'Lecturer Resources' on the Online Resource Centre, complete a simple registration form which allows you to choose your own password, and access will be granted within 72 hours (subject to verification).

Test bank

A fully customizable resource containing ready-made assessments to test your students' understanding of key concepts as they progress through the course. The test bank contains over 150 questions with full answers and feedback linked back to the textbook. It offers versatile testing tailored to the contents of each chapter and can be downloaded into virtual learning environments (VLEs).

Customizable PowerPoint® presentations

For each chapter there is a corresponding lecture presentation provided in PowerPoint®. Each presentation lists the main points for discussion and is easily downloaded for customization and use in lectures and seminars.

Scan here!
Scan here with your mobile device to go directly to the Online Resource Centre homepage.

Author blog with podcasts

www.martinpartington.com

Martin Partington's regularly updated blog, which accompanies this book, is intended to help you keep up to date with key developments in the law.

The blog has a number of aims:-

- It provides easy access to important developments in law and on-going changes in legal policy.
- It offers the author's views and ideas on topical debates in the English legal system and highlights issues and themes other media may not have picked up.
- It includes interesting and engaging podcasts, which capture the author's discussions with leading lawyers on the more controversial issues affecting the English legal system.
- And, most importantly, it invites you to post your thoughts, communicating with the author directly. We look forward to hearing from you!

Scan here!
Scan here with your mobile device to go directly to Martin Partington's blog.

Outline contents

Contents

CONCLUSION

List of boxes and diagrams

Table of cases

Tables of legislation

Statutory Instruments

EU Legislation

INTRODUCTION

1

Aims, themes, and structure

Aims

This book provides an introductory account of the English legal system, how it has developed in recent years, and how it may develop in future. I want readers to think about the legal system and to question the extent to which it is fit for purpose. I also want readers to see how the legal system relates to some of the most difficult issues facing the modern world. For example, how should the government's need to protect civil liberties be balanced with its need to reduce the risks associated with terrorism?

The book is primarily about the *English* legal system (which includes for most practical purposes the legal system in Wales). There is a quite different system in Scotland and a rather different system in Northern Ireland. There are times when it is not sensible to refer just to 'England'—thus the phrases 'Great Britain' or 'United Kingdom' are used where they seem more appropriate. Nonetheless, the focus of the book is on the English legal system.

This does not mean that the book is exclusively about institutions located in England and Wales. The English legal system is subject to important external factors, in particular the law and institutions of the European Union and Council of Europe.

Many who study law in England come from other countries. I hope readers from overseas can both learn from the issues discussed here, and relate the questions raised to the situation in their home countries. Many come from other common law countries—whose legal systems are based on the principles of the English legal system, in particular that judges have power to make law; others come from civil law countries, whose legal systems are founded on principles of law and the codification of law developed in Roman times.[1] Are the legal systems with which they may be more familiar fitted to their purpose? Are there lessons to be learned from the English experience? And, turning these questions around, what should the English be learning from experience elsewhere?

---

[1] The distinction between common law systems and civil law systems is not discussed in this book; a helpful introduction can be found in Merryman, J. H., *The Civil Law Tradition: An Introduction to the Legal Systems of Europe and Latin America* (3rd edn, Stanford, CA, Stanford University Press, 2007).

Themes

Although an introductory book, it seeks to address themes inadequately considered in other books with the same or similar titles:

- First, many current accounts of the English legal system are rather 'practitioner-oriented'; they focus primarily on those parts of the system in which professionally qualified lawyers practise law. This book adopts a more holistic approach, designed to introduce the reader to activities and functions often ignored elsewhere. This approach is adopted, not just from a desire to be different, but also to ensure that students of law start to appreciate the enormous variety of contexts in which the legal knowledge and skills they are setting out to acquire can be used. Students should be encouraged to think about law and legal practice beyond the boundaries of the legal profession. It should also benefit students who are studying law for its own inherent interest, without necessarily intending to become practising lawyers.

- Secondly, other introductory accounts are somewhat descriptive and 'static' in nature, providing a snapshot of the system at the moment of writing. As already suggested, the English legal system is considerably more dynamic and more responsive to change than is often realized. A recurring theme is on change and the forces that have shaped and are shaping the English legal system. At the same time, questions are raised about the extent to which particular changes are desirable or should be resisted.

- Thirdly, the English legal system is often portrayed as something distinct from the British system of government. Indeed, one of the important claims made for law and its practice is that it is 'independent' of government. Yet the government of the country is based in law; the institutions of law derive their power and authority from the system of government. Understanding the constitutional function of the English legal system and the relationship of the legal system to other branches of government is therefore another theme underpinning the discussion in this work.

- Lastly, the assertion is often made that 'we have the best system of justice in the world'. It may be a good system, indeed a very good system. But this conclusion should be arrived at on the basis of evidence, not mere assertion. This book is intended to provide a basis for thinking critically about the institutions and practices of the law and contemplating change where inadequacy or inefficiency is demonstrated to exist.

Structure

Having set out the themes that underpin the book, the structure of the book is as follows.

Titled *Law, Society, and Authority*, *Part I* contains two chapters that raise fundamental issues about the social functions of law and the legitimacy of law. It is impossible to study law without asking: what is the purpose of law? What impact does law have on society? Thus *Chapter 2* considers what functions law plays in the way in which society is ordered, exposing the different and conflicting functions inherent in the phrase 'law and order'. Having argued that law makes an important contribution to the ordering of society, *Chapter 3* goes on to consider how law is made, who makes it, and whence they get the authority for making it and imposing it on society. The role of Parliament, the senior courts and key European institutions are discussed.

Part II considers the institutional framework within which law is developed and practised. *Chapter 4* opens with an account of the role of government in shaping the institutions and practice of law. Primary attention is paid to the Ministry of Justice, but the role of other government departments is also considered. *Chapters 5 to 8* look in turn at the four legal systems which, for the purpose of this book, make up the English legal system. The simple distinction made in most English legal system books between criminal and civil justice is here replaced by a more nuanced delineation of four separately identifiable justice systems: criminal justice, administrative justice, family justice, and civil and commercial justice. In each chapter, a 'holistic' approach is adopted. Thus there is consideration not only of the work of the formal legal institutions such as courts, but also the informal or other processes that do not catch the public eye (and, indeed, which are often not properly understood by professional lawyers) but which form an essential part of the framework of the English legal system when seen in the round.

Part III looks at the delivery and funding of legal services. *Chapter 9* considers the role both of those professionally qualified to practise law and of other groups who provide legal services but who are not formally qualified as solicitors and barristers. It also considers the adjudicators and other dispute resolvers who play a very significant role in the working of the legal systems. And it reflects on the contribution made by law teachers, both those working in universities as well as others working in private colleges and other contexts in the formation of the legal professional. *Chapter 10* reflects on how legal services are (and should be) paid for, and considers in particular the enormous changes being made to the funding of civil litigation following changes to the system of legal aid.

Lastly, a short concluding chapter, *Chapter 11*, asks whether the English legal system is in fact fit for the purposes it is required to perform. Is the English legal system 'the best in the world' in need of little or no change? Or is the system simply not delivering what is required of it, and thus in need of fundamental change? If changes are needed, what are they? What are the forces likely to render change difficult, if not impossible?

Questions

Use the self-test questions on the Online Resource Centre to test your understanding of the topics covered in this chapter and receive tailored feedback:

www.oxfordtextbooks.co.uk/orc/partington13_14/

Weblinks

Check the Online Resource Centre for a selection of annotated weblinks allowing you to easily research topics of particular interest:

www.oxfordtextbooks.co.uk/orc/partington13_14/

Blog items

 See www.martinpartington.com (access via the Online Resource Centre)

Includes: comments on public legal education; the media treatment of legal issues; the televising of courts; court dress; young people and the legal system.

Further reading

BANKOWSKI, Z., and MUNGHAM, G., *Images of Law* (London, Routledge and Kegan Paul, 1976)

COWNIE, F., BRADNEY, A., and BURTON, M., *English Legal System in Context* (5th edn, Oxford, Oxford University Press, 2010) (6th edn forthcoming 2013)

ELLIOTT, C., and QUINN, F., *English Legal System* (13th edn, London, Longman 2012)

GILLESPIE, A., *The English Legal System* (3rd revised edn, Oxford, Oxford University Press, 2011)

GREENFIELD, S., OSBORN, G., and ROBSON, P., *Film and the Law: The Cinema of Justice* (2nd edn, Oxford, Hart Publishing, 2010)

JACONELLI, J., *Open Justice: A Critique of the Public Trial* (Oxford, Oxford University Press, 2002)

ZANDER, M., *A Matter of Justice: The Legal System in Ferment* (London, Tauris, 1988)

—— *Cases and Materials on the English Legal System* (10th edn, Cambridge, Cambridge University Press, 2007)

—— *The State of Justice* (London, Sweet & Maxwell, 2000)

PART I

LAW, SOCIETY, AND AUTHORITY

2

Law and society: the purposes and functions of law

Introduction: understanding the role of law in society

A primary aim of this book is to enable readers to understand the institutional framework within which rules of law are made and used. This book does not analyse specific rules of law, for example, 'What is the legal definition of murder?' or 'When is a contract legally binding?'. Nonetheless, it is impossible to make any sense of the institutional framework without having some idea of the *social purposes* or *social functions* of law. This chapter aims to get the reader to start thinking about these issues.

In so doing, it is helpful to distinguish between the macro and the micro functions of law. Macro functions of law are those relating to the *general* role law plays in the running and ordering of society. Micro functions—which derive from those macro functions—relate to more *specific* uses to which law is put. The distinction becomes clearer as the discussion proceeds.

Macro functions of law: law and orders

If one asks, 'What is the role of law in society?', a common response would be 'to maintain order'. Much public debate and political rhetoric links law and order. There are two problems with this response.

First, it is extremely ambiguous. There is no single concept of order, but rather a variety of orders in relation to which law may play a role. These include:

- public order;
- political order;
- social order;
- economic order;
- international order; and
- moral order.

Secondly, the relationship between law and each of these types of order is extremely complex. The ability of law to shape these different orders is not unconstrained, but is shaped by wider political and social forces. The law is not a neutral force which contributes to the organization of society, but is otherwise detached from that society. The relationship between law and orders in any given society cannot be understood without an understanding of the political, social, and economic ideologies that underpin that society. The role law plays in one society differs sharply from that which it plays in another.

The ambiguities surrounding the concept of order, and the complexity of the relationship between law and orders, are considered further in the following paragraphs.

Law and public order

Many argue that a—possibly the—primary function of law is the *preservation of public order*. It was certainly a cry widely heard at the time of the riots in London and other cities in summer 2011. But maintaining public order is not exclusively a task for law; many other factors such as pressure from family or friends or work colleagues play an important part. Nonetheless, the fact that law sets the boundaries of acceptable behaviour and prescribes sanctions for breaches of those boundaries (which is in essence the function of criminal law) makes a significant contribution to preserving public order.

The preservation of public order, however, immediately raises another but not necessarily consistent function for law: the *protection of civil liberties and human rights*. The ability of people to argue freely about their beliefs is an important aspect of life in a democratic society. Limits may need to be set to the freedom of individuals to advance unpopular views, for example, those that are obscene or defamatory or that incite racial or religious hatred. Nevertheless, within those limits, freedoms of speech and thought must be protected by law.

Until recently, the British had no formal statement of human rights, comparable to the Bill of Rights enshrined in the Constitution of the United States. Rather, they relied on long-standing principles of law allowing people to indicate dissent, for example, by peaceful demonstrations or marches. Since October 2000, when the Human Rights Act 1998 came into effect, a more formal code of human rights has applied in the United Kingdom. Protection of human rights and civil liberties can therefore be identified as another function of law.

But this function is not always consistent with the preservation of public order. There are occasions when preservation of public order results in restrictions on civil liberties. Conversely, the protection of civil liberties can on occasion limit the ability of public authorities to control public order. The tension between the two is illustrated in the responses to the occupation of land around St Paul's Cathedral in London in autumn 2011.

In highly repressive societies, of which there are a number in the modern world, the use of law to legitimize the preservation of public order may become so dominant that civil liberties and other fundamental freedoms are effectively destroyed. In more tolerant societies where dissent is permitted, there must be a balance. There is always sharp debate about the extent to which law's function is to preserve public order, as opposed to protecting other rights and freedoms. Pressure groups, such as *Liberty* and *Justice*, which seek to defend human rights and civil liberty, may not always persuade governments to change their minds on proposals relating to the development of law. But their ability to challenge and criticize government is fundamental in a democratic system based on the rule of law.

The Protection of Freedoms Act 2012 provides an illustration of the difficulties in getting the balance right between control and liberty (*see Box 2.1*). Two current bills, one before Parliament—the Justice and Security Bill—the other in draft—the Draft Communications Data Bill, provide yet further illustrations of this challenge; both measures are strongly defended by the government but are equally strongly attacked by civil liberty organisations.[1] The law's function in relation to the maintenance of public order is, thus, highly contingent upon the nature of the society in which law operates.

Box 2.1   Reform in progress

Protection of Freedoms Act 2012

This Act of Parliament deals with a somewhat miscellaneous series of matters, but ones which had caused political controversy, where it was argued (and the Coalition government had accepted) that the balance between the rights of the individual and the interests of the state was not right. (It had, indeed, been preceded by the Identity Documents Act 2010, which abolished measures relating to the introduction of iden-tity cards, introduced by the previous Labour administration.) Among the measures included in the 2012 Act are:

• reducing the maximum period of pre-charge detention (without trial) for terrorist suspects to 14 days;
• deleting the DNA samples and fingerprints of more than one million people from police databases;
• abolishing a law to permit trials without juries in serious fraud cases;
• ending the fingerprinting of children in schools without parental consent; and
• introducing a code of practice for CCTV and Automatic Number Plate Recognition systems.

For more detail of these and other provisions, go to <www.homeoffice.gov.uk/media-centre/news/protection-of-freedoms> and follow the links.

---

[1] These are not discussed in detail here, but I have some comments on both measures in my blog, www.martinpartington.com.

Law and political order

Another primary function of law is to underpin the political order of the country—the constitutional function of law. In this context, the United Kingdom is an oddity. It is one of a very few countries that does not have a written constitution. Many important practices within the British Constitution derive from unwritten 'conventions', rather than from written rules of law (*see Box 3.2*) Some crucial aspects about the way the system of government is organized in the United Kingdom fall outside the scope of law altogether, based more in political theory than in legal rules. In view of this, some may think that support for constitutional arrangements should not be regarded as one of the macro functions of law.

Nevertheless, despite the lack of a written constitution, it is right to include this topic here. It emphasizes the fact that, although the United Kingdom has no written constitution, a great deal of fundamental law regulates the way in which its political system operates. The former Labour government was engaged in a programme of constitutional reform, which included the creation of the Supreme Court and reform of the House of Lords; the current Coalition government has introduced fixed-term Parliaments and held a referendum on voting reform. (Proposals to reform the House of Lords have been shelved.) Many of the UK's constitutional arrangements are enshrined in law.

To give some examples:

- British membership of the European Union, recognized in such fundamental statutes as the European Communities Act 1972 and as amended to take account of changes to the European Treaties, has, among other things, set limits to the legislative power—the sovereignty—of the British Parliament.

- The Scotland Act 1998 and the Wales Act 1998 (supplemented by the Government of Wales Act 2006) both provide for devolution of powers from the government in London to, respectively, the Scottish Parliament and the Welsh Assembly. This provides a new legal framework for the regulation of the relationship between the government in London, and governments in Edinburgh and Cardiff.

- The Human Rights Act 1998 has significantly affected the practice of government. Legislation must be compliant with the provisions of the European Convention on Human Rights, which are incorporated in that Act.

- Following the passing of the Freedom of Information Act 2000, which came into effect in 2005, there is new law relating to official secrecy and freedom of information that determines the extent to which governments can operate openly or in secret.

- Many other examples can be given: the detailed law relating to the running of elections; or the law regulating the relationship between central and local government.

Given this rapidly growing body of law, many influential commentators now argue that the British should take the last step and adopt a written constitution, which would codify into a single legislative measure all these constitutional provisions.

Law and social order

Law also impacts upon a country's 'social order'. Defining the nature of social order is extremely complex; there are wide differences of opinion. However, it is clear that in the United Kingdom, as in many other countries in the Western democratic tradition, there are substantial differences between individuals. These may arise from differences of ability, or differences of income or wealth, or differences of birth or class. These differences are reflected in many rules of law, in particular those that define concepts of property and contract. The present social order and the law that supports that social order have the effect of protecting the rights of those with property and the economic power to enter and enforce contractual arrangements. Much criminal law also seeks to protect property rights. On this analysis, the relationship between law and social order may be seen as conservative, in the sense that it seeks to conserve established social arrangements.

However, as with the role of law in relation to public order, there are other ways of thinking about the relationship between law and social order. Many now assert that a fundamental purpose of law is to promote a more dynamic social order, designed to ensure that society is not locked into historic structures that sustain inequality, but is based on principles of equality and the prevention of social exclusion.

How to attack inequality is the subject of fierce debate. Some argue that equality can be achieved only if there is a complete removal of the differences between people—so that, for example, everyone in employment receives more or less equal pay, that there is equality in the amounts of wealth capable of being held by individuals, and so on.

Others take the view that equality in this sense is neither the right nor a sensible way to promote a new social order. They argue that the focus should be on *equality of opportunity*, for example, in the provision of education or health care or work opportunities.

Many modern rules of law have the promotion of equality of opportunity as a prime objective. Both within the United Kingdom and more broadly in the European Union, there is law designed to combat discrimination based on grounds of gender, ethnicity and race, disability or age. This has been given a new focus following the coming into force of the Equality Act 2010 (*see Box 2.2*). This is driven not by simplistic notions of political correctness but by the very practical belief that our collective good is enhanced by ensuring that all citizens can play a full part in the economic and social life of those nations. To give a simple example, if women are excluded from the workforce, 50 per cent of the available talent is thereby excluded.

Box 2.2 Legal system explained

Equality Act 2010

The Equality Act 2010 replaces previous anti-discrimination laws with a single Act aiming to make the law simpler and to remove inconsistencies. The Act covers nine 'protected characteristics', which cannot be used as a reason to treat people unfairly. As every person has one or more of the protected characteristics, the Act potentially protects everyone against unfair treatment. The protected characteristics are:

- age;
- disability;
- gender reassignment;
- marriage and civil partnership;
- pregnancy and maternity;
- race;
- religion or belief;
- sex;
- sexual orientation.

The Equality Act 2010 sets out the different ways in which it is unlawful to treat someone, such as direct and indirect discrimination, harassment, victimization, and failing to make a reasonable adjustment for a disabled person. The Act prohibits unfair treatment in the workplace, when providing goods, facilities and services, when exercising public functions, in the disposal and management of premises, in education, and by associations (such as private clubs).

In addition to specific anti-discrimination legislation, a great deal of public policy is directed to devising social, welfare, and educational policies that seek to assist in the creation of a new social order. Law gives legitimacy to those policies. There is nothing new about this. Since the development of the Welfare State in the middle of the 19th century, it has been argued that it is right that governments should seek, to varying degrees, to promote equality, for example by taxing the better off relatively more than the poor. The law clearly has had and continues to have a central part to play in these developments.

However, the mere fact that policies have been developed and enshrined in Acts of Parliament does not mean that a new social order is thereby automatically created. The evidence is that in modern Britain there remain very marked inequalities—whether based on class, education, employment, health, or other life opportunities. Thus while there may be aspirations towards equality, the social reality is that equality—however defined—has not yet been fully realized.

The claim that law has a role to play in the promotion of equality is one that is frequently made. It was advanced by those who promoted the first Race Relations Act in 1965, and was also used in debate on the Equality Act 2010. Promotion of equality can thus be included as one of the macro functions of law. However, law also plays a role in maintaining the existing social order, for example through the protection of rights in property. This function may conflict with law's role in promoting greater equality. This leads some to argue that law has another, more political, function—namely, supporting the existing social order as opposed to promoting a new social order. As with the tension between the preservation of public order and the protection of civil liberty, there are tensions between the role of law in the preservation of the existing social order and its role in the promotion of a new social order.

Similarly, claims are made that a function of law is to promote social justice. The extent to which law and the legal system, by themselves, can deliver social justice is limited. Social justice is more a political concept than a legal one. Law may be able to support steps taken to achieve social justice and thus promote a new social order; but it would be unrealistic to claim that law can achieve this in isolation from other non-legal factors that underpin modern society.

Even if the ability of law directly to foster social justice or equality is limited, there is nevertheless an important claim for law: that it does have a role to play in protecting the weak against the powerful. This became a very important function for law as the concept of the Welfare State developed, not just in the United Kingdom but across the developed world.

Law and economic order

The relationship between law and economic order raises matters similar to those considered in the relationship between law and social order. The dominant economic philosophy in the United Kingdom, indeed throughout the Western world, is market capitalism.[2] Here, a very important function for law has lain in the recognition of legally enforceable rights in private property, whether in land or other forms of security. Law defines ownership rights in property as well as laying down procedures for the transfer of those ownership rights from one person to another. The law enables different property rights (e.g. tenancy or trust) to co-exist in the same piece of property. And the law provides mechanisms for the enforcement of those rights. The notions of property developed in law have, historically, assisted in the development of this economic framework and continue to sustain it.

Similar arguments apply to contract. The recognition of the principle of the legally enforceable bargain (contract), breaches of which can be litigated in the courts, has been an essential tool in the development of the modern market capitalist economy. As with its function in the maintenance of the social order, so too can law be seen as instrumental in the creation and underpinning of the economic order.

Nevertheless, there are other ways in which law is now used to regulate the economic order. It has long been recognized that market economies are bad at delivering certain socially desirable outcomes. Without legislation, those operating factories or machinery might do so without proper regard for health and safety. This certainly happened in the 19th century. A great deal of modern law creates regulatory frameworks within which capitalist entrepreneurs must operate. Currently, there is widespread

---

[2] Differences between different models of capitalism—e.g. the Anglo-American model, the European model, or the Japanese model—are not considered here. But it should not be assumed that the operation of capitalist systems is the same in all countries.

discussion about how bankers should be regulated. Here, too, regulation is argued to be justified on the ground that it fills gaps left by market failure.

Indeed, it has long been recognized that untrammelled capitalist activity contains its own contradictions. There is an inexorable tendency for capitalists to accumulate market position and, if possible, dominate that position through the exercise of monopoly power. However, the shift from competition to monopoly poses a fundamental threat to the operation of the market. Thus legal mechanisms are used to promote competition and to limit the development of monopolistic positions.

There is also an inevitable tendency for those with greater bargaining power to seek through contract to impose their wishes on parties with weaker bargaining positions. A great deal of modern law is designed to level the playing field. Thus a vast body of consumer law is designed to soften the binding nature of contractual relationships by giving rights to consumers in situations where the bargaining power between the supplier of goods or services and the consumer of those goods or services is unequal. For example, there are legal requirements that those who sell insurance policies or other expensive financial products must allow the purchaser a 'cooling-off period' within which the purchaser may change his or her mind. Housing law regulates the relationship between landlords and tenants. Employment law regulates the relationship between employer and employee. More generally, there are measures enabling the consumer to challenge terms in contracts thought to be 'unfair'.

Once again, as with law and public order and law and social order, in relation to the economic order the law performs functions that are to a degree in conflict. Law has helped to legitimate the tools essential to the commercial context within which market capitalism is able to flourish. At the same time, law is used to limit the excesses of market behaviour that can arise from unregulated operation of market capitalism.

Law and international order

Another function of law is support for international order. This is an extremely complex and controversial subject not considered in detail here. Some argue that there is really no such thing as international law; rather that maintenance of international order is sustained by international relations and diplomatic pressure. But in many respects, international bodies and politicians like to point to legal authority for what they are trying to achieve. For example:

- recent incursions by the United Nations into the world's trouble-spots—for example, the recent imposition of the no-fly zone in Libya—have been justified in part by reference to the legal framework of the United Nations Charter and its executive bodies, in particular the role of the Security Council;[3]

---

[3] Much of the controversy about the war in Iraq arose from arguments that it was not properly sanctioned under international law.

- attempts to deal with 'crimes against humanity'—a particular curse of the modern age—are being made through special War Crimes Tribunals that have been established by the United Nations and which sit in The Hague and elsewhere;

- in other areas, such as the regulation of world trade or the protection of the environment, the regulation of the use of the sea, or space, there is an increasing tendency not only to enter treaties—which historically was common practice—but also to create special institutions and mechanisms for enforcement like courts or tribunals, which are independent of particular national governments;

- the conduct of war has long been subject to international legal constraints, for example the Geneva Convention on the treatment of prisoners of war. Similarly, other constraints on behaviour in war and other situations of conflict, such as the prevention of torture, have been prescribed in instruments of international law; and

- one of the most pressing of current social issues, the protection of those seeking asylum in one country because of a well-founded fear of persecution in another, is essentially shaped by principles of international law.

These are important and controversial issues. Even though the focus of this work is on the rather more parochial subject of the 'English legal system', we cannot ignore the global context in which countries now operate. Legal instruments and institutions have played a significant part in this development; this wider dimension of the role of law should not be forgotten.

Law and moral order

Another macro function of law is to provide support for the moral ordering of society. This is also extremely controversial. Some theorists argue that there should be little, if any, distinction between law and morality; that the law should clearly and deliberately mirror those issues of morality which people think 'ought' to inform the way we should behave. Others seek to draw a clear distinction between law and morality. They argue that the mere fact that many people believe that certain forms of behaviour or activity are morally wrong (e.g. engaging in homosexual activity, or tax avoidance[4]) should not mean that they should be defined as unlawful.

There are clear dangers and considerable difficulties in seeking to equate law and morality, not least because of the problems of determining what the common morality is on any given issue. Nevertheless, many rules of law are founded on a moral view of society. Perhaps the clearest example is the moral imperative not to kill people, reflected in rules of criminal law which outlaw such activity.

In general, it may be suggested that rules of criminal law which reflect some common morality, however defined, may be more acceptable and effective in regulating

---

[4] Tax avoidance is technically legal, as opposed to tax evasion which is clearly illegal.

behaviour than those rules which do not. Even so, there may well be behaviours that many would regard as undesirable—dressing shabbily or drinking cheap alcohol in the streets—but that should not of themselves be defined as criminal.

We should also note that ideas about what should be regarded as behaviour that should be regulated by criminal law do change. For example many of the criminal offences that 200 or 300 years ago led to draconian punishments such as transportation or even the death penalty now seem very trivial, and are either not criminal at all or dealt with much less severely. Today, many argue that a less criminalized approach to the use of soft drugs might not only lead to more equitable treatment of drug users, as compared with those who use alcohol or nicotine, but also to reductions in other forms of criminality resulting from the need for drug users to break the law to obtain the money to buy their drugs. On the other hand, there are powerful political arguments that any relaxation in the government's approach to drug use would 'send the wrong signal' to the community at large.

In a different context, much of the law that seeks to regulate relationships between individuals is also based in concepts of morality, for example the law relating to marriage. (The present Coalition government's decision to promote the case in favour of the legal recognition of homosexual marriage throws the relationship between law and morality into sharp focus.) This is another context in which law provides at least some support for the moral order, a function reinforced by the principle of the protection of family life found in Article 8 of the European Convention on Human Rights.

Related to the relationship between law and moral order is the relationship between *law and religious order*. Despite the decline in religious belief in England, there are still many who argue that religion—both formal and informal—remains an important facet of society at large. However, and in contrast with discussion about the relationship between law and morality, it is not now often argued that law should be directly supportive of religion. Indeed many would argue, whether in general principle or because of their own religious (or anti-religious) beliefs, that law should *not* be used to support the religious order. Questions of spirituality and religious belief should fall within that private sphere of activity in which the law should not intervene.

Nevertheless, the historical role played by religion in the development of modern England cannot be wholly ignored. At its most basic, its calendar and major holiday festivals are based in the Christian tradition, rather than that of other religious groupings. There are a number of legal privileges that attach exclusively to the Church of England; there are others that apply to religious groups more generally. Thus it is arguable, though not often seen in this light, that present-day law still plays a residual part in the support of religious order, in particular the Christian religious order.

This is controversial, not least because of the rise in a number of countries of various forms of religious fundamentalism. These are often accompanied by degrees of intolerance towards others that are quite unacceptable in a modern pluralistic society. Indeed, it may be the case that, in order to protect social pluralism, the law should be used more to protect the ability of those of different religious beliefs to hold and practise their religion, another issue embraced in the European Convention on Human Rights in Article 9.

Other macro functions

In addition to the ways in which law may interact with the maintenance of and challenges to different types of order, law also has a number of other macro functions.

The resolution of social problems

The response of politicians and their officials to many issues perceived as social problems is to create more laws seeking to regulate the behaviour complained against. This is the expected political response. Only rarely do politicians concede that there may be enough law, and that what is needed is better understanding of or enforcement of existing law. Even more rarely are politicians willing to accept that a possible solution to a problem might be to repeal existing rules of law or to develop the law in such a way as to 'decriminalize' the activity in question. Their mindset assumes that a function of law is 'to solve social problems'. Indeed, whole careers are devoted to the promotion of legislation allegedly designed to address particular social issues—even if, as often happens, there is already a perfectly satisfactory law already available, or where changing the law is not really a solution to the problem. Recent debate about the (in)ability of law to regulate anti-social behaviour is a good example of these issues.

One obvious consequence of creating legal provisions to solve social problems is that people—ever mindful of their own self-interest—respond to new legal frameworks in ways not predicted by the law-makers. Tax law offers numerous instances where laws designed to achieve one objective (increased taxation) are thwarted by taxpayers who rearrange their affairs to avoid new tax burdens. A hidden but often inevitable consequence of using law to solve social problems is, therefore, that the very process of creating new law results not in the solution of existing social problems but rather in the creation of new social problems. The process of dealing with one issue leads to the creation of another, which in turn has to be 'solved' later.

The regulation of human relationships

Another important function of law is the regulation of the nature and extent of human relationships. The definition of and the formalities relating to the creation of marriage (and, more recently, civil partnerships between same-sex couples) are determined by legal rules, often supplementing different religious rules. (Proposals to allow homosexual couples to marry indicate that the definition of marriage is now seen by many as more of a legal issue than a religious one.) Law provides a framework for the distribution of assets on the breakdown of marriage and civil partnership. Law sets boundaries to the scope of sexual relationships, prescribing for example the minimum age of sexual consent, and making certain sexual relationships within the 'prohibited degrees of consanguinity' (incest and other close relationships) unlawful. The law also sets down a framework for the treatment of children and other family members.

The educative or ideological function of law

A further function of law, almost irrespective of its impact in particular cases, is an educative one; it contributes to the shaping of the 'ideology' of a nation. To give a simple if significant example, there is no doubt that attitudes to drinking and driving have changed dramatically over the last 25 years. In part, this is the result of powerful advertising, demonstrating the devastating impact that drink-drive accidents can have on victims and their families. But the change in attitude has also been the result of changes in the law contributing to a climate of opinion in which drinking and driving is no longer regarded as socially acceptable behaviour. Another example is the contribution law has made to the elimination of smoking in public places.

A third example is law, mentioned earlier, outlawing various forms of discrimination. When such laws come into effect, those who argue for their introduction often accept that the law does not, on its own, alter the attitudes of mind that lead to the discriminatory behaviours that result in the creation of those laws. However, those who have sponsored such laws see them as not only creating certain legal rights that may be enforceable by individuals, but also sending a more general educative signal to members of society at large that discriminatory behaviour is not acceptable.

More generally, countries that embrace the principle of the rule of law are, in effect, asserting that powers of officials of the state must be limited and that the individual citizen should have both the right and the opportunity to challenge decisions where they are thought to be wrong or in some respect unfair.

The decision by the British government to introduce the Human Rights Act 1998, incorporating the European Convention on Human Rights directly into English law, is another example of legislation that not only creates legal rights which individuals may seek to enforce through the courts, but that also sends an important educative signal about the limits within which people, particularly those who work within government, must behave. In this sense, therefore, another macro function of law relates to the education of the public's social attitudes and responsibilities.

Micro functions of law

Turning from the 'macro' to the 'micro' level involves consideration of rather more specific functions for law, many of which derive from the 'macro' functions identified earlier. A number of examples are offered; this does not purport to be a comprehensive list. Readers may be able to think of other functions not identified here. Readers may also be able to identify other examples to illustrate the particular functions which are set out in the following paragraphs.

Defining the limits of acceptable behaviour

Most people have some awareness of the *criminal law*. A major objective of this branch of the law is to prescribe the limits of socially acceptable behaviour. The criminal law prohibits many kinds of activity about which there would be widespread agreement, such as murder and violent crime. It also outlaws a wide range of other activities about which there may be more debate, such as the use of particular types of drugs. The following points may be made in this context:

- Not all behaviour that may be regarded by many as undesirable is characterized in legal terms as criminal. Thus there is no law preventing a person over the age of 18 from drinking alcohol. However, where the consequences of that conduct may impinge on others the law often steps in. There is strict law making it unlawful for persons who have been drinking alcohol or taking drugs to drive.

- Human conduct is regulated in many ways in addition to the use of law. Codes of morality, religious principles, pressures of friends and family all constrain the ways in which people behave.

- Different countries set the boundaries of their criminal law in different places: what is criminal in one country is not necessarily criminal in another.[5] Although there is a great deal of commonality between different bodies of criminal law, in important respects the boundaries of criminal law are *culturally determined*, set by the demands of the specific society. There are particularly important distinctions in societies with different religious traditions or moral backgrounds: laws applying in Islamic countries are in many respects quite different from those in countries founded on the Judaeo-Christian tradition.

- The boundaries of the criminal law are *dynamic*. Activity which has historically been regarded as criminal is not necessarily regarded as criminal forever. The prohibition of alcohol in the United States during the 1920s is a good example.

However, the function of law in regulating human behaviour is not exclusively through the criminal law. Areas of *civil law* have a similar function. For example, if a party to a contract breaks that contract, rules of law allow the party affected to claim compensation from the person in breach. The law of negligence prescribes situations in which a person who has negligently injured another has to compensate that other for the injury. In short, law defines the scope of obligations that exist between individuals and provides remedies for breach of those obligations. Although the objective of civil law is not

---

[5] This has the important practical consequence that, if a person commits a criminal act in one country and flees to another country where that act is not criminal, this is often the basis for successfully resisting extradition proceedings—official proceedings to bring the alleged miscreant back for trial to the country where the original act took place.

to punish an offender, in the sense used in considering criminal law, nevertheless rules of civil law clearly signal that a contract cannot be breached with impunity, nor can one person act negligently in relation to another. In this sense, the rules of civil law also send the message that certain types of behaviour are unacceptable or undesirable.

Defining the consequences of certain forms of behaviour

Law does not simply define forms of behaviour that are unacceptable. It also prescribes consequences. In the case of criminal law, these are the punishments that attach to a finding of guilt. Similarly, in the area of civil law, law prescribes the remedies that the person affected by a breach of contract or a negligent act may obtain from the perpetrator.

In some situations the same facts may generate a variety of legal consequences. For example, a road accident may be caused by a person driving a car carelessly or recklessly. This may result in the police seeking to get that person prosecuted through the criminal courts; if found guilty this may result in the imposition of a fine or even imprisonment. If the accident causes damage to another, that other person may seek compensation by bringing an action for damages in negligence against the driver. The driver may argue that the accident occurred because her car was improperly serviced, and may therefore bring an action for breach of contract against the garage. Three different legal consequences have arisen from the same incident.

Defining processes for the transaction of business and other activities

A rather different function of law is to define procedures by which certain transactions must be carried out. Some of these are quite straightforward, such as those relating to the making of simple contracts. In other cases, particularly where there is concern to prevent fraud, considerable formality may be required. Many of these relate to transactions dealing with the transfer of property rights. For example, the process of buying and selling houses is subject to a number of formal legal requirements, known collectively as the rules of conveyancing. There are detailed rules relating to the creation of leases. There are special rules for the creation of wills. Similarly, there are detailed requirements for the creation of trusts or settlements of property. These are all designed to protect valuable assets and prevent fraud.

One of the problems with prescribing formal requirements is that, whatever the law states, in practice people attempt to carry out these transactions in ignorance of the rules. The law must then develop supplementary principles to prevent injustice occurring, notwithstanding the existence of procedural irregularity. Many of the principles of the law of equity have developed in response to this problem.

Creating regulatory frameworks

A great deal of modern law seeks to regulate those who provide services to the public. For example, much law now regulates the professional activities of lawyers, doctors, architects, nurses, or estate agents. There is a vast regulatory framework designed to control the activities of those who provide financial services to the public to prevent fraud and other breaches of trust. Another branch of regulatory law relates to the promotion of health and safety in the workplace and other contexts. A consequence of the privatization of formerly nationalized industries has been to create an extensive body of law designed to regulate the activities of companies now in the private sector (such as telecommunications, utilities—gas, water, and electricity—and transport) including the promotion of competition and the regulation of prices. And specific areas of economic activity are subject to the most detailed legal regulation designed to promote standards and give the consumer value for money. The regulation of the housing market through housing law is a prime example.

A different form of regulatory law, but one that has been in existence for many years, is planning law regulating the use to which land in the United Kingdom can be put. Law that seeks to regulate industry in order to protect the environment is another example. In this context, the law operates at an international as well as a national level.

Regulatory law also serves another purpose. It defines the categories of persons able to make representations to government about a particular policy or decision. For example, again in the context of planning law, the relevant law determines who may challenge decisions of the planning authorities and who may appear to make their case at any public inquiry resulting from a planning decision.

Complaints are frequently heard that the burden of regulation is too great; governments often assert that they are trying to cut back on regulation. But in practice there is no escaping regulation. Whenever politicians say that they want to protect consumers, how do they do that? Through regulation!

Giving authority to agents of the state to take actions against citizens

Another function of law is to give power to state officials to take action against members of the public. There are numerous examples: the powers of the police to stop, search, question, arrest, and caution members of the public is one; the power of doctors to detain in mental hospitals those diagnosed as suffering from acute mental illness is another; the power of social workers to remove children from families where they are thought to be at risk and to place them in the care of the local authorities is a third. Similarly, agents of both central and local government are given power to take money away from members of the public through taxation.

A rather different example is the power given to government and other agencies of the state to acquire land compulsorily in the public interest.

Preventing the abuse of power by officials

In contrast to the previous head, much law is designed to prevent abuses of power by public servants. For example, the police are required to operate within a framework of powers prescribed by the Police and Criminal Evidence Act 1984, which limits their powers of arrest, search, and questioning, considered further in *Chapter 5*.

The essence of administrative law, discussed in *Chapter 6*, relates to the importance of officials acting within a framework of law which prescribes their power; not allowing officials to use discretionary powers in an abusive way; and giving people the opportunity to take advantage of certain procedural safeguards—for example a right to put their case—before adverse decisions about them are taken. These are further examples of rules of law setting boundaries to the power of state officials.

Giving power/authority to officials to assist the public

The law also sets down a vast range of requirements for agencies of the state to provide services or other goods to the public. At the most general level, all public expenditure has to be legitimated by special Acts of Parliament known as Appropriation Acts. These give general authority for the expenditure of public money on the whole range of programmes run by government.

More specific bodies of law deal with the details. Social security law is one example, setting out as it does the entitlements to social security benefits which have been created by government. Many other examples could be given: entitlement to free education is one, free treatment within the National Health Service is another. All these activities, of the social security, education, and health authorities, are underpinned by detailed legal frameworks.

Prescribing procedures for the use of law

In addition to prescribing procedures for conducting different types of transaction, there is another important body of law—procedural law—which seeks to control the ways in which courts and other adjudicative bodies operate. This body of law may set limits to the evidence that can be brought in different types of cases. It also prescribes the way in which different types of proceedings, whether in the courts or other legal fora, are to be conducted.

Conclusion: law and society

It is not claimed here that these examples of the macro and micro functions of law in society are exhaustive. Readers should ask themselves whether there are other functions for law and whether they should be regarded as macro or micro in character. There is a huge literature on the relationship of law and society of which the foregoing is only a very limited summary. However, a number of points can be noted:

(1) All the functions of law, whether macro or micro, are *contingent* upon the stage in the development of that society and the pressures and challenges facing that society. While many of these functions of law are common to very many societies, others are not.

(2) The laws that exist and the ways in which they are used are dependent on the ideology and politics of the particular country. For example, current notions of social justice and equality in the United Kingdom have developed in the light of particular socio-political and economic theories. They will change in the future. The list of functions proposed here should not, therefore, be regarded as set in concrete; it reflects broader changes in the social and political ideas and ideals of that society.

(3) The functions of law are by no means always consistent with each other: preservation of social order may, on occasion, be in sharp conflict with the function of protecting civil liberties; the role of law in advancing equality or social justice may be in conflict with its role in supporting current social and economic orders.

(4) It should be remembered that there are still activities that are not currently the subject of legal regulation. Governments frequently claim that they are seeking to limit the encroachment of law. Interestingly, however, when a new technology arrives that actually enables activities to occur outside conventional regulatory frameworks—the rise of internet use or developments in biotechnology are good examples—politicians and others quickly become agitated.

(5) There are many mechanisms, outside law, that are used to regulate and alter people's behaviour. Much of the practice of economics is based on the assumption that, if financial incentives are right, behaviours change. An interesting example is the proposal that problems of global pollution and global warming must be tackled not just by laws saying what should or should not be done, but also by getting financial incentives right— higher taxes paid by those who pollute, for example.

(6) More fundamentally, there are significant issues about the way in which we order our society that are either not touched on at all by law or only in relatively insignificant ways. For example, one of the major social issues of our time relates to the extent to which groups in the community are excluded from the mainstream of social life, whether through lack of money or other material resources, such as housing. To be sure, there are legislative provisions relating to the provision of social security benefits or to the provision of accommodation to the homeless. However, the entitlements contained in these bodies of law are not absolute but are highly contingent on legal tests being met. Those claiming benefits or access to housing have a substantial list of conditions that they must satisfy before they can be helped. The fact that the rhetoric of law employs concepts such as liberty or justice does not mean that substantive law actually delivers social justice to all citizens of the United Kingdom.

(7) Perhaps the most important point to stress is that although the discussion has, perhaps, been somewhat abstract, the issues considered are central to many of the most serious challenges facing the United Kingdom. One obvious example is how governments should respond to terrorist attacks, such as the bombings in London in July 2005. How should this be handled? By giving the Home Secretary new powers to detain people for longer periods without being charged for any offence, or new powers to deport those felt to be promoting religious intolerance? By allowing courts to receive evidence obtained as the result of covert surveillance? Or will these developments undermine freedoms essential to British values and the British way of life?

Questions

Use the self-test questions on the Online Resource Centre to test your understanding of the topics covered in this chapter and receive tailored feedback:

www.oxfordtextbooks.co.uk/orc/partington13_14/

Weblinks

Check the Online Resource Centre for a selection of annotated weblinks allowing you to research easily topics of particular interest:

www.oxfordtextbooks.co.uk/orc/partington13_14/

Blog items

See www.martinpartington.com (access via the Online Resource Centre)

Includes: a note on the Protection of Freedoms Act 2012; the challenge of promoting the rule of law internationally; a discussion (podcasts) of the work of JUSTICE in the promotion of human rights; the importance of empirical research on law to understand how law works in the real world; the role of government in promoting UK legal services internationally.

Further reading

ABEL-SMITH, B., and STEVENS, R., *In Search of Justice: Society and the Legal System* (London, Allen Lane, 1968)

ALLAN, T. R. S., *Constitutional Justice—A Liberal Theory of the Rule of Law* (Oxford, Oxford University Press, 2003)

BINGHAM, T., *The Rule of Law* (London, Penguin Books, 2010; paperback and Kindle edns, 2011)

BRAKE, M., and HALE, C., *Public Order and Private Lives: the Politics of Law and Order* (London, Routledge, 1992)

COTTERRELL, R., *The Sociology of Law: An Introduction* (2nd edn, Oxford, Oxford University Press, 1992)

DELUPIS, I., *The International Legal Order* (Aldershot, Dartmouth, c. 1994)

DICKSON, B., and CONNELLY, A., *Human Rights and the European Convention: the Effects of the Convention on the United Kingdom and Ireland* (London, Sweet & Maxwell, 1997)

DYZENHAUS, D. (ed.), *Recrafting the Rule of Law: The Limits of Legal Order* (Oxford, Hart Publishing, 1999)

HUDSON, A., *Towards a Just Society: Law, Labour and Legal Aid* (London, Continuum International Publishing Group, 1999)

KENNEDY, H., *Eve Was Framed: Women and British Justice* (London, Random House digital, 2011)

JACOBS, F. G., WHITE, R. C. A., and OVEY, C., *The European Convention on Human Rights* (5th edn, Oxford, Oxford University Press, 2010)

MANSELL, W., THOMSON, A., and METEYARD, B., *Critical Introduction to Law* (3rd edn, London, Cavendish Publishing, 2004)

PLANT, R., *The Neo-liberal State* (Oxford, Oxford University Press, 2009)

ROBERTS, S., *Order and Dispute: an Introduction to Legal Anthropology* (Harmondsworth, Penguin, 1979)

SCHACHTER, O., and JOYNER, C. C. (eds), *United Nations Legal Order* (Cambridge, Grotius, 1995)

SEDLEY, S., *Ashes and Sparks: Essays on Law and Justice* (Cambridge, Cambridge University Press, 2011)

WARD, I., *Introduction to Critical Legal Theory* (2nd edn, London, Cavendish Publishing, 2004)

3

Law-making: authority and process

Chapter 2 considered a number of functions that law plays in the ordering of society. Here we consider how law is made in the United Kingdom. Before getting into any detail, we ask: what gives the law-making institutions their authority? What gives law-makers their legitimacy?

Power, legitimacy, and authority in the law-making process

One of the macro functions of law identified in *Chapter 2* was support for the political order. Law provides much, if not all, of the legal framework within which power is exercised. But simply stating that constitutional principles provide governments or other executive agencies with the power to make law begs a more fundamental question: from where do these constitutional legal principles derive their authority?

The answer is far from easy. Different societies base claims for the legitimacy of their law-makers on different theoretical foundations. In broad terms, however, law-makers may be said to derive their authority from two principal sources:

(1) the basic constitutional framework or constitutional settlement that operates within that country; and

(2) the underlying political ideology of that country.

The reasons why people are more or less willing to accept these as bases for the exercise of power are complex. One is that most people, while accepting that certain services such as education and health need to be provided, do not want to run them themselves. They are happy to let politicians and bureaucrats get on with the job. Furthermore, once a government has established a claim to exercise power, particularly coercive power, it invariably creates the machinery—police, security services, and the like—to enforce the law which results from the exercise of that power.

But it should always be remembered that even the most fundamental of constitutional arrangements fail if significant groups within a particular society find that constitutional basis unworkable. The fact that in some countries in the world there have been civil wars, that in others there have been *coups d'état*, demonstrates the point. The destruction of the Berlin Wall, the collapse of apartheid in South Africa, and more recently events in countries such as Tunisia, Egypt, and Libya, can all be cited as modern examples. Even countries that now enjoy the most stable and secure of constitutional arrangements such as the United Kingdom or the United States, can trace their present situation to resistance to or rebellion against historically unacceptable constitutional arrangements.

In the United Kingdom, and in many other developed countries, that consent is more taken for granted than actively sought (save on particular issues which are the subject of referendums (*see Box 3.1*)). In these countries, free and regular elections are seen as the primary mechanism through which continuing consent to govern is implied. What concerns many people today, particularly in countries where democratic process is well established, is that voter apathy weakens the legitimacy of law-making institutions. This leads some to argue that voting in elections should be made compulsory; this is already the law in Australia, for example. Whether or not this step is taken, it is vital that cynicism with politicians should not prevent citizens from participating in this fundamental constitutional process. It is also important that electoral processes are as efficient and corruption free as possible.[1]

Box 3.1   Legal system explained

Referendums

Referendums are a mechanism for giving the electorate a chance to vote on a specific question of policy. In countries, such as the United Kingdom, where referendums are neither mandatory nor binding there may, nonetheless, exist an unwritten convention that certain important constitutional changes will be put to a referendum and that the result will be respected. There have been two national referendums. The first concerned the United Kingdom joining the Common Market; the vote went in favour. The second was on changing the system for voting in General Elections from first past the post to a form of proportional representation; that was defeated.

Two important national referendums are in prospect: one relating to Scottish Independence, which will take place in 2014; and one on the continued membership of the United Kingdom in the European Union, for which a date has not yet been decided.

Referendums on local issues are more common. For example, in 2011, 37 local authorities asked their citizens whether they should in future be run by an elected Mayor; only Bristol voted in favour of the idea.

Advocates of referendums argue that certain decisions are best taken out of the hands of representatives in Parliament and determined directly by the people. Critics argue that voters in a referendum are not sufficiently informed to make decisions on complicated or technical issues, being swayed by strong personalities, and expensive advertising campaigns. They also argue that voter apathy may result in low turnout so that in reality the results of referendums do not reflect general public opinion.

---

[1] The Electoral Registration and Administration Bill 2012, currently before Parliament, makes further technical changes to the electoral process. For more detail, see my blog, www.martinpartington.com.

Lastly, the authority and legitimacy of a country's law-making institutions must not be squandered. The recent scandals concerning the expenses claimed by Members of Parliament (MPs) proved a big challenge for the UK Parliament. New legislation, the Parliamentary Standards Act 2009, was enacted to try to address the issue. It created the Independent Parliamentary Standards Authority and a new Commissioner for Parliamentary Investigations, whose task is to monitor the propriety of MPs' expense claims and other financial interests.

Constitutions and constitutionalism

One basis for the authority given to the law-makers can therefore be found in a country's constitution and its related principles of constitutionalism. What are these?

In most countries there exists a *written constitution* or other form of 'basic law' that defines the powers of the law-making institutions of the country. The constitutional arrangements of the United Kingdom are unusual in that there is no formal written constitution. Many of the most important constitutional principles are found not in any written document but in unwritten practice, known as *constitutional conventions* (*see Box 3.2*).

Box 3.2   Legal system explained

Constitutional conventions

There is a substantial literature on constitutional conventions and the extent to which they have changed over the years. Some examples of constitutional conventions may be noted, as follows.

Constitutional monarchy. The theoretical Head of State remains the monarch. The principle of constitutional monarchy means that the Queen takes no active part in the running of the country. Although the parliamentary year starts with the 'Queen's speech' and although bills are given 'royal assent', the Queen does not intervene in the politics of the law-making programme. The Queen is kept informed about what is happening in Parliament and, through audiences with the Prime Minister of the day, is briefed about significant developments. It would be surprising if, on occasion, she did not offer her views on particular issues. But the monarch is not the source of political decision taking or law-making.

Prerogative powers. Nevertheless, there are still certain functions of government that are based not in legislative authority, but on the historic exercise of power by the monarch. These are known as 'prerogative powers'. The most dramatic and controversial example of this is the power to go to war. This is exercised by ministers not under the authority of an Act of Parliament, but by exercise of prerogative powers. The Home Secretary's 'prerogative of mercy' to reduce a sentence imposed by the courts after a criminal trial is another example.

Box 3.2 *Continued*

Cabinet government and collective responsibility. The very existence of the Cabinet—the central committee of ministers chaired by the Prime Minister and responsible for determining the government's programme—is another aspect of the British Constitution based in convention, rather than legislation. The related doctrine of collective responsibility, whereby ministers who do not agree with the policy of the government as determined in Cabinet are supposed to resign, is also based in constitutional convention, not constitutional law.

Individual ministerial responsibility. Another constitutional convention is that ministers should take ultimate responsibility for what goes on in their departments. This means that they must answer questions in Parliament or select committees about the work of their departments. On occasion, this may also lead ministers to resign, where something has gone very seriously wrong, though in practice this is now a rare occurrence.

These unwritten principles are nevertheless supplemented by an increasing number of statutory provisions that have constitutional effect (*see Chapter 2, Law and political order*). Devolution of powers to government in Scotland and Wales, human rights, and freedom of information have required legislation which has transformed the constitutional legal landscape. The Constitutional Reform Act 2005 went further, significantly changing the role of the Lord Chancellor, making the Lord Chief Justice the head of the judiciary, and making provision for the new Supreme Court. The Constitutional Reform and Governance Act 2010 made further changes, for example on the process of ratifying international treaties by requiring treaties to be laid before Parliament before ratification.

The current Coalition government has made further constitutional change, legislating for changes to the size of Parliament, and introducing fixed-term (five-year) Parliaments (*see Boxes 3.3 and 3.4*). It also proposed reform of the House of Lords, but this is not being taken forward. The relative ease with which these important changes to the structure of government in the United Kingdom may be made may, paradoxically, arise from the fact that the United Kingdom does *not* have a written constitution.

Box 3.3   Reform in progress

Parliamentary Voting System and Constituencies Act 2011

This Act required the holding of a referendum, in May 2011, on a proposal to change the voting rules for general elections. The proposal was soundly defeated.

Less publicized, but still important, the Act contains provisions to reduce the number of seats in the House of Commons from 650 to 600. The Act also created new rules for

Box 3.3 *Continued*

the redistribution of seats needed for the 600 constituencies. The rules made numerical equality the core principle, in that there was to be a uniform electoral quota for the United Kingdom. The size of constituencies could not vary by more than five per cent from the quota, with only limited exceptions. Regular redistributions would take place every five years.

In the case of England there would be 502 MPs rather than the current 533. The number of electors in each constituency would be no smaller than 72,810 and no larger than 80,473. The Boundary Commission for England stated: 'Early indications are that the changes will have to be significant in order to reduce the number of constituencies by 31 and to ensure that they are of equal size. The majority of existing constituencies are likely to be affected.'

It should not be thought that this is a simple mathematical question; it has important political consequences. Because urban constituencies (many of which are held by Labour) have historically had fewer constituents than rural ones, the redistribution would be likely to work against the Labour Party and in favour of the Conservative Party.

At present, it is unlikely that these changes will be made before the 2015 General Election. A consequence of the Coalition government abandoning its plans for reforming the House of Lords is that the Liberal Democrat members of the Coalition have stated that they will delay the final proposals.

Box 3.4 Reform in progress

Fixed-term Parliaments Act 2011

One of the peculiarities of the British system of government is that the duration of the Westminster Parliament—i.e. the length of time a government lasts following a general election—was not fixed. The maximum duration of a UK Parliament was five years, determined by the Septennial Act 1715, as amended by the Parliament Act 1911. Under those provisions, if a Parliament was not dissolved in the period up to five years after the day on which it was summoned to meet, it automatically expired.

These provisions gave the Prime Minister of the day considerable flexibility on when he or she 'goes to the country'—a decision that may well be determined by the state of the public opinion polls.

The Coalition government enacted the Fixed-term Parliaments Act 2011, which provides for fixed days for polls for parliamentary general elections. The polling day for elections will ordinarily be the first Thursday in May every five years. The first such polling day is 7 May 2015. The Prime Minister is given power to alter, by statutory

> **Box 3.4**   *Continued*
>
> instrument, the polling day for parliamentary general elections but only to a day not more than two months earlier or later than the scheduled polling day.
>
> The holding of early parliamentary general elections outside this time frame can be triggered either by a vote of no confidence in the government following which the House of Commons did not endorse a new government within 14 days, or a vote by at least two-thirds of all MPs in favour of an early election. Where such an early election occurs, the next scheduled election after that will be five years from the previous first Thursday in May.

British *constitutionalism*—the principles which underpin the constitution—rests on three principal concepts: the *sovereignty of Parliament*, the *rule of law*, and the *separation of powers*. Definitions of these concepts have, over the years, been fiercely contested (*see Further reading* for examples). For present purposes:

- The *sovereignty of Parliament* asserts that the ultimate legal authority for law-making in the United Kingdom should be Parliament.

- The *rule of law* insists that power should not be exercised by persons acting by or on behalf of the state, without their being able to point to some form of legal *authority* for their actions. Further, the process by which decisions are reached should be fair. The Constitutional Reform Act 2005, for the first time, gave statutory recognition to the concept of the rule of law.

- The *separation of powers* suggests that, to prevent any particular arm of government from becoming too powerful, there should be separation between the legislative (law-making), executive, and judicial functions of government. Thereby each branch of government is subject to *checks and balances*. This in turn leads to the proposition that the judges in particular, and lawyers in general, must act independently of government—a principle also recognized in the Constitutional Reform Act 2005.

These principles relate to the central issues of power: who may exercise it, how it can be controlled, and how those who exercise power can be called to account.

Political ideology

Stating these constitutional principles still leaves unanswered the question: what is the theoretical basis on which power to make law may be asserted by political institutions? To answer this it is necessary to consider the underlying political ideology of the country.

In the United Kingdom, and many other countries, the currently dominant political ideology is *representative democracy*, expressed principally through the holding of regular elections. Democratic theory suggests that society is unable to function as effectively as it might if everyone retained their unique power to control their own life or the lives of others. Instead, political parties set out their ideas for the policies they would like to deliver in election manifestos. By electing MPs who are members of those political parties to *represent* the views of electors, individuals pass to those elected some of the control or *sovereignty* that gives them the authority to govern on behalf of the people. In practice, that authority extends not just to issues set out in manifestos, but to the much wider range of issues that inevitably arise during the course of any period of government.

Those in power are also subject to the principle of *accountability*. Thus politicians are regularly called to account when general elections are held. The electoral process gives those elected to political office their authority to make laws on behalf of the citizens of the country. But they know that if their actions are not approved of by the electorate they will be defeated at the next general election. They are also subject to accountability through the *checks and balances* that exist, both within Parliament (such as parliamentary debates or questions to ministers) and outside (including the essential part played by the press and other mass media in exposing things that go wrong within government).

Principles in practice

The application of these principles is not as clear in practice as theory might imply:

- First, in the British system, the work of Parliament is strictly controlled by the political party (currently the Coalition) that forms the government of the day. There are very few issues on which MPs vote independently of their party. There is the occasional backbench revolt; and the occasional 'free vote' on a matter of conscience where the party 'whip' is not applied. But these are the exception, not the rule. The experience of the Coalition government appears not to have fundamentally changed things, although there have been instances where backbench divisions between the Coalition partners have caused policies to be changed—the dropping of proposals for reform of the House of Lords is the most striking example to date.

- Secondly, all legislation in the United Kingdom passes through not only the elected House of Commons, but also the non-elected House of Lords. Although the House of Lords rarely exercises the power it theoretically has to delay bills from becoming law, on many occasions the House of Lords amends, often very substantially, legislation coming to it from the House of Commons. The threat of delay may also lead to significant amendment or even the dropping of legislative proposals. While there is in the Commons a clear link between the democratic process of election and the outcomes of the legislative process, in the Lords this is not so.

- Thirdly, knowing the extent to which the electoral process actually represents the will of the people is very difficult. In the United Kingdom, the 'first past the post' voting system has meant that nearly all recently elected governments have attained power with less than 50 per cent of the popular vote. This leads many, particularly those in the smaller parties who struggle to get elected under the present system, to argue that a fairer voting system would incorporate proportional representation, with seats in Parliament distributed in proportion to votes cast. The primary argument against this apparently attractive proposition is that this tends to lead to coalition governments, in which small minority parties acquire a disproportionately powerful position. Nevertheless, proportional representation has been introduced in the United Kingdom in the context of elections of members to the European Parliament and elections to the devolved Parliaments in Wales and Scotland. The attempt by the Liberal Democrat partner in the Coalition to get a change to the voting rules failed when the public rejected the idea in a referendum held in 2011.

- A fourth issue said to weaken the democratic process is a decline in the percentage of the population voting in elections. This has led to procedural changes making it easier for people to vote by post; it has also led to suggestions to make it easier for people to vote, for example by setting up electronic voting systems in supermarkets. There have even been calls to make voting compulsory, as happens in some other countries.

- Fifthly, there are important sources of law other than Parliament. Under the British system of separation of powers, judges in the higher courts have power to make new rules of law. They do this through the development of rules of 'common law'—long-standing principles of law developed over the years, in some cases centuries, by the judges (*see Judges and the courts*) Yet judges are not elected; they do not get their authority from any theory of representative democracy. The legitimacy for their law-making is found in other constitutional principles, in particular the separation of powers. The judges are recognized to be both a part of the machinery of government and, paradoxically, at the same time independent of it.

The law-making institutions

With these points in mind, we take a closer look at the functions of a number of the law-making institutions that exist in the United Kingdom and consider: (1) the British Parliament and central government; and (2) judges and the courts.

The British Parliament and central government

The principal law-making body in the United Kingdom is the British Parliament. Its legislative programme is at the heart of the law-making process. By no means all legislative measures are the subject of detailed parliamentary scrutiny (*see Box 3.5*), but the vast bulk of legislative measures derive their authority from the parliamentary process. Even the European measures that the British government is required to put into law are given the stamp of parliamentary approval.

Box 3.5   Legal system explained

Statute law: the classification of legislative measures

The vast bulk of new law brought into effect in England is statute law, that is law that has been enacted by Parliament following debate in the House of Commons and the House of Lords, or law made under the authority of statutes. Statute law comes in a variety of forms:

- primary legislation;
- secondary legislation;
- tertiary legislation; and
- (though not strictly statute law) 'quasi-legislation' or 'soft law'.

Primary legislation comprises the *Acts of Parliament* that are passed by Parliament. Most Acts are 'Public General Acts', which apply generally in England. They also apply in Wales if they relate to matters not devolved to the Welsh Assembly Government. They often apply in Scotland, though not on matters devolved to the Scottish Parliament. (Each Act contains a section detailing the precise extent of its coverage.) Some are 'Local or Personal Acts' applying only in particular localities or to specific people (*see further Box 3.6*).

Primary legislation is supplemented by a vast body of *secondary legislation*—regulations and orders made under the authority of an Act of Parliament. These are known generically as *statutory instruments*. There are typically over 3,000 of these made each year, running to many thousands of pages of text. They are not subject to detailed parliamentary scrutiny, though in many cases statutory instruments cannot be made by the government without consultation with specialist advisory committees (*see Box 3.9*).

Besides primary and secondary legislation, there is a huge amount of *tertiary legislation*—legislative instruments, made under the authority of an Act of Parliament, but which are subject to no parliamentary scrutiny at all. For example, in housing law, numerous powers are given to ministers to issue 'directions' or other instruments, drafted in the form of legislation and which effectively have the force of law, but which are simply issued by the government department in question. Similar examples are found in many other areas of government.

There is, lastly, a fourth category of instrument, sometimes referred to as *quasi-legislation* or *soft law*, which comprises statements of good practice or guidance. These may be made under the authority of an Act of Parliament and are in some cases subject to parliamentary approval. But, as with tertiary legislation, they get no detailed parliamentary discussion. Examples include the Highway Code or the codes of practice relating to police behaviour made under the Police and Criminal Evidence Act 1984 (*see Chapter 5*). Many other examples could be given.

Box 3.5 *Continued*

There is a practical problem with tertiary and quasi-legislation. It is not published through the National Archive—the official outlet for legislative publications. An important issue of principle flows from this. It is frequently asserted that because legislation is published by a single authoritative source, 'everyone is deemed to know the law'. Such a claim is simply not sustainable in the case of such instruments.

The legislative process has undergone significant though inadequately publicized change in recent years—an example of the often understated dynamism that characterizes many developments in the English legal system. The discussion here focuses on the process of enacting an Act of Parliament. Apart from the inherent importance of the subject, there is a good practical reason why lawyers need to know about this. There are now circumstances—albeit limited—in which what was said about a bill as it passed through Parliament may be used in court when dealing with a question of statutory interpretation (*see Pepper v Hart* [1993] AC 593 (HL); *see further, Statutory interpretation*)

Primary legislation

All Acts of Parliament start as bills. Most bills are accompanied by an Explanatory Note, a detailed note drafted by the bill's sponsors, which sets out the background to the bill and explains what it is trying to achieve. (Since 1999, Explanatory Notes have also been published alongside new Acts of Parliament.) Although some lawyers do not like this practice, arguing that interpretation of statutes is a matter for the courts, the notes are in reality the key to any public understanding of legislation. They are written in plain language and are designed to explain the policy and legal context to non-lawyers. This is possibly the most important procedural innovation of recent years. All bills and notes are published on the internet. Four distinct types of bill may be identified (*see further, Box 3.6*):

Box 3.6 Legal system explained

Acts of Parliament: Public General Acts and Local and Personal Acts

Most Acts of Parliament are Public General Acts. Each Public General Act contains a section which defines to which parts of the United Kingdom the Act applies. Since the devolution of legislative powers to Scotland and Wales, this is not always straightforward. But all such Acts are of general application in those parts of the countries to which they are stated to apply. There are special rules relating to legislation which is effective in Northern Ireland.

Box 3.6 *Continued*

By contrast, Local and Personal Acts (together called 'Private Acts') apply only to a local area (say a town), to a specific institution (say a body such as a university), or a particular individual. The procedure by which Local and Personal Acts become law is quite different from the procedure by which Public General Acts become law. The detail is not considered here, but in essence such Acts use a procedure involving committees of the House, not the full House of Commons.

Private Acts must be sharply distinguished from Private Members' Acts (*see Box 3.7*).

(1) Government bills, which are designed to advance the political programme of the party in government. These bills are sponsored by individual ministers and absorb the bulk of parliamentary time spent on legislation.

(2) Law reform bills, which arise from recommendations made by law reform agencies, such as the Law Commission (*see further, Chapter 4, The Law Commission*). These are less politically controversial.

(3) Consolidation bills, which bring together into a single place a wide range of legislative provisions scattered through many Acts of Parliament and thus difficult to find. These measures do not introduce new law but tidy up and re-present what is already on the statute book. Failure to consolidate adds to the complexity of carrying out legal research, since printed versions of Acts of Parliament that have been substantially amended can be very misleading. New computer technology makes it easier to keep texts of statutes up to date. In the United Kingdom this is achieved in part by commercial legal information providers such as Westlaw, in part by government through its Statute Law Database. This does not reduce the need for regular consolidation bills. A special procedure enables these bills to reach the statute book without going through the full parliamentary process discussed later.

(4) Private Members' bills, which are a special type of bill introduced by backbench MPs (*see Box 3.7*).

Box 3.7   Legal system explained

Private Members' Acts

Private Members' Acts start as bills introduced by individual MPs who are not members of the government. They are subject to special rules relating to their content. The most important is that they cannot contain any provision that would result in the

Box 3.7 *Continued*

expenditure of public money. These bills are also subject to special procedural rules, which mean that only a very few such measures reach the statute book in any given year.

The backbenchers who bring these bills forward are selected following a ballot—a process that takes place early in each parliamentary session. Private Members' bills are debated only on Fridays—a day when the pressure of government business is usually less. Twenty private members are able to introduce their measures following the ballot; those near the top of the list have a greater chance of seeing their bills introduced into law. For a bill to have any chance of success it must either be supported by the government, or at least not actively resisted by the government.

The Housing (Homeless Persons) Bill 1976 is a good example: as originally drafted it would have given a range of legal rights to the homeless that the government regarded as wholly unacceptable. In that case, the government offered the bill's sponsor, the late Stephen Ross, an alternative bill, which he took forward. With this government support the bill passed into law.

Private Members' bills can be used to introduce measures on which there are fierce divisions of opinion, but where those divisions are not the subject of party political debate. An example is the Abortion Act 1967, which was a very important, obviously controversial, measure introduced by David Steel, in relation to which none of the main political parties wished to tie their political reputations. The willingness of a private member to take such an issue forward means that the political parties, in particular the government party, can to an extent distance themselves from the issue.

Over the last 15 years or so, about eight out of 20 Private Members' bills have reached the statute book each year. There are three other means by which backbenchers may attempt to introduce legislation: 'presentation bills', Ten Minute Rule bills, and bills from individual members of the House of Lords. The numbers of such bills passing into law are tiny and are not considered further here.

Preparatory stages

Before being presented to Parliament, many bills start the process of becoming law by being included in the political manifesto of the party that won the last general election. Political parties want power to turn their ideas into legislative form. Issues that involve a good deal of specialist know-how are frequently the subject of consultation with persons or other agencies outside government. There are various ways in which this is carried out.

Commonly, ideas for new policies and related changes in the law are floated in *green papers*, so called because years ago they were published with green covers. (These days, image-conscious governments produce green papers with multi-coloured covers.)

They set out policy proposals and ask the public for comments on them. The government often attempts to steer responses by indicating its preliminary view on what should happen.

Following initial consultation, a further and firmer statement of the government's policy objectives may be published in *white papers* (which are also no longer white) that summarize responses to consultations and set out what the government plans to do.

Until a few years ago, parliamentary practice required all bills to be presented first to Parliament. Failure to do this was regarded as an insult to Parliament. The process of enacting bills has recently undergone two important changes.

Firstly, *consultation*. The wisdom of the principle that bills must not see the light of day until they are brought to Parliament became subject to increasing criticism. As the result of important procedural changes recommended by the House of Commons Select Committee on Modernisation in 1997, an increasing number of bills are now published in draft and circulated for comment and criticism by those most likely to be affected, prior to their formal introduction into Parliament. The Select Committee on Modernisation recommended that this procedure be followed as much as possible. The former Labour government increasingly used this procedure; the Coalition government currently has eight draft bills under consideration.

Secondly, *hearings*. In some cases, a draft bill is the subject of special hearings by a committee of MPs—a practice common in the United States and other countries but not until recently used in the United Kingdom. An early example was the pre-legislative scrutiny by the Social Security Select Committee of the government's draft bill on pension sharing on divorce, published in June 1998. The Financial Services and Markets Bill 1999 was subject to even more scrutiny. First, a consultation paper was issued in July 1998, with a draft bill attached to it. Comments were sought in particular from those likely to be affected by it. Secondly, the draft bill was the subject of hearings before two parliamentary committees: one, the Treasury Committee of the House of Commons; the other, a joint committee of the House of Commons and House of Lords, both of which issued reports on the draft bill. All this work led to further changes to the bill being made before it was formally introduced into the House of Commons in June 1999.

The Queen's speech

Each session of Parliament, now usually in May, opens with the Queen's speech. Written by the government, it sets out the legislative priorities for the coming parliamentary session. Getting a slot in the Queen's speech is a key objective for ministers seeking to introduce a bill into Parliament. Without it, their legislative ambitions cannot be advanced. (The only exception is emergency legislation needed urgently to deal with an important but unexpected issue.) The details of the Queen's speech are determined each year by a Cabinet committee.

As with bills, until recently, considerable care used to be taken by ministers not to reveal the content of the speech until it was read out in Parliament. However, once again, the procedure has changed. A draft legislative programme is announced well in advance of the Queen's speech. The intention is that those particularly likely to be affected by proposed measures can start to consider their potential impact.

The advantage of these developments is clear. Those likely to be affected are given the opportunity to comment on proposed legislation before it reaches its final form.

Parliamentary stages

Once a bill's policy objectives have been determined by government, those policies are transformed into legislative form—the bill—by specially trained lawyers known as parliamentary counsel. Most measures designed to advance the political objectives of the government are presented first in the House of Commons; less controversial measures (including consolidation bills) may start in the House of Lords. *Diagram 3.1* sets out the different stages.

The *first reading* is purely formal. The House orders the bill to be printed. (All bills are printed on a light-blue-coloured paper, to distinguish them from the subsequent Act, which is printed on white paper.) No further progress can be made until it has been printed.

At the *second reading*, the minister responsible sets out the main policy objectives; the opposition parties set out their objections. This is followed by comments from other MPs. At the end of the debate, there is a summing-up by a government minister. It is rare for a government bill to be defeated at this stage, though this happened to the Shops Bill 1986, designed to deregulate Sunday trading. If a bill requires either the raising of taxation or the expenditure of public money, Parliament also has to pass (respectively) a ways and means resolution or a money resolution.

The *committee stage* involves detailed scrutiny of the text. This is carried out by one of several *public bill* committees of MPs, which may range in size from 16 to 50. Unlike the standing committees they replaced, public bill committees have the power to take written and oral evidence from officials and experts outside Parliament. They consider the clauses of the bill, as drafted, consider amendments proposed to those clauses, and determine whether or not such amendments should or should not be accepted. This

Diagram 3.1 Passage of a bill

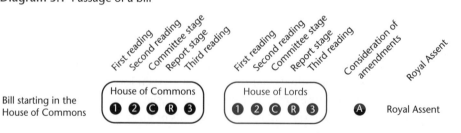

A bill can start in the House of Commons or the House of Lords and must be approved in the same form by both Houses before becoming an Act of Parliament.

is a highly 'political' stage in the legislative process. Not only do opposition members put down amendments that they have thought of, but members of the public bill committee are also subject to intense lobbying from groups outside Parliament, seeking to persuade them to put down amendments that reflect their interests. These groups also exert pressure in other ways, through press releases, interviews on TV and radio, and so on.

Given that the governing party always has a majority on the committee, and that MPs from the government side are instructed to vote as the whip tells them, the government usually either gets its way, or makes only those concessions which it is prepared to accept. Nevertheless, bills are frequently amended and often emerge from the overall process significantly changed from the form in which they were first advanced. Very occasionally, where a bill is being rushed through Parliament, or involves significant constitutional change, the committee stage takes place in the whole House.

The *report stage* is where what happened to the bill in committee is reported to the main House. This gives the government the chance to undo anything that the committee may have done to the bill which the government does not like. It is often the point at which amendments which the government itself wishes to introduce into the bill (perhaps following debate in committee) are introduced.

Lastly, the *third reading* is a more formal stage in which the bill in its amended form is brought together but no more amendments are made. The bill then goes to the House of Lords, where it begins a similar process.

The progress of a bill through Parliament is regulated by a *programme order*, formally approved by Parliament following the second reading. This sets out the dates by which each stage of the bill must be completed. One effect of programme orders is that, not infrequently, substantial parts of a bill may pass into law without any debate.

The House of Lords

Procedure in the House of Lords is broadly similar to that in the Commons. The major differences are:

(1) the committee stage is taken on the floor of the House. There are no separate committees of peers which report back to the House as a whole;

(2) there is no programme order, and thus debate on amendments is not restricted; and

(3) amendments can be made at the third reading stage.

These potentially can be, and on occasion are, a source of delay. In theory the House of Lords is able to wreck or seriously delay legislation. But peers are aware that, given their status as a non-elected legislative body, the ultimate decision on legislation must lie with the elected House of Commons. While they do not in practice wholly destroy bills, there have been a number of occasions in recent years where they have secured significant amendments or even caused a bill to be withdrawn. (For a case study on the work of the House of Lords, *see Box 3.8.*)

Box 3.8 Reform in progress

House of Lords consideration of the Constitutional Reform Bill 2004

As part of the former Labour government's programme of constitutional reform, in June 2003, it was decided to abolish the post of Lord Chancellor, establish a new mechanism for the appointment of judges, and create a new Supreme Court. This generated considerable controversy, not least among the senior judiciary who feared that such a step could undermine the conventional constitutional balance of power between the judicial and executive branches of government. It was also discovered that, in any event, simple abolition of the office of Lord Chancellor without legislation was not technically possible.

There followed a period of public consultation on the three principal elements of reform, and the government published summaries of the responses on 26 January 2004. The Supreme Court and judicial appointments issues were also considered by the Constitutional Affairs Committee of the House of Commons, which reported on 3 February 2004. One of its recommendations was that the Constitutional Reform Bill would be 'a clear candidate for examination in draft'. A number of speakers in the House of Lords on 12 February 2004 made the same point.

Nevertheless, the government decided to introduce the Constitutional Reform Bill into the House of Lords without prior discussion. It became clear that, such was the degree of opposition to the bill, it stood little chance of being passed by the House of Lords. However, the Lords was also conscious that to deny progress to what the government regarded as an important measure would be a risky step to take.

The compromise was to 'rediscover' a procedure—not used in relation to a government bill for about 90 years—of referring the bill to a specially constituted select committee of the House of Lords. The Committee spent nine days hearing evidence and a further 11 days deliberating. It made numerous drafting changes to the bill, though on the two main issues—abolition of the post of Lord Chancellor and creation of the Supreme Court—the committee remained divided.

The effect of the process was that people outside Parliament had a chance to comment on the bill. The Committee also made detailed changes to the bill, as public bill committees of the House of Commons do.

Although the select committee did not agree on everything, the bill, as amended, was recommitted to the House of Lords, from which it finally emerged as the Constitutional Reform Act 2005.

One of the most important features of the select committee's report is that it published the hitherto unpublished agreement reached by the Lord Chancellor and the Lord Chief Justice on the guarantees needed to ensure the continuing independence of the judiciary. For further information about the concordat, as the agreement is known, *see Chapter 4, Support for the judiciary: the concordat.*

Once the Lords' stages are complete, there is a further process in the Commons and the Lords for all the amendments to be agreed to produce a single version of the text.

Particularly towards the end of the parliamentary year, this can lead to dramatic horse-trading (called, unbelievably, 'ping-pong') between Lords and Commons, especially where measures are very controversial. In the last resort, the House of Lords has power under the Parliament Act 1911 to delay a Commons bill (though not a money bill) for up to one year. If there is an ultimate impasse, then the view of the elected legislature, the House of Commons, prevails. The most recent occasion on which the Parliament Act was invoked was in relation to the passing of the Hunting Act 2004.

Carry forward. This further procedural change enables a bill to be considered over two parliamentary sessions. It used to be the case that if the passage of a bill through Parliament was not completed before the end of the parliamentary session it fell and had to start the whole process again in the following session. Carry forward enables bills to be carried into the next session without having to start again. It should be noted, though, that carry forward is only possible within a Parliament; bills not enacted before a general election is held cannot be carried forward to the new Parliament, even if the new government is formed by the same political party as the outgoing government. In such cases, the bill must start the parliamentary process anew.

Carry forward has the practical advantage that there can be greater flexibility over the dates on which bills can be introduced into Parliament. Before the procedural change, the presentation of new bills was front-loaded into the first half of each parliamentary session to try to ensure that there was sufficient parliamentary time to enable them to become law. This pressure is eased by carry forward. It also represents a sensible attempt to prevent the detail of complex legislation being rushed through Parliament, at the end of a parliamentary session, often with undesirable drafting consequences.

Royal assent and commencement

Lastly comes *royal assent*. This has not been withheld since 1707, but, reflecting the fact that the United Kingdom is a constitutional monarchy, remains a formal step that has to be completed. It is at this point that the *clauses* in the bill become the *sections* in the Act.

The mere fact that an Act has completed the legislative process does not mean it becomes effective at once. Commonly, new administrative arrangements have to be made before an Act can become operational. In such cases, the legislation is effective only when a *commencement order*—a special type of statutory instrument (*see Secondary legislation*)—is made. (The Easter Act 1928 has still not been brought into force.) It is essential that those who wish to use new rules of law discover whether or not statutory provisions are in force. This can involve difficult detailed research. However, the availability of statutes online, through legislation database services such as Westlaw or *LexisNexis* and the government Statute Law Database, has made it much easier to discover whether new legislation is in force.

Reports of debates

The debates on all the parliamentary stages are the subject of verbatim reporting in the Official Reports of the Houses of Parliament (known collectively as*Hansard*).

Thus it is possible to research what was said and by whom at each stage of the parliamentary process. These reports also detail how MPs voted. These reports are available online.

Secondary legislation

Because of the time needed to ensure the passage of legislation through Parliament, modern Acts of Parliament tend to contain the essential principles of legislation only. The detail is filled in by *secondary legislation* made under the authority of the Act, but which is not subject to the full parliamentary scrutiny that a bill faces. Secondary legislation is technically known as *statutory instruments*, which come in two forms, *regulations* (the most common) and *orders*.

   Underpinning the creation of secondary legislation is a number of controls designed to ensure that governments only introduce measures for which they have authority:

(1) regulations are subject to formal vetting by the Joint Committee on Statutory Instruments;

(2) many categories of statutory instruments also have to be shown in draft to particular bodies or organizations detailed in the 'parent' Act. Many governmental advisory committees are given the specific task of commenting on and vetting proposed regulations (*see Box 3.9*). Some parent Acts require the government not just to consult with a specific nominated body, but with 'such bodies as appear to have an interest in the legislation'. This is code for requiring the government to discuss the content of proposed delegated legislation with a range of interested groups;

(3) there is the potential for some parliamentary input, though this rarely happens. All regulations are subject either to a *negative resolution procedure* or to an *affirmative resolution procedure*. (Two particular types of statutory instrument, commencement orders—which bring Acts of Parliament, or parts of Acts of Parliament into effect—and orders in council, are not subject to any parliamentary procedure.) The *negative resolution procedure* is the more common. It means that, once laid before Parliament, a new regulation becomes effective on the date stated in the regulation, *unless* Parliament passes a resolution stating that the regulations should be annulled. Given that regulations are introduced by government and that (usually) the government has a majority in the House of Commons, annulment happens very infrequently. By contrast, the *affirmative resolution procedure* means that a regulation laid before Parliament cannot become effective unless Parliament adopts a resolution that states *positively* that the regulation should become effective. It cannot be said that this process gives the House of Commons much control over the detail, since debate is permitted only on the underlying issues, not the specific details. But affirmative resolution debates give some opportunity for opposition parties to make broad political points about the regulation in question. An example is found in the annual

uprating of social security benefits. The relevant regulations are subject to the affirmative resolution procedure. Debate on whether the new amounts should be 50p more or less is not permitted; but general debate about social security provision and social welfare policy is allowed;

(4) in an extreme case, the validity of a statutory instrument may be challenged in the courts and, if found to be *ultra vires* (outside the legal framework provided by the parent Act), will be declared by the courts to be a nullity. Although a relatively rare occurrence, it can happen. (See, e.g. *R v Secretary of State for Trade and Industry, ex p Thomson Holidays, The Times*, 12 January 2000, CA and *R v Secretary of State for the Environment, Transport and the Regions and Another, ex p Spath Holme Ltd* [2000] 1 All ER 884, HL.)

Box 3.9   Legal system explained

Case study: consultation on regulations: the case of social security

An interesting example of the use of a specialist committee to review delegated legislation is found in the work of the Social Security Advisory Committee, which looks at draft regulations relating to social security. It not only considers the proposals, but also consults on them with a wide range of bodies and pressure groups outside government. It reflects on these comments before making its own report to the government. The government then decides whether or not to accept the advice of its Committee.

When it brings forward the final version of the regulations, the government is required to publish a special report which not only reproduces the report from the Advisory Committee, but also details why the government has (or more often has not) followed the advice of the Committee.

This represents a particular form of accountability which to some extent replaces normal parliamentary debate; arguably it is more relevant since most of those consulted have a specialist interest in and knowledge of the area. This is a model that, it has been forcefully argued, should apply in other regulation-making contexts.

Amending legislation

The process of amending legislation is usually done by passing a new Act that alters an Act already on the statute book. Thus amending legislation must take its turn in finding a slot in the legislative programme. On occasion, ministers have sought to make their lives easier by providing that provisions in an Act of Parliament can be amended by statutory instrument, thereby avoiding Parliament. These provisions are called 'Henry VIII clauses', reflecting the propensity of that monarch to ride roughshod over Parliament. However, they are not regarded with favour.

One consequence of the passing of amending legislation is that it can make it hard to find out what the current law is on a particular subject. The Statute Law Database provides details of how and when legislation has been amended. It is not yet complete, in the sense that not all legislation on the statute book is currently in the database; but its scope is expanding. It is a very important new legal resource.

Regulatory reform

In recent years, it has been accepted that where legislation has imposed unnecessary regulatory burdens on business or individuals, they should be able to be removed without waiting for a full parliamentary legislative slot. The first Act to move in this direction, the Deregulation and Contracting-Out Act 1994, provided that, subject to detailed safeguards, ministers could lay orders before Parliament that had the effect of amending legislation. The power was used 48 times to remove burdens that might not otherwise have received parliamentary time. The Regulatory Reform Act 2001 gave ministers wider powers to lay orders before Parliament to amend legislation, again so long as any such amendment removed burdens. This Act was replaced by the Legislative and Regulatory Reform Act 2006, which came into force at the start of 2007.

The passage of all these bills was very controversial. MPs and commentators outside government feared the powers could allow ministers to make significant legislative change without exposing their arguments to parliamentary scrutiny. Many of these fears were, arguably, overstated; certainly ministers' powers to amend legislation are significantly circumscribed (*see Box 3.10* for further detail).

Box 3.10   Legal system explained

Legislative and Regulatory Reform Act 2006: scope of the Act

In relation to powers to amend legislation, ministers are given power to make any provision by order, called a legislative reform order, that would remove or reduce any burden, or remove or reduce the overall burdens, to which any person is subject as a direct or indirect result of any legislation. Burdens are defined as: a financial cost; an administrative inconvenience; an obstacle to efficiency, productivity, or profitability; or a sanction, criminal or otherwise, which affects the carrying on of any lawful activity. Each of these concepts is defined further in the legislation. One clear limit is that ministers can only use their power to reform an area where there is already a legislative framework. It could be used to replace one statutory regime with another where this removes or reduces burdens. But it cannot be used to introduce an entirely new regulatory regime. So, for example, it would not be possible to create an entirely new legislative framework relating to a new area of consumer protection, employment rights, or environmental protection simply because there are considered to be good policy reasons for doing so.

Box 3.10 *Continued*

Ministers are also given power to amend the powers of regulators so that their functions comply more closely with defined Principles of Good Regulation. These are that: regulatory activities should be carried out in a way that is transparent, accountable, proportionate, consistent, and should be targeted only at cases in which action is needed.

Save where a minister wants simply to restate existing law, he or she must meet six conditions:

(1) There are no non-legislative solutions that will satisfactorily remedy the difficulty that the order is intended to address.

(2) The effect of the provision made by the order is proportionate to its policy objective.

(3) The provision made by the order, taken as a whole, strikes a fair balance between the public interest and the interests of the persons adversely affected by the order.

(4) The provision made by the order does not remove any necessary protection.

(5) The provision made by the order will not prevent any person from continuing to exercise any right or freedom that he or she might reasonably expect to continue to exercise.

(6) The provision made by the order is not constitutionally significant.

The Act sets out the procedures ministers must follow. First, the minister must consult on his proposals for an order. He must then lay a draft order and an explanatory document before Parliament. The order must be made by statutory instrument in accordance with the negative resolution procedure, or the affirmative resolution procedure (*see Secondary legislation*) or the super-affirmative resolution procedure. The minister's recommended procedure applies unless either House of Parliament requires a higher level of procedure.

Super-affirmative procedure

The super-affirmative procedure affords greater parliamentary scrutiny than the ordinary affirmative resolution orders procedure. First, the minister must lay a proposed legislative reform order before Parliament in draft, together with a full explanatory document. Following a 60-day period of parliamentary consideration, during which time the proposal is referred automatically and simultaneously to two parliamentary committees, the committees make their first reports to their respective Houses. If the reports are favourable, the next stage is for the minister formally to lay a draft order in each House, along with an explanation of any changes made to the original draft proposal. If the minister accepts any changes proposed to the draft order by the committees or others between this stage and the final vote on the order, he must formally withdraw the draft order he has laid and replace it with another which incorporates the changes. The ability to make changes (minor or otherwise) to the draft order is a

Box 3.10   *Continued*

key feature of the order-making power, which is not available to statutory instruments dealt with in the usual way.

The final procedural stages for parliamentary scrutiny of draft regulatory reform orders are set out in standing orders. The Commons committee produces a report on the draft order within 15 days. The Lords committee has no set time period but usually reports within the same time period. Each House then considers the relevant committee report on the draft order (this is the main feature that makes this form of parliamentary consideration 'super-affirmative').

The use of parliamentary time: a comment

Given the domination of the parliamentary timetable by the government machine, it is sometimes asked whether the amount of time spent debating proposals in relation to which the outcome is totally or largely predictable is worthwhile. Elected MPs do not, in general, have any detailed control over the content of Acts of Parliament; indeed, there is no guarantee that all provisions of bills are subject to considered debate. The vast bulk of legislation—secondary legislation—reaches the statute book with no consideration by MPs at all.

Nevertheless, it should be remembered that much of the detail of the parliamentary process was developed in an age where the party machine and the discipline over the parliamentary party provided by the whips was not as it is today. But the enormous power of the government to dominate the legislative process is perhaps the best reason for retaining the detailed process that currently exists. This arises from the very political theories, noted earlier, that underpin the British Constitution and its system of government. Although ministers may be able to achieve their desired goals in the end, the process ensures that they will have been subject to challenge by elected MPs. Without these procedures it would be far harder for ministers seeking to defend a particular measure to claim legitimacy for their legislative acts.

Judges and the courts

It should be stressed at the outset that only the higher courts—the Supreme Court, the Court of Appeal, and the High Court—have authority to make law (*see further, Chapter 8*). There are three principal ways in which English courts develop English law:

- *Development of the common law.* England is a 'common law' country. This means that many of the principal doctrines of law have been established, not by Parliament, but through cases determined in the higher courts. Many examples of judicial law-making can be given:
  - the fundamental law of contract, on which much economic activity is based;
  - the law of negligence, which relates (among other matters) to dealing with the aftermath of accidents and other forms of injury; and
  - the development of the principles of *judicial review*, which is the basis on which judicial control of the administrative arm of government is achieved.

- *Statutory interpretation.* Courts play a crucial role in the interpretation of the statutes that Parliament has enacted.

- *Procedural law.* Courts also make important contributions to the development of procedures that the courts follow.

Development of the common law

It may seem odd today, but judicial power to make law was, for many years, not acknowledged. Judges said their power was merely to 'discover' basic principles of the common law. No one seriously believes this now; judges do, in fact, make law. There is, however, often unease about the theoretical basis for this power. Certainly it cannot derive from any theory of representative democracy; judges are not elected. Rather, the power of the judiciary depends on the doctrine of the *separation of powers*, that to prevent dictatorial powers from being asserted by any one branch of government there must be checks and balances in the constitution. Judges have the primary task of ensuring adherence by ministers and other agents of the state to the principles of the *rule of law*. This cannot be achieved without an independent judiciary (*see further, Box 3.11*).

Box 3.11   Legal system explained

Independence of the judiciary

The key claim made for the judges, indeed for adjudicators of all kinds (*see Chapter 9*), is that they must not only be, but be seen to be, independent. Judicial independence relates centrally to the constitutional function of judges in interpreting and applying law outside the constraints of internal government departmental policies. Judges and adjudicators not perceived as independent are fatally compromised in the eyes of the public, particularly by those whose disputes are being resolved by them. One of the strong claims for adjudicators in the English legal system is that, with rare exceptions,

Box 3.11 *Continued*

they both appear to be independent and act independently. This is not to say that they may not bring their own views of the world into play when reaching decisions or determining facts. But claims of corruption of those who hold judicial office—which would fatally compromise judicial independence—are not heard in England.

The Constitutional Reform Act 2005 made judicial independence, for the first time, subject to statutory protection. Section 3 states, in part:

(1) The Lord Chancellor, other ministers of the Crown, and all with responsibility for matters relating to the judiciary or otherwise to the administration of justice must uphold the continued independence of the judiciary....

(4) The following particular duties are imposed for the purpose of upholding that independence.

(5) The Lord Chancellor and other ministers of the Crown must not seek to influence particular judicial decisions through any special access to the judiciary.

(6) The Lord Chancellor must have regard to—

   (a) the need to defend that independence;
   (b) the need for the judiciary to have the support necessary to enable them to exercise their functions;
   (c) the need for the public interest in regard to matters relating to the judiciary or otherwise to the administration of justice to be properly represented in decisions affecting those matters.

When one hears government ministers criticizing the senior judiciary, it is sensible to bear these provisions in mind.

The law-making powers of the judiciary are supported by two other fundamental principles: the hierarchical structure of the courts, and the doctrine of precedent.

The hierarchical structure of the courts

The idea of courts being arranged within a hierarchical framework is quite straightforward. The courts are organized on the basis of seniority (*see Diagram 3.2*); the higher the level of seniority, the greater the authority of the court. Thus the decisions of the Supreme Court (formerly the House of Lords) are the most authoritative; those of the Court of Appeal are next; those of the High Court third. Decisions of courts at lower levels are not regarded as precedents, though very occasionally the judgment of a county court judge on a novel point of law may get reported (*see Box 3.12* on the importance of law reporting).

Diagram 3.2 An outline of the court structure in England and Wales

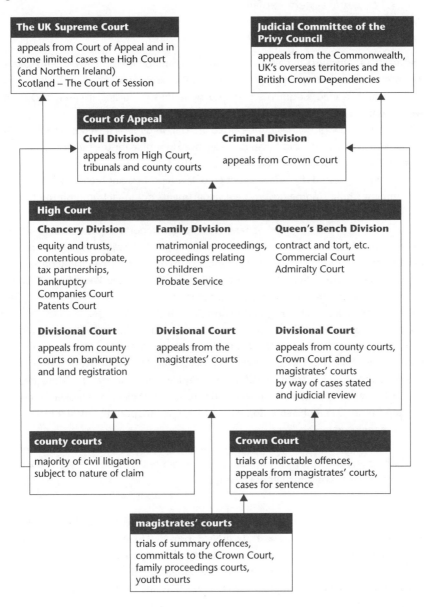

The UK Supreme Court

appeals from Court of Appeal and in some limited cases the High Court (and Northern Ireland)
Scotland – The Court of Session

Judicial Committee of the Privy Council

appeals from the Commonwealth, UK's overseas territories and the British Crown Dependencies

Court of Appeal

Civil Division

appeals from High Court, tribunals and county courts

Criminal Division

appeals from Crown Court

High Court

Chancery Division

equity and trusts, contentious probate, tax partnerships, bankruptcy
Companies Court
Patents Court

Family Division

matrimonial proceedings, proceedings relating to children
Probate Service

Queen's Bench Division

contract and tort, etc.
Commercial Court
Admiralty Court

Divisional Court

appeals from county courts on bankruptcy and land registration

Divisional Court

appeals from the magistrates' courts

Divisional Court

appeals from county courts, Crown Court and magistrates' courts
by way of cases stated and judicial review

county courts

majority of civil litigation subject to nature of claim

Crown Court

trials of indictable offences, appeals from magistrates' courts, cases for sentence

magistrates' courts

trials of summary offences, committals to the Crown Court, family proceedings courts, youth courts

Source: Judicial and Court Statistics 2010 (see <www.justice.gov.uk/downloads/publications/statistics-and-data/courts-and-sentencing/judicial-court-stats.pdf>)

This diagram is, of necessity, much simplified and should not be taken as a comprehensive statement on the jurisdiction of any specific court.

Box 3.12   Legal system explained

Law reporting

The ability of the courts to develop principles of common law or to give authoritative interpretations of statutory principles relies on the publication of law reports, which contain the reasoned judgments prepared by judges in particular cases, and from which general principles are then drawn.

Decisions as to which cases get reported are not, in general, taken by members of the judiciary themselves, but by editorial teams responsible for the publication of law reports. Many sets of law reports are now published.

It should be stressed that the production of law reports is not seen as a function of government (though some government departments do, in fact, publish the text of decisions in specialist areas, such as taxation and immigration).

The most authoritative of the generalist sets of law reports are those published by the Incorporated Council of Law Reporting, which publishes a range of reports, including: Appeal Cases (decisions of the Supreme Court), the Queen's Bench Reports, and the Chancery Division Reports. The Council also publishes the *Weekly Law Reports*. There is a requirement that if a case is reported in these reports, that is the version that must be used, at least in the High Court and Court of Appeal.

Other sets of law reports are published by commercial publishers. The most widely available generalist set is the *All England Law Reports*, published by LexisNexis. In addition, there is now a wide range of specialist reports available in areas ranging from local government to housing, from education to family law, from criminal appeals to judicial review. Many sub-specialisms in legal practice now have their own sets of law reports. Law reports are also reported in some broadsheet newspapers; the most widely used are those reported in *The Times*.

Maintaining a complete library of all sets of reports is very expensive, only possible for the best-endowed university libraries, the libraries of the Law Society and the Inns of Court, and the most prosperous law firms.

Legal electronic databases

In addition to reports in paper format, more and more law reports are now published in electronic format. For many years, LexisNexis provided full-text versions of decisions from a range of the most senior courts. Initially, their use was limited by the refusal of judges to take into account judgments that appeared only in the Lexis format. This has now changed. Other companies, such as Westlaw and Justcite also offer extensive legal databases.

A great deal of source legal material is also available free online. The Supreme Court/House of Lords has placed all judgments since 14 November 1996 online; Her Majesty's Courts and Tribunals Service website carries reports from the Court of Appeal and Administrative Court. There are also other online sources available (*see the Online Resource Centre, list of websites*). For those who have access to the internet, the costs of obtaining the report of a particular case are limited to the costs of going

Box 3.12 *Continued*

online and printing the text. The provision of the reports themselves is at present free. To facilitate use of these sources, the 'neutral citation' of judgments has been introduced *(see Box 3.13)*.

Box 3.13   Legal system explained

Neutral citation of judgments

Since 11 January 2001 every judgment of the Court of Appeal and of the Administrative Court, and since 14 January 2002 every judgment of the High Court, has been pre-pared and issued as approved with single spacing, paragraph numbering (in the margins), and no page numbers. In courts with more than one judge the paragraph numbering continues sequentially through each judgment and does not start again at the beginning of each judgment. A unique reference number is given to each judgment.

   Each Court of Appeal judgment starts with the year, followed by EW (for England and Wales), then CA (for Court of Appeal), followed by Civ (for Civil) or Crim (for Criminal) and finally the sequential number. For example *Smith v Jones* [2001] EWCA Civ 10.

   In the High Court, abbreviated as HC, the number comes before the divisional abbre-viation and, unlike Court of Appeal judgments, the latter is bracketed: (Ch(ancery)), (Pat(ent)), (Q(ueen's) B(ench)), (Admin(istrative)), (Comm(ercial)), (Admlty(Admiralty)), (TCC (Technology and Construction Court)), or (Fam(ily)) as appropriate. For example, [2002] EWHC 123 (Fam) or [2002] EWHC 124 (QB) or [2002] EWHC 125 (Ch).

   Paragraph numbers are referred to in square brackets. Thus paragraph 59 in *Green v White* [2002] EWHC 124 (QB) would be cited: *Green v White* [2002] EWHC 124 at [59]; paragraphs 30–35 in *Smith v Jones* would be *Smith v Jones* [2001] EWCA Civ 10 at [30]–[35]. Page numbers are not given.

   This 'neutral citation' is the official number attributed to the judgment and must always be used at least once when the judgment is cited in a later judgment. It is designed to facilitate the use of websites so that the confusion that is caused by differ-ences in pagination that occur when information is downloaded to different comput-ers with different printers is avoided.

There have been occasions on which this hierarchical structure has been challenged, most notably by the late Lord Denning when, as Master of the Rolls, he was the senior judge in the Court of Appeal. He argued that, since most appeals ended in his court and did not proceed to the House of Lords/Supreme Court, his court should have similar law-making power to the top court. His arguments did not prevail, though they provoke a broader question: do we need all the levels of court, in particular all the levels of appeal, that currently exist?

The doctrine of precedent

This is also a simple idea, though not always easy to apply in practice. The essence of precedent is that a principle of law, established in one case, must be applied in a similar situation in a later case. Such a rule of law continues to be applied until either another court decides that the case was incorrectly decided, or for some other reason cannot be allowed to stand; or until a court higher in the hierarchy overturns the decision; or until Parliament decides to change the law by passing a new Act of Parliament that overrules or alters the rule laid down by the court.

There have long been arguments for and against the use of precedent. Against, it is argued that precedent introduces unnecessary rigidity into the law, thereby preventing legal doctrine from developing as society develops. In its favour, the use of precedent is said to bring certainty to the law by enabling people to know how issues in the future will be resolved. The principle of law in one case that forms the precedent is known by the Latin phrase, the *ratio decidendi*. Any part of a judgment that does not form part of the *ratio* is not part of the precedent, and thus not relevant in later cases. These are referred to as *obiter dicta*.

There are many reasons why these apparently straightforward ideas can be exceptionally hard to apply in practice:

(1) The facts on which the *ratio* of one case is based never replicate themselves precisely in a later case. Thus lawyers wishing to argue that a particular precedent does not apply to the later case will seek to *distinguish* the two fact situations, thereby, they hope, rendering the earlier decision irrelevant.

(2) Given the large number of reported decisions, there may be situations where a decision reached in one case was reached in ignorance of other relevant decisions. The argument is then made that the precedent in question was made incorrectly or, again to use the Latin, *per incuriam*.

(3) Because of the large numbers of cases that are now reported, there may be two decisions in the law reports that are simply inconsistent, so that straightforward application of a particular decision to a new situation is not possible.

(4) Since 1966, the House of Lords/Supreme Court has asserted the authority, in very exceptional circumstances, to change its mind and alter a precedent. It may, therefore, on occasion and notwithstanding the existence of clear precedents, decide that earlier cases were wrongly decided and that the law should now be changed.

There are also more technical reasons why the doctrine of precedent is not always simple to apply in practice. It can be very hard to decide what the precedent is. When, in the famous case of *Donoghue v Stevenson* [1942] AC 562 the House of Lords found that a manufacturer of ginger-beer was negligent after it allowed a decomposed snail to enter a ginger-beer bottle, was this a case about not allowing snails to get into ginger-beer bottles? Or about not allowing foreign bodies in general to get into manu-facturing processes? Or was it about the duty of care that any person—including a professional person giving advice to a client—should demonstrate towards others? In short, what was the 'level of generality' at which the particular instance of snails in ginger-beer bottles was to be treated in future cases?

Even if the principle of law that can be derived from the cases is clear—such as the principle of negligence, that one person owes a 'duty of care' to his or her 'neigh-bour'—who will be categorized for these purposes as a neighbour? And what will be the standard of behaviour that will result in a conclusion that the 'duty of care' has been broken? If teachers take a party of teenage pupils to the seaside, and one of the pupils is washed out to sea by a freak wave, were the teachers in breach of a duty of care in those circumstances to the pupil who drowned? Or did the fault lie with the pupil who ignored advice and went clambering onto the rocks from which he was swept?

Much of the litigation that arises out of the principles of the law of negligence is not seeking to redefine the principles of the law, but rather exploring the extent to which those principles should apply in new situations of risk. This is not the place for a detailed analysis of the law of negligence. The point to be stressed here is that, even though at one level the law may be quite clear, the situations to which the law may be applied in future can be far from clear. And the development of the law is in the hands of the senior courts, not legislators.

Statutory interpretation

Statutory interpretation is another way in which courts with authority within the hier-archical structure develop the law. The work of the courts interpreting statutes may not be as dramatic at developing principles of common law, as judges clearly have to work within the texts that have been prescribed by Parliament through the legislative process. Nevertheless, the interpretative process can lead to the clarification of words in statutes, and thus in the implementation of those statutory rules (*see Box 3.14* for an example).

Box 3.14   System in action

Case study: statutory interpretation: the case of Mr Fitzpatrick

In current housing law, a tenant can pass his or her right to occupy premises on death to a 'member of his family'. The question has arisen in a number of cases over the last 50 years: who is a member of the family? Initially, in the 1940s, it was held that the phrase was limited to blood relatives; thus the former mistress of a deceased tenant could not take over the tenancy, despite having lived together with her partner for many years. Later, in the 1960s, it was held that, with changes in the nature of relationships

Box 3.14   *Continued*

and society's attitudes, the mistress of a deceased male tenant could in such a circumstance be regarded as a member of the family and thus take over the tenancy.

More recently still, in 1999, the House of Lords decided that the long-standing homosexual partner of a deceased tenant could similarly take over the tenancy. The judges found that, in terms of love and affection and thus the attributes of family, a distinction could no longer sensibly be drawn between a couple of the same sex living together and a couple of different sexes. Reference was made to the provisions of the European Convention on Human Rights protecting family and family life. (See *Fitzpatrick v Sterling Housing Association* [1999] 3 WLR 1113, HL.)

This case illustrates that, even within a single statutory framework, there is scope for developing statute law by interpretation that reflects changes in social practices and attitudes.

The power of the court to interpret statutes has increased now the Human Rights Act 1998 is in force. British courts not only interpret legislative provisions, but also test the substance of legislative provisions against the standards laid down in the Human Rights Act 1998, which derive from the Articles of the European Convention on Human Rights (*see European Convention on Human Rights*). In cases where the courts find that they must declare a statute or provision within a statute to be incompatible with the Convention—effectively requiring ministers to change the law—the courts acquired a significant new power to develop English law.

One question that may be asked is: why—if Parliament has passed legislation—is there any need for the courts to intervene at all? There are two basic reasons why this needs to happen: the unpredictability of fact situations, and the ambiguity of language.

The unpredictability of fact situations

However detailed statutory provisions may be, they can only set down rules at a certain level of generality. There will always be those whose particular situation is not captured *precisely* by the legislative provisions. In such cases the facts need to be determined by the courts—in itself not always a straightforward task—and, once this has been done, a judgment reached as to whether or not the relevant legislative provision applies. Particularly where legislative provisions seek to impose some burden or penalty on the citizen, there is a general judicial policy that this should not happen unless those provisions quite clearly 'bite' on the individual circumstances concerned. To give an example: the 'tax avoidance industry' engages in the detailed analysis of tax legislation to see whether arrangements can be made to enable those who might otherwise have to pay tax quite legitimately to avoid paying it.[2]

Many apparently pedantic points taken in some criminal trials are, similarly, the result of the principle that a person should not be convicted of a crime unless the facts found by the court are clearly caught by the relevant statutory provisions.

The ambiguity of language

The other justification for the role of the courts is that the meaning of language is not itself precise. There may be ambiguities arising from the way particular rules have been drafted. There may be differences in the meaning of words chosen. Some statutory provisions are deliberately drafted using words such as 'reasonable' or 'fair' that do not have a precise meaning and that therefore give scope to officials and others for the exercise of discretion or judgement. There may be changes in the meaning of a word (*see Box 3.14*) resulting from broader developments in society.

There is, in the literature on statutory interpretation, a set of principles—rather inaccurately described as 'rules'—designed to be of assistance. These include:

- the literal rule;
- the golden rule;
- the mischief rule; and
- the 'unified common approach'.

The *literal rule* is what it implies. The words of a statute should be given their literal meaning. However, this does not solve the problem of linguistic ambiguity—words may have more than one literal meaning.

The *golden rule* suggests that the courts should use the literal rule unless this would lead to manifest absurdity.

The *mischief rule* asks the judge to consider what was the legislative purpose of the Act— what was the 'mischief' the Act was trying to deal with. Any question of interpretation should be resolved in such a way as not to thwart that purpose. The problem with this view is: does it undermine the independence of the judiciary? If the mischief rule is rigidly adhered to, does this not result in the judges losing their independence and doing the government's job for it? On the other hand, if legislative intention is wilfully ignored by the judges, how does that square with the constitutional principle that the primary law-making authority should rest with the democratically elected Parliament, not the unelected judiciary?

It will be quickly appreciated that these principles are not consistent with each other; they offer great scope for reaching different conclusions. The reality is that different judges favour different approaches; indeed individual judges are themselves not consistent.

---

[2] The distinction between tax avoidance, which if successful is lawful, and tax evasion, which is clearly unlawful, should be noted. In recent years, governments have become increasingly adept in their attempts to thwart tax avoiders. Tax incentives—schemes that attract tax advantages and are part of the government's fiscal policy, for example tax relief on pension premiums—are quite different.

The *unified common approach* is the label now used to suggest that judges should adopt a broader, less specific approach. It implies that judges should start by considering the literal meaning of the words; but if they are really not clear or would lead to absurd results then the judge should consider what the purpose of the Act was and interpret the Act so as to advance that purpose.

The inference should not be drawn from this discussion that the bases on which the judiciary interprets legislation are so varied that there is no principle at all. Reading reported judgments in decided cases reveals that judges in the higher courts go to great lengths to try to ensure that their decisions are founded in rationality and principle. But that there are different approaches cannot be denied, and the inevitable consequence is that there is some inconsistency of outcome. The ability of different judges to arrive at different decisions in individual cases is seen most clearly in cases that go to appeal, when courts are quite frequently divided in their views.

Procedural law

A third way in which judges make law is by the development of new procedures. A number of examples may be briefly mentioned:

- the day-to-day practice of litigation is regulated by rules of procedure that are drafted by the judiciary—in Rules Committees—acting under legislative authority. Many rules of court are supplemented by practice directions, also made by the judiciary (*see Chapters 6, 7, and 8*);

- rules of evidence—what evidence is or is not admissible in a court of law—has to an important degree been developed by the judiciary, though supplemented by very important statutory provisions, for example the Police and Criminal Evidence Act 1984, the Civil Evidence Act 1991, or the Criminal Justice Act 2003 (*see Chapter 5*);

- a number of powers of the court are asserted on the basis of what it claims as its 'inherent jurisdiction'—the High Court's powers of wardship over children may be given as an example (*see Chapter 7*); and perhaps the most important judicial development of the last generation has been the shaping of the rules and practice relating to judicial review, which goes to the heart of the powers of the judiciary to render government departments and other public bodies legally accountable for their actions (*see Chapter 6*).

Europe

So far the discussion has considered the law-making process in the United Kingdom as though it was a completely domestic process. But no student of the modern English legal system can ignore the impact of international law in general, and European law in particular on law-making in the United Kingdom. Despite the United Kingdom's long engagement with Europe, the European institutions and their practices and procedures still remain poorly understood. The following pages offer a brief introduction to the law-making functions carried out in Europe, the role of the courts in Europe and their overall impact on the United Kingdom. We also consider the question of where the European institutions get their law-making authority.

Before proceeding, we must be clear that, in talking about 'Europe', two completely separate entities are involved which are frequently confused: the Council of Europe and the European Union.

The Council of Europe

The Council of Europe was established after the end of the Second World War. Its primary aim was to prevent a repeat of the human rights outrages of the Second World War period. More recently it has engaged in assisting countries of the former Eastern Bloc to develop institutional arrangements that will support their move to democracy. The Council now has 47 member countries and is based in Strasbourg.

European Convention on Human Rights

The Council of Europe's most significant achievement, insofar as its impact on English law is concerned, was the creation of the European Convention on Human Rights. This document, drafted with considerable input from British lawyers, is a charter of fundamental rights and freedoms agreed by all the member states of the Council of Europe. In common with all international treaties, the Convention could not come into effect until it had been ratified by a specified number of governments. This happened in 1953. The Convention has been amended a number of times since then. The current version, amended by Protocol 11, came into effect in November 1998. Adherence to the standards set out in the Convention is the responsibility of the European Court of Human Rights which has power to decide cases raising alleged breaches of the European Convention by member states of the Council of Europe.

Normally, treaties seek to regulate relationships between nation states. They may provide that one country may take action against another where there is an alleged breach of an international treaty obligation. The European Convention on Human Rights is unusual. In it, provision is made for *individuals* to take proceedings to the European Court of Human Rights where it is alleged that a government is in breach of its obligations under the treaty. Individuals cannot start proceedings unless the government in question has agreed that this can take place. In the case of the United Kingdom, the right of individuals to take proceedings against the British government for alleged breaches of the Convention was accepted by the British government in 1966.

The European Union

The European Union, originally called the European Economic Community, came into being on 1 January 1958. Starting with just six members, it has now expanded to

27 members. Its founding document was the Treaty of Rome, 1957. The fundamental purpose of the European Union is to create a free market for the provision of goods and services in all EU countries. To achieve this, the European Union seeks to provide a framework within which trade between the member countries of the European Union can take place fairly. For example, there are policies on the promotion of competition and the regulation of anti-competitive practices; similarly, there are policies to liberalize industries, such as telecommunications or the airlines, to allow greater freedom of consumer choice. It prescribes EU-wide standards for the manufacture of goods, both to protect consumers and to try to ensure that industry overheads are broadly similar. The laws of the European Union are designed to promote those policies. It also sets common standards for social security provision for workers, as well as entitlements for citizens of one country in the European Union to work in other countries of the Union. There are specific rules relating to employment protection, including safety at work and the prohibition of discriminatory employment practices.

In recent years, the European Union has developed other wider areas of activity, for example, the promotion of human rights and supporting measures for social cohesion. In response to criticism about the inability of the European Union to intervene in situations of conflict that might seem to warrant a Europe-wide approach, moves have been made towards the creation of a common foreign and security policy and a common defence policy. It is seeking to develop supra-national responses to challenges posed by climate change and environmental degradation. There have also been important initiatives in the area of justice and home affairs. And, of course, at present the European Union is seeking ways to resolve the financial problems that exist in the euro-zone.

The impact of the Council of Europe and the European Union on law-making in the United Kingdom

The Council of Europe

The impact of the Council of Europe on the law-making process in the United Kingdom has been indirect. The European Convention on Human Rights sets out a list of principles against which the actions of governments may be tested. Where cases are taken before the European Court of Human Rights in Strasbourg that result in a decision that a rule of British law or some practice of the British government is contrary to the provisions of the Convention, this leads to a requirement that the British government change the law to bring it into line with the Convention, as interpreted by the Court. There have been over 30 decisions of the Court adverse to the British government. One of these led to the passing of the Interception of Communications Act 1985, which regulates phone-tapping.

Following enactment of the Human Rights Act 1998, most of the articles of the European Convention on Human Rights became directly enforceable in the English courts. Indeed, it is arguable that the Human Rights Act 1998 did not so much change the law, as make it easier to use because cases can be brought in the United Kingdom without the need to go to Strasbourg.

The Human Rights Act 1998 has had two principal effects on the law-making process in the United Kingdom.

First, in presenting bills to Parliament, ministers must declare that in their opinion proposed legislation complies with Convention provisions. Policy-makers within government have become conscious of the need to ensure that policies are Convention-compliant. New legislation is scrutinized for compliance by the Parliamen-tary Joint Committee on Human Rights. To that extent the Act has had significant impact.

Secondly, under section 4 of the Human Rights Act 1998 British courts have power to declare a provision of UK law to be incompatible with the provisions of the Convention. This formula was adopted to preserve the notion of the sovereignty of Parliament. This is in effect a direction to the government of the day that a particular statutory provision must be amended in order to comply with the provisions of the European Convention on Human Rights. Although not declaring an Act of Parliament, or a provision in an Act, unlawful, any such judicial ruling puts overwhelming pressure on ministers to introduce changes so that the incompatibility is removed. In this important sense, the legislative freedom of ministers is reduced.

Legal arguments based on the Human Rights Act 1998 have been advanced in a significant number of cases in the upper courts (High Court, Court of Appeal, and Supreme Court). However, the extent to which these arguments have been upheld in the courts has so far been relatively limited. The major exception to this generalization has been in the area of counter-terrorism where the New Labour administration of Tony Blair sought to extend significantly, to 90 days, the length of time terror suspects could be detained without trial. The House of Lords ruled in *A and Others v Secretary of State for the Home Department* [2004] UKHL 56 that this was contrary to the provisions of the European Convention on Human Rights. The present Coalition government has now decided, in its Protection of Freedoms Act 2012, that the normal period of detention without trial should be 14 days.

One feature of the Human Rights Act 1998 is that it provides that, in interpreting its provisions, English judges must take account of the jurisprudence developed by the European Court of Human Rights in Strasbourg. One possibly unexpected consequence is that judges in the court in Strasbourg now appear to take more notice of what British judges say on human rights issues and their interpretation of the Convention.

The basis for establishing the legitimacy and authority of the Council of Europe and the European Court of Human Rights to make rules of law which have an effect in the United Kingdom is quite hard to analyse.

The Council of Europe is not a parliamentary body to which individuals are elected. The Council was established by International Treaty, which the UK government ratified. Similarly, the European Convention on Human Rights and the related powers of the European Court of Human Rights were ratified by the UK government by exercise of its prerogative power to sign up to international treaties. There are no elections for membership of the Council of Europe.

As regards the authority of the European Court, it is clear that any allegation of breach of the European Convention on Human Rights must now be determined first in the English Courts. Nevertheless, there remains a residual right for parties to go to the European Court on Human Rights.

Paradoxically, some now claim that the Human Rights Act 1998 has to an extent undermined the legitimacy and authority of the European Court of Human Rights. They argue that if issues under the European Convention on Human Rights can be argued in the UK Supreme Court, there should be no need for a further tier to appeal to the European Court. On the other side, there are still those who strongly defend the right of the European Court to be the ultimate authority in the interpretation of the European Convention, not least because this ensures that there are consistent standards applied throughout all the members states of the Council of Europe.

The Council of Europe itself has recognized that there is a need to reform the relationship between the European Court of Human rights and member states, though this is more for the practical reason that the Court has a huge backlog of cases which lead to unacceptable delay. In 2012, an important conference was held in Brighton, which set out the framework for a programme of reform to the Court (*see Box 3.15*).

Box 3.15   Reform in progress

Reforming the European Court of Human Rights:
the Brighton Declaration

The question of the relationship between the English legal system, in particular the UK Supreme Court, and the European Court of Human Rights has generated a lot of political controversy—much of it deriving from the decision in the case involving the terror suspect Abu Qatada. The British government wanted to deport him to Jordan for trial. The European Court feared that evidence obtained by torture could be used against him. This would be contrary to the European Convention on Human Rights. The European Court decided that he could not be deported until this question had been resolved. The political fallout from this very controversial case has been significant, with many people demanding that the United Kingdom no longer acknowledge the jurisdiction of the European Court.

In April 2012—during the UK Presidency of the Council of Europe—a conference was held in Brighton to consider proposals for the reform of the court, designed to rebalance the relationship between Strasbourg and national supreme courts.

In outline, the Brighton Declaration makes proposals for:

- amending the Convention to include the principles of subsidiarity and the margin of appreciation; this should give more power to domestic courts to decide matters without intervention from Strasbourg;

Box 3.15   *Continued*

- amending the Convention to tighten the admissibility criteria, so that trivial cases can be thrown out and the focus of the Court can be on serious abuses;
- reducing the time limit for making claims from six months to four;
- improving the selection process for judges;
- setting out a roadmap for further reform.

The full text of the Brighton Declaration is at <https://wcd.coe.int/ViewDoc. jsp?id=1934031>.

While these may be useful first steps, the final implementation of the reform proposals will take some time to complete.

Further developments may result following publication of the report of the Independent Commission on a UK Bill of Rights, set up by the Coalition government in 2011.

The European Union

The law-making processes of the European Union are extremely complex. They are not at all like the parliamentary processes we are familiar with in the United Kingdom. Under the European Treaties, the European Commission has the exclusive right to initiate proposals for legislation. Whether or not its proposals become law and, if so, on what terms, depends on the outcome of complex negotiations and consensus-building between the Commission, the Council of Ministers[3], and the European Parliament. The nature of the legislative process is more like that in the United States, where the President proposes legislation and the Congress decides whether or not it passes into law—the whole process relying on negotiation between the White House and Capitol Hill.

A number of technical points need to be made about the different types of law that emerge from the EU institutions.

First, all the institutions of the European Union draw their ultimate authority from the treaties that underpin the establishment of the European Union, in particular, the Treaty of Rome, the Single European Act, the Treaty of Maastricht, the Treaty of

---

[3] Although in the formal descriptions of the European Union there is only one Council of Ministers, there is in fact a substantial number of Councils of Ministers reflecting the different portfolios of those ministers, for example agriculture, foreign policy, economic matters, trade matters, and the like. The supreme Council of Ministers is that which comprises the leaders of the governments of the European Union, brought together to determine the most fundamental issues affecting the Union. Initially, decisions of the Council of Ministers had to be unanimous; a single vote against a proposal would result in its not being adopted. As the European Union has expanded, the principle of unanimity has been replaced in a large number of policy areas by the principle of qualified majority, which enables measures to be introduced despite the opposition of some ministers.

Amsterdam, the Treaty of Nice, and the Treaty of Lisbon. These may be regarded as the *primary legislation* of the European Union. (An attempt to create a formal Constitution for the European Union foundered because citizens of a number of European countries voted against the idea in referendums.)

While many of these fundamental provisions of Community law are designed to deal with obligations between states, some have been held by the European Court of Justice to have 'direct effect' on the law of individual members states in the determination of individual rights and duties. For treaty provisions to have this effect, the content of the provision must be clear; the provision must be self-executing, in the sense that it imposes a specific duty; and the provision must not contain any conditions or qualifications. There are many European Court of Justice decisions that have held particular treaty Articles to be of direct effect; for example Article 81, which outlaws anti-competitive agreements, or Article 141, establishing the principle of equal pay between men and women.

Secondly, where a treaty provision is found to be of direct effect it may be both vertically and horizontally effective. 'Vertical' effectiveness arises when an individual uses a treaty provision to challenge an act of the government or some other public body. 'Horizontal' effectiveness arises where one individual or other body wishes to use EU law to challenge the behaviour of another individual body of similar status.

Thirdly, more detailed legislative measures that seek to implement the detailed policies of the European Union can collectively be described as the *secondary legislation* of the European Union. This emerges in three different guises: regulations, directives, and decisions.

Under Article 249 of the Treaty establishing the European Community, *regulations* are—like the treaty provisions considered earlier—of 'direct effect', that is to say they automatically become part of the internal law of each of the member states of the European Union. An example is Regulation 1408/71, which deals with aspects of social security law and the need to insure workers under a scheme of national insurance. As with treaty provisions, regulations may have both vertical and horizontal effectiveness.

Directives are more general in tone. They set down standards towards which member states are required to aim, but some discretion as to the detail of how that is to be done is left to the member states. The implementation in the United Kingdom of the Working-Time Directive, which regulates the number of hours worked each week, provides a good example. The principle of direct effect may arise if there is a complaint that a government has failed so to incorporate the provision into national law. In the United Kingdom, directives are usually brought into effect in statutory instruments.

Decisions are rulings on particular matters addressed to either governments of member states, corporations, or individuals. For example, an argument about whether a particular take-over bid was or was not anti-competitive could be the subject of a decision. Decisions are binding on those to whom they are addressed (Article 249).

In addition to these forms of secondary legislation, the European Union may also make *recommendations* and *opinions*, but these do not have any direct effect.

One of the fundamental principles of membership of the European Union is that the institutions of the Union, in particular the European Commission and the European Court of Justice, have power to force member states to obey EU law. This gives the Union power to intervene directly in the law-making processes of member states. This raises important but difficult questions about the authority of the Union as a law-making body.

The UK government, in an attempt to ensure the perceived legitimacy of the European Union's law-making powers in the United Kingdom, decided that before joining the Union—which happened in 1973—this step should be preceded by two important events. First, there was a national referendum (*see Box 3.1*) which sought, and obtained, a majority vote in favour of entry into the Union. Secondly, the UK government enacted the European Communities Act, 1972, a British Act of Parliament which committed the UK government to implementing and abiding by EU law, if necessary without the any intervention of the UK Parliament.

In practice, the British government seeks to incorporate rules of European law into British law, whether or not it likes them. Furthermore, the House of Lords decided in *Factortame v Secretary of State for Transport (No. 2)* [1991] 1 AC 603 that if the provisions of a British Act of Parliament are in conflict with European law, then the British Act is to be regarded as of no effect. Until then, the British courts had never sought to overrule an Act of Parliament, since Parliament was always regarded as the sovereign law-making authority.

These developments have led eurosceptic critics of the UK's involvement in the European Union to make two specific arguments which challenge the authority of the Union's law-making institutions: democratic deficit; and loss of sovereignty.

Under the first heading—'democratic deficit'—it is argued that too many of the institutions established to run the European Union operate without the authority/legitimacy bestowed by democratic accountability. For example, the exclusive right to initiate legislation is held by the European Commission. But Commissioners are appointed to their positions. They have not been directly elected by the people of the European Union on the basis of a legislative manifesto such as occurs in elections in the United Kingdom. In practice, the powers of Commissioners are constrained by the European Council of Ministers, comprising elected ministers from each of the member states, and whose approval of legislative proposals is always required. But this does not satisfy those who think that there should be a closer link between the exercise of a vote by the ordinary citizen, and the making of legislation.

The European Parliament—the only body with directly elected members—does have a part to play in the law-making process. Indeed, over the last 20 years, successive treaties (Maastricht (1992), Amsterdam (1997), Nice (2001), and most recently, Lisbon (2007) (*see Box 3.16*)) have given the European Parliament increasing amounts of power to control the content of legislative measures. It still cannot initiate legislative proposals, but the majority of European law-making must be approved by a majority of the European Parliament as well as the Council of Ministers. (The poor participation by the British electorate in European elections may be explained, at least in part, by widespread ignorance about the role of the European Parliament and how it has changed.)

In addition, a further principle has been developed within the European Union—'subsidiarity'—which is designed to ensure that the European institutions exercise their law-making powers only in relation to those matters that are truly essential to the working of the aims and objectives of the European Union and that can only be achieved by inter-governmental co-operation. Other, subsidiary, matters are to be left to the law-making bodies in member states. It is beyond the scope of this work to assess the extent to which the principle of subsidiarity has in fact reduced the amount of law-making activity undertaken in the institutions of the European Union.

At the same time, other institutional reform has been designed to make the working of the European Union more efficient, particularly with the increase in the size of the Union to 27 member states. This has, arguably, had the effect of distancing still further the European institutions from the principles of representation and accountability, mentioned earlier.

Box 3.16   Reform in progress

Principal features of the Lisbon Treaty

The changes introduced by ratification of the Lisbon Treaty are not well understood. The Treaty:

- created the post of President of the European Council, who is elected for two and a half years. This replaced the former system whereby the Presidency of the European Council circulated every six months between the 27 heads of government who are the members of the European Council;
- created the post of High Representative for the Union in Foreign Affairs and Security Policy. The post-holder is also Vice-President of the Commission. A new European External Action Service will provide back up and support to the High Representative. The European Union will also have a single legal personality designed to make its international negotiating power more effective;
- gave the European Parliament new powers over EU legislation, the EU budget, and international agreements, designed to ensure the European Parliament is placed on an equal footing with the Council for the vast bulk of EU legislation. It also limits the size of the European Parliament to 751, with no country having more than 96 nor fewer than six Members of the European Parliament;
- makes qualified majority voting the default voting method in the European Council of Ministers, save where treaties require a different procedure (e.g. unanimity). This means that qualified majority voting has been extended to many new policy areas, such as immigration and culture. From 2014, a new voting method will be introduced—double majority voting. To be passed by the Council, proposed EU laws will

---

Box 3.16 *Continued*

then require a majority not only of the Union's member countries (55 per cent) but also of the EU population (65 per cent);

- gives national parliaments greater opportunities to be involved in the work of the Union, in particular to monitor the principle of subsidiarity whereby the Union only acts where results can be better attained at Union level;
- explicitly recognizes for the first time the possibility of a member state withdrawing from the European Union.

Source: <www.europa.eu/lisbon_treaty/index_en.htm>.

In addition to the suggestion that there is a democratic deficit, eurosceptics also argue that UK membership of the European Union (and indeed of the Council of Europe) has been accompanied by what they regard as an unacceptable loss of sovereignty—the ability of the British Parliament to determine its own laws. Eurosceptics decry the loss of sovereignty involved in the United Kingdom's membership of the European Union; they do not regard the principle of subsidiarity as offering any meaningful return of power to the United Kingdom. By contrast, europhiles argue that the transfer of sovereignty is in the national interest as it adds to the ability of the United Kingdom—in partnership with other European countries—to negotiate with the other substantial political and economic powers.

Ultimately, the issue of the relationship between the United Kingdom and Europe will be determined, not by academic analysis of democratic deficit or loss of sovereignty, but by practical economic and political concerns. Will the interests of the United Kingdom be served better inside or outside membership of these bodies?

Development of European law: the role of the European courts

The European Union has, as one of its constituent bodies, the European Court of Justice, which sits in Luxembourg. The Council of Europe has the European Court of Human Rights, which sits in Strasbourg. Both courts have played a significant role in the development of the jurisprudence of, respectively, the European Union and the European Convention on Human Rights.

It is hard to summarize the 'European' approach of the judges in these courts. The legal instruments of both the European Union and the Council of Europe, with which the European courts have to deal, are drafted in the relatively more broad-brush European continental tradition than in the more linguistically precise tradition familiar in the United Kingdom. As a consequence, the approach of judges in the European courts has been to decide cases very much bearing the purposes of the relevant treaty provisions in mind. British legal minds often regard this as rather distinct from the approach favoured in the United Kingdom. Perhaps more accurately the European approach may represent something of a hybrid between the British approaches to common law and statutory interpretation. Decisions of the European courts lead to the development of legal principle on a case-by-case basis, not dissimilar to the common law tradition. At the same time, these developments are set within the framework of treaties and other instruments that have emanated from the institutions of the European Union and the Council of Europe and that require interpretation by the courts.

Other sources of law-making

At the end of this lengthy account, the existence of other sources of law-making will be mentioned only briefly.

Local and regional government

Local government has long had power to make by-laws—a form of tertiary legislation (*see Box 3.5*)—since by-laws are made under the authority of Acts of Parliament but apply only in the area of the local authority in question.

Under the terms of the Scotland Act 1998 the Scottish Parliament was granted authority to pass legislation in areas within its competence. Under the Government of Wales Act 1998, the National Assembly for Wales was given power to pass secondary legislation, again within the scope of its areas of competence. Limited powers to make primary legislation have been granted to the Welsh Assembly Government by the Government of Wales Act 2006. The Northern Ireland Act 1998 similarly grants legislative power to the Northern Ireland Assembly.

Other rule-making agencies

A great deal of rule making is also undertaken by industry regulators: for example the Civil Aviation Authority or the regulators of the privatized utilities. Under the Financial Services and Markets Act 2000, major rule-making powers were conferred on the Financial Services Authority. The rules made by these bodies fall outside the parliamentary framework though in most cases they are based on legislative authority conferred by Act of Parliament.

Other international institutions and bodies of international law

We have considered the Council of Europe and the European Union in context. Many other international institutions also have an impact on detailed rules of English law. There are many industries, for example aviation and telecommunications, where at least some of the legislative framework results from the provisions of international treaties. Increasing globalization of economic activity combined with increasing pressure to deal with some of the major issues of the day—the environment, genetic engineering, global warming, international trade—ensures that this trend will develop.

Lastly, it is relevant to note the existence of a separate body of private international law—in essence rules of English law, designed to assist in the determination of private law rights and entitlements that have an international dimension.

Conclusion

Law-making is a central feature of modern government. It is theoretically based in democratic principles, though by no means all sources of law derive their authority from those principles. Law-making and other normative statements also occur in a variety of formats. This all makes for considerable complexity that has increased enormously in recent years. It is unlikely that the ordinary person in the street is aware of more than a fraction of the law which in theory affects him or her. It is fanciful to claim that ordinary people can be assumed to know the law. One of the challenges facing modern society is how new technologies can be used to transform this vast mass of legal information into knowledge that can actually be used by the ordinary citizen.

Questions

Use the self-test questions on the Online Resource Centre to test your understanding of the topics covered in this chapter and receive tailored feedback:

www.oxfordtextbooks.co.uk/orc/partington13_14/

Weblinks

Check the Online Resource Centre for a selection of annotated weblinks allowing you to research easily topics of particular interest:

www.oxfordtextbooks.co.uk/orc/partington13_14/

Blog items

See www.martinpartington.com (access via the Online Resource Centre)

Includes notes on: the Independent Commission on a British Bill of Rights; the reforms to the electoral system; fixed-term parliaments; the role of the courts in developing the law of privacy; the value of the BBC website 'democracy live'; House of Lords reform; the impact of the Human Rights Act 1998; the limitations of the Regulation of Investigatory Powers Act 2000 to protect privacy; the Protection of Freedoms Act 2012.

Further reading

BALDWIN, R., *Rules and Government* (Oxford, Oxford University Press, 1995)

BENOIT-ROHMER, F., and KLEBES, H., *Towards a Pan-European Legal Area* (Strasbourg, Council of Europe, 2005)

BIRCH, A. H., *Representative and Responsible Government: an Essay on the British Constitution* (Ann Arbor, MI, University of Michigan, 1989)

BIRKINSHAW, P., *Freedom of Information: The Law, the Practice and the Ideal* (3rd edn, Cambridge, Cambridge University Press, 2001)

—— *Government and Information: The Law Relating to Access, Disclosure and Their Regulation* (3rd edn, Haywards Heath, Tottel Publishing, 2005)

BOGDANOR, V. (ed.), *The British Constitution in the Twentieth Century* (Oxford, Oxford University Press, 2004)

—— *The New British Constitution* (Oxford, Hart Publishing, 2009)

BRAZIER, A. (ed.), *Parliament, Politics and Law Making: Issues and Developments in the Legislative Process* (London, Hansard Society, 2004)

BRAZIER, R., *Constitutional Practice: the Foundations of British Government* (3rd edn, Oxford, Oxford University Press, 1999)

—— *Constitutional Reform: Reshaping the British Political System* (3rd edn, Oxford, Oxford University Press, 2008)

—— *Ministers of the Crown* (Oxford, Clarendon Press, 1997)

BUTLER, D., BOGDANOR, V., and SUMMERS, R. (eds), *Law, Politics and the Constitution* (Oxford, Oxford University Press, 1999)

CARR, H., CARTER, S., and HORSEY, K., *Skills for Law Students* (Oxford, Oxford University Press, 2009)

COSGROVE, R. A., *The Rule of Law: Albert Venn Dicey, Victorian Jurist* (London, Palgrave Macmillan, 1980)

CRAIG, P., *The Lisbon Treaty: Law, Politics, and Treaty Reform* (Oxford, Oxford University Press, 2010)

FINCH, E., and FAFINSKI, S., *Legal Skills* (2nd edn, Oxford, Oxford University Press, 2009)

FINE, B., *Democracy and the Rule of Law: Liberal Ideals and Marxist Critiques* (London, Pluto Press, 1984)

FREEMAN, N., *The Art of the Loophole: Making the Law Work for You* (London, Coronet Books, 2012)

HARDEN, I., and LEWIS, N., *The Noble Lie: the British Constitution and the Rule of Law* (London, Hutchinson, 1986)

HARTLEY, T. C., *Constitutional Problems of the European Union* (Oxford, Hart Publishing, 1999)

—— *The Foundations of European Community Law: an Introduction to the Constitutional and Administrative Law of the European Community* (7th edn, Oxford, Oxford University Press, 2010)

HOLLAND, J. A., and WEBB, J., *Learning Legal Rules* (7th edn, Oxford, Oxford University Press, 2010)

HUTCHINSON, A. C., *Laughing at the Gods: Great Judges and How They Made the Common Law* (Cambridge, Cambridge University Press, 2011)

MARSHALL, G. (ed.), *Ministerial Responsibility* (Oxford, Oxford University Press, 1989)

PAGE, E. C., *Governing by Numbers: Delegated Legislation and Everyday Policymaking* (Oxford, Hart Publishing, 2001)

PULZER, P., *Political Representation and Elections in Britain* (London, Taylor & Francis Ltd, 2009)

ROBINSON, C., *Electoral Systems and Voting in Britain* (Edinburgh, Edinburgh University Press, 2009)

SCHUTZE, R., *An Introduction to European Law* (Cambridge, Cambridge University Press, 2012)

SYRPIS, P., *The Judiciary, the Legislature and the EU Internal Market* (Cambridge, Cambridge University Press, 2012)

TWINING, W., and MIERS, D., *How to do Things with Rules: a Primer of Interpretation* (5th edn, Cambridge, Cambridge University Press, 2010)

VILE, M. J. C., *Constitutionalism and the Separation of Powers* (2nd edn, Indianapolis, IN, Liberty Fund, c. 1998)

WASS, D., *Government and the Governed* (London, Taylor & Francis Ltd, 2009)

PART II

THE INSTITUTIONAL FRAMEWORK

4

Shaping the institutional framework: the role of government

Introduction: shaping the system

One way in which the English legal system has changed over the years has been the increased involvement of government in shaping and reforming it. Central government now provides substantial levels of funding not only for running court services and publicly funded legal services, but also for the huge array of other services which are part of or impact upon the legal system. The police, prison and probation services, and administrative tribunals are obvious examples. All governments are concerned with keeping levels of public expenditure under control and securing value for money; they are always looking for ways of delivering services in a more cost effective way.

These concerns are now far more acute, given the 2010 Coalition government's commitment to significant reductions in public expenditure. Cuts are affecting the legal system. Many regard any cuts as by definition leading to changes that are retrograde and undesirable. However, this is to assume that all public moneys are currently wisely and efficiently spent. If this assumption is not accepted, then some curbs on public expenditure could in fact promote changes that are actually beneficial to the system. There may be opportunities to improve, as well as threats to existing provision. It is not obvious that, for example, more intensive use of some court buildings and closure of others is necessarily a bad thing.

This chapter considers the principal government departments that have been and will continue to be shaping the English legal system:

- the Ministry of Justice (MoJ);
- the Home Office; and
- other central government departments.

Lurking behind all of them is the Treasury.

The Ministry of Justice

The MoJ plays the central role in the development of policy relating to the legal system. It was established in 2007. This was the culmination of a dramatic process of constitutional change that had seen the former Lord Chancellor's Department (LCD) become the Department for Constitutional Affairs (DCA) (in 2003).

There had long been calls for the creation of an MoJ. Many argued that the former split between the LCD/DCA and the Home Office (with the latter largely responsible for criminal justice) prevented the development of a coherent justice policy.

There was also concern about the post of the Lord Chancellor. Historically, the Lord Chancellor had always been a member of the non-elected House of Lords, not the House of Commons. He (there have been no female Lord Chancellors) was always a qualified lawyer. And he embodied a peculiar position in the government, apparently breaching the principle of the separation of powers, since he was simultaneously a member of the executive (the Lord Chancellor is a member of the Cabinet); the head of the judiciary; and, as Speaker of the House of Lords, a member of the legislature.

When the 2003 changes were made, it was originally intended that the historic post of Lord Chancellor should simply disappear, and that the chief minister should become a Secretary of State, just like any other head of a government department. Closer analysis revealed that legislative change was needed to achieve this outcome. When first published, the Constitutional Reform Bill contained a clause that would have abolished the post of Lord Chancellor. This became one of a number of issues that were fiercely contested during the passage of the bill through Parliament. In the end a political compromise was achieved (*see Box 3.8*). It was agreed that the post of Lord Chancellor would be retained, but he would no longer be the Speaker of the House of Lords; nor would he remain the head of the judiciary—this responsibility would pass to the Lord Chief Justice. Nor would the posts of Secretary of State and Lord Chancellor necessarily be held by the same person. In future, the Secretary of State would be exclusively a member of the executive branch of government.

The government also secured the principle that the office would in future no longer have to be held by a member of the House of Lords. But the Constitutional Reform Act 2005 uniquely limits the power of the Prime Minister in relation to the person who may be appointed Lord Chancellor. The convention that the Lord Chancellor should always be a senior barrister is dropped. Instead, the Act states that the Prime Minister must appoint someone 'qualified by experience'. This is defined in section 2 of the Act as experience as a minister of the Crown; as a member of either House of Parliament; as a qualifying legal practitioner; as a teacher of law in a university; or with 'such other experience that the Prime Minister considers relevant'. The present Secretary of State/ Lord Chancellor, Chris Grayling MP, is the third to be appointed under the new law.

The MoJ (and its predecessors) is a department that has grown markedly in both size and importance within government. There was an occasion in the 1920s when its Permanent Secretary—the head civil servant—was able to record that not one item of post had been received! For many years the former LCD was seen as a bit odd in the overall government structure. In most government departments, lawyers are used as specialists advising on questions of law, drafting bills and regulations and the like, rather than being closely involved in the development of policy. In the LCD, the Permanent Secretary was required by law to be qualified as a practising lawyer, unlike his counterparts in other departments, who were not required to have specific professional qualifications. This rule was abolished in 1997. Since then the Permanent Secretary has not been a lawyer.

Over the last decade, the MoJ (and its predecessors) have come to operate much more like other large service-delivery departments. It employs around 76,000 people (including probation services) and has a budget of about £9 billion. As is discussed in this chapter, the department radically altered the management of the courts, through the creation of Her Majesty's Courts Service (HMCS) and a new Tribunals Service. In April 2011, these were merged into Her Majesty's Courts and Tribunals Service (HMCTS). It has made major changes to the ways in which the legal profession is regulated. No longer can the MoJ be regarded as at the periphery of government.

Responsibilities

The MoJ's website sets out a frightening list of responsibilities (see <www.justice.gov.uk/about/moj/what-we-do/our-responsibilities.htm>). These include: administration of correctional services in England and Wales through Her Majesty's Prison Service and the Probation Service, under the umbrella of the National Offender Management Service; youth justice and sponsorship of the Youth Justice Board; criminal, civil, family, and administrative law; criminal law and sentencing policy, including sponsorship of the Sentencing Council; sponsorship of the Law Commission; sponsorship of HMCTS; legal aid; and regulation of the legal profession.

It also has responsibility for constitutional affairs, including electoral reform and democratic engagement, civil and human rights, freedom of information, management of the United Kingdom's constitutional arrangements, and relationships including with the devolved administrations and the Crown dependencies. And the list does not mention its very important role in commissioning and undertaking the empirical research needed to inform its policy-making.

No aspect of the justice system has remained unchanged in recent years. It is the MoJ that has driven that change and that will shape future policy. In short, government injects into the English legal system a dynamism that is often not fully appreciated—both in the sense of its not being understood by those outside the system, and its not being welcomed by those inside.

Most of the activities listed earlier are considered in their appropriate context. Here we consider those that do not fit easily into other chapters.

Her Majesty's Courts and Tribunals Service

HMCTS is an executive agency of the MoJ. It started operation, as HMCS, on 1 April 2005. It was formed by merging the Court Service (set up in 1995) and the Magistrates' Courts Service (which had been run separately). The creation of HMCS was one of the main recommendations of a review of the criminal justice system carried out by Sir Robin Auld in 2001. He argued that a unified court service should be able to offer a more coherent and flexible court system. Her Majesty's Tribunals Service was created in 2006 (*see Chapter 6*). In April 2011, the two services were merged into the single HMCTS.

In common with other areas of government, HMCTS is required to deliver defined standards of service to all those who come through the doors of the courts and tribunals—whether as claimants, those defending claims, those appearing as witnesses, jurors, other friends and relatives, or general members of the public—standards unheard of only a few years ago. Many of the key tasks required of HMCTS are those of administrative efficiency: dealing with people courteously; dealing with issues expeditiously but fairly; handling matters as economically as possible and seeking to reduce costs; and—in the civil courts—recovering from parties to proceedings the costs associated with the provision of court services.

HMCTS is engaged in a programme of investment in computerization and new information technologies. This will not be complete for a number of years, but the implications for the more efficient running of the system are enormous. Increasingly sophisticated telecommunications and information technologies allow for routine proceedings to take place without the need for personal attendance at court. Professional lawyers can be relieved from wasting time attending court on purely procedural matters. Parties to proceedings can similarly be allowed to 'attend' court from a distance.

HMCS completed the roll out of its XHIBIT service in March 2006. This is a website providing up-to-date information about the progress of criminal cases listed in courts. In addition, HMCTS now runs Money Claim Online, which enables persons to bring an action for debt using the internet; Possession Claim Online, which similarly enables certain possession proceedings to be started online; and payments of fines online.

Clearly, parties are still required to attend trials. But a great deal of routine procedural work does not require attendance; it just wastes resources. Similarly, facilities are being developed to enable more evidence to be presented through video links, thus making it easier for witnesses, who may be unable or reluctant to attend a particular court, to appear.

New forms of electronic data collection also have the potential for reducing the amounts of paper that have to be brought to court for major trials. Use of legal databases is transforming the library facilities available in courts to the judiciary—outside the principal courts these were woefully inadequate.

HMCTS has also taken a hard look at the location of its court buildings and their configuration. It is creating more unified court centres where both criminal and civil cases are dealt with. At the same time it is in the process of closing 93 magistrates' courts and 49 county courts (out of a total of 530 court buildings).

Support for the judiciary: the concordat

Reforming the post of Lord Chancellor to make it more democratically accountable may initially have seemed straightforward. But it generated enormous controversy (*see Box 3.8*). The senior judiciary was extremely worried that an office, which had historically been a strong defender of the independence of the judiciary, might lose its effectiveness. The outcome of protracted and often heated discussions between the then Lord Chancellor, Lord Falconer, and the then Lord Chief Justice, Lord Woolf, resulted in publication of a concordat. This sets out how the judiciary-related functions of the Lord Chancellor would in future be carried out. There are three specific issues to be drawn from the concordat.

First, the concordat establishes the basis of the division between the functions of the Secretary of State and the Lord Chief Justice. Broadly, the Secretary of State has responsibility for determining fundamental issues, such as the level of resource available to enable the courts and tribunals to operate. These include obvious matters such as pay and pensions and the provision of accommodation. The Lord Chief Justice has responsibility for ensuring the effective deployment of the judicial resources that are available.

Secondly, the importance of the Secretary of State continuing to guarantee the independence of the judiciary was recognized. A section in the Constitutional Reform Act 2005 enshrines the principle in law (*see Box 3.11*).

Thirdly, there was to be greater transparency in a number of areas in which, hitherto, it had been argued this was lacking. The making of judicial appointments (*see Judicial appointments*) is the obvious example. (It was also important to ensure that judicial appointments would not be subject to political intervention.) There were also other issues where, in future, there would be greater procedural transparency. These included matters such as the disciplining of judges and dealing with complaints against them.

The principles set out in the concordat were subject to severe test when the announcement of the creation of the MoJ was made in 2007. Judges particularly feared that the inclusion of the National Offender Management Service in the overall activity of the new Ministry would result in resources being taken away from courts and tribunals to fund shortfalls in prisons and probation budgets. Eventually, agreement was reached that appropriate levels of funding would be guaranteed.

Judicial Office

To reinforce the institutional separation of the judiciary from the executive, a new Judicial Office was established in 2006. Its officials provide administrative support to the Lord Chief Justice. Among their most important tasks is the upholding of the concordat. They support the Lord Chief Justice's responsibilities for the disposition of the judiciary around the court system. In addition, the Office has taken over personnel functions associated with the judiciary. It also enables the development of new management processes such as appraisal of judicial performance.

For the first time, senior members of the judiciary are involved in the management of judges—a role that for many is novel, requiring the acquisition of new skills. Following the enactment of the Constitutional Reform Act 2005, a new Judicial Executive Board was set up, which supports the Lord Chief Justice in his executive and leadership roles. The Board receives secretarial support from the Judicial Office. Standing behind the Executive Board, which is a relatively small body of the most senior judges, stands the Judges' Council, first established in the 19th century. It is a larger body than the Board, and is representative of judges at all the different judicial levels. It has changed its role over the years, and now provides input to the work of the Board. It meets four times a year.

The Judicial Office is also responsible for ensuring that complaints about the judiciary are properly dealt with. This function in particular involves a complex interaction between the Lord Chancellor and the Lord Chief Justice, especially where a serious complaint about a judge is upheld and the question arises whether that individual should remain a judge. Detailed investigation of complaints about judicial conduct is undertaken by the Office for Judicial Complaints, which operates under the provisions of a concordat designed to ensure its independence from both the MoJ and the Judicial Office. In most cases it can reach a decision about a complaint itself; serious cases may be referred for review by a specially nominated senior judge. In 2011–12, 30 judges were removed from office, of whom 19 were magistrates. This is a tiny percentage of the total numbers of judicial appointments (*see Chapter 9*).

Judicial College

The Judicial Office also has formal responsibility for the work of the Judicial College (formerly the Judicial Studies Board (JSB)). The College is another part of the English legal system that has developed significantly in recent years. For a long time, many judges assumed that they knew all that there was to know about law and legal process, and that therefore judicial training was unnecessary; some regarded it as an impertinence to suggest otherwise. Notwithstanding this complacent view, there has been increasing acceptance that judicial training is needed. As early as the 1960s, judicial conferences were convened to address the particular issue of inconsistency in sentencing by the judiciary.

The scope of judicial training was put on a more formal footing in 1979 with the creation of the JSB. Over the following 30 years the Board grew in size and stature to deliver a very considerable programme of judicial training, not only to judges sitting in criminal trials, but also those handling civil trials, and to the chairs of a wide range of tribunals. It also set the framework for the training of magistrates. With the merger of HMCS and the Tribunals Service, the training resources of both were combined and, in April 2011, the JSB was renamed the Judicial College.

In delivering its programmes, the College provides both *induction* courses, which must be taken before a judge begins to sit, and *continuation* courses, which are offered as refresher courses for sitting judges. In addition, the college may arrange special programmes (as, e.g. the JSB did to introduce the judiciary to the Human Rights Act 1998 prior to its coming into force in October 2000). Most controversial was a programme, in 1995–96, to provide ethnic awareness training to the judiciary—an issue that arose from perceived differences in the ways in which people from different ethnic groups might be treated in the courts.[1] This remains an issue of great importance for the work of the courts, as well as other actors in the legal system.

Besides courses, the College provides written guidance on the running of trials in *Bench Books*—loose-leaf volumes of information that judges keep beside them for easy reference while performing their judicial functions. It has also produced a number of publications offering guidance on the skills needed by judicial office holders. Through its Equal Treatment Advisory Committee (formerly the Ethnic Minorities Advisory Committee) it has developed advice and training for judges to ensure that parties to proceedings in courts or tribunals feel they have been treated equally and not been subject to any form of discrimination. The College also sponsors one or two more practical books, notably the *Guidelines for the Assessment of Damages in Personal Injury Cases*, designed to ensure greater consistency in reaching awards for damages in personal injury cases.

The development of the role of the JSB/Judicial College is a fascinating example of the evolution of policy and practice in the English legal system. It did not stem from ministerial action or the enactment of special legislation. Rather, senior officials in the former LCD, working quietly with influential members of the judiciary, saw this as an important part of the management of a modern judicial system. Pockets of resistance among the judiciary—which undoubtedly existed years ago—have been replaced by an acceptance, reflected in professional life more generally, that continuing education is a proper, indeed essential, part of professional development. Newly appointed judges now expect training; and those in post acknowledge the need for opportunities to reflect on their work.

This is not to say that the model so far developed is perfect. The amount of training that English judges receive is still modest. Unlike the situation in some other jurisdictions, there is no university law school that offers a specialist post-graduate diploma or degree in judicial science, though an Institute for Judicial Studies was created at University College, London, in 2010. There is always more that can and should be done. Nevertheless, the development of professional judicial studies has been one of the most significant developments in the English legal system in the past two decades. It has not attracted the public attention that it deserves.

Judicial appointments

The process of making judicial appointments is another feature of the English legal system that has undergone rapid change. For many years, it was shrouded in secrecy.

Appointments were offered to a relatively small circle of barristers, mostly practising in London. The expansion of the legal profession and the opening of judicial appointments to solicitors were among the factors that meant such procedures were no longer viable. Written criteria for judicial appointment have been in the public domain

---

[1] See Hood, R., in collaboration with Cordovil, G., *Race and Sentencing: a Study in the Crown Court: A Report for the Commission for Racial Equality* (Oxford, Clarendon Press, 1992).

for well over 15 years. But this was not enough for critics of the system. Over recent years, there has been substantial further reform.

It started in 1999 when the Lord Chancellor invited Sir Leonard Peach to review the process of judicial appointments. (He was also asked to look at the process of selection of QCs.) He found that while many judicial recruitment practices had developed in accordance with the best personnel management practice, in other respects, particularly the process of consultation that went on about the merits or otherwise of those seeking judicial appointment, he found it too secretive.

While Sir Leonard did not recommend that the whole process should be taken outside the government machine, he proposed the creation of a post of *Commissioner for Judicial Appointments*, which would both provide an ombudsman function for disappointed individuals and organizations, and undertake a regular audit of applications for appointment.

The Commission for Judicial Appointments was created in 2001. The Commissioner's functions included: reviewing procedures to ensure that selection was on merit and investigating any complaints arising out of the application of appointment procedures. In his first report, published in 2002, the Commissioner noted that much had been done to make the appointment process more transparent. But he also stated that applicants for judicial appointment needed to understand: the criteria against which their applications were assessed; the processes by which their applications were assessed; the weight placed on different aspects of their applications; the role played by consultees in the assessment process; the identity of those who were consulted; and the process by which consultees' comments were taken into account. Consultees needed to understand: their role in the appointment process; the criteria against which applications will be judged; the importance of relating their comments to the criteria; and the process by which their comments will be taken into account. Failure to do this might lead to a perception of unfairness.

These changes still did not satisfy the critics. It was argued that so long as judicial appointments were the responsibility of the Lord Chancellor, this undermined the independence of the judiciary. When the DCA was created in 2003, it was decided more needed to be done.

Thus a key feature of the Constitutional Reform Act 2005 was the creation of a *Judicial Appointments Commission* (JAC), supported by a *Judicial Appointments and Conduct Ombudsman*. The JAC began work in April 2006. One of its particular aims is to increase judicial diversity. Some interpret this focus on judicial diversity as meaning that those targeted—women, members of ethnic minorities, and people with disabilities—will receive preferential treatment. This is not what the JAC wants or is allowed to do. What it is, quite properly, doing is encouraging all those qualified to apply for judicial appointment to do so. Thus it runs road shows and takes other steps to draw to the attention of members of the legal profession that the process of appointment has changed and is more open.

A number of important changes have also been made to the threshold qualification for being able to apply for judicial appointment. The Tribunals, Courts and

Enforcement Act 2007 provides that, rather than eligibility for office being based on possession of rights of audience for a specified period, those who wish to apply for judicial office have to show that they possessed a relevant legal qualification for the requisite period and that while holding that qualification they have been gaining legal experience. In respect of many of the offices, the number of years for which a person must have held such qualification before becoming eligible for judicial office is also reduced. There is evidence (from the JAC) that with greater flexibility, a wider variety of candidates has started to emerge. Published figures relating to diversity in the judiciary indicate that there has been modest improvement in the gender balance of appointments in the lower tiers of the judiciary; but the numbers of women in the top judicial jobs remains very small (*see Diagram 4.1*). The numbers of ethnic minority origin remain extremely small. In February 2010, the JAC's Advisory Panel on Diversity in the Judiciary published an important report. Its vision was that by 2020 there should be a much more diverse judiciary at all levels which:

- is as talented, respected, and independent as it was in 2010;
- recognizes the concept of a judicial career;
- seeks and finds talent in more unusual places;
- gives opportunities to a wider range of individuals, and
- is more flexible in its working practices.

To achieve these objectives, the panel made 53 recommendations for improving judicial diversity. Among these was the proposal for a judicial diversity taskforce

Diagram 4.1 Judicial appointment diversity statistics: as at 1 April 2012 (2011 figures in brackets)

Post	Total	Female no.	Female %	Of ethnic minority origin no.	Of ethnic minority origin %
Heads of Division	5 (5)	0 (0)	0.0 (0.0)	0 (0)	0.0 (0.0)
Lord Justices of Appeal	38 (37)	4 (4)	10.5 (10.8)	0 (0)	0.0 (0.0)
High Court Judges	110 (108)	17 (17)	15.5 (15.7)	5 (4)	4.5 (4.5)
Circuit Judges	665 (665)	114 (106)	17.1 (15.9)	11 (15)	1.7 (2.5)
Recorders	1155 (1221)	188 (201)	16.3 (16.5)	59 (61)	5.1 (6.5)
District Judges	447 (444)	117 (113)	26.2 (25.5)	23 (21)	5.1 (5.1)
Deputy District Judges	754 (788)	247 (259)	32.8 (32.9)	38 (39)	5.0 (6.2)
District Judges (MC)	141 (137)	41 (38)	29.1 (27.7)	4 (4)	2.8 (3.9)
Deputy District Judges (MC)	134 (143)	37 (41)	27.6 (28.7)	6 (6)	4.5 (6.4)

Source: Adapted from Judicial Diversity Statistics 2012

to oversee progress. In May 2011 the taskforce reported that there had been some progress, but there was still more to be done. A core feature of the panel's report was that there should be a shift away from the idea of *judicial appointment* that focuses on the individual seeking appointment towards the idea of a *judicial career* which anyone engaged in the law might be encouraged to consider. This development will be enhanced as the integration of courts and tribunals becomes more embedded; there will be more opportunities to acquire judicial skills that can be transferred from one part of the justice system to another.

In order to take this work forward, in late 2011 the Ministry of Justice issued a consultation paper—*Appointments and Diversity: A Judiciary for the 21st Century*—proposing changes to the way in which the JAC functions and the division of responsibilities as between the JAC, the Lord Chief Justice, and the Lord Chancellor. These were broadly supported by those who commented on the consultation paper. The Crime and Courts Bill currently going through Parliament will, when enacted, give legislative force to the proposed changes (*see Box 4.1*), The government wants moves towards improving judicial diversity to be enhanced. The figures in *Diagram 4.1* reveal that this will be very challenging; over the last two years, progress towards a more diverse judiciary seems, on those figures, to have been extremely limited. (*See Chapter 9* for further consideration of the encouragement of greater diversity in the legal profession.)

Box 4.1   Reform in progress

Crime and Courts Bill 2012: Part 2

Provisions in this bill include:

- changing the rules to extend part-time working patterns for senior judges, intended to help balance work and family lives;
- enabling 'positive action' for appointments—meaning that if two candidates are completely equal in their abilities, a selection can be made on the basis of improving diversity.

The government states that these moves will not change the overriding principle of appointments based on merit but are intended to promote career progression, and to encourage applications from a wider talent pool to create a judiciary which reflects society.

There are also proposals designed to make the judicial appointments process more efficient. These include:

- having an independent lay person as chair of the selection panels for both the Lord Chief Justice and President of the UK Supreme Court, rather than a judge;
- increasing JAC involvement in the selection and appointment of the judges who are authorized to sit as Deputy High Court Judges;

Box 4.1 *Continued*

- providing the Lord Chancellor with an increased and more effective role in appointing the most senior judges—through the use of pre-selection consultation in appointments to the Court of Appeal and Heads of Division and sitting on the selection commission for the appointment of the Lord Chief Justice and President of the UK Supreme Court;
- reducing the role of the Lord Chancellor in the appointment of less senior judges, by transferring his powers for judicial appointments below the High Court and Court of Appeal to the Lord Chief Justice;
- introducing flexible deployment so judges can move between working in the courts and tribunals systems, to help judicial career development. This was seen as a key step in the report published by the Advisory Panel on Judicial Diversity.

The Law Commission

The Law Commission was established by Act of Parliament in 1965 to keep the law of England and Wales under review. (There is a separate Law Commission for Scotland.) It is the most important standing body devoted to questions of law reform. Though independent in character, it falls within the overall responsibility of the MoJ. The Commission is chaired by a Court of Appeal judge, currently Lord Justice Lloyd Jones. He is supported by four other commissioners, who in turn are assisted by teams of lawyers, research assistants, and a small secretariat.

In carrying out its functions it does not attempt to review all the law all the time. Rather it determines, on a regular basis, programmes of work it intends to carry out. (At any one time, the Commission is engaged on between 20 and 30 projects, at different stages of development.) In addition, the Commission seeks to *codify* areas of law that have become extremely complex, and to *repeal* legislation that is no longer of practical use. (Since 1965, over 5,000 measures have been removed from the statute book as a result of this work.) The current 11th programme contains new projects on the law on contempt of court; electoral law; European contract law; misconduct in public office; and offences against the person. It also contains work brought over from the preceding 10th programme.

Its projects are selected on the basis of: importance—how unsatisfactory is the current state of the law; suitability—whether the topic is one of high political sensitivity (which might make it unsuitable); and resources—whether both the financial and human resources are available to enable the job to be done. Selection of topics also results from an extensive programme of consultation and negotiation with government departments.

Its work starts with analysis of the existing law, including, where relevant, consideration of how other countries have dealt with the issue in question. It then drafts a preliminary consultation paper setting out a statement of the existing law, explaining why that area of law needs reform, and indicating its preliminary views on how the law might be reformed, on which it seeks comments from members of the public. Having analysed those comments, the Commission develops its ideas into recommendations for the reform of the law. It usually commissions the drafting of a bill designed to capture the outcome of these policy formulations. One of the particular features of the Law Commission is that Parliamentary Counsel are seconded to it for the purpose of drafting Commission bills.

However, the mere fact that this stage in the law-making process has been reached by no means guarantees that the bill so drafted becomes law. It still has to go through the parliamentary process discussed in *Chapter 3*. And no further progress can be made if parliamentary time cannot be found. About two-thirds of the Commission's proposals for reform have reached the statute book (*see Box 4.2*).

Box 4.2   Reform in progress

Law Commission Act 2009 and Protocol

The Law Commission Act 2009 is designed to ensure that government departments take notice of and act upon recommendations arising from the work of the Law Commission. The Act:

- requires the Lord Chancellor to prepare an annual report, to be laid before Parliament, on the implementation of Law Commission proposals;
- requires the Lord Chancellor to set out plans for dealing with any Law Commission proposals that have not been implemented and provide the reasoning behind decisions not to implement proposals;
- allows the Lord Chancellor and Law Commission to agree a protocol about the Law Commission's work, designed to provide a framework for the relationship between the UK government and the Law Commission. The Lord Chancellor has to lay the protocol before Parliament.

The protocol was agreed in March 2010. It is intended to increase the number of Law Commission proposals implemented by government and to reduce the time in taking reform forward.

Under the protocol, government departments will:

- give an undertaking that there is serious intention to take forward law reform in any relevant area of law included in the Commission's programme of work;
- keep the Commission up to date on other developments in policy that may impact on its proposals;
- provide an interim response as soon as possible or in any event within six months of the Law Commission publishing its proposals and a full response as soon as possible or in any event within a year.

> **Box 4.2** *Continued*
>
> The Law Commission will:
>
> - consult departmental ministers about potential law reform projects in their areas;
> - support all its final reports with an impact assessment;
> - take full account of the minister's views in deciding whether and how to continue with a project at agreed review points.
>
> The second report from the Lord Chancellor was published in March 2012. The 11th programme was settled on the basis set out in the protocol.

Research

Unlike many other large-spending government departments, the former DCA did not invest heavily in empirical research. Specific policy-related research projects were commissioned from time to time. But policy initiatives too often derived from anecdotal evidence, pressure from influential individual or groups of judges, powerful professional bodies such as the Law Society and the Bar Council, or the ideas or even prejudices of government ministers or Members of Parliament.

The former DCA had a research unit with control over a (modest) budget dedicated to the development of specially commissioned policy-related research. Initially, all the research was carried out by academics or other research agencies on a research contract basis. This was later supplemented with an in-house research team.

One of the consequences of the creation of the MoJ is that the very much larger research activity formerly within the Home Office has been brought into the new Ministry. The bulk of the research published relates to aspects of criminal justice. This is supplemented by research carried out by the Youth Justice Board and the National Offenders Management Service.

The research work of the MoJ is further complemented by that of the Legal Services Research Centre, which currently works within the Legal Services Commission. It has done pioneering work on the need for legal and advice services, how people use those services, and the gaps in service provisions.

It must be right in principle to attempt to develop policy that is going to affect large numbers of people on the basis of hard information rather than soft anecdote. There are, however, significant challenges to the undertaking of empirical research on law, not least the narrowness of vision of many lawyers and their inability to understand the crucial links between the discipline of law and the disciplines of the social sciences. Meeting these challenges requires strong intellectual leadership from the academic community and from policy-makers within government.

The Home Office

The Home Office is the other government department with a central role in shaping the institutional framework of the English legal system, particularly in relation to the development of the criminal justice system considered further in *Chapter 5*. Much of the drive for increased efficiency within the criminal justice system, leading to signifi-cant changes to the ways in which criminal processes operate, has derived from Home Office initiatives.

One of the key features of policing in England and Wales is that there is no national police force, but rather 43 different police forces operating throughout the coun-try. Arguments in favour of the creation of a national police force are met by the counter-argument that that would lead to too great a centralization of police power and a lack of local accountability. The Coalition government has decided to make police forces more accountable at local level. Part 1 of the Police Reform and Social Responsibility Act 2011 abolishes police authorities (which are appointed bodies), replacing them with directly elected Police and Crime Commissioners. The first elec-tions were held on 15 November 2012.

It is recognized, however, that issues such as serious organized crime and economic fraud cannot be dealt with effectively by fragmented local forces. In relation to the former, the Serious Organised Crime and Police Act 2005 created the Serious Organised Crime Agency (SOCA), which brought together the National Criminal Intelligence Service, the National Crime Squad, that part of Her Majesty's Revenue and Customs that dealt with drug trafficking, and part of the UK Immigration Service dealing with organized immigration crime. SOCA was however criticized for lack of effectiveness. The Coalition government is currently creating a new National Crime Agency, to include within it the work of the Child Exploitation and Online Protection Centre.

Although most of its functions relating to the criminal justice system were trans-ferred to the MoJ, the Home Office still takes the lead in relation to a number of issues that have an important impact on law-making and the role of law in England and Wales. These include: crime reduction; immigration and nationality; drugs prevention; and race equality and diversity, including anti-discrimination legislation. Particularly controversial areas for which it is responsible include: dealing with internal terrorist threats—which includes the issue of the extent to which people should be able to be detained without charge while inquiries are made; handling claims of asylum-seekers; and anti-social behaviour.

Other government departments

One other department, closely associated with the development of the justice sys-tem, is the Attorney-General's Department. The Attorney-General (A-G) occupies an interesting though complex position in government. Partly, the A-G acts as a kind of in-house lawyer, giving independent advice to government; the A-G is also ultimately responsible for the work of the Director of Public Prosecutions and the Crown Prosecution Service (*see Chapter 5*).

The impact of other government departments on the English legal system is less focused than the examples given earlier but is nonetheless considerable. For example, the Department for Education works closely with the MoJ on issues relating to family justice (*see Chapter 7*) and also on dealing with young offenders (*see Chapter 5*).

The new Department for Business Innovation and Skills does much work on regulation, involving detailed consideration of existing rules and regulations, how they might be simplified, and how they can be made more effective without over-burdening industry and commerce. It also has responsibility for consumer protection. Both of these streams of work underpin issues relating to civil and commercial justice (*see Chapter 8*). This department is also responsible for employment matters, including policy relating to employment tribunals (*see Chapter 6*). In addition, it provides the bulk of the funding for Citizens' Advice, a service which helps people resolve their legal, money and other problems by providing free advice (*see also, Chapter 9, Lay advisers/advocates*).

The Department for Communities and Local Government has a wide range of policy under its control. These include both planning and housing—both of which involve use of the administrative justice and civil justice systems (*see Chapters 6 and 8*).

One of the great challenges for government as a whole is to ensure that, as far as possible, policy initiatives arising in one department reflect and work with (rather than against) policies arising in other departments. While the principle of a joined-up approach to the delivery of policy is broadly accepted, it is far from easy to deliver this in practice.

Questions

Use the self-test questions on the Online Resource Centre to test your understanding of the topics covered in this chapter and receive tailored feedback:

www.oxfordtextbooks.co.uk/orc/partington13_14/

Weblinks

Check the Online Resource Centre for a selection of annotated weblinks allowing you to easily research topics of particular interest:

www.oxfordtextbooks.co.uk/orc/partington13_14/

Blog items

See www.martinpartington.com (access via the Online Resource Centre)

Items discussed include: the promotion of alternative dispute resolution and mediation; the internationalization of legal services in the United Kingdom; interactions between young people and the law; an outline of the Legal Aid, Sentencing and Punishment of Offenders Bill 2011 and the Legal Aid, Sentencing and Punishment of Offenders Act 2012; the future of legal aid; reform of the courts; courts on TV; the crisis in administrative justice; promoting judicial diversity; educating judges; regulating the legal profession and handling complaints against lawyers. *See also, Chapter 1, Blog items*, for empirical research on law.

Further reading

ABEL-SMITH, B., and STEVENS, R., *In Search of Justice: Society and the Legal System* (London, Allen Lane, 1968)

KENNEY, S. J., *Gender and Justice: Why Women in the Judiciary Really Matter* (London, Routledge, 2012)

MALLESON, K., and BANDA, F., *Factors Affecting the Decision to Apply for Silk and Judicial Office* (London, Lord Chancellor's Department, 2000)

OLIVER, D., *Constitutional Reform in the United Kingdom* (Oxford, Oxford University Press, 2003)

POLDEN, P., *Guide to the Records of the Lord Chancellor's Department* (London, Her Majesty's Stationery Office, 1988)

STEVENS, R., *The Independence of the Judiciary: The View from the Lord Chancellor's Office* (rev. edn, Oxford, Clarendon Press, 1997)

WOODHOUSE, D., *The Office of the Lord Chancellor* (Oxford, Hart Publishing, 2001)

5

The criminal justice system

Introduction: criminal justice

Criminal law is central to the relationship between law and society. It seeks to regulate behaviour; it provides sanctions against those who break those rules. It is intimately linked with key social policy objectives, such as the maintenance of law and order and preservation of the peace, security of the individual, and the protection of property. It is also linked to other objectives, especially the protection of human rights and individual freedoms. Indeed, one of the great challenges law-makers face when thinking about the development of rules of criminal law and criminal procedure is how to achieve a proper balance between the provisions of the criminal law and the preservation of liberty and the freedom of the individual. These issues are currently seen in sharp focus in discussions about how we should respond to threats of terrorist activity. Furthermore, the boundaries of the criminal law change over time. They are not always set by the outcome of purely rational debate and argument; they also reflect the preferences and prejudices of politicians. The criminal justice system is that branch of the English legal system in which the criminal law is administered.

Any idea that the criminal justice system can be understood simply by looking at the work of the criminal courts can be quickly disabused by considering the wide range of agencies involved. They include:

- the police service;
- the Crown Prosecution Service;
- the Serious Fraud Office;
- the Serious Organised Crime Agency;
- other investigating/prosecuting authorities;
- magistrates' courts;
- the Crown Court;
- the appeal courts;
- the Criminal Cases Review Commission;
- the prison service;
- the national probation service for England and Wales;

- the Criminal Defence Service;
- the Criminal Injuries Compensation Scheme for victims; and
- other victim and witness care services.

Further institutional changes are in progress. The Coalition government has decided to replace the Serious Organised Crime Agency with a new National Crime Agency, which would include the Child Exploitation and Online Protection Centre. It starts operation in April 2013. Other proposed changes are noted in context in this chapter.

Altogether, the criminal justice system affects large numbers of people.[1] It is a huge employer. It consumes a great deal of public money: currently over £19 billion a year. Huge sums are spent on policing. The prison service, the probation service, and criminal legal aid also consume large amounts. These sums are not trivial; indeed the United Kingdom spends more on these issues than most other comparable countries.

The Coalition government's commitment is to reduce public expenditure. Cost reduction is central to the development of criminal justice policy. This does not necessarily mean that the work of the criminal justice system will be undermined; there may well be ways in which, by doing things differently, expenditure can be saved while efficiency is improved. What is important is that any changes made do not compromise the core values of the criminal justice system, in particular the need for procedures to be fair and for the liberty of the individual to be protected. At the same time the public must be protected from those who would otherwise be a threat to safety and security. The efficiency of the criminal justice system—to ensure that its social objectives are met, while at the same time reducing expenditure levels—is, as in other areas of social policy, a constant challenge for government. One controversial issue is the extent to which services currently provided by government agencies should be contracted out to private or voluntary sector suppliers. (This already happens with the private provision of some prison services.)

The criminal justice system has been the subject of much political controversy, many official inquiries, and considerable change. Nearly every year there is new legislation on some aspect of the criminal justice system. To give just a few examples: a Royal Commission on Criminal Procedure reported in 1981; a further Royal Commission on Criminal Justice reported in 1993; and a review of the criminal courts was published in 2001. In the same year, there was also a major review of sentencing policy.

The Coalition government has conducted a further review of sentencing. It has introduced major changes to the organization and accountability of the police, with the creation of locally elected Police and Crime Commissioners, as well as significant cut-backs in the bureaucratic burden imposed on the police. (Her Majesty's Inspectorate

---

[1] A longitudinal study carried out by the Home Office showed that 34 per cent of *all* males born in the United Kingdom in 1953 had, by 1993, received at least one conviction for a criminal offence of a more serious nature; the figure for females was eight per cent. Reported in Taylor, R., *Forty Years of Crime and Criminal Justice Statistics, 1958–1997* (London, Home Office, Research and Development Section, 1999).

of Constabulary estimates that, at present, only around ten per cent of police are available at any one time for the delivery of frontline services to the public.)

Some argue that the system is loaded in favour of those accused of criminal activity and against those who are the victims of crime or, more generally, 'the interests of society at large'. This leads to calls for a rebalancing of the system in favour of victims and witnesses. Others strongly disagree, pointing to the serious miscarriages of justice that have occurred over the years and the need to protect individuals from wrongful involvement in the criminal justice system. In this chapter, each part of the criminal justice system is considered. First, though, we consider the social theories that underpin the system.

Theories of criminal justice

Just as the social functions of the criminal law are quite diverse, so too are the different social theories or models that underpin the criminal justice system.[2] From the criminological literature, a number of 'models' of the criminal justice system may be identified. These include:

(1) the *due process* model, in which the primary social goal is said to be 'justice', and the emphasis is on fairness, and the rules needed to protect the accused against error and the exercise of arbitrary power;

(2) the *crime control* model, in which the primary social goal is punishment, where the focus is on ensuring that the police are able to obtain convictions in the courts;

(3) a *medical* model, in which the emphasis is on the rehabilitation of the offender, giving decision-takers discretion to achieve this;

(4) the *restorative justice* model, in which the emphasis is on getting the offender to recognize his or her responsibility in committing the offence and to make amends to the victim;

(5) the *bureaucratic* model, in which the emphasis is on the management of crime and the criminal, and the efficient processing of offenders through the system;

(6) a *status passage* model, in which the emphasis is on the denunciation and degradation of the offender, involving a shaming of the offender, reflecting society's views of the offender; and

(7) a *power* model, in which the emphasis is on the maintenance of a particular social/class order, which reinforces the values of certain classes over others.

---

[2] The following is derived from the excellent book by King, M., *The Framework of Criminal Justice* (London, Croom Helm, 1981).

None of these models offers a uniquely correct interpretation of the criminal justice system. The explanatory power of each model varies, depending on the person looking at the system. The defence lawyer or the defendant will take a different view from the policeman or the prosecutor, the victim, or the Home Secretary. Thinking about these models, however, both highlights the tensions that—perhaps inevitably—exist in this complex sector of the justice system, and also helps to identify assumptions that are all too often left unstated in considering developments in the criminal justice system. The reader should reflect on how recent developments in criminal justice fit into the models thus identified.

Understanding the criminal justice system

To gain any understanding of the criminal justice system, it is necessary to break the overall structure into more manageable parts. The approach here is to look at the system in three segments:

- pre-trial stages;
- trial stage; and
- post-trial stages.

Each of these is further subdivided.

Pre-trial stages

Before any alleged criminal gets anywhere near a courtroom, a number of crucial preliminary steps are taken, each of which may affect the outcome of the case, and indeed whether a case ever reaches court at all. The following analysis of the stages that an allegation of criminal activity may go through before trial provides a structure that obviously does not occur as neatly as this in practice; but it should help the reader to see the overall shape of the criminal justice system more clearly.

The committing, reporting, and recording of crime

It may be obvious that the first step in any criminal process is that some criminal act should have been *committed*. By itself, that is not (save in the most exceptional circumstances) sufficient to launch any kind of criminal process. Unless the offence is *reported* to the authorities, either by the victim or by some other person who has seen the incident or has come to realize that some criminal activity has taken place, no further action will follow. (*See Box 5.1* for crime statistics.)

Box 5.1 Legal system explained

Crime statistics

There are two principal sources of data on crime. The first are figures for crime recorded by the police; the second are figures derived from the Crime Survey for England and Wales.

As regards the former, there are at least two potential problems:

(1) As with all data, their value is dependent on the quality of the input. There is always the possibility of error in data collection and entry. Some reporting practices may distort patterns of criminality. The thief who steals a crate of milk bottles from outside a front door may be recorded as having stolen one item (the crate); or 12 items (each individual bottle). In statistical terms, this is a very considerable difference.

(2) The figures relate to reported and recorded crime. Many factors influence reporting and recording. For example, if insurance companies insist on theft from cars or property being reported, this may lead to an increase in the rate of recorded crime; conversely, a relaxation in their practices may lead to a reduction in recorded crime.

It is not argued here that the figures for recorded crime do not reflect trends in criminality in the community. But one should be cautious about drawing the simple conclusion, as is often done in the media, that published statistics of recorded crime represent 'the crime figures'. It is more complex than that.

The latter data are derived from an annual survey in which a sample of the population is interviewed about its experience of crime as well as the criminal justice system. Although this survey by no means covers the totality of the population, the sample of over 40,000 people is drawn on the basis of accepted practices for creating social survey databases. The conclusion to be drawn from the *Crime Survey for England and Wales* is that a somewhat different picture of criminality and the individual experience of crime is presented there, compared with the picture presented by the reported crime statistics. This is illustrated clearly in *Diagram 5.1*, which shows the gap in the amount of crime estimated by the *Crime Survey for England and Wales*, and the numbers of crimes recorded by the police.

The agency to which most crime is reported is the police. But many other agencies also have criminal law enforcement responsibilities. For example:

- local authorities have responsibilities for areas like environmental pollution and public health;
- central government departments have responsibilities for investigating a wide variety of potential criminal activity—for example social security benefit fraud, tax evasion, and other types of fraudulent commercial activity;

- health and safety agencies have duties to prosecute breaches of health and safety legislation (e.g. unlawful emissions of radioactive material); and

- in very rare circumstances, an individual him- or herself may commence a criminal prosecution.

Diagram 5.1 Trends in recorded crime and CSEW, 1981–year ending June 2012

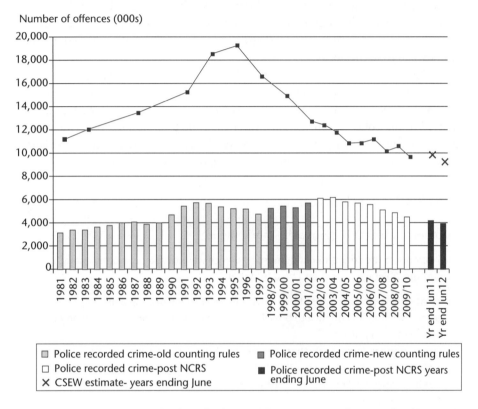

Number of offences (000s)

☐ Police recorded crime-old counting rules	▨ Police recorded crime-new counting rules
☐ Police recorded crime-post NCRS	■ Police recorded crime-post NCRS years ending June
✕ CSEW estimate- years ending June	

Source: Crime Survey for England and Wales – Office for National Statistics, Home Office, reproduced in *Crime in England and Wales, year ending June 2012* (London, Office for National Statistics, 2012), p. 3.

Although the police are the largest single agency to which crimes are reported, the total number of criminal offences committed each year that are dealt with by bodies other than the police exceeds the total offences reported to the police. Nonetheless, for present purposes we concentrate on the role of the police.

Research shows clearly that, if a victim of crime is unwilling to report a crime and get the police to investigate it, then in all save the gravest situations no effective further action will be taken in relation to that alleged offence.[3] The initial act of reporting is crucial.

Furthermore, if the police are perceived as being unsympathetic in any particular context, then this reduces the likelihood of alleged offences being reported. For

[3] Cretney, A., and Davis, G., *Punishing Violence* (London, Routledge, 1995).

example, some years ago the police were perceived as being unsympathetic to female victims of alleged rape. The police took this criticism seriously, improved training and made other efforts to demonstrate that this was not the case. The police were determined to change their practices. At the time it could be predicted that the number of reported rape cases would increase. This indeed happened. It may be that the increase in numbers of reported rapes is the result of more rapes occurring. But at least some of the increase is attributable to more reliable patterns of reporting and recording. (There is still evidence that the number of rapes is under-reported, but this may be more due to fears victims may have about how they are going to be dealt with by the courts than reluctance to go to the police.)

Another example is domestic violence. There is a widespread assumption that the police are reluctant to get involved in domestic disputes. Whether or not this perception is correct does not much matter. The number of cases of domestic violence reported to the police is considerably lower than the total number of incidents that actually take place. The Home Office estimates that, on average, a victim experiences 35 incidents of domestic violence before going to the police (*see Box 5.2*).

Box 5.2   System in action

Domestic violence: reform of law and practice

In response to the criticism that domestic violence was not taken seriously enough, the Domestic Violence, Crimes and Victims Act 2004:

- created new police powers to deal with domestic violence including making it an arrestable, criminal offence to breach a non-molestation order, with a penalty of up to five years in prison;
- gave stronger legal protection for victims by extending the use of restraining orders—giving courts the power to impose a restraining order where the defendant has been acquitted but the court believes an order is necessary to protect the victim from harassment;
- provided for a code of practice, binding on all criminal justice agencies, so that all victims receive the support, protection, information, and advice they need;
- allowed victims to take their case to the Parliamentary Ombudsman if they feel the code had not been adhered to by the criminal justice agencies;
- set up an independent commissioner for victims to give victims a voice at the heart of government and to safeguard and promote the interests of victims and witnesses, encouraging the spread of good practice and reviewing the statutory code;
- amended the Protection from Harassment Act 1997 to ensure that victims have their say if an application is made to vary or terminate a restraining order that is protecting them from abuse or harassment;
- strengthened the civil law on domestic violence so that cohabiting same-sex couples have the same protection as heterosexual couples, and extending the availability

Box 5.2 *Continued*

of non-molestation orders to couples who have never lived together or have never been married; and

- created a new offence of familial homicide for causing or allowing the death of a child or vulnerable adult.

Research published in 2008 suggested both that the number of domestic violence cases being reported had increased, as had the number of cases going through the courts.

The government has established a number of specialist domestic violence courts. Key features of the courts include:

- trained and dedicated criminal justice staff with enhanced expertise in dealing with domestic violence, including magistrates specially trained in dealing with domestic violence cases;
- tailored support and advice from independent domestic violence advisers;
- multi-agency risk assessment conferences (MARAC) to provide protection for those most at risk of harm.

New provisions designed to protect the victims of domestic violence are included in the Crime and Security Act 2010. Instead of having to go to court to seek an injunction, the Act gives the police power to issue a *domestic violence protection notice* to a person who has been violent or has threatened violence, breach of which is a criminal offence.

Source: <http://webarchive.nationalarchives.gov.uk/+/http://www.justice.gov.uk/about/domesticviolence.htm>.

Even if an alleged offence is reported, the police may not think that there is sufficient information to justify the *recording* of the alleged incident. If the matter is not recorded, no further action will be taken. Indeed, even if a crime is both reported and recorded, no effective further action necessarily results. Many reports of petty theft, for example, are not taken further by the police—they do not have the resources to carry out the required investigations.

The investigation stage: police powers

Once a crime has been reported to the relevant agency (still using the police as the main example) the next stage is the investigation. In the case of major incidents this involves the consumption of considerable resources with large numbers of police spending a lot of time on an investigation. In less important cases, the investigation stage may be extremely cursory. (There are cases where the conceptually distinct processes of reporting and investigating are in practice blurred. The police may gain intelligence that a criminal act is being planned. This leads to investigation in advance of the commission of the offence. If the offence is actually committed, the preliminary intelligence-gathering may also result in the gathering of sufficient evidence to justify the arrest of the person or persons concerned and their being charged with the commission of an offence.)

For the criminal investigation bodies to be able to do their work, they need special powers. In the case of the police, their powers were subject to major reform under the Police and Criminal Evidence Act 1984 (PACE). The statutory powers of the police are supplemented by important *codes of practice*, which should also be observed by the police (*see Box 5.3*).

Box 5.3   Legal system explained

PACE codes of practice

There are eight codes of practice:

- Code A on Powers of Stop and Search;
- Code B on Search and Seizure;
- Code C on Detention, Treatment, and Questioning of Persons;
- Code D on the Identification of Persons;
- Code E on Tape Recording;
- Code F on Visual Recording of Interviews;
- Code G on the Statutory Power of Arrest by Police Officers; and
- Code H on the Detention and Questioning of those Suspected of Terrorism.

The codes have also been adapted to apply to immigration officers in their work for the UK Border Agency.

Originally, there were just five codes, but they have been revised and added to over the years. The most recent versions came into effect at different dates between 2005 and 2012. Full details of the current codes including recent amendments are available at <www.homeoffice.gov.uk/police/powers/pace-codes/>.

The principal powers enabling the police to carry out their functions are:

- the power to stop and search;
- the power to arrest and detain;
- the power to question; and
- the power to enter and search premises.

The precise order in which these powers are used in any particular case naturally depends on the circumstances. The extent of police powers, how they are interpreted and applied by the police, and the balance between those powers and the liberty of the individual are constant sources of controversy.

Stop and search

The powers of the police to stop and search people or vehicles are contained in section 1 of the PACE. The law provides that a constable must have reasonable grounds for believing that, by exercising his or her powers, stolen goods, an offensive weapon, a knife or other bladed or sharply pointed article, articles adapted for use in burglary, theft or obtaining by deception, or a vehicle that has been taken without authority will be found.

These general powers are supplemented by many other powers to stop and search to be found in other specific Acts of Parliament—for example relating to terrorism, drugs, firearms, or alcohol at sporting events.

Thus, under section 43(1) of the Terrorism Act 2000 a constable may stop and search a person whom the officer reasonably suspects to be a terrorist to discover whether the person is in possession of anything that may constitute evidence that the person is a terrorist. These searches may only be carried out by an officer of the same sex as the person searched.

Section 60 of the Criminal Justice and Public Order Act 1994 created an extensive power to stop and search 'in anticipation of violence'. However, this power may not be exercised unless a police superintendent has authorized its use in a particular locality.

In exercising these powers, the police are required to follow procedures set down in section 2 of the PACE, which, among other things, requires the officer to give his or her name, state why the search is taking place, and record that the stop and search has occurred (unless this is not practicable). The details of what must be recorded, criticized for being over bureaucratic, were reduced following enactment of the Crime and Security Act 2010.

The language of the legislation gives considerable scope to individual police officers to decide whether or not the conditions for carrying out a stop and search are met. The exercise of the power has been controversial, in particular because of evidence that people from the ethnic minorities are significantly more likely to be stopped and searched than those from the majority white communities (*see Box 5.4*).

Box 5.4   System in action

Impact of stops and searches on crime and the community

Impact on crime

- *Detection*—evidence suggests that searches probably detect offenders for only a small proportion of all the crimes they address. However, they can make a more notable contribution to arrests.
- *Disruption*—searches can directly disrupt criminal activities, although evidence suggests this effect is likely to be small in relation to overall crime. Search arrests can also disrupt crime through the incapacitation or desistance of offenders. However, it is difficult to assess the extent to which this occurs on existing evidence.

Box 5.4 *Continued*

- *Deterrence*—there is little solid evidence that this occurs. However, police stops, more generally, may have a role in preventing crime.
- *Order maintenance*—it is possible that a focus on low-level crime problems helps prevent the development of more serious crime problems. However, the role or effectiveness of searches in this regard is unknown.
- *Intelligence*—information gained from a search encounter can be fed back into police work. This is potentially true of stops in general, as well as just searches. The research suggests that the effectiveness of searches is greatest when they are based on strong grounds for suspicion and make the best use of intelligence.

Impact on the community

The research shows that the experience of being searched is associated with reduced confidence in the police. It is likely, therefore, that this will contribute directly to lower levels of confidence in the police among those from minority ethnic groups. It also notes that people were less satisfied with stop or search encounters when they were searched, not given convincing explanations, or not treated politely or fairly.

Lower levels of satisfaction with encounters among ethnic minority people appears to occur because they disproportionately experience these problems. Problems with community relations could be reduced by making efficient use of searches, responding constructively to disproportionality, and improving the management of encounters.

Conclusions

Were it not for the controversy surrounding searches, no doubt they would be seen as one useful 'tool in the toolbox' for the police. By using stops and searches in an appropriate way, it is likely that effectiveness can be maximized and community costs can be reduced.

Source: Police Stops and Searches: Lessons from a programme of research (London, Home Office, 2000).

The Ministry of Justice publishes annual statistics on race and the criminal justice system, which includes an analysis of information about the use of stop and search powers. These show that members of ethnic minorities are stopped and searched far more than those from the white majority. However, and although somewhat inconclusive, there is some evidence that if the police take a 'softly, softly' approach to stop and search, levels of crime rise. What is clear is that, while the power is an important one, it is one that must be used sensibly and with care if it is not to exacerbate local community feelings and make the task of policing harder. The Equality and Human Rights Commission is currently working with the Association of Chief Constables to develop good practice. It is an issue that the government must keep under regular review, especially because of the tensions that arise with use of stop and search powers.

Arrest

Broadly, there are two types of arrest—with warrant, and without warrant:

- An arrest *with warrant* occurs under the authority of a warrant issued by a magistrate. A warrant may be issued after information has been given to the magistrate, on oath, that the person named has or is suspected of having committed an offence.

- There are a number of powers to arrest *without a warrant*. Section 24 of the PACE has been amended by the Serious Organised Crime and Police Act 2005 to provide that the police have a general power to arrest without warrant persons who have committed or are suspected of committing an offence and that it is necessary that the person should be arrested without a warrant. One of the following reasons must be present: (1) to enable the name of the person in question to be ascertained; (2) also the person's address; (3) to prevent the person causing or suffering, or causing loss of or damage to property, or committing an offence against public decency;[4] or causing an unlawful obstruction of the highway; (4) to protect a child or other vulnerable person; (5) to allow prompt and effective investigation of the offence or of the conduct of the person in question; (6) to prevent the disappearance of the person in question.

- The amended law clarifies the circumstances in which a citizen may make an arrest. The exercise of the citizen's power of arrest is limited to arresting those committing or suspected of committing an indictable offence.

In addition, there are a number of specific powers to arrest without warrant under particular Acts of Parliament, for example the Mental Health Act 1983. Lastly, there is a common law power to arrest where a breach of the peace is taking place or is reasonably anticipated.

For an arrest to take place without a warrant, the person making the arrest must make it clear, by words or action, that the person arrested is under compulsion. The person arrested must be informed of the ground for the arrest, either at the time of arrest or as soon as possible thereafter, for example where it is not practicable to provide the information before the person to be arrested tries to run away. There is no legal power simply to detain persons for questioning without first making an arrest. (When one hears that a person is 'helping the police with their inquiries', this is an indication that he or she has not been arrested, but is attending the police station 'voluntarily'.)

An arrest is the first stage in a process that may eventually lead to a criminal trial. Research suggests that, despite the legal framework created by the PACE, a very large number of arrests lead to no further action being taken. This raises the question of the extent to which police practice on arrest conforms to the legal rules relating to arrest.

---

[4] This applies only where members of the public going about their normal business cannot reasonably be expected to avoid the person in question.

Detention

Once a person has been arrested, that person may be detained in a police station to enable further investigation (including questioning of the person) to be carried out. The PACE contains detailed provisions to regulate the time a person could be detained in custody. Under Part IV of the Act (as amended), arrangements must be made for a staff custody officer, usually a police officer, to keep the detention under review. The police have, in general, 24 hours in which they must either charge the arrested person with an offence, or release the person, either with or without bail. Exceptionally, authorization for detention without charge for up to 36 hours may be given.

In the context of responses to terrorist events, there are now special powers to detain those suspected of these classes of offence for longer periods. These are said by the police and other investigating agencies to be needed in order that they can complete essential inquiries. Opponents of these measures argue that they are unnecessarily draconian, and likely to create more problems than they resolve. These arguments were exposed in the sharp differences of view in Parliament during debate on the Terrorism Bill, which became the Terrorism Act 2006. There a government attempt to extend the period of detention without charge to 90 days was defeated, and replaced by 28 days. The Coalition government has reduced the period to 14 days, though with the possibility of extending the time to 28 days in an emergency (Protection of Freedoms Act 2012). Because powers to detain without either charge or trial are so exceptional, PACE Code H was introduced in July 2006 to regulate police practice in this area.

Once charged, the person may be further detained but must be brought before a magistrates' court as soon as practicable. The magistrates decide whether the person can then be released on bail or remanded in custody.

Part V of the PACE, supplemented by Code C, sets out detailed provisions for the treatment of those who have been detained. Usually, a person detained is entitled to have someone informed of that fact, and to have access to legal advice, which gives the right to consult privately a solicitor at any time. There are powers to delay these rights where this is thought necessary, for example to prevent evidence being destroyed. The statutory rules and code also set out in detail the physical conditions in which people should be detained; these include details about the provision of drinks and refreshment.

The Criminal Justice Act 2003 extended the powers of the police to enable them to take fingerprints and a DNA sample from a person whilst in police detention following arrest. Fingerprints can now be taken electronically. Thus the police can confirm in a few minutes the identity of a suspect where that person's fingerprints are already held on the national fingerprint database. This prevents persons who may be wanted for other matters avoiding detection by giving the police a false name and address. Fingerprints taken under this provision can also be subject to a speculative search across the crime scene database to see if they are linked to any unsolved crime.

The DNA profile of an arrested person is loaded onto the national DNA database. It can also be subject to a speculative search to see whether it matches a crime scene stain already held on the database. Both these new powers can assist the police in the detection and prevention of crime. Currently, the database holds information on just over five per cent of the population. A senior judge recently suggested that all citizens should be required to provide a DNA sample for the national database, arguing that this would help the innocent as much as the wrongdoer; this was fiercely criticized by civil liberty groups. The Coalition government has introduced new rules relating to the destruction of DNA data, to reduce the amount of information retained (Protection of Freedoms Act 2012).

Questioning

The power to question suspects detained by the police is the subject of detailed guidance in Code C. The police regard the power to question as crucial. Questioning often leads to the suspect providing a confession. This leads to considerable savings later in the criminal process, as most of those confessing plead guilty.

Confessions raise two particular problems: 'induced' confessions, and false confessions.

Induced confessions are, as the name implies, confessions that have arisen from the police offering inducements to the suspect to confess—for example, early release on bail, the suggestion that a confession may lead to less serious charges being made against the alleged criminal, or that in some other way the outcome will be less serious than it would otherwise be. Such inducements can colour the reliability of the confession.

Rules of evidence that apply in court are designed to ensure that induced confessions are not made, by preventing the evidence obtained from them from being presented in court. Many police practices, for example the tape recording of interviews or the requirement to issue a formal caution to those who may be charged with an offence, are designed to eliminate improper police behaviour. However, it seems unlikely that the police will never seek to induce a confession, for example in a location where there are no tape recorders. Furthermore, the present form of the 'caution'[5] provides some incentive to people to make statements at an early stage.

False confessions are more problematic. Contrary to common sense and expectation there have been cases where a person being questioned by the police has confessed to a crime that he or she has not in fact committed. This can arise from the very considerable psychological pressure that people are under when detained in a police station. This was one of the issues that led to the establishment of the Royal Commission on Criminal Evidence and Procedure in 1979.[6]

---

[5] 'You do not have to say anything. But it may harm your defence if you do not mention when questioned something which you later rely on in court. Anything you do say may be given in evidence'. This form of words provoked much criticism when introduced, as it was argued that it undermined the right of silence, one of the principal sources of protection for the accused.

[6] See Irving, B., *Police Interrogation: A Study of Current Practice* (Research Study No. 2 for the Royal Commission on Criminal Procedure) (London, Her Majesty's Stationery Office, 1980).

Entering and searching premises

The last general power available to the police (and other crime investigation agencies) is the power to enter and search premises for evidence, and where relevant to seize that evidence. Many specific Acts of Parliament give power to grant warrants to the police for particular purposes, for example investigating drugs offences or theft. Section 8 of the PACE (as amended by the Serious Organised Crime and Police Act 2005) creates a general power enabling magistrates to grant warrants to search for evidence relating to a serious arrestable offence. A warrant may relate to specific premises, or more generally to all premises controlled by an individual. As with other police powers, these statutory provisions are supplemented by statutory safeguards and Code B. Certain types of material are excluded from this provision, for example items subject to legal privilege (principally, communications containing legal advice from a professional legal adviser to his or her client); and certain other categories of excluded material, for example personal records and journalistic records. (There is a procedure whereby a circuit judge may be asked to make an order granting access to such material or, in an extreme case, to grant a warrant to search for this sort of material (see section 9 of and Schedule 1 to the PACE).)

There are also circumstances where the police are empowered to enter and search premises without a warrant: for example to arrest someone suspected of committing an arrestable offence or to save life and limb or prevent serious damage to property (see section 17 of the PACE).

Comment on police powers

There can be no doubting the powers that the police have over the ordinary citizen. The range of powers may be seen as a sensible code, enabling the police to go about their business of investigating crime and catching suspects. Nevertheless, there are always concerns, backed by specific examples of police malpractice, which reveal that some police act beyond the powers given to them. This in turn means that further controls on police behaviour to prevent the exercise of powers beyond the legally prescribed limits are essential.

Where examples of the planting of evidence or the use of oppressive questioning techniques are demonstrated, some critics argue that use of illegally obtained evidence is endemic to police practice. Others, including the police themselves, argue that such abuses are simply the result of individual 'rotten apples', and that, so long as steps are taken to remove them, the basic activities of the police are undertaken within both the letter and the spirit of the law.

The police who fail to act within the scope of their legal powers may be the subject of internal disciplinary proceedings, or worse. Potentially, the most effective deterrent against breaking the rules arises from the fact that any evidence obtained improperly may not be able to be given in court. As the police know that during the investigative/information-gathering stage these rules of evidence will be applied should a case reach court and be contested, the rules should shape the ways in which evidence is obtained by the police. However, as is noted later, the law of evidence gives judges considerable discretion whether or not evidence should be excluded. The practical consequences of bending or ignoring the questioning rules are not always predictable.

As in other aspects of professional and public life, there is now much more formal accountability than was the case some years ago. The overall efficiency of police forces is the responsibility of Her Majesty's Inspectorate of Constabulary. The creation of the Independent Police Complaints Commission (which in 2002 replaced the Police Complaints Authority) has resulted in new mechanisms for individuals to pursue grievances against the police. In addition, each year a number of cases against the police are brought before the courts by individuals, for example seeking damages for false imprisonment or compensation for damage to property.

Suggestions, made by some, that police activity is characterized by wholesale malpractice and corruption are not justified. Many who have incidental brushes with the police find they operate strictly according to the book and in a perfectly proper fashion. However, it is also true that there are more circumstances than those that hit the headlines in which the police do not behave strictly according to the rule book.

Next steps

On completing the first two stages, the police have a number of choices. They may:

- take no further action, for example where insufficient evidence has been obtained;
- give an informal warning;
- issue a formal caution (for adults) or reprimand or warning (for youths) from a senior police officer—this should only follow an admission of guilt and informed consent by the offender (or his or her parents or guardian in the case of a juvenile);
- exercising powers under the Criminal Justice Act 2003, issue a conditional caution (*see Box 5.5* on conditional cautions);
- refer the papers to the prosecuting authorities for a decision on whether to charge the person with having committed a particular offence. (For all but minor and routine cases, the decision to charge is no longer made by the police, but by the prosecuting authorities. This change, made by the Criminal Justice Act 2003, resulted from pilot projects that showed that involving the prosecutor at an earlier stage led to more accurate charges and earlier guilty pleas.)

Box 5.5 System in action

Conditional cautions

Conditional cautions may be given where there is sufficient evidence to charge a suspect with an offence which he or she admits, and the suspect agrees to the caution.

Box 5.5 *Continued*

In such cases, the Crown Prosecution Service decides whether a conditional caution is appropriate; the police administer it. If the suspect fails to comply with the conditions, he or she is liable to be prosecuted for the offence. A code of practice relating to conditional cautions was published in October 2004. The conditions that may be used in this context may be:

- reparative (such as writing a letter of apology; repairing damage; paying compensation or undertaking unpaid work in the community, if the public or the wider community are the victim; mediation between the offender and the victim);
- rehabilitative (attendance at drug or alcohol awareness sessions in an effort to halt the causes of the offending behaviour); or
- restrictive (not to approach a particular area or person) if the restriction supports reparation or rehabilitation.

The use of cautions is, therefore, extensively used to divert potential cases from the courts. Under the Legal Aid, Sentencing and Punishment of Offenders Act 2012, police are given power to issue conditional cautions without reference to a prosecutor. It also changes rules relating to youth conditional cautions to make their use more flexible.

Source: Crown Prosecution Service, *Introduction to Conditional Cautioning* Quarterly data, at <www.cps.gov.uk/publications/performance/conditional_cautioning/>.

For more information about the use of out-of-court disposals, *see Diagram 5.2.*

Diagram 5.2 Use of out-of-court disposals 2002–12

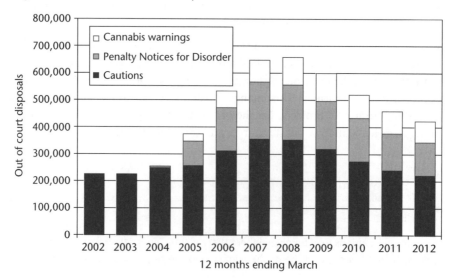

Source: <www.justice.gov.uk/statistics/criminal-justice/criminal-justice-statistics>, 2012 figure 1.

In practice, very many reported and recorded crimes are dealt with in the first four of the ways listed earlier. It is statistically much more likely that a case will end at this point and not proceed to formal prosecution. Those who argue that the criminal justice system should be based on the 'due process' model should realize that, in this majority of cases, the formal protections of that model are effectively not available to the accused.

If a person is charged with an offence, a further decision must be taken whether the person charged is to be detained in custody or released on bail (*see Box 5.6*).

Box 5.6   Legal system explained

Bail or custody

A fundamental principle of the criminal justice system is that a person is deemed to be innocent until proved guilty. It is wrong to deny an innocent person his liberty. Yet consideration of the real world suggests that some accused of crime are simply too dangerous to be allowed to remain at liberty until any case against them has been determined. They must be remanded in custody, either for their own good or for the good of society at large.

Decisions about whether to release persons on bail (i.e. subject to a requirement that they surrender to custody at a specified time and place) can be taken at any stage in the criminal trial process until the final determination of the last appeal. Thus bail may be granted by the police, magistrates' courts, Crown Courts, the High Court, and the Court of Appeal (Criminal Division). The granting of bail, by whichever agency is involved, is subject to the principles laid down in the Bail Act 1976. The Act creates a statutory presumption that bail should be granted unless specified circumstances exist that mean that bail should not be granted. These make it easier to justify remanding in custody persons charged with an offence that may result in a sentence of imprisonment, than those charged with one which would not.

In some cases, the presumption is reversed. For example, following the passing of the Criminal Justice Act 2003, there is a presumption that bail will not be granted for a person aged 18 or over who is charged with an imprisonable offence, and tests positive for a specified Class A drug, if he or she refuses to undergo an assessment as to his dependency or propensity to misuse such drugs, or following an assessment, refuses any relevant follow-up action recommended, unless the court is satisfied that there is no significant risk of his reoffending on bail. Also, when deciding whether to grant bail in respect of an offence which appears to have been committed while the defendant was on bail for another offence, courts are required to give particular weight to that fact when assessing the risk that (if granted bail) the defendant may commit further offences. Under the Legal Aid, Sentencing and Punishment of Offenders Act 2012, the law is further altered, by restricting the court's powers to remand adult unconvicted defendants in custody where it is apparent that there is no real prospect that the defendant would receive a custodial sentence if convicted. A court would still be able to remand in custody for the defendant's own protection, or where there was a risk of further offending involving domestic violence.

Box 5.6 *Continued*

In practice, the vast majority of those against whom criminal proceedings are taken are granted bail. Nevertheless, there are those who argue that bail is granted too readily. In particular, there is disquiet about the numbers of crimes committed by people while they are out on bail. Notwithstanding these fears and the apparent policy of the Bail Act 1976, numbers of those remanded in custody awaiting trial or sentencing or an appeal have increased sharply over the years and have exacerbated the problem of prison overcrowding. This has led policy-makers to consider other options, such as the electronic tagging of defendants so that the authorities can keep track of those persons even though they have not been detained in custody.

There are two types of bail: conditional bail, and unconditional bail.

Conditional bail

The police and courts can impose any requirements needed to make sure that defendants attend court and do not commit offences or interfere with witnesses whilst on bail. Conditions can also be imposed for the defendant's own protection or welfare (where he or she is a child or young person). Common conditions include: not going within a certain distance of a witness's house, or being subject to a curfew. If a defendant is reported or believed to have broken a bail condition, he or she can be arrested and brought before a magistrates' court, which may then place the person in custody.

Unconditional bail

If the police or court think that the defendant is unlikely to commit further offences, will attend court when required, and will not interfere with the justice process, he or she is usually released on unconditional bail.

Breach of bail

Defendants who do not stick to their bail conditions, or fail to attend court on the set date, are in breach of bail. They are liable to be arrested and may have their bail withdrawn. They may be remanded in custody and might not get bail in the future. Failing to appear at court as required is a criminal offence and they can also be prosecuted for this offence.

The decision to prosecute

Decisions to charge an alleged offender are, except in minor cases, taken by prosecutors. The principal prosecution authority is the Crown Prosecution Service (CPS). The CPS is a public service, headed by the Director of Public Prosecutions (DPP), answerable to Parliament through the Attorney-General. It was established in 1986 under the Prosecution of Offences Act 1985.

Before then, the decision to prosecute was usually taken by the police themselves. This led to the criticism that, in some cases that had involved miscarriages of justice, the interrelation of investigation and prosecution had resulted in the police inappropriately exercising their powers to prosecute. The Royal Commission on Criminal Procedure 1981 recommended a separation of the investigation and prosecution functions to introduce an element of independence into the latter. At the beginning of 2010, the CPS was expanded by the inclusion of the former Revenue and Customs Prosecution Office, which had responsibility for prosecuting cases involving tax. The CPS employs a considerable number of staff (around 8,250 in total). They work in 42 different areas spread across the country on a regional basis. There are five national divisions dealing with: counter-terrorism; fraud; organized crime; tax cases; and special crime.

In addition to the CPS, there are many other prosecuting agencies. For example, local authorities and the social security authorities have legal powers both to investigate criminal activities and to bring prosecutions before the courts.

The decision to create the CPS was extremely controversial. In the early years, the police in particular were very unhappy. The CPS was also confronted with many public challenges. It was said that they employed poor quality staff; their work was hampered by poor quality administration; and their decisions were often criticized. Notwithstanding these early criticisms, the role of the CPS has been retained, and it has grown in confidence and maturity. There are now fewer complaints about its role in the criminal justice system.

The basic procedure is that, after the police have investigated a crime, the case papers are passed to the CPS. One of the CPS lawyers—a Crown Prosecutor—reviews the papers to decide whether or not to go ahead with the case. The Prosecutor's decision is based on two tests set out in the *Code for Crown Prosecutors* (*see Box 5.7*), the latest edition of which was published in 2010. A further revised Code is expected in early 2013. There is much public ignorance about these tests.

Box 5.7   Legal system explained

Code for Crown Prosecutors: the decision to prosecute

Crown Prosecutors make charging decisions in accordance with the full code test, other than in those limited circumstances where the threshold test applies. The threshold test applies to cases where it is proposed to keep the suspect in custody after charge, but the evidence required to apply the full code test is not yet available. Where a Crown Prosecutor makes a charging decision in accordance with the threshold test, the case must be reviewed in accordance with the full code test as soon as reasonably practicable, taking into account the progress of the investigation.

The full code test has two stages: evidential, and public interest. If a case does not pass the evidential stage it must not go ahead no matter how important or serious it may be. If it passes the evidential stage, Crown Prosecutors must decide if a prosecution is needed in the public interest.

Box 5.7 *Continued*

The evidential stage

Crown Prosecutors must be satisfied that there is enough evidence to provide a 'realistic prospect of conviction' against each defendant on each charge. They must consider what the defence case may be, and how that is likely to affect the prosecution case.

A realistic prospect of conviction is an objective test. It means that a jury or bench of magistrates or judge hearing a case alone, properly directed in accordance with the law, is more likely than not to convict the defendant of the charge alleged. This is distinct from the test of 'beyond reasonable doubt' that the criminal courts themselves must apply.

When deciding whether there is enough evidence to prosecute, Crown Prosecutors must consider whether the evidence can be used and is reliable. There are many cases in which the evidence does not give any cause for concern. But there are also cases in which the evidence may not be as strong as it first appears. Crown Prosecutors must ask themselves:

• *Can the evidence be used in court?* There are legal rules that might mean that evidence that seems relevant cannot be given at a trial. For example, is it likely that the evidence will be excluded because of the way in which it was obtained? Is the evidence hearsay? Does the evidence relate to the bad character of the suspect? (*see Ensuring the fairness of the trial*)
• *Is the evidence reliable?* What explanation has the suspect given? Is a court likely to find it credible in the light of the evidence as a whole? Does the evidence support an innocent explanation? Is there evidence that might support or detract from the reliability of a confession? Is its reliability affected by factors such as the suspect's level of understanding? Is the identification of the suspect likely to be questioned? Are there concerns over the accuracy, reliability, or credibility of the evidence of any witness? Is there further evidence that the police or other investigators should reasonably be asked to find which may support or undermine the account of the witness? Does any witness have any motive that may affect his or her attitude to the case? Does any witness have a relevant previous conviction or out-of-court disposal that may affect his or her credibility?

Where it is considered that it would be helpful in assessing the reliability of a witness's evidence or in better understanding complex evidence, an appropriately trained and authorized Prosecutor should conduct a pre-trial interview with the witness.

Crown Prosecutors should not ignore evidence because they are not sure that it can be used or is reliable. But they should look closely at it when deciding if there is a realistic prospect of conviction.

The public interest stage

In 1951, Lord Shawcross, then Attorney-General, made the classic statement on public interest, which has been supported by Attorneys-General ever since: 'It has never been the rule in this country—I hope it never will be—that suspected criminal offences must

Box 5.7 *Continued*

automatically be the subject of prosecution' (House of Commons Debates, volume 483, column 681, 29 January 1951).

The public interest must be considered in each case where there is enough evidence to provide a realistic prospect of conviction. Although there may be public interest factors against prosecution in a particular case, often the prosecution should go ahead and those factors should be put to the court for consideration when sentence is being passed. A prosecution will usually take place unless there are public interest factors tending against prosecution which clearly outweigh those tending in favour, or it appears more appropriate in all the circumstances of the case to divert the person from prosecution. Crown Prosecutors must balance factors for and against prosecution carefully and fairly.

Some common public interest factors in favour of prosecution

The more serious the offence, the more likely it is that a prosecution will be needed in the public interest. A prosecution is likely to be needed if:

- a conviction is likely to result in a significant sentence;
- a conviction is likely to result in a confiscation or any other order;
- a weapon was used or violence was threatened during the commission of the offence;
- the offence was committed against a person serving the public (e.g. a police or prison officer, or a nurse);
- the defendant was in a position of authority or trust;
- the evidence shows that the defendant was a ringleader or an organizer of the offence;
- there is evidence that the offence was premeditated;
- there is evidence that the offence was carried out by a group;
- the victim of the offence was vulnerable, has been put in considerable fear, or suffered personal attack, damage, or disturbance;
- the offence was committed in the presence of, or in close proximity to, a child;
- the offence was motivated by any form of discrimination against the victim's ethnic or national origin, disability, sex, religious beliefs, political views, or sexual orientation, or the suspect demonstrated hostility towards the victim based on any of those characteristics;
- there is a marked difference between the actual or mental ages of the defendant and the victim, or if there is any element of corruption;
- the defendant's previous convictions or cautions are relevant to the present offence;
- the defendant is alleged to have committed the offence while under an order of the court;
- there are grounds for believing that the offence is likely to be continued or repeated, for example by a history of recurring conduct;

Box 5.7 *Continued*

- the offence, although not serious in itself, is widespread in the area where it was committed; or
- a prosecution would have a significant positive impact on maintaining community confidence.

A prosecution is less likely to be needed if:

- the court is likely to impose a nominal penalty;
- the defendant has already been made the subject of a sentence and any further conviction would be unlikely to result in the imposition of an additional sentence or order, unless the nature of the particular offence requires a prosecution or the defendant withdraws consent to have an offence taken into consideration during sentencing;
- the offence was committed as a result of a genuine mistake or misunderstanding (these factors must be balanced against the seriousness of the offence);
- the loss or harm can be described as minor and was the result of a single incident, particularly if it was caused by a misjudgment;
- there has been a long delay between the offence taking place and the date of the trial, unless the offence is serious; or the delay has been caused in part by the defendant;
- the offence has only recently come to light; or the complexity of the offence has meant that there has been a long investigation;
- a prosecution is likely to have a bad effect on the victim's physical or mental health, always bearing in mind the seriousness of the offence;
- the defendant is elderly or is, or was at the time of the offence, suffering from significant mental or physical ill health, unless the offence is serious or there is a real possibility that it may be repeated;
- the defendant has put right the loss or harm that was caused (but defendants must not avoid prosecution or diversion solely because they pay compensation); or
- details may be made public that could harm sources of information, international relations, or national security.

The CPS does not act for victims or the families of victims in the same way as solicitors act for their clients. Crown Prosecutors act on behalf of the public and not just in the interests of any particular individual. However, when considering the public interest, Crown Prosecutors must take into account the consequences for the victim of whether or not to prosecute, and any views expressed by the victim or the victim's family. It is important that a victim is told about a decision that makes a significant difference to the case in which he or she is involved.

Source: Adapted from the *Code for Crown Prosecutors* (London, Crown Prosecution Service, 2010).

Notwithstanding the general approach of the CPS there are still cases where the CPS comes under heavy criticism, either from the police or from a victim (or his or her family).

Particular problems arise in very emotive cases, which may have attracted considerable media publicity, where therefore there is a great pressure to prosecute, but where the evidence to satisfy the tests sketched out earlier may just not be there. In making its decisions, the CPS cannot always reach conclusions that attract universal approval.

One issue that is particularly controversial relates to assisted suicides. Where a person has assisted a person, often an elderly loved one with a terminal illness, to end his or her life, the question arises whether that person should face prosecution, either for murder or manslaughter. While the law on unlawful killing may be clearly in favour of prosecution, compassion for the victim and his or her assistant may work the other way. In February 2010, the DPP issued specific guidance on when it would and when it would not be in the public interest to bring prosecutions in such cases (see <www.cps.gov.uk/publications/prosecution/assisted_suicide.html>.)

Two other topics have recently been aired. First, it used to be the case that when the CPS decided not to proceed with a prosecution, that was the end of the matter. The courts are clearly unhappy that the CPS should never reconsider a decision not to prosecute. The DPP seems to agree. In a recent lecture,[7] he argued that there might be circumstances where a decision could properly be re-examined.

Secondly, in cases involving serious economic crime, experience in the United States suggests that investigations may be assisted if agreements can be reached with alleged offenders not to prosecute, in return for their providing key evidence. The government has recently launched a consultation on whether 'deferred prosecution agreements' should be introduced in the United Kingdom.[8]

Monitoring

Because of concerns about the work of the CPS, an inspectorate was established in 1996 to monitor the quality and consistency of decision taking across the country, and to try to ensure the spread of good practice. The Inspectorate was originally created by executive action; following enactment of the Crown Prosecution Service Inspectorate Act 2000, it has been placed on a statutory footing. It examines not only the CPS but also other prosecuting authorities. Particular incidents may, additionally, be the subject of special inquiry.[9]

The trial stage

As we have seen, there are many reasons why criminal offences do not all result in an offender being brought before the courts. Even when a case is brought, the public image of what happens is far removed from the typical case. The news media or TV

---

[7] Starmer, K., QC, (2012) *Criminal Law Review* 526.

[8] For further detail on both these issues, see my blog, www.martinpartington.com.

[9] See, e.g. His Honour Gerald Butler QC's report, *Inquiry into CPS Decision-Making in Relation to Deaths in Custody and Related Matters* (London, The Stationery Office, 1999).

drama series suggest that most prosecutions result in full-scale jury trials in the Crown Court. In fact, the vast bulk of criminal trials are disposed of in the magistrates' court, and the vast bulk of them—both in the Crown Court and in the magistrates' court—are determined on the basis of a plea of guilty. The trial is a statistical rarity.

All prosecutions start in the magistrates' court. Whether they finish there depends on how the case is classified (*see Box 5.8*). The most serious cases—indictable offences—are sent to the Crown Court for disposal. The vast majority of criminal cases—summary cases—are disposed of in the magistrates' court. Cases which are triable either way, i.e. either summarily or on indictment, are determined in the appropriate court, once a decision on the classification of the case has been made.

Box 5.8   Legal system explained

Classification of criminal cases

There are four potential classes of criminal case:

- *Offences triable only on indictment.* These are the most serious cases, such as murder, manslaughter, and rape. If the defendant pleads not guilty, these cases must be tried in the Crown Court, before a jury.
- *Offences triable summarily.* These are all offences created by statute, where the statute provides that they are summary offences. These cases are determined by magistrates. There is no right to trial by jury. There have been some attempts at reclassifying certain offences as summary only, in particular small thefts; but political arguments about 'taking away rights to a jury trial' have made change difficult.
- *Offences triable either way.* These are offences, also created by statute, where the Act provides that they may be dealt with either summarily or on indictment. In such cases, the accused currently chooses how he or she wishes to be tried, before magistrates or before a jury. Opting for trial in the Crown Court exposes the accused to the prospect of more serious sentences, as the Crown Court has wider powers of sentence than the magistrates' court, though the latter can commit a case to the Crown Court where it thinks its powers of sentence are inadequate.
- *Summary cases triable on indictment.* In specific cases an accused may have a charge that he or she has committed a summary offence added to a charge that he or she has committed an indictable offence. These can now both be dealt with in the same trial in the Crown Court (see sections 40 and 41 of the Criminal Justice Act 1988).

The functions of the courts

Criminal courts have two principal functions:

- dealing with the case, which includes determining guilt where the defendant has pleaded not guilty, as well as deciding on the correct sentence; and
- ensuring that, so far as possible, the trial is fair.

They may also have to deal with other procedural questions, such as whether or not to grant bail or remand a person in custody (*see Box 5.6*).

Dealing with the case

In cases where the accused pleads not guilty, the court must hear the evidence, in the light of that evidence reach findings of fact, in the light of those findings determine whether the accused person is or is not guilty of the alleged crime, and, if guilty, pass an appropriate sentence. In the magistrates' courts all these functions are performed by the magistrates. In the Crown Court, finding the facts and deciding guilt are determined by the jury. Before the jury starts its work, it is provided with a summing-up of the case by the trial judge, an exercise designed to help it focus on the issues it must decide. If a conviction results, then, subject to further pleas in mitigation and reports on the accused from other agencies such as the probation service or social services, sentence is passed by the trial judge.

Many think that the function of the court is to determine the truth about the events that have led to a person appearing in court. In practice, the function of the trial is rather different. The prosecution must prove 'beyond reasonable doubt' that the accused committed the offence alleged. The function of the defence, therefore, is to throw sufficient doubt on what the prosecution is alleging so that the burden of proof is not established. If the burden of proof is not met, the defendant must be acquitted.

Where the defendant pleads guilty, the only issue for the court, again subject to pleas in mitigation made on behalf of the accused and other reports, is to determine sentence.

Ensuring the fairness of the trial

Fairness is at the heart of the due process model of criminal justice. A great deal of the law of criminal procedure and evidence is designed to ensure that the accused gets a fair trial. It is in this context that many of the tensions between the 'due process' model and the 'crime control' model may be seen. A number of initiatives have been taken in recent years that have shifted the balance from the former to the latter. The question is whether the balance has now gone too far. The full detail of the relevant law is beyond the scope of this book. However, two examples are briefly considered: evidence, and disclosure.

Evidence. The law on criminal evidence is designed to ensure that only relevant material is put before the court and to prevent material being put before the court that would be unfairly prejudicial to the defendant. Among the rules that exclude evidence in a criminal trial are:

- *the rule against hearsay evidence*: in general, only evidence given by witnesses in court is admitted. What others said to a witness cannot be admitted, as the person who made the statement cannot be challenged (cross-examined) about its veracity. The Criminal Justice Act 2003 relaxed these principles. It provided that witness statements can be used as evidence, subject to a number of safeguards, where the witness is identified but unavailable to testify or the statement is contained in a business document. The court is also given a discretion to admit hearsay evidence where it would not be contrary to the interests of justice for it to be used. In addition, witnesses' previous statements have been made more widely admissible at trial. This enables witnesses to refer to their statement whilst giving evidence in court and permits greater use of video-recorded statements for crucial evidence in serious cases;

- *the rule preventing the giving of information about an accused person's past record*: in general, the prosecution was not able to disclose to the court evidence about the defendant's history, particularly criminal record, unless that person wished to challenge the veracity of a prosecution witness, say a policeman. Under the Criminal Justice Act 2003, this principle is also relaxed. Judges are given power to let juries hear about a defendant's previous convictions and other misconduct where relevant to the case. The court can exclude evidence of previous misconduct if it thinks that the jury will give it disproportionate weight (in other words, if the relevance of the evidence to the case is outweighed by any prejudicial effect). The starting point, however, is that relevant evidence is admissible. To give an example: if X was being prosecuted for rape, the fact that X had previous convictions for robbery would not be admitted; however, evidence that X had previously been found guilty of other charges of serious assault against women would be. This proposal, which derived in part from a detailed study of the issue by the Law Commission, was extremely controversial. Lawyers' organizations and civil liberty groups argued that a person should be tried only for the crime for which he or she has been prosecuted; to introduce evidence of previous misconduct would undermine the presumption that a person should be regarded as innocent until proved guilty. Those in favour of the proposal argued that, as such evidence will not be admitted generally, but only where it is relevant to the case in question, it should be able to be taken into account.

In some circumstances, there are precise rules of law which relate to the admissibility of evidence. For example, where it is proposed to rely on a confession, section 76 of the PACE requires the prosecution to demonstrate beyond reasonable doubt that the confession was not made by oppression of the person who made it, or as a result of inducements made to the person giving it that might render the confession unreliable.

Section 78 of the PACE also gives the judge/magistrate a general discretion to exclude evidence that would otherwise be admissible and relevant 'where the admission of the evidence would have such an adverse effect on the fairness of the proceedings that the court ought not to admit it'. Evidence obtained by the police in breach of the rules relating to questioning and interrogation can fall into this category.

Disclosure. A separate issue relates to the question of what evidence should be disclosed by the prosecution to the defendant and vice versa. One of the most significant causes of serious miscarriages of justice arises when the prosecution withholds evidence that it has acquired during the process of its investigation but that weakens the case that the prosecution is seeking to build against the accused.

This was a central issue considered by the Royal Commission on Criminal Justice which reported in 1993. As a result of, though not fully accepting, its recommendations, the government introduced a new legal regime relating to disclosure, contained in Parts I and II of the Criminal Procedure and Investigations Act 1996 (*see Box 5.9*). Disputes about whether or not documents should be disclosed are resolved by the court at a pre-trial hearing.

Box 5.9   System in action

Disclosure of evidence

The Royal Commission on Criminal Justice was appointed in 1991 against a background of cases where there had been clear miscarriages of justice: the 'Guildford four', the 'Maguire seven', the 'Birmingham six', and the Judith Ward cases are amongst the best known. In addition, the courts in a number of cases had been developing the (then) common law relating to disclosure. The result had been to place increased responsibility to disclose on the police. This provided an opportunity to the defence to mount fishing expeditions to find out what information the police had. The Royal Commission sought to strike a balance between the duties of the prosecution and the rights of the defence. It proposed that a new scheme for disclosure should be enshrined in statute, accompanied by a code of practice or a more detailed statutory instrument.

In May 1995, the then government published a consultation paper, which led to the Criminal Investigations and Procedure Act 1996, now amended by the Criminal Justice Act 2003. In outline, this provides:

(1) the investigator (usually the police) must preserve material gathered during the investigation and make available to the prosecutor material falling into defined key categories, plus a list of other material that has been acquired;

(2) the prosecutor must serve on the defence material on which the prosecutor intends to rely to found the case;

(3) the prosecutor must also disclose prosecution material that has not previously been disclosed and that might reasonably be considered capable of undermining the case for the prosecution against the accused, or of assisting the case for the accused. There is a continuing duty on the prosecutor to disclose material that meets the new test. The prosecutor is specifically required to review the prosecution material on receipt of the defence statement and to make further disclosure if required under the continuing duty; and

(4) the defence statement must set out the nature of the defence including any particular defences on which the defence intends to rely. It must also indicate any points of law the defence wishes to take, including any points as to the admissibility of evidence or abuse of process. The judge is required to warn the accused about any failure to comply with the defence statement requirements. There is also a requirement

Box 5.9 *Continued*

for service of an updated defence statement to assist the management of the trial, requiring the accused to serve, before the trial, details of any witnesses he or she intends to call to give evidence (other than him- or herself) and also details of all experts instructed including those not called to give evidence. The new obligation on the defence to provide details of the witnesses it intends to call will be accompanied by a code of practice governing the conduct of any interviews by the police or non-police investigators with defence witnesses disclosed in accordance with the requirement.

Any disputes about disclosure are to be resolved by the court in a pre-trial hearing.

The main features of the process are: (1) that it is statute-based; (2) that it puts the responsibility on the prosecution to decide what should be disclosed; and (3) that it requires that the defence should make disclosure of its case before the start of the trial.

The accompanying *code of practice* (made under the authority of Part 2 of the 1996 Act) requires the appointment, in any criminal investigation, of an 'officer in charge', plus a separate 'disclosure officer' who will be responsible for the administration of the investigation, including the operation of the disclosure scheme. The 'investigator'—the police or other officer carrying out the investigation—is made responsible for retaining material gathered or generated by the inquiry. The disclosure officer prepares the schedule of unused material, together with a list of any sensitive material (e.g. relating to national security or information given in confidence). The disclosure officer must send these schedules to the prosecutor, accompanied by copies of any material relating to the unreliability of witnesses or confessions or containing any explanation by the accused for the offence. Once the defence statement is filed, the disclosure officer must look at all the files again and draw attention to any that may assist the defence. The officer must then certify to the prosecutor that, to the best of his or her knowledge and belief, the duties imposed by the code have been complied with.

In a decision by the European Court of Human Rights, *Rowe and Davis v United Kingdom* (*The Times*, 1 March 2000), it was held that where the prosecution withheld evidence because it was claimed to be immune from disclosure on the grounds of public interest, the failure to put it before a trial judge so as to permit him to rule on the question of disclosure deprived an accused person of the right to a fair trial.

The effectiveness of these arrangements depends to a large extent on the willingness of particular individuals, on both the investigation and prosecution sides, to operate the scheme in accordance with the statutory provisions and code of guidance. A report, published in 2000 by the CPS Inspectorate,[10] gave a disturbing account of routine failures to follow the rules.

An important innovation in the way the courts work was the creation, in 2004, of a Criminal Procedure Rules Committee, whose task is to create a code of criminal

---

[10] Crown Prosecution Service Inspectorate, *Report on the Thematic Review of the Disclosure of Unused Material* (London, Crown Prosecution Service, 2000).

procedure and related practice directions that apply throughout the criminal courts. Modelled on the Civil Procedure Rules Committee (*see Chapter 8, Civil Procedure Rules 1999*), it is designed to give judges greater authority to manage the progress of criminal trials. The Rules were published in 2005 and brought together some 50 pre-existing sets of procedural rules. They are now consolidated annually; the latest edition, the 2012 rules, came into effect in October 2012. The rules, which govern the practice and procedure of the criminal courts, are designed to change some of the culture of the criminal trial process, in particular through judicial case management.

Magistrates' courts

Magistrates' courts have a long history. They have a distinct character in that they depend very heavily on volunteer/lay persons to determine decisions. Much of the claim to legitimacy for the magistrates is that benches are composed of persons who come from the community affected by the alleged criminal activity. (*See Box 5.10* for types of magistrates' courts. Magistrates' courts also decide certain family law matters, *see Chapter 7, Family proceedings courts.*)

Box 5.10   Legal system explained

Types of magistrates' courts

There are two distinct types of magistrates' courts that operate in England and Wales: *lay justices'* courts, and *district judge* (formerly *stipendiary*) *magistrates'* courts. Lay justices' courts are made up of (usually) three lay persons (i.e. persons with no specific legal qualifications), known as *justices of the peace* (JPs), who sit and determine criminal cases. They receive legal advice on their powers from the *justices' clerk*, a specially appointed official who is legally qualified. JPs provide their services on a voluntary basis; they receive expenses, for example for travel and subsistence, and, where appropriate, can claim a loss of earnings allowance. Apart from that, however, they are unpaid. By far the majority of magistrates' courts are lay justices' courts.

District judge magistrates' courts are run by district judges, who are qualified lawyers and sit on their own, rather than in panels of three. They used to sit only in those areas of the country designated by the government as appropriate for such courts. As the result of a change in the law (section 78 of and Schedule 11 to the Access to Justice Act 1999), they are now able to sit in any magistrates' court in the country, thus giving court managers greater flexibility in the use of this judicial resource.

Functions

All criminal trials start in the magistrates' courts. In carrying out their judicial function, there are two distinct types of procedure that they control: *committal proceedings*, and *summary trials*. In addition, they have responsibility for enforcing non-custodial penalties, especially fines.

Committal proceedings and sending for trial

Historically, committal proceedings were a formal stage in a criminal trial designed to ensure that, even though a case was going to be tried in the Crown Court, magistrates were satisfied that there is a case for the defendant to answer. Indeed, years ago committal proceedings were fully reported in the press and other mass media; but this led to the criticism that such publicity made it difficult to find members of a jury who had not heard about the case. The law was therefore changed; publicity to committal proceedings could be given only where the defendant permits this.

From January 2001, all indictable-only cases are automatically sent for trial in the Crown Court following the appearance of the defendant before magistrates. Traditional committal proceedings would only take place in the case of an offence triable either way, where it is decided that the trial should be on indictment. The government has now decided that committal proceedings for these cases should also be abolished. They started to be phased out in June 2012; this process will be completed in 2013. It is estimated that this will save about 60,000 hearings a year.

The reason for the abolition of committal proceedings, as seen by the government, is that it is rare for magistrates to find there is no case to answer. It is, therefore, argued that formal committal proceedings merely add delay and expense to the process of the criminal trial.

Under section 49 of the Criminal Procedures and Investigations Act 1996, accused persons must enter a plea—guilty or not guilty—in the magistrates' court. Those who, before this rule came into force would have been committed to the Crown Court for trial and who would then have pleaded guilty, are now no longer committed for trial, though they may be committed for sentence. Despite this change in the rules, 72 per cent of those appearing in the Crown Court (who by definition pleaded not guilty before the magistrates) plead guilty (i.e. change their plea) when they get to Crown Court.

Summary trials

All other prosecutions are dealt with summarily, that is to say by the magistrates themselves. In the year ending March 2012, some 1.53 million defendants were proceeded against in the magistrates' courts: around 95 per cent of prosecutions are dealt with in this way.[11] The vast majority are determined by a plea of guilty, rather than following a trial. In 2011, there were only 163,000 trials in the magistrates' courts and of these less than half were effective trials.[12]

---

[11] Figures derived from <www.justice.gov.uk/downloads/statistics/criminal-justice-stats/criminal-justice-stats-march-2012.pdf>.

[12] Figure derived from <www.justice.gov.uk/statistics/courts-and-sentencing/judicial-annual-2011>, chapter 3. Effective trials are those where the case is disposed of after a full hearing of the evidence.

Committals for sentence

In all cases where guilt is established, whether or not there is a trial, the magistrates must impose a penalty. The powers of magistrates to impose sentences are limited. However, where they decide that their powers of sentence are inadequate they can commit a case to the Crown Court. The number of cases committed to the Crown Court for sentence in the year ending March 2012 was around 21,000. These numbers may reduce in future as the government, under the Legal Aid, Sentencing and Punishment of Offenders Act 2012, is removing the current £5,000 limit on fines that can be imposed by magistrates. (For sentencing more generally, *see Sentencing.*)

Fine enforcement

In many cases where the penalty imposed is a fine, the magistrates must follow this up with enforcement proceedings.

Youth courts

A vast amount of criminal activity is carried out by people, mainly male, at a relatively early age. Juvenile delinquency and measures to try to deal with it—not always with conspicuous success—have been high on the policy agendas of governments for many years. Current debates about anti-social behaviour, drug and alcohol abuse, and general fear of violent crime, are fuelled at least in part by a perception that we live in a 'yob culture'. There are major tensions between the desire to prevent juvenile crime and deal firmly with those young persons found guilty of criminal activity, and the desire not to blight young lives unnecessarily by giving them criminal records that may prevent them entering the job market or otherwise making a positive contribution to society.

There have also been fierce debates about where the responsibility for youth crime should lie—with individual offenders, with their parent(s), with schools and teachers, or with the wider society, which is said to fail to provide the educational and employment opportunities that might make youth offenders more productive members of society.

The issue was reviewed by the former Labour government in 1997 in the white paper *No More Excuses.*[13] This led to two Acts of Parliament, the Crime and Disorder Act 1998 and the Youth Justice and Criminal Evidence Act 1999. These contained provisions, not only to process young offenders (those under the age of 18) through the criminal justice system more quickly, but also to try to demonstrate to them the effect their actions have on the lives of others.

The Crime and Disorder Act 1998 led to the creation of *youth offending teams*— multi-disciplinary agencies brought together at the local level to devise effective programmes to prevent offending and reoffending by young people. Their work is kept under review by a *Youth Justice Board.*

[13] (Cm 3809) (London, The Stationery Office, 1997).

The 1998 Act also replaced a non-statutory policy, whereby police could merely decide to caution a young offender, with a new statutory 'final warning'. Once an offender has received one, any further offence leads to criminal proceedings in court.

When dealing with young offenders, magistrates' courts are technically known as *youth courts*. When sitting as a youth court, magistrates are subject to special procedural rules designed to ensure that cases are dealt with as speedily as possible. In 2001, the Home Office published a *Good Practice Guide for Youth Courts*.[14] This evolved from an experiment in two courts that sought to achieve four key objectives:

- effective engagement with defendants and their parents to probe the reasons for offending and to encourage plans to change behaviour;
- changing courtroom layouts to facilitate better communication;
- making the court process more open by lifting reporting restrictions where appropriate, and exercising discretion to allow others such as victims to attend court; and
- giving feedback to sentencers on the outcome of sentences.

The guide is designed to encourage youth courts to respond positively to such initiatives to counter public perceptions that they were not delivering effective justice.

Magistrates also have a special range of sentencing options now brought together in the generic youth rehabilitation order (*see Box 5.11*).

Box 5.11   Legal system explained

Youth rehabilitation orders

As a result of the Criminal Justice and Immigration Act 2008, there is now a generic 'youth rehabilitation order' available to the courts. This enables the court to impose one or more of the following: (1) an activity requirement; (2) a supervision requirement; (3) in a case where the offender is aged 16 or 17 at the time of the conviction, an unpaid work requirement; (4) a programme requirement; (5) an attendance centre requirement; (6) a prohibited activity requirement; (7) a curfew requirement; (8) an exclusion requirement; (9) a residence requirement; (10) a local authority residence requirement; (11) a mental health treatment requirement; (12) a drug treatment requirement; (13) a drug testing requirement; (14) an intoxicating substance treatment requirement; and (15) an education requirement.

A youth rehabilitation order may also impose an electronic monitoring requirement, and in some cases must do so. In addition, a youth rehabilitation order may be made with intensive supervision and surveillance, or with fostering.

The Act sets out in detail what each of these requirements involves and when it can be used. The Legal Aid Sentencing and Punishment of Offenders Act 2012 has made detailed amendment to the rules on youth rehabilitation orders.

---

[14] *The Youth Court: Changing the Culture of the Youth Court* (London, Home Office, 2001).

As a result of the Youth Justice and Criminal Evidence Act 1999, magistrates may make a referral order to refer first-time offenders to a *youth offender panel*. The power to refer is available only in the youth court. Where a young offender has been tried in the Crown Court, the trial judge may, on conviction, refer the offender to the youth court for sentence in a case where that seems to be appropriate. The youth court may in turn refer the offender to the panel.

A youth offender panel consists of two volunteers recruited directly from the local community, working alongside a member of the youth offending team. The aim of the panel is to agree a programme of behaviour for the young offender to follow. The programme is explicitly based on the theory of 'restorative justice', to ensure that the offender takes responsibility for the consequences of his or her offending behaviour; makes restoration to the victim; and achieves reintegration into the law-abiding community. It must be questioned whether the theory of restorative justice is the only theory behind the new programme; other 'justice models'—including the 'crime control' and the 'bureaucratic'—appear to be in play as well.

In addition to the work of the youth courts, other measures designed to curb anti-social behaviour have also been introduced. These include: local child curfews; anti-social behaviour orders; and acceptable behaviour contracts. As in other areas of the justice system the pace of change has been extremely fast. There is now a strong case for a period of consolidation and evaluation of what has been done rather than yet more change.

The Crown Court

Jurisdiction and organization

The Crown Court is where the most serious criminal cases—cases tried on indictment—are disposed of. The Crown Court works from 76 court centres, grouped into six circuits: Midland and Oxford; North Eastern; Northern; South Eastern; Wales and Chester; and Western. The 'Old Bailey' is the name given to the Central Criminal Court in London, a Crown Court in the South Eastern Circuit. The Court is divided into three tiers:

- First-tier courts are those in which High Court judges, circuit judges, and recorders sit. They have higher levels of security to deal with the most difficult prisoners. The full range of criminal work, together with High Court civil work (*see Chapter 8*), is dealt with in these courts.
- Second-tier courts are the same, though no civil work is conducted in them.
- Third-tier courts are presided over only by circuit judges or recorders.

The offences dealt with in the Crown Court are themselves divided into three classes, under directions given by the Lord Chief Justice:

- Class 1—Generally heard by a High Court judge, these are the most serious offences which include treason and murder.

- Class 2—Offences which include rape that are usually heard by a circuit judge under the authority of the presiding judge.

- Class 3—Includes all other offences, such as kidnapping, burglary, grievous bodily harm and robbery, which are normally tried by a circuit judge or recorder.

The obvious intention is that the most serious offences should be dealt with by the most senior judges.

The Crown Court also has powers to sentence persons convicted in the magistrates' court where the magistrates have decided that their own powers of sentencing are inadequate. In addition, the Crown Court hears appeals from decisions of the magistrates' court.

Work-load

Committals and cases sent for trial. In the year ending March 2012, the Crown Court had around 98,000 cases committed to it.[15] In 2011, in 70 per cent of cases the defendant pleaded guilty. Only 30 per cent of cases were dealt with following a plea of not guilty. Thus considerably less than a third went to trial. Of these trials, 40 per cent of trials were 'cracked trials', i.e. cases originally listed for trial, but where the accused changed his plea from not guilty to guilty, most commonly on the day of the trial. Another 14 per cent of trials were 'ineffective' trials, the majority where the defendant was absent, or unfit to stand trial or because a prosecution witness is absent.[16]

These represent a considerable drain on resources, for two reasons. First, when judges cannot hear a cracked or ineffective case, it is usually too late to give them something else to do. Secondly, cases that collapse at the last minute waste enormous amounts of work put in by the CPS in preparing a case for trial. The DPP announced in October 2010 that he would be reviewing current practice to find ways of bringing cases to court more efficiently. Although the outcome of this process is not yet known, it will again highlight the tension between the 'due process' and the 'bureaucratic' models of criminal justice.

Of those pleading not guilty to all charges, 62 per cent were acquitted. Of these, about 30 per cent were acquitted as the result of a not guilty verdict from the jury; 61 per cent were discharged by the judge, and nine per cent were acquitted on the direction of the judge.

Of the defendants who were convicted after pleading not guilty (about ten per cent of all those dealt with in the Crown Court), only 19 per cent were convicted on the basis of a majority verdict; the rest were convicted by the unanimous decision of the jury.

Committals for sentence. Around 42,000 committals for sentence were made; and around the same number of cases were dealt with.

---

[15] See <www.justice.gov.uk/downloads/statistics/criminal-justice-stats/criminal-justice-stats-march-2012.pdf>.

[16] See <www.justice.gov.uk/statistics/courts-and-sentencing/judicial-annual-2011>, chapter 4.

Appeals. 13,359 appeals from magistrates' courts were made, and a similar number were dealt with. Of these, 43 per cent were allowed or resulted in a variation of the sentence.

Hearing times. The average hearing times were:

- for not guilty pleas in sent for trial cases, 18.9 hours;
- for not guilty pleas in committed for trial cases, 7.9 hours;
- for guilty pleas, 1.7 hours;
- for sentence, 0.5 hours;
- for appeals from magistrates' courts, 1.1 hour.

Comment on crown court work

The most obvious point is that, as in the magistrates' courts, full-scale trials following a plea of not guilty are a statistical rarity:

- A significant percentage of those who plead not guilty are ultimately acquitted, though far more are on the direction of the judge rather than as the result of a jury verdict.
- The newspapers may give the impression that cases in the Crown Court take significant amounts of time, particularly where there is a full trial. Although trials take longer than other forms of disposal, sent for trial cases (the most serious) on average last under 20 hours.
- The 'success rate' in appeals could be seen as raising some questions about the quality of magistrates' decisions, though the total number of appeals is a tiny proportion of the total number of cases dealt with by the magistrates.

Issues in the criminal justice trial system

Charge and plea bargaining

The high level of guilty pleas in both the magistrates' and Crown Courts may suggest that the police and prosecution allow only the strongest cases to come before a court. But it may nonetheless seem surprising that, in a system where the theory is that all are innocent until proved guilty, so few accused actually take advantage of the due process model of criminal justice and submit the evidence presented by the prosecution for testing before either the magistrates or a jury.

Of course there are cases where the evidence is so overwhelming that a guilty plea is the only sensible option for the accused. But in less clear-cut cases, at least part of the answer to this puzzle arises from the fact that those within the criminal justice system work quite hard, through various forms of bargaining, to ensure that accused persons plead guilty. This saves considerable amounts of court time (as the statistics for average hearing times set out earlier clearly show) and thus expense and other resources. There are various practices that may occur to assist the accused in deciding what plea to enter.

First, there may be a negotiation between the prosecutor and the defence about the charge to be proceeded with before the courts. If the accused is willing or can be persuaded to plead guilty to a charge that carries a less severe penalty, the prosecution may then decide not to pursue an alternative charge that could arise from the same factual situation, which might attract a more severe penalty.

Secondly, there may be an indication that if a plea of guilty is entered, then, in passing sentence, the judge may reduce the sentence he might otherwise have imposed. Direct negotiations between defence lawyers and judges on sentence, commonplace in the United States, do not take place in the United Kingdom. Further, the decision in *R v Turner* ([1970] 2 QB 321, CA) makes it clear that judges may not indicate the sentence they are planning to impose, nor indicate how that sentence might change were the defendant to plead guilty.

However, at the end of a hearing, section 48(2) of the Criminal Justice and Public Order Act 1994 requires a judge to give reasons for any reduction in the sentence from what would normally be expected for the offence in question taking normal sentencing guidelines into account. The Criminal Justice Act 2003 also requires courts to take into account the stage in the proceedings at which the guilty plea was offered, and the circumstances in which it was made. In practice, judges allow a discount of between 25 and 33 per cent in cases where the defendant pleads guilty: the earlier the plea, the higher the discount. During 2012–13, Crown Courts in the London area are developing Early Guilty Plea Protocols. These are designed to ensure that those accused of offences are encouraged to plead guilty early. A similar protocol also operates in magistrates' courts.[17]

The formal legal position is that undue pressure must not be put on defendants to enter any particular plea, as this may lead the innocent to plead guilty to a crime he or she did not commit. Such practices do not fit with the due process model of the criminal justice system. The reality is, however, that justice is frequently negotiated, a practice justified by the added efficiency that it brings to the system, thus fitting the crime control model. The extent to which such practices should be condoned is the subject of considerable debate in the criminal justice literature.

Jury trial

A second issue of considerable current importance relates to the use of juries to determine the facts in Crown Court trials. Three issues can be considered separately: Are juries competent to decide cases? To what extent should the accused be entitled to choose trial by jury in those cases where a choice is open to them? Should the classification of indictable offences (for which the right to trial by jury arises automatically) be altered?

---

[17] For more detail, see my blog, www.martinpartington.com.

The competence of juries. Jury trial is perceived by many as one of the great strengths of the English criminal justice system. There is an enormous literature on juries, asserting their importance as a defender of civil liberty and a bulwark against oppression by the state. Indeed, the use of juries may be said to legitimate decision taking in the criminal justice system by enabling decisions to be taken by ordinary lay people. This reinforces the independence of the judicial system in this context and thus fits with the constitutional separation of the courts from other decision-making bodies (*see Box 5.12*).

Box 5.12   System in action

Case study: the case of Mr Ponting

There have certainly been historically significant, if rare, cases where juries appear, despite the weight of evidence, to have acted on their conscience to protect civil liberty by finding persons not guilty of crimes which may be said to have significant political overtones. The example of the acquittal of Clive Ponting is often cited. Ponting was a former civil servant, accused of offences under the Official Secrets Act 1911 after he had passed to a Member of Parliament confidential documents relating to the sinking of an Argentinian battleship during the Falklands War in 1982. Despite a ruling from the judge that Ponting had no authorization to pass the documents on, and that there was no other lawful justification for his action, the jury acquitted him. It was assumed that the jury had decided that the moral arguments in favour of his doing what he did outweighed the legal arguments that what he did was unlawful.

Important changes to the constitution and functions of juries have been made over the years. Before 1972, occupation of a house with a prescribed rateable value was one of the criteria for selection. Since then most of the restrictions on jury qualification have gone (with the exception of those relating to mentally disordered persons and certain groups of convicted persons). This has led to profound changes in jury composition, certainly in terms of their class composition. Since 1981, selection for jury service has been by random selection using a computer. Perhaps the most significant change occurred in 1967 when the ability of juries to determine cases on the basis of majority verdicts was introduced.[18]

Despite the arguments in favour of jury trial, which have considerable force, little is actually known about how juries function. Direct research into the work of the jury is not permitted. The only research currently available is through the use of 'surrogate' juries dealing with hypothetical situations, or secondary analysis of data on the outcomes of trials. In 2010, an important study—which had used both these research methods—was published by the Ministry of Justice (*see Box 5.13*).

---

[18] See the Juries Act 1974, s. 17. Majority verdicts are subject to an important *Practice Direction* [1967] 1 WLR 1198, and [1970] 1 WLR 916 which regulates their use. Data on the use of majority verdicts are in the text.

Box 5.13   System in action

Are juries fair?

Professor Cheryl Thomas sought to discover whether juries were fair, in particular toward defendants from the black and ethnic minority communities who are statistically over-represented in the criminal courts. The research found no evidence of jury bias, though the report also acknowledged that where all-white juries dealt with black defendants, there might be a perception of bias.

The report dealt with some misconceptions about jury verdicts. For example, in rape cases, contrary to popular belief and previous government reports, juries actually convict more often than they acquit in rape cases (55 per cent jury conviction rate); other serious offences (attempted murder, manslaughter, GBH) have lower jury conviction rates than rape.

Jury conviction rates for rape vary according to the gender and age of the complainant, with high conviction rates for some female complainants and low conviction rates for some male complainants. This challenges the view that juries' failure to convict in rape cases is due to juror bias against female complainants.

Further, the research found that in courts with over 1,000 jury verdicts in 2006–08, the conviction rate ranged from 69 per cent to 53 per cent. There were no courts with a higher jury acquittal than conviction rate. This dispels the myth that there are courts where juries rarely convict.

More worrying was the ability of jurors to understand directions given by judges. The study involved 797 jurors at three courts who all saw the same simulated trial and heard exactly the same judicial directions on the law. Most jurors at Blackfriars (69 per cent) and Winchester (68 per cent) felt they were able to understand the directions, while most jurors at Nottingham (51 per cent) felt the directions were difficult to understand.

Jurors' actual comprehension of the judge's legal directions was also examined. While over half of the jurors perceived the judge's directions as easy to understand, only a minority (31 per cent) actually understood the directions fully in the legal terms used by the judge. Younger jurors were better able than older jurors to comprehend the legal instructions, with comprehension of directions on the law declining as the age of the juror increased.

A written summary of the judge's directions on the law given to jurors at the time of the judge's oral instructions improved juror comprehension of the law: the proportion of jurors who fully understood the legal questions in the case in the terms used by the judge increased from 31 per cent to 48 per cent with written instructions.

Professor Thomas argued that the judiciary should reconsider implementing the Auld recommendations for issuing jurors with written aide-memoires on the law in all cases.

Source: <www.justice.gov.uk/downloads/publications/research-and-analysis/moj-research/are-juries-fair-research.pdf>.

There have been many suggestions that particular types of case—lengthy and complex fraud trials are given as the prime candidate—are not suitable for jury trial. This has led to alternative proposals being adopted, for example judges sitting with a panel of lay assessors, or such cases being heard by a panel of judges rather than just a single judge. (There are significant dangers in allowing facts to be found from disputed evidence by a single adjudicator.)

Part 7 of the Criminal Justice Act 2003 made provision for the possibility of trials without a jury. First, it would have enabled the prosecution to apply for a trial of a serious or complex fraud case to proceed in the absence of a jury. The section of the Act that would have enabled this to happen was never brought into effect, and the Coalition government has repealed the relevant law.

Secondly, the Act provided for a trial to be conducted without a jury where there was a real and present danger of jury tampering, or continued without a jury where the jury has been discharged because of jury tampering (*see Box 5.14* for a case study). The Act also provided a right of appeal to the Court of Appeal for both prosecution and defence. Where a trial is conducted or continued without a jury and a defendant is convicted, the court is required to give its reasons for the conviction.

Box 5.14   System in action

Case study: the case of the Heathrow bullion robbers

Although the law came into force in 2006, it was not until 2010 that, for the first time, a court used the power to hold a criminal trial without a jury. The case involved four persons who had been accused of armed robbery at Heathrow Airport in 2004, involving the theft of more than £1,750,000 in a variety of foreign currencies. An earlier trial had been stopped because there was evidence of jury tampering. In this case, the court accepted the prosecution's argument that there was still a very real threat of jury tampering, which justified the case being tried by a judge sitting on his own.

Despite concerns expressed, this procedure has hardly been used. The CPS has provided a very detailed note setting out the conditions on which they might argue for a trial to proceed without a jury.

Source: <www.cps.gov.uk/legal/l_to_o/non_jury_trials/>.

While some believe that juries are too ready to acquit defendants, the reality is that far more acquittals are ordered by the trial judge. There are no serious proposals that jury trial should be abolished. Such a step would be politically quite unacceptable, and too great a move from the due process model to the crime control model of criminal justice.

Choice of mode of trial. A quite distinct issue, though also a matter of considerable controversy, is the question of who should have the right to choose jury trial in those cases that are triable either way. Following the Royal Commission on Criminal

Procedure's report in 1993, the Blair government proposed that the decision should be made by the magistrates before whom all such cases initially come, and not left to the discretion of the accused. Powerful voices dissented, arguing that such a change would involve a fundamental issue of principle, which, once conceded, would further undermine the due process model of criminal justice. Having unsuccessfully tried twice to get such a proposal through Parliament, the government decided not to pursue this issue.

Should the classification of indictable offences be altered? There is a quite distinct argument that the present classification of offences allows some cases to be tried by juries where this does not seem warranted by the seriousness of the offence. There have been examples of reclassification happening in recent years. For example, the Criminal Justice Act 1988 reclassified a number of motoring offences as summary only. There have been other attempts to reclassify certain types of minor theft as summary offences, thereby denying those accused of them the right to trial by jury. Proposals for change are always countered by the 'thin end of the wedge' argument, that any step in this direction will encourage governments to take further steps in the same direction, thereby reducing the scope of jury trial still further. The Criminal Justice Act 2003 contains a provision enabling the sentencing powers of the magistrates' courts to be raised from six to 12 months. This has not however been brought into effect.

Representation

For a discussion of the criminal defence service, *see Chapter 10, Criminal Defence Service: criminal legal aid.*

Sentencing

In the same way that the criminal justice system as a whole may be seen to depend on a variety of conflicting social theories, so too is sentencing policy and practice based on a variety of conflicting theories. The literature on theories of sentencing is extensive. Ashworth has classified the approaches under five main headings:

- desert (retributive) theories;
- deterrence theories;
- rehabilitative theories;
- incapacitative theories; and
- restorative (reparative) theories.

Desert or retributive theories take as their focus the idea that punishment is a natural or appropriate response to crime, at least so long as it is proportionate to the crime committed. It is assumed that a person who commits a crime deserves to be punished; and that society is entitled to see that retribution is exacted from the offender. The problem of determining whether sentences are in fact proportional to the offence is, of course, a matter on which there can be great room for debate—and often is when the press criticize judges for apparently light (occasionally over-harsh) sentencing.

Deterrence theories offer a slightly different view. Here the perspective is on deterring future offending behaviour by punishing the offender currently before the authorities. Such a theory would then justify harsher penalties being imposed on an offender who has committed the same offence on more than one occasion than would be the case for a first offender. The research literature does not offer great confidence that, in practice, policies of deterrence work. Nonetheless, they are very important politically, and indeed have led to the adoption of mandatory sentences for certain categories of repeat offenders.

Rehabilitative sentencing focuses on the offender and efforts to change his or her behaviour so that he or she can become a full and productive member of society. It may be assumed that offenders are in some way unable to cope with life and thus need professional support to change. It involves elements of diagnosis and treatment; it also implies that particular decisions need to be tailored to the individual offender.

Incapacitative sentencing focuses on the need to identify particular individuals or groups who are likely to do serious harm in the future, and who therefore need to be removed from society ('incapacitated') to prevent such harm occurring. The difficulties of imposing what may be severe penalties on the basis of what may happen in the future are obvious, but arise, for example, in the context of convicted paedophiles.

Restorative approaches concentrate more on the victim and the need for the offender to make amends to the victim. Restorative justice shares with rehabilitative models the belief that such outcomes will encourage the offender to change his way of life, but the focus on the victim is distinctive. The use of these approaches in youth justice has been noted earlier.

The Criminal Justice Act 2003 sets out a statutory list of the principles and purposes of sentencing, reflecting the approaches outlined above (*see Box 5.15*). Given the conflicting nature of these theories, it is not entirely obvious what the purpose of doing this was. As with general theories of criminal justice, different rationales for sentencing practice need to be understood so that not only the present law but also possible alternatives to it can be assessed.

Box 5.15 Legal system explained

Purposes of sentencing

The Criminal Justice Act 2003 listed the following as the purposes to which the court must have regard: (1) the punishment of offenders; (2) the reduction of crime (including its reduction by deterrence); (3) the reform and rehabilitation of offenders; (4) the protection of the public; and (5) the making of reparation by offenders to persons affected by their offences.

Box 5.15 *Continued*

In relation to young offenders, the Criminal Justice and Immigration Act 2008 has a different list reflecting a different approach. Here, the court must have regard to: (1) the principal aim of the youth justice system (which is to prevent offending (or reoffending)) by persons aged under 18; (2) the welfare of the offender; and (3) the purposes of sentencing. These are: (1) the punishment of offenders; (2) the reform and rehabilitation of offenders; (3) the protection of the public, and (4) the making of reparation by offenders to persons affected by their offences.

Determining sentencing policy is extremely hard. Politicians seek to reassure the public that they are taking crime seriously and therefore place emphasis on the deterrent effect of penalties, particularly custodial sentences. They are supported in this by sections of the mass media that make rational discussion of sentencing policy and practice extremely difficult. Research tends to show that, in many cases, so-called deterrent sentences do not in general deter. This leads to arguments that there should be more emphasis on rehabilitation and reparation. Certainly, the range of penalties available to the courts has grown in recent years. In particular new forms of 'community sentence', in which the offender is obliged to undertake some form of reparative work in the community and for the victim, have been introduced. The problem with community sentences is convincing the public that they are not a 'soft-option'. (*See Box 5.16* for some basic facts on current sentencing outcomes.)

Box 5.16 System in action

Sentencing: some basic facts

In the year ending March 2012, 1.28 million offenders were sentenced, having been found guilty of indictable or summary offences. 101,200 were sentenced to immediate custody, with an average sentence length of 14.8 months. 47,200 Suspended Sentence Orders were handed down in the same period. 170,000 were given a community sentence. 839,700 were fined.
Source: <www.justice.gov.uk/downloads/statistics/criminal-justice-stats/criminal-justice-stats-march-2012.pdf>.

Current sentencing policy is based on provisions in the Criminal Justice Act 2003. Further change will follow the introduction of the Legal Aid, Sentencing and Punishment of Offenders Act 2012. (*See Box 5.17* for the principal features of the current sentencing regime.)

Box 5.17 System in action

Criminal Justice Act 2003: the principal features

Generic community sentences. The Act created a single community sentence under which a range of measures formerly attached to different types of community orders remain available. It also set out the tests that must be met before a community order is made. The statutory tests are supplemented by guidance from the Sentencing Council (*see Box 5.18*).

Short custodial sentences. These were identified as particularly problematic. They were too short to offer the offender any rehabilitation but when the offender came out from prison, there was no further supervision for him or her. Recidivism was common. The 2003 Act offered three alternatives. The first is 'custody minus'. A short prison sentence can be suspended for up to two years while requirements to do some work in the community that is set by the court are undertaken. If the offender breaches any of the requirements, the custodial term is activated, and the sentence becomes one of custody plus. Committing a further offence during the period of suspension also counts as breach.

The other two, 'intermittent custody', where the custodial element would be served intermittently, for example at weekends, and 'custody plus', where those sentenced to less than a year could have a mix of prison and community sentence, were never implemented, and are repealed by the Legal Aid, Sentencing and Punishment of Offenders Act 2012.

Sentences of over 12 months. For offenders serving a sentence of over 12 months (apart from the sentences for dangerous offenders outlined in the next paragraph) release is made automatic at the half-way point. They remain on licence until the end of the sentence.

Sentences for dangerous offenders. The Act introduced a controversial scheme for the sentencing of dangerous adults. Offenders who committed a specified sexual or violent offence and were assessed as dangerous were subject to a life sentence, if the maximum penalty is life. If the maximum penalty for the offence was less than this (but was for ten years' imprisonment or more), the offender could be subject to a sentence of 'imprisonment for public protection'. The court may impose an 'extended sentence' where the maximum term is between two and ten years' imprisonment. The Coalition government has repealed these provisions and replaced them with wider use of life sentences where people are convicted for the second time for defined serious offences. This removes the element of indeterminacy which was found not to work well in practice.

Legal Aid, Sentencing and Punishment of Offenders Act 2012

The headline features of the latest legislation are:

- it imposes a duty on courts to consider the imposition of compensation orders for certain types of offence;

Box 5.17 *Continued*

- it simplifies the provision setting out the court's duty to give reasons for and to explain the effect of a sentence imposed by the court;
- it adds transgender identity to the personal characteristics which will be statutory aggravating factors in sentencing where any offence is motivated by hostility to the victim on this basis. It also provides for a starting point of 30 years for the minimum term for a life sentence for murder aggravated on the grounds of the victim's disability or transgender identity;
- it makes a number of changes in relation to community orders for adults. It clarifies when community orders come to an end and enables a court to impose a fine for breach of a community order.
- it makes amendments to certain requirements that may be imposed as part of community orders and suspended sentence orders, in particular, curfew requirements, and mental health, drug rehabilitation and alcohol treatment requirements. It also creates new powers to prohibit foreign travel and to impose alcohol abstinence and monitoring requirements as part of an order.
- it amends the court's power to suspend a prison sentence by increasing the length of sentences that can be suspended, giving the court discretion not to impose community requirements as part of the sentence and enabling it to impose a fine for breach of a suspended sentence order.
- in relation to the sentencing provisions that apply to youths, it enables a court to impose a penalty for breach of a detention and training order even where the order has finished its term.

Box 5.18   Reform in progress

Establishment of Sentencing Council

The Coroners and Justice Act 2009 established the Sentencing Council. It replaced the rather cumbersome structure of a Sentencing Guidelines Council advised by a separate Sentencing Advisory Panel that was created by the Criminal Justice Act 2003. The new Council is required by statute to consult the Justice Select Committee on any sentencing guidelines it may contemplate making. This is designed to ensure that there is at least some democratically elected input into the guidelines-making process. It publishes guidelines for judges, designed to increase consistency in judicial sentencing practice.

Sentencing practice is frequently the subject of (usually adverse) press comment, much of which is ill-informed. Judges and magistrates are often criticized for sentencing too lightly. Yet there are proportionately more people in prison in England and Wales than in almost any other European country. Although more community sentences are now handed down than custodial ones (particularly by magistrates) prison overcrowding remains a source of considerable tension in the criminal justice system. Judges are told both to impose severe sentences where necessary and not to send people to prison unless absolutely essential. Both the design and implementation of sentencing policy is extremely controversial. At least in part this is because there are strongly held assumptions about the effectiveness of particular forms of case disposal that are not borne out either in practice or in the results of research. It is a topic on which rationality is often found to be in short supply.

Assets recovery

An additional form of penalty arises from the principle of assets recovery. Although this has been possible in specific contexts (e.g. seizing the proceeds of drug trafficking) for some time, the principle was put on a more general basis in the Proceeds of Crime Act 2002. This Act created the Assets Recovery Agency. Following criticism that its impact had been limited with only modest amounts of assets being recovered, the Agency was abolished in 2008, its work being moved into the Serious Organised Crime Agency (SOCA) (*see Chapter 4, The Home Office*). Where it will go when SOCA is replaced by the National Crime Agency is currently not clear. Nonetheless, assets recovery has become a more central aspect of criminal policy, particularly in relation to serious organized crime.

The post-trial stages

Criminal appeals[19]

Those convicted in magistrates' courts can appeal to the Crown Court, either against conviction or against sentence. In 2011, there were 13,359 appeals from the magistrates' courts to the Crown Court. Forty-four per cent of the appellants dealt with either had their conviction quashed or their sentence varied. Thirty-one per cent of appeals were dismissed. The remaining 25 per cent were otherwise disposed of.

Appeals from the Crown Court can be made to the Court of Appeal (Criminal Division), but only with the leave of the court. In 2011, the Court of Appeal dealt with 7,475 applications for permission to appeal, of which 5,623 were against the sentence imposed, and 1,535 were against conviction. Of these, permission was granted in 1,284 cases. Sentence appeals were allowed in 1,386 of cases heard; conviction appeals led to 197 convictions being quashed.

There is the possibility of a further appeal to the Supreme Court, but this can only be exercised with the permission of the court. The Supreme Court gives permission in only a handful of cases.

[19] For consideration of appeals in civil cases, *see Chapter 8, The appeal courts.*

Criminal Cases Review Commission

One of the most serious challenges facing the criminal justice system is ensuring that miscarriages of justice do not occur. Notwithstanding the opportunities for appeal and the outcomes of appeals, there will always be cases where the full facts have not emerged at trial or on subsequent appeal, possibly because there have been failures by the police or prosecution to put evidence before the court.

The Criminal Cases Review Commission was established in 1997 under Part 2 of the Criminal Appeal Act 1995.

The Commission usually considers only those cases that have been through the normal judicial appeal process. It started undertaking casework at the end of March 1997. By the end of September 2012 it had received 15,332 applications. Many of the applications are rejected as being not admissible. Of 14,465 cases closed (which include inadmissible cases), only 463 have been dealt with by the Court of Appeal, 325 cases resulted in the conviction being quashed or the sentence reduced, and in 138 cases the original decision was upheld.

Reviews are conducted by case review managers. Decisions on the outcome of the work of the case review managers are taken by the Commission. The Commission has nine members, appointed from a variety of backgrounds. Any decision to refer a case to the Court of Appeal is taken by a committee of at least three members.

The function of the Commission is to consider whether there would be a real possibility that a conviction, finding of fact, verdict, or sentence would not be upheld by the court, were a reference back to be made. In relation to reviews of convictions, there has to be either a legal argument or evidence that had not been raised at the trial or on appeal, or other exceptional circumstances; in relation to sentencing, again there has to be legal argument or information about the individual or the offence that was not raised during the trial or on appeal.[20]

Parole and the work of the Parole Board

Even though the court may have imposed a custodial sentence in a particular case, this does not mean that the convicted person will serve the whole period of the sentence. Sentences are subject to review by the Parole Board. This body was established under the provisions of the Criminal Justice Act 1967 and has been in operation since 1968. Its primary function is to make risk assessments that inform decisions whether prisoners can be released back into the community early. While protection of the public is crucial, the Board seeks to enhance the rehabilitative effect of prison in cases where that seems possible. The responsibilities of the Board vary, depending on different types of case. Important changes to the work of the Board were made by the Criminal Justice Act 2003.

---

[20] A detailed account of the work of the Commission can be found in its *Annual Reports* (London, Criminal Cases Review Commission, annual).

Determinate sentence cases

Cases determined under the Criminal Justice Act 1991. Where a convicted person was sentenced to a fixed term of imprisonment on or after 1 October 1992, he or she becomes eligible for parole half-way through the sentence, backdated to include any time spent in custody on remand before the trial. (For those sentenced before 1 October 1992, the date of eligibility for parole arose one-third of the way through the sentence.) Thus a prisoner sentenced to four years on 2 January 1994, who had also spent six months in custody on remand, became eligible for parole on 2 July 1996—the parole eligibility date (PED).

Six months before the PED, officers of the Parole Board begin gathering information to enable a panel from the Parole Board to take an initial decision on whether the prisoner may or may not be suitable for parole. The prisoner may also be interviewed by a Parole Board member. In addition to written reports, the panel is required to take into account *directions* made by the Home Secretary. These give guidance on particular issues on which the panel must be satisfied before finding in favour of the prisoner. While the decision to grant parole is formally one for the Secretary of State, he has delegated his decision-taking powers to the Board in all cases where the prisoner was sentenced to a period of less than 15 years. At this stage the decision of the Board is a discretionary one; cases are referred to as *discretionary conditional release* (DCR) cases. The latest annual report from the Board records that in 2011–12 parole was granted in 22 per cent of the 875 DCR cases it considered in the year.

Whether or not prisoners are released following a Parole Board review, determinate prisoners are automatically released two-thirds of the way through their sentence. However, all those released either after a parole decision or under the automatic process remain subject to supervision by the Probation Service and are subject to recall either for reoffending or for other breaches of the probation supervision until 75 per cent of the period of the sentence has expired. (The recall rate is about four per cent of those serving determinate sentences who have been released on parole.) Although the supervision of the Probation Service ends at that point, the remaining 25 per cent of the sentence can be reactivated if the person is subsequently committed for another criminal offence.

The Criminal Justice Act 2003 made recall to custody an executive decision—by the prison and probation services—rather than by the Parole Board itself. The offender has the right of appeal to the Parole Board and, even if the offender chooses not to exercise this right, the Parole Board scrutinizes all recall decisions to ensure they are fairly taken. By allowing the Parole Board to focus on assessing decisions of recall, the Act removed an anomaly whereby the Parole Board used to both advise on the decision to recall and act as the appeal body against those same recalls.

Cases determined under the Criminal Justice Act 2003. For these cases, prisoners are automatically released on licence once they have served half their sentence. They remain on licence until the end of their nominal sentence. Thus the Board is no longer involved in the initial decision to release. However, they retain a key role in deciding what should happen should a decision be taken to recall a prisoner for breach of the licence. The Parole Board now reviews such cases; 14,977 recall cases were reviewed in 2011–12. The House of Lords held in the case of *Smith and West* [2005] UKHL 1 that those recalled had the right to make oral representations. There were 928 oral hearings in 2011–12. The role of the Board has, therefore, become more like that of an administrative tribunal, less like that of a decision-taking agency.

Life sentences

The Parole Board also has important responsibilities in relation to life sentences. There are two sorts of life sentence: *mandatory* life sentences, where the judge must impose a life sentence (as in the case of a conviction for murder); and *discretionary* life sentences, where this was the sentence that the judge decided was appropriate because of the risk that the offender would commit another offence.

The starting point is a decision on *the tariff*. This is the minimum period that the prisoner is to serve. Under the provisions of the Crime (Sentences) Act 1997, the tariff for mandatory lifers was fixed by the Home Secretary taking into account a recommendation of the trial judge. Following a decision of the European Court of Human Rights (*Stafford v United Kingdom*, Application No. 46295/99, 28 May 2002), the House of Lords declared that the imposition of the tariff was indistinguishable from sentencing, and thus in effect part of the trial process (*R v Secretary of State for the Home Department, ex p Anderson* [2002] UKHL 46). As Article 6 of the European Convention on Human Rights requires tribunals deciding criminal trials to be independent, the role of the Home Secretary was held incompatible with Article 6. The tariff in all cases is now set by the trial judge.

Three years before the expiry of the tariff, the case is reviewed by the Parole Board. It considers whether or not a prisoner is suitable to be moved to the more relaxed regime of an open prison. On expiry of the tariff, the Parole Board considers whether the prisoner is suitable for release on licence. If it decides to release on licence, the prisoner is still subject to supervision by the Probation Service for at least four years. At that point (or later) the Home Secretary may decide that the supervision requirements can be lifted. The prisoner remains liable to recall and for the balance of his sentence to be reactivated for the rest of his life, should there be reason for so doing, such as subsequent offending.

If the Parole Board concludes that, on the expiry of the tariff, release would not be appropriate, the case is reviewed, normally every two years.

Procedure

The process of reaching these decisions does, however, vary. In the case of *mandatory* lifers, the decision-taking process is similar to that for determinate sentences. Reports are prepared; an interview is held by a member of the Parole Board with the prisoner; and a decision is reached on the papers. Mandatory lifer panels are specially constituted to include a judge and a psychiatrist. Again the panel is required to take into account *directions* prescribed by the Home Secretary. Originally, the actual decision was taken by the Home Secretary; the Parole Board panel could only make a recommendation. The Criminal Justice Act 2003 provides that the Board should take the decision.

For *discretionary* lifers, the process of review involves the compilation of a dossier of reports. But there is then a fundamentally important difference. An oral hearing (rather like a tribunal hearing) is listed before a discretionary lifer panel of the Parole Board (which includes a judge and a psychiatrist). The prisoner is entitled to legal representation at this hearing. At the conclusion of the hearing, the panel may recommend transfer to open prison conditions, or may in appropriate cases direct release. In 2011–12, the Board arranged 1,549 hearings relating to lifers and 1,957 hearings for those subject to indeterminate sentences who were seeking release on parole.

The place of the victim

One of the ways in which the criminal justice system has been transformed in recent years is through increased recognition of the victims of crime. As has already been noted, the position of the victim is fundamental to the whole criminal justice system since the victim's report that a crime has been committed is, save for the most serious offences, the key to further steps being taken in the criminal process. Further, as also noted, the viewpoint of the victim is one of the factors taken into account by the CPS in reaching a decision whether or not to prosecute a case. There are respects in which sentencing policy reflects the impact the criminal activity may have had on the victim. Much of the activity in the youth justice system is designed to make the offender aware of the victim's perceptions of what he or she has done. The Home Office sought to bring support for victims (and witnesses) together in its *Victims' Charter* (originally published in 1997).

In recent years the place of the victim has been given greater statutory recognition. Many of the provisions in the Criminal Justice Act 2003, for example those relating to bail or the use of video links, are designed to assist victims and other witnesses to give evidence. More specifically, the Domestic Violence, Crime and Victims Act 2004 contains a number of provisions designed to ensure that the victim is kept informed about the progress of a case, and about the release of a prisoner.

Among the measures included are, first, the Victims' Charter is transformed into a statutory code of guidance, which must be endorsed by Parliament. Secondly, it provides that, where a court convicts a person (the 'offender') for a sexual or violent offence and imposes a prison sentence of a minimum of 12 months, the local probation board must take reasonable steps to establish whether the victim of the offence wishes to make representations about whether the offender should be subject to conditions on release (and, if so, what conditions), or wishes to receive information about those conditions. If the victim does express such a wish, the relevant local probation board becomes responsible for forwarding any representations the victim makes to the authority responsible for making the decisions about release. The board is also responsible for informing the victim whether the offender will be subject to any conditions in the event of release; for providing details of any conditions about contact with the victim or his family; and for providing any other information it considers appropriate. Similar provisions apply where an offender has been detained under the provisions of the Mental Health Act 1983.

Thirdly, the jurisdiction of the Parliamentary Commissioner for Administration is expanded so that she can investigate and report on complaints that a duty under the code of practice for victims has been breached. These relate to complaints that any person has failed to comply with a duty to victims relating to the need to keep victims informed. The Parliamentary Commissioner has the same powers to obtain evidence and examine witnesses as she has in relation to complaints of maladministration. (*See Chapter 6, Ombudsmen.*)

Fourthly, the Act provided for the creation of the post of Commissioner for Victims and Witnesses. The Commissioner's primary functions are: to promote the interests of victims and witnesses of crime and anti-social behaviour; and to take steps to encourage good practice in their treatment and to keep the code of guidance under review. The Commissioner is given various ways in which she can carry out these functions, including making reports to the Secretary of State, commissioning research, and making recommendations to an authority within his remit (a broadly defined group of those working in and around the criminal justice system). Further, the Commissioner must provide advice on issues relating to victims and witnesses of crime and anti-social behaviour when requested to do so by any government minister. The authorities within the Commissioner's remit may also ask the Commissioner to give specific advice in connection with the information they provide, through whatever medium, to victims and witnesses. The post was held, since July 2010, by Louise Casey, who came to the job with a formidable reputation for speaking up about the consequences of anti-social behaviour. She brought this outspoken approach into her new role. She issued several reports and made a number of important speeches about how the criminal justice system fails the victims of crime, particularly serious violent crime. In October 2011 alone she published reports on research into the view of victims on their experience of court and sentencing, and on the needs of families suffering bereavement because of homicide. In 2012, she announced her resignation to take up a new role. Recruitment of a new Commissioner has recently been completed. (See my blog for details.)

Fifthly, the Act provided for the appointment of a Victims' Advisory Panel, which the Home Secretary could consult on matters relating to victims and witnesses of crime and of anti-social behaviour. The Coalition government decided to abolish the Panel.

Three further developments may be briefly noted: victim support schemes; the criminal injuries compensation scheme; and compensation orders.

Victim support schemes

There are now about 365 local victim support schemes with some 15,000 volunteers offering help to over 1.5 million victims. In the Crown Court, there are another 1,500+

volunteers helping over 120,000 victims and witnesses who have to attend court. These do a great deal of work trying to reassure the victims of crime that they have not been targeted, but are simply the victims of opportunistic criminal activity. They also help victims and other witnesses cope with the stress and strain of appearing in court.

The Criminal Injuries Compensation Scheme

This has been in operation for many years. This state-funded scheme was revised in 2001, and 2008. It was further revised from November 2012. It is administered by the Criminal Injuries Compensation Authority. In 2011–12, the scheme paid about £449 million compensation to successful claimants. (Around 50 per cent of applications are unsuccessful.) The scheme is limited to victims injured as the result of violent criminal activity directed towards them. Critics point out that other negative consequences of being the victim of crime are not thus compensated.

Two specific points may be noted. First, the amounts of compensation paid are defined in a statutory tariff; they are not assessed in the same way as damages for personal injury in civil litigation. This leads to complaints that the scheme under-compensates the victims of crime, particularly where they have suffered other than by way of physical injury. Secondly, as a result of amendments in the Domestic Violence, Crime and Victims Act 2004, it is now provided that the courts, when making a compensation order, can require sums obtained from the offender to be used to compensate the Compensation Injuries Fund (in cases where an award from the fund has been made).

Compensation orders

In addition to this statutory scheme, since 1972 the criminal courts have had power to order those convicted of crimes to pay compensation to their victims. These powers have been developed so that there are circumstances in which a compensation order may be imposed as the sole penalty. Since 1988, the courts have been required to consider making compensation orders in defined groups of cases involving death, injury, loss, or damage, and to give reasons where an order is not made. Since 1991 the limits on the sums that magistrates may order as compensation have been increased. The Legal Aid, Sentencing and Punishment of Offenders Act 2012 has created a duty on the courts to consider making a compensation order in such cases. These developments may be seen as more reparative forms of outcome for the criminal justice system.

A strategic approach to criminal justice?

Underpinning all the reforms of the criminal justice system that have been considered earlier has been the recognition by successive governments of the need for a more integrated approach to dealing with crime. Numerous initiatives have been taken in recent years to try to deliver this. Indeed the pace of change has been breathtaking. Things have moved so quickly that it is often hard to assess the impact of all this change on the ground. The objective of a more integrated approach is clearly sensible. But these often involve getting those working in the criminal justice system to work in new ways. Unless there is a clearly defined and well-run programme of change management, the outcomes may not be as fully integrated on the ground as system planners may hope. At present, the effects of all these changes are not clear; too much has happened too recently.

There are complaints from many quarters about the pace of change. But clearly the government wants results, not least to satisfy political demands to be seen to be getting on top of crime. A number of emerging themes may be noted in this final section. First, a new approach to the delivery of criminal justice was the subject of an important trial in Liverpool—the Community Justice Centre (*see Box 5.19*). However, plans for creating a number of similar centres in other towns are currently on hold.

Box 5.19   Reform in progress

Case study: the North Liverpool Community Justice Centre

This new initiative was designed, in the government's words, 'to improve quality of life in the area by reducing criminal activity and the fear of crime, while providing advice and support to the community'. It is based on a successful project in New York city. The centre, which opened fully in 2005, works in partnership with local people to provide help with a wide range of problems and deal with offences committed against the community that affect quality of life, for example vandalism, fly-tipping, and graffiti. The centre also provides access to support, social, and education services for both offenders and local residents. It contains a courtroom, run by a single judge, who works closely with the community, to provide consistency for offenders and check that they carry out the sentences they have been given. Over 200 North Liverpool residents including parents, teenagers, senior citizens, the long-term unemployed, and local business people joined with probation officers and ex-offenders to help develop plans for the Community Justice Centre and discuss how a more holistic approach to low-level offending can have a positive impact on their local neighbourhoods.

Findings from independent research among a number of residents, which covered the wards of Anfield, Everton, Kirkdale, and Walton within the Atlantic Partnership area, give a clear indication of how the Community Justice Centre could provide a new approach to dealing with criminals damaging the quality of life for residents. Research showed that the overall perception is that crime in the area is a problem, with major areas of concern being drugs and youth gangs. Against this background, over three-quarters of those participating believed that the Community Justice Centre is, or could be, a good idea. Nearly three-quarters of the residents interviewed were concerned that offenders should be sent to court, be sentenced, and rehabilitated quickly. They also believed that sentences should be set that involve completing work to benefit the local neighbourhood. Over half thought that the community should have a say

Box 5.19 *Continued*

in the type and location of unpaid work done as part of a sentence. Two-thirds of those interviewed supported the idea of a single judge who will make sure that offenders carry out their sentences and three-quarters thought the community should be able to report what is going on in their area, safely. There is clear agreement that the centre should place an emphasis on dealing with anti-social behaviour-type offences, like car crime, criminal damage, and fly-tipping.

Judge David Fletcher, who leads the centre, has said:

> There is a lot of support out there for the idea of community justice. Residents are telling us they want improvements to their quality of life, including the need for people to feel safer, have better support, and a better environment to live in. The centre represents the most radical change to occur in the justice system for decades. While focusing on reducing crime through tackling its root causes and offering long-term support to the community, we can help all law-abiding citizens to be heard, without fear of reprisal or intimidation.

Merseyside Police, the CPS, probation and youth offending teams all have offices on-site to provide a joined-up, problem-solving approach to offending. The centre also aims to bring a number of other community advice and support services under one roof. Recent research suggests that the Centre has not had as positive an impact as had been hoped for.

Secondly, there is a lot of emphasis on the use of inspectorates to oversee the work of agencies involved in the criminal justice system (*see Box 5.20*).

Box 5.20   Legal system explained

Inspectorates in the criminal justice system

The current inspection regime comprises: Her Majesty's Inspectorate of Constabulary (HMIC); Her Majesty's Crown Prosecution Service Inspectorate (HMCPSI); Her Majesty's Inspectorate of Prisons (HMI Prisons); and Her Majesty's Inspectorate of Probation (HMI Probation). Although constituted differently, they all predominantly ensure the safe and proper delivery of the services inspected and promulgate good practice:

- HMIC has a stated purpose to promote the efficiency and effectiveness of policing through inspection of police organizations and functions to ensure agreed standards are achieved and maintained, good practice is spread, and performance is improved. It has a developing remit, with its inspection responsibilities growing to include Her Majesty's Revenue and Customs (HMRC) enforcement work and the SOCA—two large non-police agencies. It also provides advice and support to the Home Secretary, police authorities and forces and plays a role in the development of future leaders.

Box 5.20 *Continued*

- HMCPSI has a stated purpose to promote continuous improvement in the efficiency, effectiveness, and fairness of the prosecution services within a joined-up criminal justice system, through the process of inspection, evaluation, and identification of good practice.
- HMI Prisons has a remit to inspect prison establishments and to report on the conditions of those establishments, the treatment of prisoners and other inmates, and the facilities available to them. The Inspectorate also undertakes inspection of immigration removal centres and, by invitation, the military corrective centre.
- HMI Probation reports on the work and performance of the National Probation Service and of Youth Offending Teams (YOTs), particularly on the effectiveness of work aimed at reducing reoffending and protecting the public. It contributes to policy and service delivery by providing advice and disseminating good practice.

HMI Prisons and HMI Probation are jointly developing a shared approach to inspection of offender management as it is developed by the National Offender Management Service (NOMS). A fifth inspectorate, Her Majesty's Inspectorate of Court Administration (HMICA) was abolished by the Coalition government in its review of public bodies.

The remaining inspectorates undertake both single agency inspection and joint inspection:

- *Single agency inspection*: the statutory remit of each inspectorate requires it to inspect and report on the performance of its relevant organization (or for prisons the treatment and conditions of those in custody). This can be done via cyclical inspection of an area, risk-based inspection of an area, or thematic inspections on a particular topic. Given the current remit of the four inspectorates, their primary attention is on the safe and proper delivery of services within their separate organizations.
- *Joint inspection*: this can take the form of either routine or thematic inspections conducted by more than one inspectorate, on a particular topic involving more than one inspected organization. These can be done both within the criminal justice system and outside in areas such as education, health, or local services; for example HMI Prisons routinely inspects with OfSTED, the Royal Pharmaceutical Society, and the British Dental Board. Currently joint inspections are resourced from existing budgets and must take into account the resource demands of single agency inspection. To facilitate cross-criminal justice system inspection, in 1998 the Chief Inspectors established a Criminal Justice Chief Inspectors Group (CJCIG) to undertake inspections within the criminal justice system on a joint basis. Since then the number of joint inspections has increased; initially they were thematic in nature, but since 2003 the inspectorates have combined to start inspecting criminal justice areas (or local criminal justice boards).

In 2005, a consultation paper argued that there was a need for institutional reform:

Box 5.20 *Continued*

- the police reform programme had introduced fundamental changes to the police service that call for the examination of the remit of HMIC, to consider how police inspection can support a modernized police service and fit with new bodies such as the National Policing Improvement Agency (a body also abolished by the Coalition government);
- the changes to the charging process, which involves CPS lawyers in police stations deciding on charges in all but minor cases, and providing the police with early legal advice before and during the charging process, have introduced a new partnership approach between the police and the CPS (the prosecution team). This involves the CPS working with the police locally to implement performance measures and procedures. These new arrangements require a joined-up inspection regime to support effective implementation and delivery; and
- the creation of a NOMS has initiated major change in the delivery of correctional services, introducing end-to-end management of offenders, whether they serve their sentence in prison, the community, or both. The creation of a purchaser–provider split in the provision of services means that NOMS will focus on specifying service standards and procuring services rather than running them directly, a shift a new inspection regime needs to address.

Notwithstanding the arguments for bringing together the large number of existing inspection functions, proposals for a new 'super-inspectorate' have not been taken forward.

Source: Adapted from *Inspection Reform: Establishing an Inspectorate for Justice and Community Safety* (London, Criminal Justice System, March 2005).

Thirdly, there has been an increase in the powers to deal with people outside the formal criminal justice system, through cautions and penalty notices for disorder (PNDs) issued by the police (*see Diagram 5.2*). These forms of disposal have been designed to provide officers with a means of dealing with simple, straightforward cases in a prompt and effective way, saving police time, reducing bureaucracy, and reserving courts for more complex cases. It also avoids the offender acquiring a criminal record. However, while it may be sensible, such procedures are starkly at odds with the due process model of criminal justice referred to at the start of this chapter. The government is concerned that PNDs are being used too freely and is devising criteria to ensure more consistent usage.

Comment on criminal justice

There can be little doubt about the importance all governments attach to reform of the criminal justice system. Should there now be a period of reflection before the introduction of any further institutional or legislative change? Ideally, this might be desirable.

However, it is inevitable that, as the Coalition government seeks to find savings in its expenditure on criminal justice, there will be more change to come. The unanswered question—and the challenge for government—is whether the system can be delivered more cheaply without compromising the important values on which the criminal justice system is based.

Questions

Use the self-test questions on the Online Resource Centre to test your understanding of the topics covered in this chapter and receive tailored feedback:

www.oxfordtextbooks.co.uk/orc/partington13_14/

Weblinks

Check the Online Resource Centre for a selection of annotated weblinks allowing you to easily research topics of particular interest:

www.oxfordtextbooks.co.uk/orc/partington13_14/

Blog items

See www.martinpartington.com (access via the Online Resource Centre)

Items discussed include: the abolition of committal hearings; the increased use of out-of-court disposals; CPS review of decisions not to prosecute; deferred prosecution agreements; the work of the Commissioner for Victims; the rescue of the Youth Justice Board; the possibility of televising crime court proceedings; a summary of the sentencing and punishment of offenders provisions in the Legal Aid, Sentencing and Punishment of Offenders Bill 2011 and the Legal Aid, Sentencing and Punishment of Offenders Act 2012; encouraging guilty pleas; discussing changes to crime statistics.

Further reading

ASHWORTH, A., *Sentencing and Criminal Justice* (5th edn, Cambridge, Cambridge University Press, 2010)

—— and REDMAYNE, M., *The Criminal Process* (4th edn, Oxford, Oxford University Press, 2010)

AULD, LORD JUSTICE, *A Review of the Criminal Courts of England and Wales* (London, The Stationery Office, 2001)

BALDWIN, J., and MCCONVILLE, M., *Jury Trials* (Oxford, Clarendon Press, 1979)

BARCLAY, G., and TAVARES, C. (eds), *DIGEST 4—Information on the Criminal Justice System* (London, Home Office, 1999)

CLEMENTS, P., *Policing a Diverse Society* (2nd edn, Oxford, Oxford University Press, 2008)

CORNISH, W. R., *The Jury* (Harmondsworth, Penguin, 1971)

CRAWFORD, A., and NEWBURN, T., *Youth Offending and Restorative Justice: Implementing Reform in Youth Justice* (Cullompton, Willan Publishing, 2003)

DAVIES, M., CROALL, H., and TYRER, J., *Criminal Justice: An Introduction to the Criminal Justice System in England and Wales* (4th edn, Harlow, Pearson Longman, 2009)

ELKS, L., *Righting Miscarriages of Justice? Ten years of the Criminal Cases Review Commission* (London, JUSTICE, 2008)

ELLISON, L., *The Adversarial Process and the Vulnerable Witness* (Oxford, Oxford University Press, 2002)

HALLIDAY, J., *Making Punishments Work: Report of a Review of the Sentencing Framework for England and Wales* (London, Home Office, 2001)

HAWKINS, K., *Law as Last Resort: Prosecution Decision-making in a Regulatory Agency* (Oxford, Oxford University Press, 2003)

HENHAM, R., *Sentence Discounts and the Criminal Process* (Aldershot, Dartmouth, 2001)

HOOD, R., in collaboration with Cordovil, G., *Race and Sentencing: A Study in the Crown Court: A Report for the Commission for Racial Equality* (Oxford, Clarendon Press, 1992)

MCCABE, S., and PURVES, R., *The Jury at Work: A Study of a Series of Jury Trials in which the Defendant was Acquitted* (Oxford, Blackwell for the Oxford University Penal Research Unit, 1972)

—— *The Shadow Jury at Work: an Account of a Series of Deliberations and Verdicts where 'Shadow' Juries were Present During Actual Trials* (Oxford, Blackwell for the Oxford University Penal Research Unit, 1974)

MCCONVILLE, M., and MIRSKY, C. L., *Jury Trials and Plea Bargaining: A True History* (Oxford, Hart Publishing, 2005)

—— and WILSON, G. (eds), *The Handbook of the Criminal Justice Process* (Oxford, Oxford University Press, 2002)

MACPHERSON OF CLUNY, SIR WILLIAM, *The Stephen Lawrence Inquiry Report* (Cm 4262) (London, The Stationery Office, 1999)

MAGUIRE, M., MORGAN, R., and REINER, R. (eds), *The Oxford Handbook of Criminology* (5th edn, Oxford, Clarendon Press, 2012)

MORGAN, R., and RUSSELL, N., *The Judiciary in the Magistrates' Courts* (London, Home Office, 2000)

NAUGHTON, M. (ed.), *The Criminal Cases Review Commission: Hope for the Innocent?* (London, Palgrave Macmillan, 2009; paperback edn, 2010)

PADFIELD, N., *Text and Materials on the Criminal Justice Process* (4th edn, Oxford University Press, 2008)

ROBERTSHAW, P., *Jury and Judge: the Crown Court in Action* (Aldershot, Dartmouth, 1995)

SANDERS, A., YOUNG, R., and BURTON, M., *Criminal Justice* (4th edn, Oxford University Press, 2010)

SPENCER, J. R., *Evidence of Bad Character* (2nd edn, Oxford, Hart Publishing, 2009)

WALKER, N., *Policing in a Changing Constitutional Order* (London, Sweet & Maxwell, 2000)

6

The administrative justice system

Introduction: administrative justice

Although the criminal justice system, discussed in *Chapter 5*, is institutionally extremely complex, the primary focus of the system—on the regulation of forms of social behaviour, and dealing with those who transgress the rules—is relatively clear. By contrast, the very concept of 'administrative justice' is controversial, meaning different things to different people. Traditional analyses of the legal system, focusing on the distinction between criminal and civil law, fail to acknowledge a separate system of 'administrative justice'. Instead, it gets wrapped up in general discussion of the civil justice system.

In part, this reflects the continuing influence of the 19th century writer A. V. Dicey, who argued that there should not be a separately identifiable body of *droit administratif* (administrative law). He thought that this would result in public officials being given legally preferential treatment and thus offend against the fundamental principle of the rule of law, that all should be equal under the law.

Over 100 years on, the reality is that the state plays a large part in the regulation of society; and there is a vast array of institutions employing individuals who provide public services. Although there may still not be a conceptually distinct branch of the law that may be described as administrative law, as there is for example in many of the countries in Continental Europe, any understanding of the modern English legal system must involve recognizing the distinct concept of administrative justice.

The primary focus of this chapter is on the institutions in which administrative law is practised. First, however, we reflect on the nature of administrative law and the role it plays in modern society.

The role of administrative law: authority and values

As already noted, one feature of the modern world is the significant role of government in developing and implementing a vast range of social policies. Implementation of social policy depends on law. Administrative law:

- provides authority for public servants to deliver government policy, whose legitimacy is enshrined in the laws (primary, secondary, and tertiary—*see Box 3.5*) passed through the parliamentary system;

- authorizes the raising and expenditure of public funds;
- sets limits to the powers of public officials;
- creates the institutional mechanisms for calling public officials to account; and
- provides means for the redress of individual grievances or resolution of complaints by the citizen.

In addition to the functional attributes of administrative law, administrative justice embraces certain *values* or *principles*, which should underpin good administration by those who deliver services on behalf of the state. These include: openness (or transparency); fairness; rationality (including the giving of reasons for decisions); impartiality (independence) of decision-takers; accountability; the prevention of the exercise of arbitrary power and the control of discretion; consistency; participation; efficiency; equity; and equal treatment. (*See also, Box 6.1.*)

Box 6.1   System in action

Principles of administrative justice

In 2011, the Administrative Justice and Tribunals Council published its own statement of Principles of Administrative Justice. The Principles say that a good administrative justice system should:

- make users and their needs central, treating them with fairness and respect at all times;
- enable people to challenge decisions and seek redress using procedures that are independent, open, and appropriate for the matter involved;
- keep people fully informed and empower them to resolve their problems as quickly and comprehensively as possible;
- lead to well-reasoned, lawful, and timely outcomes;
- be coherent and consistent;
- work proportionately and efficiently;
- adopt the highest standards of behaviour, seek to learn from experience, and continuously improve.

While these may seem in many ways obvious, it is surprising how often these basic messages are forgotten. Their report also contains a self-assessment toolkit, which administrators can use as a template against which they can measure their organization. This is the sort of valuable work that will be lost once the Council, as the Coalition government has decided, is abolished.

As with the underlying values of criminal justice, the underlying values of administrative justice are not wholly consistent with one another. There may be circumstances in which openness may properly yield to confidentiality; where fairness of process may conflict with efficiency. Each of these values is contingent upon the context in which it is asserted. One of the challenges for those who govern, and for those who criticize government, is to achieve an appropriate balance between conflicting values.

The details of particular areas of substantive public law (e.g. rules relating to social security) are not for discussion here. Rather, the focus is on the mechanisms of account-ability which exist to keep officials in check and which provide means of resolving disputes when things go wrong. But readers should reflect on the tensions between the different values in administrative justice in the context of particular administrative activities—for example, the determination of asylum applications; or the collection of taxes; or the granting of planning permissions; or the payment of social security benefits.

Administrative justice: the institutional framework

A great variety of bodies and processes make up the institutional framework of administrative justice. They include:

- courts;
- tribunals;
- inquiries;
- ombudsmen;
- complaints procedures.

As with the criminal justice system, these employ thousands of people and cost millions of pounds to run. It is also necessary to consider the role of Parliament in this context, as well as the impact of the Freedom of Information Act 2000. Each is discussed in this chapter. Administrative justice is another area where there has been rapid development over the last 60 years and is one of the most dynamic parts of the English legal system.

This way of conceptualizing the framework of administrative justice is not wholly orthodox. Practising lawyers tend not to think about administrative justice in the broad sense used here, but rather more narrowly about administrative law and in particular the special process available in the High Court known as *judicial review*. Academic administrative lawyers go beyond this court-focused approach to include in their analyses comments on other mechanisms for the resolution of disputes. But the treatment of topics other than judicial review tends to be somewhat superficial.[1] There are perfectly good reasons for this:

(1) The *qualitative* importance of the law of judicial review is clear. It is in the reported decisions of judges in the Administrative Court (now also the Upper

---

[1] There are honourable exceptions to this generalization: see e.g. Harlow, C. and Rawlings, R., *Law and Administration* (3rd edn, Cambridge, Cambridge University Press, 2009).

Tier Tribunal, *see Diagram 6.1*) and above that the jurisprudence of judicial review has been developed. Fundamental principles—of procedural fairness, and limiting the exercise of discretionary power by officials—are the creation of the courts. The courts have also defined: who can bring proceedings by way of judicial review; the bodies and institutions which are subject to the principles of judicial review; and the grounds on which judicial review may be sought. The principles of judicial review provide the legal background to the administrative justice system. In doing this work, the judges assert that fundamental constitutional principle, the independence of the judiciary. The importance of this work has been expanded by the Human Rights Act 1998, which enshrines further principles against which official actions can be tested in the courts, in particular that UK laws must be compatible with the European Convention on Human Rights and that public authorities must act in compliance with the Convention.

(2) It is in the courts that practising lawyers earn good money and develop formidable reputations. With rare exceptions, legal aid is not available to pay for legal representation before tribunals or other dispute resolution/grievance handling fora. This reduces the incentive for legal practitioners to get to know about the wider world of administrative justice.

(3) The work of this wider range of bodies is often not the subject of formal published documentation. Legal scholars find it hard to access the material needed for a full review of the administrative justice system as a whole.

Nevertheless, concentration on judicial review—a procedure that in 2011 resulted in 11,200 applications being brought to the Administrative Court, although with only a much smaller number going on to a full hearing—means that other procedures for the delivery of administrative justice are not paid the attention they deserve. By contrast with the case-load in the courts, in 2011–12 the Tribunals Service received 739,600 new cases and dealt with 732,600 cases in the same period. The large number of ombudsmen that now exist handle thousands more cases in a year. A variety of complaints procedures deal with countless other grievances. *Quantitatively* tribunals, ombudsmen, and complaints procedures are far more significant than the courts. This account seeks to redress the balance.

There are two important reasons for making this argument, which arise not just from a desire to be different. First, what the administrative justice system—taken as a whole—provides is a vast test bed for the development and evaluation of new procedures:

- decisions being taken on the papers;
- decisions by a single judge;
- decisions by three- (or more) person tribunals; and
- procedures involving the unrepresented and inarticulate.

It is one of the great wasted opportunities that those who have sought in recent years to introduce change into the civil justice system should have paid such scant attention to what goes on in practice in the administrative justice system. The latter has provided a rich source of ideas for how things might be done differently. Those who in the past may have looked down their noses at the administrative justice system as 'not being proper courts' should think again. It is here that alternative procedures are to be found, often working extremely well.

Secondly, the failure to see the administrative justice system in a more holistic fashion prevents people from seeing the enormous variety of ways that exist for seeking the redress of citizens' grievances. This is a theme that was taken up by the National Audit Office (NAO) in an important report on citizen redress (*see Box 6.2*).

Box 6.2   Reform in progress

Citizen redress

An important and distinctive feature of public services are the arrangements in place for getting things put right, remedying grievances, or securing a second view of a disputed decision. We use the 'citizen redress' label to denote all the administrative mechanisms that allow citizens to seek remedies for what they perceive to be poor treatment, mistakes, faults, or injustices in their dealings with central government departments or agencies. Of course, redress mechanisms may not find in favour of the citizens making complaints or bringing appeals. Indeed, in a well-run administrative system the large majority of cases investigated should prove to be unfounded. Yet even in such cases the redress processes used should provide people with assurance that they have been fairly and properly treated or that a disputed decision has been correctly made under the relevant rules.

The systems currently in place for the citizen to seek remedy when things go wrong have developed over time and for a variety of different purposes. Inevitably, this has resulted in complexity and variations in attitude and approach.

The main mechanisms for achieving redress currently are: customer complaints procedures; appeals and tribunals systems; references to independent complaints handlers or ombudsmen; and resort to judicial review (and other forms of legal action).

In cases where something is found to have gone wrong, one important outcome of such mechanisms may be the payment of compensation. The different redress mechanisms interconnect strongly. From the citizens' point of view they offer a range of different options and opportunities for trying to achieve very similar or connected outcomes. And from government organizations' points of view, the efficacy of some redress procedures may imply fewer cases running through other routes. For instance, good basic complaints-handling systems should minimize the number of cases referred on to ombudsmen or leading to legal actions.

Yet public sector redress systems have developed piecemeal over many years and in the past they have rarely been systematically thought about as a whole. Central

Box 6.2   *Continued*

government organizations make a strong distinction between complaints and appeals. Complaints concern processes and how issues have been handled. They have traditionally been considered as part of the internal business arrangements of departments and agencies. They are often thought about primarily in terms of customer responsiveness and business effectiveness. Appeals systems and tribunals concern the accuracy or correctness of substantive departmental or agency decisions. They conventionally form part of the administrative justice sphere. They are often considered primarily in terms of citizens' legal rights, natural justice, and a range of related quasi-judicial criteria. This bifurcated approach may have some advantages, but it is very distinctive to the public sector and has no counterpart in private sector firms. Rigidly separating complaints from appeals also means that many public service organizations are essentially providing two different basic systems of redress, which are set up and organized on different lines. And citizens also have to grapple with two very different concepts of redress, instead of a more integrated concept of 'getting things put right'.

Citizen redress procedures have an importance for the overall quality of public services that goes far beyond their direct costs. Complaints are an important source of feedback to central departments and agencies about where things are perceived by citizens as going wrong, a view also stressed by the Parliamentary Ombudsman. Hence they are a significant source of information on possible improvements in organizational arrangements. Similarly, the availability of appeals and tribunals options is intended to provide an effective incentive for officials to make considered decisions that are right first time. Providing a range of administrative procedures for citizens to seek remedies or redress is also a key area of civil rights, providing vital safeguards against arbitrary or ill-founded decision making by government organizations. So it is clearly essential that any changes made to citizen redress arrangements do not restrict established rights to independent review and an opportunity to state one's case.

However, it is also possible that the current workings of citizen redress institutions may not be optimally configured to deliver what the public most want. Current arrangements have built up over long periods, largely in separated ways, often specific to one policy sector or one government organization. So the existing ladder of redress options may not be as accessible or as useful to citizens as it could be. It also may well not deliver what citizens most want. Redress systems should be purposefully targeted to deliver valued benefits to citizens in a timely way, rather than just following through on established procedures whose added value for citizens remains unclear.

In the past there were separate channels in government for dealing with complaints, appeals, and ombudsmen processes. The complaints route has mostly been seen as a matter for departments or agencies to run in a decentralized way as they see fit, with only the general discipline provided by ombudsmens' comments. Appeals and tribunals confer important citizens' rights and are legally mandated and so in business terms are an inescapable cost. They were previously regulated in a separate, more legal manner by the then Lord Chancellor's Department with input from the Council

Box 6.2 *Continued*

of Tribunals. As a result, citizen redress arrangements have apparently not been monitored or costed in any systematic way by central departments (such as the Cabinet
Office or the Treasury). The onus has been on departments and agencies to consider
the effectiveness and efficiency of their own redress schemes as part of their wider
drive to improve efficiency.

Source: Extracted from National Audit Office, *Citizen Redress: What citizens can do if
things go wrong with public services* (HC 21, 2004–05) (London, The Stationery Office,
2005).

Cost

Although most of the dispute-resolution procedures (save the courts) are provided
free to the individual, they clearly cost money to run. The relationship between that
cost and the output of the bodies and procedures funded cannot be ignored. In the
same report, the NAO provided some first estimates of the costs of the administrative
justice system, as broadly conceived here (*see Box 6.3*). It may be argued that, though
significant, these costs are small compared with expenditure on public services taken
as a whole. But this is not sufficient reason for not thinking critically about the present
system and whether it could be made more efficient. A consequence of the failure to see
administrative justice in the round is that it makes it hard to appreciate the amount of
money spent on the provision of administrative justice systems.

Box 6.3 System in action

Cost of the administrative justice system

In 2005, research undertaken for the NAO estimated that nearly 1.4 million cases are
received through redress systems in central government annually and are processed
by over 9,300 staff at an annual cost of at least £510 million. Appeals and tribunal cases
account for just under three-fifths of the redress load, seven-tenths of the annual costs,
and two-thirds of the staff numbers. Complaints are much cheaper to handle, account-
ing for two in five redress cases but an eighth of the annual costs. Cases handled by
independent complaints handlers or ombudsmen are a small part of the total. But
because they often concern more complex or hard-to-resolve issues they are perhaps
inevitably more resource-intensive than basic complaints handling.

There are currently very wide differences amongst departments and agencies in
the ways that they define and record complaints. The NAO survey shows that around
half of central government organizations, including departments operating in areas
of major interest to many citizens, cannot effectively answer how many complaints
they have received in either of the last two years. In some cases complaints are not

Box 6.3   *Continued*

distinguished from 'enquiries'. Even when complaints are systematically monitored in some way, departments and agencies vary greatly in how they define an interaction with citizens as 'a complaint'.

Even the apparently clearer concept of 'an appeal' has important variations in meaning in different administrative settings. In some organizations a large number of customer interactions are processed into the appeals system with minimal effort on citizens' part, whereas in other cases citizens must make more of an effort to initiate an appeal. So our findings here are necessarily qualified by difficulties in measurement and inadequacies in many government organizations' recording systems, especially for the costs of redress.

The overall public expenditure costs of handling complaints and appeals can be assessed very roughly as the cost per new case and research suggests the following data:

- complaints cost an average of £155 per new case;
- appeals cases cost an average of £455 per new case;
- the costs for independent complaints handlers and for ombudsmen vary a lot, ranging between £550 and £4,500 per case, but mostly around £1,500 to £2,000.

There are very wide variations around these average numbers.

In addition to the direct administrative costs of complaints, appeals, and other redress systems, processing these cases can indirectly create substantial additional expenditures for some particular areas of the central government, via legal aid costs paid to those people eligible for this assistance. From information supplied by the Legal Services Commission the NAO can say that these additional costs are a minimum of £198 million in central government (primarily in the area of immigration and asylum appeals), plus a small amount in welfare benefit appeals. A minimum additional £24 million is incurred in the National Health Service. The actual full costs involved here are likely to be much greater than this.

Cutting down the initial numbers of complaints or appeals, resolving more complaints and appeals more speedily and proactively, and improving the cost efficiency of current redress arrangements, could all make appreciable savings in public money, savings that could then cumulate with every passing year. If reductions of five per cent could be made in the current costs of redress systems, the NAO estimates that the Exchequer would save at least £25 million per year less the cost of implementation.

Source: Adapted from National Audit Office, *Citizen Redress: What citizens can do if things go wrong with public services* (HC 21, 2004–05) (London, The Stationery Office, 2005).

The costs of administrative justice, particularly tribunals, have not gone unnoticed by government. The Coalition government's desire to find public expenditure savings has led to its proposing that fees should be charged to those wishing to take cases to tribunal. Fees are already charged in many types of immigration and asylum cases, fees in employment tribunal cases are introduced from the summer of 2013. The Administrative Justice and Review Council has argued that other financial models should be considered, in particular that government departments against which successful appeals have been made should themselves make a contribution towards the costs of the appeal process (*see Box 6.6*).

The courts

The heart of the administrative justice system is the Administrative Court, part of the High Court, where the fundamental principles of *judicial review* have been developed. The essence of judicial review is straightforward. Public officials must act within the constraints of the law. The primary tasks of judges in judicial review cases are:

- *to interpret statutory provisions*: there are many situations, particularly after new legislation has been passed, when the law needs clarification. Deciding the limits of the law, and whether or not a person acted within the law or outside it, is clearly a judicial task;

- *to control discretion*: in some situations legislation is deliberately drafted to give officials flexibility in the application of the law. Where a statute states that the minister 'may' act in a certain way or reach a 'reasonable' decision, these are examples of discretionary power. The judges have developed the principle that the exercise of discretion must not be 'unreasonable' (*Associated Provincial Picture Houses Ltd v Wednesbury Corporation* [1948] 1 KB 223, CA);

- *to determine the validity of secondary legislation*: the UK Supreme Court does not decide, as does the Supreme Court in the United States, that particular items of legislation are unlawful; that would offend the principle of the sovereignty of Parliament. This is subject to one exception, where UK legislation is contrary to the law of the European Union (*Factortame v Secretary of State for Transport (No. 2)* [1991] 1 AC 603). Under the Human Rights Act 1998, the courts have power to declare a provision in an Act of Parliament incompatible with the rights set out in the Human Rights Act 1998. The courts have long asserted the power to declare secondary legislation unlawful, on the basis that the statutory instrument was beyond the powers of the minister as established by the primary Act of Parliament (see, e.g. *R v Secretary of State for the Environment, Transport and the Regions, ex p Spath Holme Ltd* [2000] 1 All ER 884, HL);

- *to determine the fairness of procedures*: the courts have also determined fundamental principles of fairness in the lower courts, in other tribunals, and in a range of other contexts in which decisions affecting the citizen are made. Where these principles apply, the person must know the basis of the case against her, and be given an opportunity to be heard;

- *to prevent bias*: in addition, judges have insisted that adjudicators in the courts and other fora must not be 'biased', in the sense that they must not have a personal interest in the outcome of any particular case; and

- *to provide a remedy*: where the court finds that the law has been broken, it has a range of remedies available to it (*see Box 6.4*). The courts can use one or more of them in their decisions. A particular feature of judicial review proceedings is that the courts have discretion whether or not to make an order or grant a remedy. They may find that there has been a technical breach of the rules, but will not make an order if the consequences of the breach are trivial, or the other side has behaved improperly.

Box 6.4 Legal system explained

Judicial review remedies

The remedies available to the courts include:

- *quashing orders*: this is the most commonly used remedy. The courts rarely make their own decision; they usually quash the decision and send it back to the original decision maker to retake;
- *prohibiting orders*: preventing a body from taking a decision it might be contemplating taking;
- *mandatory orders*: requiring a body to carry out a duty imposed by statute;
- *declarations*: clarifying the rights and obligations of the parties to proceedings;
- *injunctions*: an order to stop a body acting in a particular way; and
- (rarely) *damages*.

Source: Adapted from *Public Law Project Information Leaflet 5*, available at <www.publiclawproject.org.uk/Publications.html>.

Judicial review has not developed in a vacuum. It is a response to the fact that people no longer accept official decisions as readily as they once did. The reasons for this are complex: better public education; a more consumerist society; the development of this type of legal practice by legal practitioners. But government has also expanded its activities. It seeks to regulate large tranches of human activity. It is not surprising that use of judicial review, or the threat of such use, should now be part of the reality of modern public administration.

One consequence of the development of judicial review has been an increased use by pressure groups of the courts for testing the validity of legislation or its interpretation. The taking of test cases has become a part of contemporary legal practice.[2] The Human Rights Act 1998 provided a new focus for such work as challenges about the compliance of legislation and policy with the European Convention on Human Rights are made.

---

[2] See, e.g. the work of the Public Law Project: <www.publiclawproject.org.uk/>.

The Administrative Court has a significant case-load. In 2011, there were over 11,200 applications for permission to apply for judicial review; the majority related to immigration or asylum matters. However, permission was granted in only 1,220 cases. Of these, about two-thirds were decided by a judge sitting alone; the rest were decided by courts comprising two or three judges—known as Divisional Courts.

One of the reforms introduced by the Tribunals, Courts and Enforcement Act 2007, discussed in the next section, is that in some cases the Administrative Court must, and in other cases may, transfer to the new Upper Tribunal cases that the Upper Tribunal has power to decide. In February 2010, the Immigration and Asylum Chamber of the Upper Tribunal was established. It has taken over many of the cases that used to go to the Administrative Court.

Tribunals

The vast majority of disputes between the citizen and the state get resolved, not in courts but in tribunals. Some, such as the General Commissioners of Income Tax, trace their history back to the late 18th century. Most are the creation of the 20th century, reflecting increased involvement of the state in the lives of its citizens.

For the first 20 to 30 years of that century, there was considerable concern about the use of tribunals as a mechanism for the resolution of disputes. It was argued that only courts had the constitutional authority to perform this function. (One of the advantages of the lack of a written constitution was that, despite this claim, there was no written constitutional principle that *required* all dispute resolution bodies to have the status of 'court'.) The development of tribunals was a pragmatic response to the problems caused for the court system when, at the end of the 19th century, jurisdiction to deal with disputes arising under the Workmen's Compensation Acts was given to the county courts. This resulted in those courts drowning in that work, preventing them from dealing effectively with other business. When the National Insurance Act 1911 was passed, creating the first social security benefits, appeals against decisions were not to the courts, but to a tribunal, the sportingly named *Committee of Referees* with a further right of appeal to the equally sporting *Umpire*.

Criticism of the use of bodies other than the courts for resolving disputes led to fierce criticism, not least from the then Lord Chief Justice, Lord Hewart, who in 1929 published his famous polemic *The New Despotism*. This resulted in the establishment of the Committee on Ministers' Powers, under the chairmanship of Lord Donoughmore, which in 1932 reported that, in its view and subject to safeguards, tribunals were a necessary if not desirable part of the fabric of the English justice system.

The issue was revisited after the Second World War when, in 1955, another committee under Sir Oliver Franks was established to review tribunals and inquiries, following a scandal known as the Crichel Down affair. His committee reported in 1957. By this time many more tribunal systems were in existence. Franks accepted that, subject to basic principles of openness, fairness, and impartiality, tribunals should be acknowledged as a part of the adjudicative structure. Since that time, there has been

no serious discussion about the need for tribunals. Indeed, their number has continued to grow (alongside other institutional developments, discussed later). The position
of tribunals is even more secure following enactment of the Human Rights Act 1998,
since Article 6 of the European Convention on Human Rights requires the existence
of courts or tribunals to determine a person's civil rights.

Reforming the tribunals system

This is the background against which the Tribunals Service was created. In May 2000,
Lord Irvine, the then Lord Chancellor, appointed Sir Andrew Leggatt (a retired Court
of Appeal judge) to undertake a review of tribunals. His report, *Tribunals for Users:
One System, One Service*, was published in August 2001. It set out a long list of recommendations, the central one being the creation of a unified Tribunals Service.

Publication of the report caused considerable consternation in the corridors of
Whitehall. Government departments came to see that implementation of the review's
proposals would involve some transfer of their functions to another department, never
an attractive prospect. However, after protracted discussion, the Lord Chancellor
announced early in 2003 that this central recommendation was accepted. The white
paper setting out the government's intentions was published in the summer of 2004.
This not only set out the framework for the new service, but also argued that it was
important to look at dispute resolution in the round. There should be clear and flexible
pathways for the citizen to obtain redress when things went wrong.[3]

The new Tribunals Service came into being in April 2006. It started work using
powers transferred to it by statutory order. The Tribunals, Courts and Enforcement
Act 2007 gave the reform programme further impetus. The new structure began to
operate in November 2008. On 1 April 2011, the Tribunals Service merged with the
Courts Service to form Her Majesty's Courts and Tribunals Service (HMCTS).

The Act created two new, generic tribunals: the First-Tier Tribunal dealing with the
bulk of cases arising from official decision taking; and the Upper Tribunal, hearing
appeals from decisions taken by the First-Tier Tribunal, as well as judicial review cases
referred to it by the Administrative Court. Tribunals are grouped into 'chambers';
pre-existing tribunals have been brought together in a practically functional way (*see
Diagram 6.1*). New tribunal jurisdictions can be brought into this generic framework.

The Act created the post of Senior President, currently the Court of Appeal judge,
Sir Jeremy Sullivan. Following the creation of HMCTS, it has been decided that the
Lord Chief Justice, who is now head of the judiciary, should also be the formal head of
the tribunal judiciary. This development is being legislated in the Crime and Courts
Bill 2012. However the post of Senior President is being retained so that he can con-
tinue to provide judicial leadership to the Tribunals Service.

The 2007 Act provided that legal members of tribunals have the title of judge.
Tribunal judges can be assigned to more than one chamber. This development enabled

[3] See *Transforming Public Services: Complaints, Redress and Tribunals* (Cm 6243) (London, The Stationery
Office, July 2004).

Diagram 6.1 Structure of the tribunals system

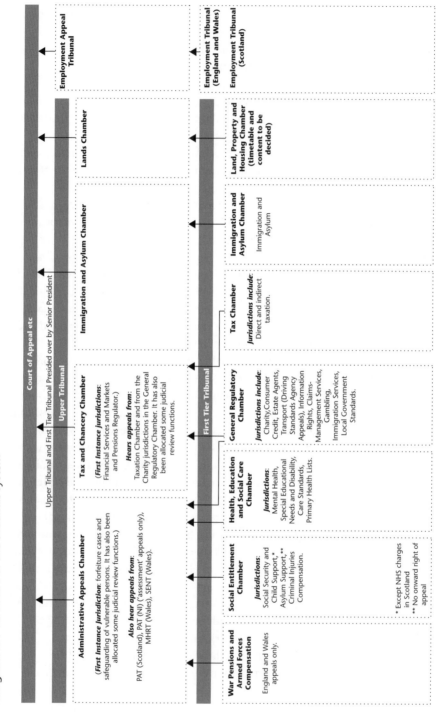

Source: Annual Report of the Senior President of Tribunals (2012), p. 3.

the Judicial Appointments Commission to start thinking more strategically about the creation of a judicial career (*see Chapter 4, Judicial appointments*). Prospective judges can start in one jurisdiction, for example in the Tribunals Service, but then contemplate moving to other judicial work in other judicial contexts, for example the courts. This flexibility will be developed still further as the result of further provisions in the Crime and Courts Bill 2012.

To reduce the bewildering variety of practices and procedures of pre-existing tribunals, the tribunals now work to a single set of procedural rules, created by the Tribunals Rules Committee.

Tribunals have two distinctive characteristics. Most important is that that they have specialist expertise. The qualifications of tribunal judges and members should be appropriate for the cases they deal with. Thus, in addition to the legal qualifications of tribunal judges, other relevant professional expertise is used as well, for example valuers or accountants or doctors.

Secondly, tribunals make extensive efforts to deal with appellants who—as the result of a lack of availability of legal aid—either have to represent themselves or have to rely on lay advocates. Unlike the adversarial approach of the courts, where the judges tend to take a back seat while arguments, for and against, are presented by advocates for both sides, members of tribunals take a more interventionist role, seeking to draw relevant information from the parties by appropriate questioning. Leggatt called this 'the enabling role' of the tribunal. This is one example of the procedural innovation of the tribunal system. The courts—if they knew what went on in the best-run tribunals—would have much to learn from tribunals. It is essential that the creation of HMCTS does not result in the disappearance of these characteristics.

Inquiries

Historically, there was an important conceptual distinction between a tribunal and an inquiry. Whereas a tribunal usually had statutory authority to adjudicate a dispute and reach a final decision which, subject to any right of appeal, determined the matter, an inquiry gathered information, in the light of which a government minister would decide the issue.

In practice, this distinction became increasingly blurred. For example, Mental Health Review Tribunals (now in one of the First-Tier Tribunal chambers), when dealing with mental patients who were detained in a mental hospital as a result of a court order, can only recommend to the Home Secretary that a patient should be released from hospital; it is the Secretary of State (or his officials) who takes the final decision. By contrast, many inquiries lead directly to a decision being taken, rather than a report to a minister which would form the basis for a decision.

Planning inquiries and related procedures

The principal use of the inquiry in the administrative justice system is found in the context of land use planning. In a geographically small country with a substantial population, it has long been accepted that the state has an interest in determining how land should be used. The planning process seeks to balance the competing interests relating to land use of urban dwellers, rural dwellers, farmers, industrialists, scientists, the pursuers of leisure interests, the providers of transport systems, and other utility providers (gas, electricity, water), to give just some examples. The bulk of planning decisions are taken by local authorities, acting as local planning authorities. Strategically important decisions—for example over the siting of a new airport—may be 'called in' for determination by the Secretary of State within central government.

Once a planning decision has been reached, rights of appeal are provided. Whereas in other contexts tribunals deal with appeals, in the planning context appeals are dealt with by planning inspectors. Originally, planning inspectors held inquiries and made recommendations to the Secretary of State in central government. These were inquiries in their original sense. As a result of changes in the law, planning inspectors now make the final determination in all but the most complex or important cases, where they still make recommendations to the Secretary of State. Thus, in most cases, the functions of the planning inspectorate are indistinguishable from the functions of a tribunal. Planning inspectors have three ways of proceeding:

- written representations;
- hearings; and
- inquiries.

Statistically, the inquiry is the least frequently used mode for determining planning appeals:

- *Written representations* are, as the name implies, a means of dealing with an appeal purely through written representations. This is the speediest and cheapest of the procedures and is particularly suitable for the determination of relatively small matters, for example an extension to a dwelling.

- *Hearings* involve the appellants and the local planning authority in a hearing before a planning inspector, but the process is consciously 'low-key'. Planning inspectors are trained to run hearings proactively to try to avoid the need for the use of expensive legal representation. The inspector shapes the hearing by assisting the parties to identify the issues that need to be addressed. Typically, the hearing is used in cases slightly more significant than those dealt with by written representation, but not as large scale as those going to inquiry.

- *Inquiries* are used primarily for major planning issues. Inquiries are also used to determine the shape of local planning authorities' local plans, which provide the background against which individual planning applications are decided. Inquiries involve hearing a wider range of persons with an interest in the decision—for example environmental groups or trade associations—than written representations or hearings. Procedurally, they are more formal, with the parties usually using barristers or solicitors to represent their interests. Inquiries can take a very long time and be very expensive; the public inquiry into the fifth terminal at London Heathrow Airport took over five years to complete.

Particular and ad hoc inquiries

In addition to planning inquiries, which are held on a regular basis, other forms of inquiry are set up as the need arises, for example, inquiries into serious rail accidents or other disasters.

The government may also use an ad hoc inquiry to deal with the aftermath of a particular incident. Recent examples include the Chilcot inquiry into the Iraq war, or the Leveson inquiry into the culture, practice, and ethics of the press. The Council on Tribunals issued advice on matters that government should take into account when establishing ad hoc inquiries.[4] Local authorities and other public bodies may also establish inquiries into a range of issues, as they arise.[5]

Review

Another form of redress of grievance is review. This involves officials who took the initial decision reviewing that decision to see whether or not it is correct or should be revised. In some cases, the reviewer is the initial decision-taker; in others the reviewer is another official, usually more senior. Reviews may lack the independence that characterizes an appeal to a tribunal or an inquiry. But they can provide an easy and quick means of rectifying a decision where something has clearly gone wrong. Reviews are found in two basic forms: formal and informal:

- *Formal* reviews are those that are required by law to be carried out.[6]
- *Informal* reviews are not required by law but officials nonetheless carry them out as part of their routine administrative procedures. In the case of social security appeals, for example, any appeal by a social security claimant triggers an internal official review to check whether the decision appealed against is or is not correct. There is evidence that more cases are revised in favour of claimants at this stage than at the appeal stage.[7]

Reviews as a feature of the administrative justice system have been the subject of considerable criticism. In the same way that, in the context of criminal justice, decisions by the police to deal with suspects administratively—for example, by issuing a caution—are criticized for undermining the due process model of criminal justice, so

---

[4] *Advice to the Lord Chancellor on the Procedural Issues arising in the context of Public Inquiries set up by Ministers,* July 1996 (HC 114) (London, Her Majesty's Stationery Office, 1996).

[5] Some of the issues are discussed in Law Commission, *In the public interest: Publication of Local Authority Inquiry Reports* (Law Com 289) (Cm 6272) (London, The Stationery Office, 2004).

[6] In some cases, such as review of decisions relating to the Social Fund, there is no tribunal process available—all appeals go through the review process. The Social Fund review procedure is abolished from April 2013.

[7] See Baldwin, J., and others, *Judging Social Security* (Oxford, Clarendon Press, 1992).

too is review seen by some as undermining the due process model of administrative justice.[8]

Against this, others suggest that models of administrative justice should be based not just on due process but also on other values, such as cost-effectiveness and efficiency. This leads to the conclusion that review is not so objectionable, but is a sensible way of ensuring that mistakes are corrected without the expense and delay of a tribunal hearing. Indeed, when well organized, reviews can have all the hallmarks of independence and due process.[9]

Experience suggests that the primary reason decisions taken by officials are later found to be wrong is not that the official has misunderstood the law to be applied to the case in question, but that the factual information on which the decision is based is in some respect wanting. It therefore makes sense to find ways of getting at the relevant facts other than by the relatively expensive and long-drawn-out process of a tribunal hearing. In this context, review may be particularly valuable. However, if the way in which the review works is that no effort is made to see whether new evidence is forthcoming, or that those who may have a case to take to a tribunal become so disheartened that they fail to pursue their claims in full, then review may be criticized as not adding value to the administrative justice system.

Whatever the theoretical objections, review will remain a part of the administrative justice system. The question is not whether review should be part of the system, but rather, in what contexts is or is it not appropriate?

Ombudsmen

The Parliamentary and Health Service Ombudsman

The Ombudsman concept was introduced into the United Kingdom from Scandinavia in 1967. The first Ombudsman was formally known as the Parliamentary Commissioner for Administration (PCA), though she is now described as the Parliamentary Ombudsman. The Ombudsman's original function was to investigate complaints and allegations of *maladministration* in UK government departments and related agencies that may have resulted in injustice.

Two particular features of the Parliamentary Ombudsman's jurisdiction should be noted. First, members of the public are not entitled to complain directly to the PCA; they must get their complaint referred to the Ombudsman by a Member of Parliament (MP). MPs are not actually obliged to refer cases to her if they think they can deal with the matter themselves. This is because, when the Ombudsman concept was introduced, some argued that it might undermine the primary responsibility of Parliament

---

[8] Sainsbury, R., 'Internal Reviews and the Weakening of Social Security Claimants' Rights of Appeal', in Richardson, G., and Genn, H. (eds), *Administrative Law and Government Action* (Oxford, Clarendon Press, 1994).

[9] Harris, M., 'The Place of Formal and Informal Review in Administrative Justice', and Scampion, J., 'New Procedures', in Harris, M., and Partington, M. (eds), *Administrative Justice in the 21st Century* (Oxford, Hart Publishing, 1999).

and its members to call ministers (and their officials) to account. The MP filter, as it is known, was not part of the original Scandinavian Ombudsman concept, where direct access by the public was permitted. In November 2011, the Ombudsman published a report recommending abolition of the MP filter.

Secondly, the Parliamentary Ombudsman cannot order that any particular consequence should follow a finding of maladministration. She can only persuade a government department, for example, to pay compensation to an aggrieved citizen. Again, in other countries, the Ombudsman has power to enforce his decisions. This limitation emerged very clearly in the context of her decision in the Equitable Life case. There she found that policyholders in the company had suffered as the result of official administration, but her recommendations for financial compensation were for a long time resisted by government. The present Coalition government has recently decided that compensation should be paid. In an important case decided by the Court of Appeal in 2008, *R (Bradley) v Secretary of State for Work and Pensions* [2008] EWCA Civ 36, it was held that while rulings of the Ombudsman were not binding, a finding of maladministration should only be rejected if there were cogent reasons for so doing.

The Ombudsman has drawn up guidance on the principles to be adopted when considering what remedies should be offered to those who are found to have suffered maladministration. The range of remedies is much wider than those offered by the courts. They include: making apologies; offering explanations; taking remedial action; in some cases offering financial compensation.

Since first established, the scope of the Ombudsman's work has been broadened considerably, first to deal with complaints about the National Health Service (NHS), more recently to deal with complaints about the Victims' Charter.

As Health Service Ombudsman she investigates complaints about failures in NHS hospitals or community health services, about care and treatment, and about local NHS family doctor, dental, pharmacy, or optical services. Members of the public may refer a complaint direct to her, i.e. there is no MP filter, though normally she pursues a complaint only if a full investigation within the NHS complaints system has been carried out first. She can only consider issues arising in the NHS in England.

Since April 2006, when the Victims' Code took effect (*see Chapter 5, The place of the victim*) the Ombudsman has provided a complaints-handling service for victims of crime who have a complaint about the way in which any of the criminal justice agencies has carried out its obligations under the code. Such cases are subject to the MP filter.

Besides investigating and, where appropriate, redressing grievances, the Ombudsman sees her function as improving the quality of administration. Her reports contain guidance on good practice from which government or health departments should learn. In March 2007, she published general principles of good administration. There are six: getting it right; being customer focused; being open and accountable; acting fairly and proportionately; putting things right; and seeking continuous improvement. Though seemingly obvious, these basic principles are often ignored in practice.

Summaries of her investigations are available on her website. She also publishes an *Annual Report*, as well as specific reports on particular issues. Her report on the treatment of the elderly is a recent example. For the first time in 2011, she produced a review of complaints handling within government departments and other public bodies. Unsurprisingly, she found unacceptable variations in practice and procedure.

In 2005, she published a joint report covering both her parliamentary and health service work. Issues particularly considered were: problems with the new tax credits system; the operations of the Child Support Agency; NHS funding of continuing care for people with long-term health care needs; and the need for a truly patient-focused NHS complaints procedure.

The *Annual Report* is considered by the specialist Public Administration Select Committee of the House of Commons, who interview her as well as senior civil servants from departments that have been criticized by her. Thus Parliament is kept informed about the Ombudsman's work and the impact it has had on government departments.

Public service ombudsmen in Wales and Scotland

Following devolution, the arrangements for Wales and Scotland have changed. In Wales, complaints originally went to four separate ombudsmen: the Commission for Local Administration in Wales, the Health Service Commissioner for Wales, the Welsh Administration Ombudsman, and also the Social Housing Ombudsman for Wales. These were brought together into a single scheme, the Public Service Ombudsman for Wales, operational from 1 April 2006.

In Scotland there is a Scottish Public Service Ombudsman. Established in 2002, he deals with complaints about Scottish public bodies previously dealt with by the Scottish Parliamentary Ombudsman, the Health Service Ombudsman for Scotland, the Local Government Ombudsman for Scotland, and the Housing Association Ombudsman for Scotland. He has also taken over the Mental Welfare Commission for Scotland's function of investigating complaints relating to mental health and complaints against Scottish Enterprise and Highlands and Islands Enterprise.

Local government ombudsmen

The Ombudsman concept has been extended to local government. There are two local government ombudsmen covering all local authorities in England. They investigate complaints against principal councils (not town, parish, or community councils) and certain other bodies in England, in particular, adult social care providers. By law, some kinds of complaint cannot be considered. Examples are personnel complaints and complaints about the internal running of schools.

As with other ombudsmen, the objective of the local government ombudsmen is to secure, where appropriate, satisfactory redress for complainants and better administration by local authorities. Since 1989, they have had power to issue advice on good administrative practice, drawing lessons from the cases they have handled. To date, six guidance notes have been published: on setting up complaints procedures; good administrative practice; council housing repairs; local authority members' interests; the disposal of land; and remedies when things have gone wrong.

Following a review of the Parliamentary and Health Services Ombudsman and the English local government ombudsmen, the government recently agreed that, where a complaint raises matters relating both to central and to local government, the two organizations could investigate it jointly (see the Regulatory Reform (Collaboration between Ombudsmen) Order 2007).

Comment on ombudsmen

The variety of processes and procedures that characterize the work of the Ombudsmen, particularly in England, has resulted in increasing numbers of calls for reform. In addition to the question of whether or not the MP filter should be retained, questions have also been raised about whether the process of going to an ombudsman can be made easier and also about whether findings of the Ombudsmen should be enforceable. In 2011, the Law Commission made recommendations for reform of the legislative framework within which these various public sector ombudsmen operate (*see Box 6.5*). The response of government is currently awaited.

Box 6.5   Reform in progress

Modernizing ombudsman services

The Law Commission's principal recommendations were that:

- The appointment of the Parliamentary Commissioner should be made following nomination of an individual by Parliament.
- Parliament, and the National Assembly for Wales in the case of the Public Services Ombudsman for Wales, should develop close links between all the public services ombudsmen and appropriate select committees.
- The legislative provisions requiring complaints to be made in writing should be repealed.
- The statutory bars that restrict the ability of citizens to choose the institution for administrative redress they prefer should be removed.
- The MP filter should be reformed, so that citizens can make complaints direct to the Parliamentary Commissioner.
- The findings of the public services ombudsmen, except the Housing Ombudsmen, should be made binding.
- All of the public services ombudsmen should have powers allowing them to publish and distribute their reports and other materials widely.

In addition, the Law Commission recommended that the government establish a wide-ranging review of the public services ombudsmen and their relationship with other institutions for administrative redress, such as courts and tribunals.

Source: Public Service Ombudsmen (Law Com 329) (2011).

Other ombudsmen offices

Increasingly, more specialist Ombudsman or Ombudsman-type offices have been created. For example, an Office for Legal Complaints handles consumer complaints in respect of all bodies providing legal services, subject to oversight by the Legal Services Board (*see Chapter 9, Dealing with complaints*); a Judicial Appointments and Conduct Ombudsman, created by the Constitutional Reform Act 2005, deals with complaints about judicial appointments and judicial conduct; the Independent Police Complaints Commission deals with complaints against the police; a Prisons and Probation Ombudsman deals with complaints about the prison and probation service; and the Housing Ombudsman deals with complaints against (primarily) registered social landlords (housing associations). (From April 2013, his jurisdiction expands to include council housing.) These are not considered further here, but more information is available on their websites, listed in the Online Resource Centre.

The rise of private sector ombudsmen

Over the last 20 years or so, a distinctively British phenomenon has emerged. A considerable number of private sector industries have set up their own ombudsman schemes to deal with those customer complaints that cannot be resolved within a particular company. These include the Property Ombudsman, the Banking Ombudsman, the Insurance Ombudsman, and the Building Societies Ombudsman. By contrast with the PCA and the other public sector ombudsmen, where the levels of complaints have been relatively low, many of these private sector ombudsmen have had large case-loads to deal with. They offer a 'mass-market' dispute resolution procedure, as opposed to the more 'Rolls-Royce' work of the PCA.[10]

Following the Financial Services and Markets Act 2000 a Financial Services Ombudsman scheme brought together many of these private schemes. It operates under statutory rather than industry-determined powers. It has a substantial case-load and is able to award compensation up to £150k. It has effectively replaced the courts as the forum for the resolution of consumer disputes with financial services providers.

Process

A common feature of all ombudsmen's procedures is that they operate on an 'inquisitorial' or 'investigative' basis. The complaint is made; the relevant ombudsman's staff investigates the complaint, taking further evidence both from the government department or other agency concerned and the complainant. In the light of the investigation a conclusion is reached on whether or not there was in fact maladministration. Many investigations result in a finding that the department or agency in question behaved perfectly responsibly, and the complainant was being unreasonable. Where there is a finding of maladministration, there is comment on whether the response

---

[10] Williams, T., and Goriely, T., 'A Question of Numbers: Managing Complaints Against Rising Expectations', in Harris, M., and Partington, M. (eds), *Administrative Justice in the 21st Century* (Oxford, Hart Publishing, 1999).

of the department was appropriate. Many findings of maladministration lead to no more than the writing of a letter of apology, which is often all that the complainant wanted in the first place. Usually, there is no possibility of an oral hearing (though the Pensions Ombudsman is required to offer this).

The European Ombudsman

In addition to developments in England and Wales, the Ombudsman concept also extends to the work of the European Union. The creation of a European Ombudsman was approved in the Maastricht Treaty; the statute giving him his authority was agreed in 1994. He took up office in 1995 and has been issuing annual reports on his work since 1996.

The Ombudsman operates on the basis of *The European Ombudsman Implementing Provisions*. These not only set out in general terms the principles on which the Ombudsman carries out his work, but also list the powers he has when determining cases: these include the possibility of making 'critical remarks' where no more general conclusions can be drawn from the case under investigation; and the making of a 'report with draft recommendations', where it appears that some more general lessons may be learned.

In addition, and unlike the national ombudsmen in England and Wales, the European Ombudsman has a very broad power to instigate his 'own-initiative' inquiries. One fruit of this, to date, has been the preparation of a set of draft recommendations, which have been put both to the European Commission and to the European Parliament and Council of Ministers, relating to the adoption of a *Code of Good Administrative Behaviour*. His reason for doing this was the result of reflecting on many of the individual complaints he had received, which indicated that maladministration might have been avoided had clearer information been available about the administrative duties of Community staff towards its citizens. The code was approved by the European Parliament and published in March 2002.

Other complaints-handling bodies

It might be thought that, with the creation of ombudsmen to deal with issues at a high level and with the more recent development of a wide variety of complaints-resolution procedures in individual government departments, there were now adequate means for the redress of citizens' complaints. In fact, many other bodies and procedures have been created with more specific remits than the ombudsmen's but more general authority than an internal complaints procedure. Only a few examples are given here:

- The *Adjudicator* investigates complaints from people and businesses about the work of Her Majesty's Revenue and Customs, the Insolvency Service, the Public Guardianship Office, and the Valuation Office Agency. The Adjudicator does not look at issues of law or of tax liability, because tribunals resolve these problems. But she does look into excessive delay, mistakes, discourtesy of staff, and the use of discretion.

- The *Independent Complaints Reviewer* deals with complaints about an eclectic mix of government agencies, including (currently) the Land Registry, the Audit Commission, the Charity Commission, the Homes and Communities Agency, the National Archives, and the Northern Ireland Youth Justice Agency.

- The *Independent Case Examiner* investigates complaints about the Child Support Agency, when clients are dissatisfied with the outcome of the Agency's internal complaints service. He also deals with complaints about the Pension, Disability and Carers Service, and about Jobcentre Plus. He also deals with complaints about the Northern Ireland Social Security Agency.

- The *Independent Adjudicator for Higher Education* operates an independent student complaints scheme to which all higher education institutions must adhere. The adjudicator handles individual complaints against those institutions, and may publish recommendations about how they deal with complaints and what constitutes good practice.

- The *Immigration Services Commissioner*, set up under the Immigration and Asylum Act 1999, is responsible for ensuring that all immigration advisers fulfill the requirements of good practice. His office is responsible for regulating immigration advisers in accordance with the Commissioner's Code of Standards and Rules, including taking criminal proceedings against advisers who are acting illegally.

The number and variety of these bodies has grown significantly over the last ten years and now looks very haphazard. There is scope for rationalization.

'Collective' administrative justice: regulators of privatized utility providers

Another context for the resolution of disputes arises from the privatization of the main utility providers—water, gas, electricity, and telecommunications—whereby the provision of services by state monopolies was replaced by private companies. New regulatory offices—including OFWAT, OFGEM, and OFTEL (now OFCOM)—were established to regulate these new industries to prevent abuse of market power in the setting of prices, and to create the conditions in which other suppliers could come into the market to provide the competition essential for consumer protection. These regulatory offices have also had some responsibility for the development of procedures for dealing with individual customer complaints and complaints from others wishing to enter particular market sectors.[11]

This is not the place to consider the work of these industry regulators in detail. But their existence and the fact that they too play a part in the administrative justice system need to be noted.

---

[11] See McHarg, A., 'Separation of Functions and Regulatory Agencies: Dispute Resolution in the Privatised Utilities', in Harris, M., and Partington, M. (eds), *Administrative Justice in the 21st Century* (Oxford, Hart Publishing, 1999).

Getting it right first time: putting people first

Notwithstanding all these dispute resolution procedures, there is a powerful argument that they would not be necessary if those who delivered public services were fully focused on delivering a high-quality service themselves. 'Getting it right first time' should be preferable to making the citizen complain, or appeal, or go to an ombudsman. This general issue has been a concern of government for many years. First was the concept of the Citizens' Charter, later rebadged by the Blair government as *Service First*. By contrast with the Ombudsman, where the concept moved from the public sector to the private, the Citizens' Charter involved private sector ideas about standards of customer care and service delivery being brought into the public sector. Though the initial introduction of the charter, in 1991 by the government of Mr Major, was seen as rather gimmicky, it provided further impetus to promoting service standards in the public sector.

Since then much attention has been given to improving the quality of public service delivery. Under the Blair government, the Office of Public Sector Reform defined four principles for public service delivery: national standards to ensure that people have the right to high-quality services wherever they live; devolution to give local leaders the means to deliver these standards to local people; more flexibility in service provision in light of people's rising expectations; and greater customer choice. Much of this was driven by the desire to enhance the use of information technology in the delivery of public services.

Many issues of considerable political importance derived from these initiatives, for example, the desirability of government setting standards and targets (and dealing with the consequences of failing to meet them); or the extremely controversial issue of the extent to which private sector companies should be involved in the delivery of public services. (Particularly contentious examples arise in relation to the provision of health care, education, and prison services.) The approach of the Coalition government is to focus less on the former, and more on the latter.

It is difficult to gauge the extent to which these principles are delivered in practice. The nature of political debate and reports in the media is to focus on things that are not happening rather than on the positive developments that are occurring. There are often good reasons to think that progress is slower than ministers would like. In many parts of the country, public service pay levels make it hard to recruit staff of adequate quality. Some forms of public service are very stressful to deliver, which increases the problems of staff recruitment and retention. And, some areas of social administration are very complex; however well staff do their jobs, there will be grounds for appeal or seeking reviews of decisions. Examples of services being delivered to much higher standards do not attract the same attention, though reports of the many official inspectorates suggest that good services are offered in many areas of government.

There seems little doubt that there will continue to be a focus on the need for public services to deliver a better service to the public. Administrative justice should be based on a desire to ensure that official decisions are right first time. If officials get the initial decision right, then the consumers of public services should be better satisfied and have less need to use the myriad appeal and complaints mechanisms discussed in this chapter. (Indeed, one of the criticisms that can be made of many of the processes discussed earlier is that there is rather little institutional commitment to the idea of considering what *general* lessons might be drawn from the resolution of *individual* appeals or complaints. The very process of encouraging disputes to be resolved on an individual basis may disguise structural questions which, if addressed by the government department or other agency, might have prevented the problem arising in the first place.)

This is the subject of the 2011 report from the Administrative Justice and Tribunals Council, *Right first time (see Box 6.6)*.

Box 6.6   Reform in progress

Right first time

The Administrative Justice and Tribunals Council argue that there are too many successful appeals before tribunals, the result of poor decision taking within government. It argues there should be more emphasis on 'getting it right'; and that departments that have unacceptably high levels of successful appeals should be made to help fund the tribunals and ombudsmen that sort incorrect decisions out. Public bodies could save money and improve the quality of service by making fewer mistakes and learning more from those they make.

Incorrect decisions impact significantly on the lives of those directly concerned. Compounding the problem is the repetition of these expensive errors. Too few public bodies have in place feedback mechanisms to ensure that the outcomes of appeals and complaints are understood throughout the organization.

'Right first time' means:

- making a decision or delivering a service to the user fairly, quickly, accurately, and effectively;
- taking into account the relevant and sufficient evidence and circumstances of a particular case;
- involving the user and keeping the user updated and informed during the process;
- communicating and explaining the decision or action to the user in a clear and understandable way, and informing the user about his or her rights in relation to complaints, reviews, appeals, or alternative dispute resolution;
- learning from feedback or complaints about the service or appeals against decisions;
- empowering and supporting staff through providing high quality guidance, training, and mentoring.

The report identifies the fundamentals of right first time as leadership, culture, responsiveness, resolution, and learning. It also highlights practical steps that should be

Box 6.6 *Continued*

adopted and followed by leaders of public bodies when reviewing their services and attempting to establish a right-first-time approach. All such bodies should carry out a review of their systems, procedures and decision-making structures, to ensure that they are doing all they can to get decisions right first time.

The report argues that it is time to adopt a 'polluter pays' approach to help promote a right-first-time culture. Tribunals (including, but not limited to, those within the Tribunals Service) are currently carrying a heavy share of the financial burden caused by incorrect decisions. It recommends the development of funding models by which original decision-making organizations contribute to the cost of running tribunals through direct reference to the volume of successful appeals they generate.

To the extent that the institutional procedures considered in this chapter are needed, this may reflect the fact that standards of administrative justice are not as high as they should be.

Audit and quality control

The discussion of administrative justice has so far focused on the wide variety of procedures, ranging from courts to informal complaints-handling procedures, available to individual citizens, dissatisfied with some aspect of public administration. Other mechanisms have also been introduced to try to ensure quality of performance and the provision of good public services that provide value for money.

Among alternative techniques used to try to achieve these more general objectives are:

- auditing: to ensure that value for money in the provision of public services is achieved;
- inspectorates: to ensure the quality of service provision;
- benchmarking: statistics to provide baseline data against which performance by public sector agencies may be measured; and
- public service agreements: designed to encourage the modernization of service delivery, support proposals for reform, and increase accountability by the setting of clear aims and objectives.

These techniques should also be seen as components of the administrative justice system.

Parliament

It has been argued in this chapter that our understanding of administrative justice should be seen as offering something more than the resolution of individual disputes between the citizen and the state. It should embrace other methods by which officials and other public servants are called to account. In this context, it must not be forgotten that Parliament—in addition to its legislative functions considered in *Chapter 3*—has important responsibilities. Three particular mechanisms may be noted here:

- MPs' questions;
- Debates;
- Select Committees.

MPs' questions

The easiest way for an MP to try to get information or to get something done by a minister is to ask a Parliamentary Question (PQ). A small number of PQs are answered orally by the minister concerned; the vast majority of PQs receive a written answer. All answers—whether oral or written—are printed in *Hansard*, the official transcript of proceedings in Parliament. Although the issues on which questions are asked range very widely, many are designed to call ministers to account, and in that sense can be seen as within the landscape of administrative justice.

Debates

A great deal of parliamentary time is spent debating legislative proposals, as noted in *Chapter 3*. This use of parliamentary time is controlled by the government. But there are also opportunities for Parliament to debate other issues, not directly related to the law-making process, and some of these opportunities are outside the control of the government. They can be used by backbench MPs to raise issues about how government is working.

For example, at the end of each parliamentary day, there is a short 30-minute adjournment debate, introduced by a backbench MP. One innovation—introduced in November 1999—is that of *backbench debates*. Because of the amount of time the legislative process takes in the House of Commons, backbenchers had only limited opportunity to raise matters of more general concern. Three days each week are now available for backbench debates on matters not related to the legislative programme. These take place not in the chamber of the House of Commons, but in Westminster Hall, which for these purposes is arranged in a horse-shoe formation—thought to be less confrontational than the familiar 'head-on' arrangements in the House of Commons.

The ability of backbenchers to control the issues considered in backbench debates has been increased by the decision, taken by the Coalition government, to create a Backbench Business Committee, which has responsibility for scheduling the subjects for debates raised by MPs. The days available for this are controlled by the government. A number will take place in the House of Commons; the rest in Westminster Hall. Around 35 days will be made available to the Committee.

Select committees

Lastly, Parliament appoints a wide range of select committees to keep the work of central government departments under review. There are also a number of select committees that cut across departmental boundaries. These include: the Public Accounts Committee, the Public Administration Select Committee, and the Procedure Committee.

In addition to those in the House of Commons, there are also select committees in the House of Lords. They do not look at individual departments, but address more general issues. There are currently five major Lords Select Committees: the European Union Committee; the Science and Technology Committee; the Communications Committee; the Constitution Committee; and the Economic Affairs Committee.

Each select committee works by inquiring into topics which it selects for investigation. The committees work by gathering written and oral evidence, and in the light of this write a report which is presented to Parliament. They can call for named individuals (including ministers and civil servants) to attend the committee to be questioned. A particular feature of select committees is that many of them are chaired by MPs who are not members of the governing political party. For the most part, they seek to write unanimous reports, whatever the party political composition of the particular committee.

Select committees have become much more important in recent years as a mechanism by which MPs try to call government to account, although a lot of their detailed work is not well understood by the public at large.

Freedom of information

Lastly, note should be taken of the Freedom of Information Act 2000, which came fully into force at the beginning of 2005. The Act covers all central government departments, and a number of other bodies closely related to central government, including, for example, the Charity Commission, the Crown Prosecution Service, the Serious Fraud Office, and the Treasury Solicitors Department. The government produces regular statistical reports on the use of the Act. The most recent shows that between April and June 2012, over 11,000 requests for information were received. This number has been increasing since 2007.

The impact of this method of calling officials and other public servants to account can be extremely dramatic; the exposure in 2009 of information about the use (and abuse) of allowances by MPs was the result of investigative work undertaken through use of freedom of information requests.

Overview of the administrative justice system

The Administrative Justice and Tribunals Council

Since 1959, tribunals and inquiries were kept under review by the Council on Tribunals. It had a statutory responsibility to advise government on the work of the tribunals and inquiry systems under its jurisdiction; to comment on drafts of procedural regulations, on which the Council must be consulted; and to deal with such other matters as might be referred to it. In addition, the Council prepared a number of reports relating to general issues about the operation of tribunals and inquiries.

A particular feature of the Council was that its members had, in the vast majority of the tribunal systems under its authority, a statutory right to attend hearings. As a result of these visits many items of concern to the Council emerged, which translated into proposals for reform. They included:

- the need for training of tribunal chairmen and members;
- the importance of the role of the clerk and administrative support generally in ensuring the smooth running of tribunals; and
- the need for adequate levels of resource to enable the work of the tribunals to be done effectively.

The Leggatt review of tribunals saw the Council as a key part of the administrative justice system and recommended that its role should be enhanced.

From November 2007, the Council was transformed into the Administrative Justice and Tribunals Council. Details of the Council's powers were set out in the Tribunals, Courts and Enforcement Act 2007. Notwithstanding this history, the Coalition government decided that, following its review of public bodies, the Council should be abolished. This could be a mistake. There are a number of issues facing the administrative justice system:

- bringing coherence to the huge range of ombudsmen and complaints-resolution processes;
- determining who should pay for tribunals;
- dealing with the impacts in cuts in legal aid and general advice provision;
- developing more proportionate dispute-resolution procedures.

Indeed, in another report, published in 2011, the Council asks whether administrative justice may be under threat. It argues that this is not the time to abolish totally an independent voice that could encourage constructive debate on challenges to the administrative justice system. The final demise of the Council has still, at the time of preparing this edition, not been achieved. According to evidence given to the Public Administration Select Committee, the Ministry of Justice has already announced that, when the Council is abolished, an informal expert advisory committee will be established to help the development of government policy. The details of this development are not yet fully available.

The Ombudsman Association

Formerly called the British and Irish Ombudsmen's Association, this is a private organization founded by the ombudsmen in 1995 to ensure that only those bodies that subscribe to certain procedural standards use the label 'ombudsman'. In particular, they wanted to ensure that ombudsmen in the private sector of the economy, who are privately financed, are truly *independent* of their paymasters. It has also undertaken other activity, such as developing principles for the training and procedures to be adopted by individual ombudsman systems. One feature particularly worthy of note—and which it is surprising does not exist in other parts of the English legal system—is its link with the neighbouring common law jurisdiction, Ireland. (There would be advantage in thinking of other areas of the justice system where there might be opportunities for the British and the Irish to learn from each other.) However, it does not see its function as keeping the whole of the administrative justice system under review.

Questions

Use the self-test questions on the Online Resource Centre to test your understanding of the topics covered in this chapter and receive tailored feedback:

www.oxfordtextbooks.co.uk/orc/partington13_14/

Weblinks

Check the Online Resource Centre for a selection of annotated weblinks allowing you to easily research topics of particular interest:

www.oxfordtextbooks.co.uk/orc/partington13_14/

Blog items

See www.martinpartington.com (access via the Online Resource Centre)

Items discussed include: charging fees for accessing tribunals; the implications of merging courts and tribunals; the proposals for reform of the Ombudsman system; removing the MP filter; the principle of 'right first time'; the crisis in administrative justice; interviews with Sir Robert Carnwath and Judge Alison McKenna; interviews with the Ombudsman and the Legal Services Ombudsman; interview with the Independent Complaints Reviewer; interview with the Chair of the Administrative Justice and Tribunals Council.

Further reading

BRIDGES, L., MESZAROS, G., and SUNKIN, M., *Judicial Review in Perspective* (London, Cavendish, 1995)

CANE, P., *Administrative Tribunals and Adjudication* (Oxford, Hart Publishing, 2010)

ELLIOTT, M., *The Constitutional Foundations of Judicial Review* (Oxford, Hart Publishing, 2001)

GENN, H., *Tribunals for Diverse Users* (DCA Research Series) (London, Department for Constitutional Affairs, 2006)

—— and GENN, Y., *The Effectiveness of Representation at Tribunals: Report to the Lord Chancellor* (London, Queen Mary College, Faculty of Law, 1989)

HARLOW, C., and RAWLINGS, R., *Law and Administration* (3rd edn, Cambridge, Cambridge University Press, 2009)

HARRIS, M., and PARTINGTON, M. (eds), *Administrative Justice in the 21st Century* (Oxford, Hart Publishing, 1999)

LEWIS, N., and Birkinshaw, P., *When Citizens Complain: Reforming Justice and Administration* (Buckingham, Open University Press, 1993)

National Audit Office, *Citizen Redress: What citizens can do if things go wrong with public services* (HC 21, 2004–05) (London, The Stationery Office, 2005)

RICHARDSON, G., and GENN, H. (eds), *Administrative Law and Government Action* (Oxford, Clarendon Press, 1994)

SENEVIRATNE, M., *Ombudsmen—Public Services and Administrative Justice* (Cambridge, Cambridge University Press, 2002)

SMITH, R. G., *Medical Discipline, The Professional Conduct Jurisdiction of the General Medical Council, 1858–1990* (Oxford, Oxford University Press, 1994)

WOOLF, LORD, JOWELL, J., LE SUEUR, A. P., and DONNELLY, C. M., *De Smith's Judicial Review of Administrative Action* (6th edn, London, Sweet & Maxwell, 2009)

7

The family justice system

Introduction: law and the family

The role law should play in the regulation of family relationships is controversial. Some argue that law should have only a residual function leaving people to structure their lives as a matter of private choice and personal morality. Others argue that society has a legitimate interest in family policy, particularly where children are involved. Furthermore, if support is not given to families, this leads to other undesirable social consequences, for example anti-social behaviour, youth crime, and teenage pregnancy.

The institutional framework within which family policy is developed has undergone considerable change in recent years. Ministerial boundaries have been redrawn and new agencies created. To give just a few examples:

(1) Following the terrible case of Victoria Climbié, in 2003 a Children's Minister was appointed within the (then) Department for Education and Science. There are currently two ministers, within the Department of Education, responsible for policies relating to children and families.

(2) The flagship scheme, established in 1999, under the former Labour government, is the *Sure Start* programme. This aims to: increase the availability of childcare for all children; improve health and emotional development for young children; and support parents as parents and in their aspirations towards employment. Sure Start covers children from conception through to the age of 14, and up to the age of 16 for those with special educational needs and disabilities. One of the principal ways of delivering these objectives is through the creation of Sure Start Children's Centres. These bring together childcare, early education, health, and family support services for families with children under five years old. The programme has been taken forward by the Coalition government, though with some reduction in the number of centres.

(3) Under the Children Act 2004, the post of Children's Commissioner was created. Her function is to ensure that ministers are continually reminded of and advised about the child's perspective in policy-making. The continuation of this

post was subject to review by the Coalition government. In July 2011, the government announced plans to strengthen the independence of the Commissioner's function and bring her functions together with those of the Children's Rights Director, currently based in Ofsted—the Office for Standards in Education, Children's Services and Skills.

Law and the family

Within this complex and changing context, we turn to the principal functions of the law that relate to the family. These are:

(1) defining the rules for the validity of marriage;

(2) setting the bases on which marital relationships may be brought to an end through divorce or nullity;

(3) dealing with the consequences of divorce and other relationship breakdown, in particular questions of responsibility for children, financial support, and the division of property rights;

(4) providing a framework for the protection of children, including care and adoption;

(5) creating a framework for dealing with issues of domestic violence.

The last two are not dependent on the existence of a marriage; the first two are. The third is largely dependent on the existence of a marriage, though there is a limited though complex involvement of the law on the breakdown of *de facto* relationships.

The extent to which the law should be involved in the regulation of *de facto* relationships is currently the subject of considerable debate. For example, there has been fierce argument about the extent to which, if at all, the provisions for distributing property on the breakdown of a marriage should or should not apply to (heterosexual) *de facto* relationships where parties have lived together as a family, but without formally getting married.

Equally controversial have been questions of the extent to which, if at all, those involved in homosexual relationships might be subject to analogous principles. The Civil Partnerships Act 2004 provides a legal framework within which same-sex couples can obtain legal recognition of their relationship by forming a civil partnership. They may do so by registering as civil partners of each other provided: they are of the same sex; they are not already in a civil partnership or lawfully married; they are not within the prohibited degrees of relationship; they are both aged 16 or over (and, if either of them is under 18 and the registration is to take place in England and Wales or Northern Ireland, the consent of appropriate people or bodies has been obtained). The Act also sets out the legal consequences of forming a civil partnership, including the rights and responsibilities of civil partners. It is now argued that the concept of marriage itself should be amended to cover same-sex couples, and the Coalition government is developing proposals to legislate for this.

Underpinning much development of the domestic law of England and Wales, there is an important international law dimension, particularly relating to the law that affects children. Although the International Convention on the Rights of the Child 1989 does not have direct impact on English law (unlike the law of the European Union or the European Convention on Human Rights) it has considerable political significance. The effect of the Convention is kept under review by the Committee on the Rights of the Child, part of the United Nations Human Rights Commission. The proposed enhancement of the role of the Children's Commissioner, mentioned earlier, is designed in part to reflect the government's desire to be able to report positively on the protection of the rights of children.

Four particular issues have emerged in the last 20 years as factors that should influence not only the structure of the family justice system, but also the roles that people who work within that system should perform:

- First, there has been the important realization that if a marriage (or indeed other long-term relationship) breaks down, the process of bringing that relationship to a formal end should—wherever possible—reduce the inevitable feelings of stress, rejection, and failure that accompany such a process, rather than add to them.

- Secondly, there is a clear acceptance in law that, as far as possible, the welfare of the child must be protected.

- Thirdly, there is much concern about the extent to which parents who have separated should be able to maintain contact with their children.

- Fourthly, there is much greater awareness of the problem of domestic violence and other forms of abuse that occur in the family home. There have been important legal developments designed both to assist victims of abuse, and to send the broader educational message that such behaviour is not acceptable.

These issues have informed much recent development of the family justice system and the attitudes of those who practise within it.

Family justice: the institutional framework

Unlike many other countries, England and Wales currently has no specialist family court. Instead, there are complex arrangements with different courts determining the different issues that may arise in family law. Over the last few years, policy initiatives have been taken which can be seen as preliminary steps towards the creation of a separate family justice system:

(1) It has been accepted for some time that the relevant judiciary should be specially suited to undertake family work. In many instances judges must undergo specialist training before they can determine family cases, particularly those relating to children. The training embraces not only instruction on the law and

legal procedures, but also theories of child development and principles of social work. The difficulty of resolving cases relating to children can hardly be over-stated, since the outcome of such cases may be that children are removed from one parent and transferred to another, or are removed from the parent(s) alto-gether and placed under the care and supervision of others. Judicial training is designed to ensure that as appropriate decisions as possible are taken.

(2) More recently, the government decided that there should be a single code of pro-cedure for the different courts dealing with family matters. Under the Courts Act 2003, a Family Procedure Rules Committee was established with the ultimate objective of writing a new uniform set of Family Procedure Rules. At the end of 2005, the Committee completed the first stage of the process with the intro-duction of uniform rules relating to adoption arising from the Adoption and Children Act 2002. In 2010, the full set of rules was completed and was brought into effect in April 2011. While the primary objective of the new rules was to restate the existing rules in a clearer way (similar to the Civil Procedure Rules discussed in *Chapter 8*), a number of changes of procedure have been introduced. In particular, there is now a procedural requirement that anyone wishing to apply to a court either for an order relating to their children or an order relating to their finances must first attend a mediation information and assessment meeting to explore whether a result can be reached outside the formal court setting.

(3) One important, and controversial, respect in which the family courts operate differently from most other courts and tribunals is that much of their work is closed to the public. This has long been justified on the ground that publicity, especially between warring parents, could be extremely damaging to children. On the other hand, there have been counter-arguments that private hearings enable judges to reach decisions that do not always appear to be fair. The former Labour government struggled with this issue. Following two consultation exer-cises in 2006 and 2007, it announced at the end of 2008 that there would be a pro-gramme of changes to family court procedures designed to improve openness (*see Box 7.1*). The Coalition government has decided that further change should await the outcome of decisions on the review of family justice that reported in 2011 (*see Box 7.3*).

Box 7. 1   Reform in progress

Openness in the family courts

In December 2008, the Secretary of State for Justice announced that:

(1) From 27 April 2009, all courts which do family work have been made accessible to members of the media who are holders of a UK press card. The courts can restrict attendance if, for example, the welfare of the child requires it, or for the safety and

Box 7.1 *Continued*

protection of parties or witnesses. The media cannot identify the parties but can report the issues raised in particular cases.

(2) In November 2009, a 12-month pilot project was launched in three courts designed to improve the information coming out of the courts. It involves:

  • placing anonymized judgments online from some family cases so that the public can see how family courts work and how decisions were reached;

  • giving parties involved a copy of the judgment at the conclusion of their case so that they have a record of what was decided and why; and

  • looking at the practicalities of retaining judgments so that children involved in proceedings can access them when they are older.

(3) The government would consult on whether adoption proceedings can be made more open.

Source: Adapted from <www.official-documents.gov.uk/document/cm75/7502/7502.pdf>.

(4) The government created the Family Justice Council to keep the family justice system as a whole under review (*see Box 7.2*).

Box 7.2   Reform in progress

Family Justice Council

The Council was established in July 2004. Its terms of reference require it to facilitate the delivery of better and quicker outcomes for families and children who use the family justice system by:

• promoting improved interdisciplinary working across the family justice system through inclusive discussion, communication, and coordination between all agencies;

• identifying and disseminating best practice throughout the family justice system by facilitating a mutual exchange of information between local committees and the Council, including information on local initiatives;

• consulting with government departments on current policy and priorities and securing best value from available resources;

• providing guidance and direction to achieve consistency of practice throughout the family justice system and submitting proposals for new practice directions where appropriate;

• promoting commitment to legislative principles and the objectives of the family justice system by disseminating advice and promoting inter-agency discussion, including by way of seminars and conferences as appropriate;

> **Box 7.2** *Continued*
>
> - promoting the effectiveness of the family justice system by identifying priorities for, and encouraging the conduct of, research;
> - providing advice and making recommendations to government on changes to legislation, practice, and procedure, which will improve the workings of the family justice system;
> - the Family Justice Council has been retained, following the Coalition government's review of public bodies; it now has the same chief executive as the Civil Justice Council (*see Chapter 8*).
>
> *Source:* Adapted from <www.judiciary.gov.uk/about-the-judiciary/advisory-bodies/fjc>.

Following publication of the Norgrove Review of Family Justice in November 2011, a complex package of very controversial reforms is being taken forward that will formally create a family court, and lead to a radical change in the ways in which family cases are dealt with, as recommended.

First, the government has decided that the time has now come to create a separate Family Court. The Crime and Courts Bill 2012 contains provisions that, when enacted, will result in this reform.

In terms of more fundamental change to the operation of the system, what particularly struck Norgrove were the delays in the current system, which could have very serious consequences, particularly where decisions relating to young children had to be made. The review wanted to encourage all those who work in the family justice system to think critically about the contribution they make to it and ask themselves whether there were ways in which their role might alter to make the whole process more efficient. The package of reforms that Norgrove recommended was complex (*see Box 7.3*). In February 2012, the government broadly accepted the recommendations. They will be implemented in a new Children and Families Bill. This is currently the subject of pre-legislative scrutiny being led by the Justice Select Committee. The bill will not be introduced into Parliament until May 2013.

> **Box 7.3**   Reform in progress
>
> Review of the family justice system
>
> The Norgrove review recommended the following.
>   *Changes to the system* including:
>
> - the creation of a new Family Justice Service to make sure agencies and professionals work together to make positive improvements in the system for children and families;

Box 7.3 *Continued*

- more judges who are specialists in family law to hear cases from start to finish to ensure consistency and confidence in the system;
- a simplified court structure making it easier for people using the courts to know where to go;
- more child focus and better training for professionals to make sure children's views are heard.

Changes to public law (which deals with the protection of children and taking them into care) to deliver results more quickly for children, including:

- a six-month time limit for all cases, save in exceptional circumstances;
- reducing reliance on unnecessary expert witnesses and reports;
- refocusing the courts on the core issue of determining whether the child should go into care.

Changes to private law (arrangements about children and money following separation and divorce) to create a simpler service for families who are separating, aimed at helping them and their children focus on reaching a safe, joint agreement, if possible, without going to court:

- a single online and phone help service to make it simpler for people to decide the most appropriate way forward and increase clarity of understanding;
- use of parenting agreements and a new 'child arrangements order' to bring together arrangements for children's care after separation, focusing on the child rather than 'contact' and 'residence';
- increased provision of mediation to prevent cases going to court unnecessarily.

The rest of this chapter considers current legal arrangements for dealing with family cases; but readers will realise that a lot of the detail will change during the next two or three years.

Children

From October 1991 (when the Children Act 1989 came into force) there has been a common jurisdiction across all the tiers of the court structure for dealing with issues relating to children. The structure is designed to enable cases to be disposed of at the most appropriate court level. Three levels of courts need to be considered:

- family proceedings courts;
- county courts; and
- the High Court.

Family proceedings courts

Family proceedings courts are magistrates' courts that deal with family matters. The lay magistrates who sit in them are drawn from specially selected family panels, whose members have all been trained and receive on-going training. The district judges who sit in family proceedings are also specially trained. In this jurisdiction they sit with lay justices. Family proceedings courts have jurisdiction to deal with both public and private law cases relating to children (*see Box 7.4*). All public law cases start in the family proceedings court. (Despite their name, family proceedings courts do not deal with divorce.)

Box 7.4   Legal system explained

Public law and private law children cases

In relation to children, it is essential to distinguish between public law cases and private law cases. *Public law* cases are brought by public authorities—in particular the social services departments of local authorities—or other agencies such as the National Society for the Prevention of Cruelty to Children (NSPCC). They may be seeking orders from the court relating to the care, supervision, or emergency protection of children. *Private law* cases are those brought by private individuals, usually the parents of the child, seeking orders relating to the child in the context of a divorce or the separation of the parents.

One of the principal objectives of the Children Act 1989 was to ensure that the voice of the child was heard. Therefore, in most public law applications, the court appoints a children's guardian to assist the child, unless the court is satisfied that this is not needed to protect the interests of the child. The role of the guardian is to ensure that the court is fully informed of facts relevant to determining the best interests of the child. The guardian also seeks to ensure that the court is made fully aware of the child's feelings and wishes. Guardians are provided by Children and Family Court Advisory and Support Service (CAFCASS), established in 2001 by the Criminal Justice and Court Services Act 2000. In defined cases, the guardian is also required to appoint a solicitor to act for the child, to ensure proper legal representation.

In private law cases, an analogous role is played by the Children and Family Reporter, also appointed by CAFCASS.

This is a busy jurisdiction. In 2011, public law applications involving nearly 22,500 children were made; private law applications involving just under 19,500 children were also made to the Family Proceedings Court during the same period.

The county court

County courts are divided into five distinct categories:

- non-divorce county courts, with no power to deal with any family law matters;

- divorce county courts, which can issue all private law family proceedings but from which, if a matter is contested, it is referred to a family hearing centre for trial;
- family hearing centres, which can issue and hear all private law family cases whether or not they are contested;
- care centres, with full powers to deal with all private law and public law matters;
- specialized adoption centres, which have power to issue, hear, and process adoption applications under guidance issued by the President of the Family Division.[1]

The circuit judges and district judges who deal with matters relating to children under the Children Act 1989 are specially nominated for family work. They are not so nominated without receiving special training and guidance. (One exception is that circuit judges who are not nominated can still hear cases involving requests for injunctions arising from allegations of domestic violence and some other matrimonial work.) They are formally known as 'nominated care judges'.[2] The circuit judges who are nominated have full powers to deal with all public and private law matters. District judges who have been nominated as care judges can hear uncontested public law cases, and contested private law cases. In addition to the nominated care judges there is also a group of circuit family judges who can deal with private law matters, but not public law matters.

County courts have a very large case-load. In 2011, they received private law applications relating to just under 90,000 children, plus public law applications relating to just over 6,500 children.

The High Court

Although there are no formal training requirements for High Court judges who do family work, nonetheless they sit in a separate division of the High Court—the Family Division. There are 17 such judges, plus a President, specially appointed to give leadership to this specialist group of judiciary. The smallness of their number enables them to operate in a collegiate style with a fair degree of common purpose and approach.

The High Court has power to hear all cases relating to children. It has exclusive power to decide matters relating to wardship, whereby the court assumes responsibility for the child, taking over from the parents. It also hears appeals from family proceedings courts. The work-load of the High Court is numerically trivial by comparison with those of the other two courts—public law applications affecting just 378 children and private law applications affecting 873 children in 2011. But its more

---

[1] *Adoption Proceedings—A New Approach* (London, Lord Chancellor's Department, 2001).
[2] There are also designated family judges who, besides undertaking normal judicial duties as nominated care judges, also chair local Family Court Business Committees and Family Court Forums—both intended to improve working relationships between the courts and their users.

important decisions are reported and thus develop the jurisprudence of the family justice system.

Orders

The Children Act 1989 provides for a wide range of orders that can be made by the courts. They include:

- care/supervision orders;
- emergency protection orders;
- exclusion requirements; and
- 'section 8' orders.

Care/supervision orders

These are made on application by either a local authority or the NSPCC (which is the only 'authorized person' under the Children Act 1989 able to bring such proceedings). Before an order may be made, the court must be satisfied either that a child is suffering or is likely to suffer significant harm, and that the harm or likelihood of harm is attributable to:

(1) the care given to the child; or

(2) the likelihood of the care not being what it would be reasonable to expect a parent to give a child;

or that the child is beyond parental control.

If the court is so satisfied, it may make an order:

(1) placing the child in the care of a designated local authority; or

(2) putting the child under the supervision of a designated local authority or probation officer.

Such orders cannot be made in relation to a child who has reached the age of 17 (16 if the child is married).

The effect of a *care order* is to impose a duty on the local authority to keep the child in care, to exercise parental responsibility over the child, and determine the extent to which a parent or guardian may meet his or her parental responsibility towards the child. The effect of a *supervision order* is to impose a duty on the supervisor to advise, assist, and befriend the child, and to take the necessary action to give effect to the order, including whether or not to apply to vary or discharge it.

Emergency protection orders

These are made where the court is satisfied that there is reasonable cause to believe that a child is suffering, or is likely to suffer, significant harm if not removed to accommodation provided by the applicant, or that the child should not remain in the place where she is currently living. Emergency protection orders may be sought where any-one, including a local authority, believes that access to a child is being unreasonably refused.

Exclusion requirements

From October 1997, the courts have had power to order the exclusion of a suspected abuser from a child's home, where ill-treatment of the child is alleged, and either an interim care order or an emergency protection order has been made. A power of arrest can be added to the exclusion requirement, so that anyone in breach may be instantly arrested. Before an exclusion requirement can be ordered, the court must be satis-fied that there will still be a person remaining in the premises with the child, and that that person has agreed to care for the child and has consented to the exclusion requirement.

'Section 8' orders

Orders made under section 8 of the Children Act 1989 include:

- *residence* orders, determining where the child should live;
- *contact* orders, deciding whom the child may see;
- *prohibited steps* orders, to prevent a defined action(s) taking place; and
- *specific issue* orders, dealing with particular aspects of a child's upbringing.

During 2011, well over 114,000 section 8 orders were made,[3] the vast bulk of them relating to residence and contact.

Problems with the enforcement of these orders resulted in the government intro-ducing new rules for dealing with parental separation. The Children and Adoption Act 2006 has two objectives.

First, it wants to promote the quality of contact between parent and child. The Act gives the court power to direct a party to take part in an activity that would promote contact with a child. Contact activities include attendance at programmes, classes, or counselling sessions designed to improve the quality of contact time, or to address a person's violent behaviour. This may occur during the proceedings, even if the court does not make a contact order, or by making such activity a condition in a contact order.

Secondly, it gives the court wider powers in cases involving breach of a contact order by adding: a power to make enforcement orders imposing an unpaid work require-ment; and a power to order one person to pay compensation to another for a finan-cial loss caused by a breach. These powers are in addition to their powers relating to

---

[3] Data in this chapter, save those relating to adoptions, are derived from Ministry of Justice, *Judicial and Court Statistics, 2011* (London, Ministry of Justice, 2012), available at <www.justice.gov.uk/statistics/courts-and-sentencing/judicial-annual-2011>, Chapter 2, and related Tables.

contempt of court and their ability to alter the residence and contact arrangements relating to a child.

Adoption

The other main activity of the courts in relation to children concerns adoption, whereby the rights, duties, and obligations of a child's natural parents are legally extinguished and are vested, by order of the court, in the adoptive parents. It is essential that the court is satisfied that the adoptive parents are suitable and have consented to the adoption. Where possible it is also necessary to obtain the consent of the parents (including any guardian with parental responsibility), though this may be dispensed with if there is evidence that the natural parent has persistently ill-treated the child or that consent is being unreasonably withheld. Once again, the primary objective of the courts is to safeguard and promote the welfare of the child. This includes taking the views of the child into account.

After a long period of gestation, major changes to the law of adoption were made by the Adoption and Children Act 2002. The intention was, while continuing to protect children, to make it easier for those wishing to adopt children to do so, thereby increasing the number of adoptions currently sanctioned by the legal process. The government is particularly anxious that more children, currently in the care of local authorities, should be adopted. Statistics from the Office for National Statistics show that the number of adoptions in England and Wales in 2011 was 4,734, an increase of six per cent since 2010; in 2011, most children adopted (62 per cent) were aged between one and four years, rising from 58 per cent in 2010; the percentage of children adopted who were born outside marriage increased slightly to 82 per cent in 2011, up from 80 per cent in 2010. Following Norgrove, the government remains determined to raise these figures and make the process less drawn out.

Matrimonial matters

The other principal work of the courts in the context of the family relates to the dissolution of marriages. For these purposes the courts are the county courts, except those designated as *non-divorce county courts*.

A marriage may be dissolved in two ways: divorce and nullity. *Divorce* is much more frequently used. To obtain a divorce, the petitioner must prove that the marriage has broken down irretrievably. This can be demonstrated by proof of: adultery; behaviour that the petitioner cannot reasonably be expected to live with; desertion for at least two years; two years' separation where the respondent consents; five years' separation where there is no such consent. Evidence of irretrievable breakdown is usually considered by a district judge. If proved, a provisional measure, the *decree nisi*, is made. The divorce becomes final only after a final decision, the *decree absolute*. The existence of this two-stage process is to provide an opportunity, albeit rarely used, for second thoughts. Most cases are disposed of on the basis of paper evidence without the need for a hearing.

Where children are involved, the court must be satisfied with the arrangements for their welfare. These must be written down and, if possible, agreed between the parents. If agreement is not possible, the judge may order the parents to come to court so that the issues may be resolved. If the issues are uncontested at this point, the judge may issue a *section 8 order* (*see 'Section 8' orders*).

The divorce case-load is enormous. In 2011, just under 130,000 petitions for divorce were filed, a decline of three per cent on the previous year; 119,610 decrees absolute were granted.

Nullity is the other mode of dissolving a marriage. However, this can be used only where there is proof that the marriage either was void in the first place (e.g. because one of the parties was under the age of 16 or was already married), or was voidable (e.g. because one of the parties was pregnant by someone else at the time of the marriage or the marriage was not consummated due to incapacity or wilful refusal). To obtain a decree of nullity, a two-stage process, similar to the divorce process, must be gone through. By contrast with divorce, this mode of dissolution is rare: around 350 petitions were filed in 2011, and around 200 were granted.

Judicial separation is an alternative procedure for those who do not wish to or who for some reason cannot get divorced. It does not terminate the marriage, but legally absolves the parties to a marriage from the obligation to live together. Just 227 applications for separation decrees were filed in 2011; 155 were granted.

Ancillary relief

Ancillary relief refers to the powers of the court to make orders linked to divorce or other matrimonial proceedings. These relate to maintenance (periodical payments to an ex-spouse) and to lump sum payments or property orders (usually dealing with the matrimonial home). As with divorce, the courts for these purposes are the county courts.

The powers of the courts to deal with maintenance orders relating to the children of the marriage have to a certain extent been taken over by the child support system (*see Child support*). Since April 1993, most new applications for maintenance have been dealt with by the Child Support Agency (now part of the Child Maintenance and Enforcement Commission). Initially, the plan was to transfer then existing court orders to the Agency. However, the controversies and operational chaos that surrounded the Agency led to an indefinite deferment of this plan. Thus county courts still have to make a significant number of orders relating to the maintenance of or other financial provision for children. In 2011, just over 12,000 such orders were made.

In 2011, the courts made over 50,000 orders relating to the payment of a lump sum or the transfer of property and around 10,000 orders relating to the division of pension rights or attachment of earnings (which requires an employer to pay a proportion of a person's wages to his former spouse). The large majority of applications were uncontested by the parties, requiring no court hearing.

Procedural reform

Detailed reform of procedures relating to ancillary relief was introduced in June 2000. These were designed to promote early settlement between the parties, to eliminate unnecessary delay, and to keep costs down. As with broader reforms to the civil justice system (*see Chapter 8*), the key is active judicial case management, combined with the need for proportionality—ensuring that the costs of the proceedings are proportionate to the assets in dispute. Both sides are required to make the other party aware of how costs are mounting up, particularly if there is unnecessary delay in reaching a conclusion. A further innovation is that the parties are required to undergo a financial dispute resolution appointment in which, with the assistance of a judge, an attempt is made to help the parties agree an outcome, rather than have a solution imposed on them by the judge.

Child support

One of the most controversial structural changes made to the family justice system has been the creation of the child support system by the Child Support Act 1991.

The principle behind its establishment in 1993 was straightforward. Far too many single parents, mostly women, found it impossible either to obtain an order for the maintenance of their children or, if they did obtain one, to enforce it. A consequence of this was that lone parents were heavily dependent on the provision of social security benefits for the financial resources needed to bring up their children, rather than being supported by the child's natural but absent parent. Indeed during the preceding decade, while the number of children living in lone-parent families increased substantially, the proportion of children receiving maintenance fell. In 1989, 23 per cent of lone parents claiming income support were receiving maintenance, compared to around 50 per cent in 1979. The child support system was intended to reverse this decline, by providing consistent rules for assessing maintenance liability and a readily accessible means for collecting and enforcing payment that was due. A system for getting absent parents to pay for their children had been introduced in Australia in the 1980s, apparently with great success. Thus, it was argued, a similar scheme could be introduced in the United Kingdom.

From the outset the British scheme was dogged by controversy. One crucial difference between the British and Australian models was that, in the former, for every pound paid by the absent parent a pound of social security benefit was lost; in Australia, for every dollar of maintenance paid by the absent parent, the parent with care lost only 85 cents of her social security payments. Although the Australian model was less advantageous from a purely public expenditure point of view, it had the supreme psychological advantage that the absent parent felt that (usually) he was, by making the payments, actually improving the quality of life for his child(ren). In the United Kingdom, there was no such positive incentive.

The force of these criticisms was to a limited degree acknowledged in the Child Support Act 1995. This introduced the *child maintenance bonus*, intended as an incentive to encourage parents with care into work, and the *departures* scheme that allowed for the normal rules for the assessment of child support liability to be departed from in order to take account of exceptional circumstances not recognized in the formula-based assessment.

However, these changes did not go far enough. In 2000, the Labour government passed further legislation—the Child Support, Pensions and Social Security Act 2000—to enable reform of the child support system to be put in place. The principal problems to be dealt with were:

- while the Child Support Agency (CSA) had almost 1.5 million children on its books, only around 300,000 gained financially from child support payments;
- the complexity of the formula led to long delays in assessing liability;
- the CSA had little time to help parents understand what they should pay or to chase up non-payment; and
- families living on income support did not gain from the payment of maintenance as their benefit was reduced by an amount equal to the maintenance paid.

The Child Support, Pensions and Social Security Act 2000:

- replaced the formula for assessing child support with a simpler system of rates;
- simplified the processes for applying for child support and the way in which child support liability was decided;
- set clear penalties for parents who deliberately misrepresented their circumstances to the CSA—and for those who refuse to provide the information needed to calculate liability and collect maintenance;
- established the possibility of varying the normal rate of maintenance liability to recognize certain exceptional costs and sources of income; and
- improved provisions for establishing paternity.

Given the history, there was much scepticism as to whether the problems that attracted so much criticism would in fact be addressed, particularly given the reluctance of absent parents to co-operate with the working of the scheme. Indeed, implementation of the new scheme was delayed because of problems with the supporting information technology. The reformed scheme started, for new cases only, in March 2003.

The Agency continued to be subject to serious criticism, with constant and critical comments from the Independent Case Examiner, and adverse reports from the Parliamentary Ombudsman. It was the subject of an investigation by the Work and Pensions Select Committee of the House of Commons. All these pressures led to the government, in 2006, commissioning a special review of the child support scheme by Sir David Henshaw. He argued for a fresh start with a redesigned scheme. The government accepted many of his recommendations and published a further white paper—*A New System of Child Maintenance*—in 2006. In June 2007, the Child Maintenance and Other Payments Bill was introduced into the House of Commons. The resulting Act established the Child Maintenance and Enforcement Commission.

Unfortunately, these reforms have not been as successful as the present Coalition government would like. It has therefore decided to abolish the Commission.

It has, instead, developed further proposals designed to encourage separating parents to reach their own family agreements about how maintenance should be provided. This is supported by the Child Maintenance Options service, designed to assist parties to reach these agreements.

Where an agreement cannot be reached, there will be a new statutory Child Maintenance Service, run within the Department for Work and Pensions, which will, in the last resort, impose an outcome on parents. A feature of the new service will be that charges for using the service will be imposed. Thus there will be financial incentives on parents to reach agreements, rather than rely on the statutory system. The Coalition government has recently completed a consultation on details of the new scheme which is intended to start operations more or less at once, with all the old CSA cases being closed by 2017.

The Child Support scheme never worked as it was intended to do. Indeed, there is evidence that, notwithstanding the efforts in other parts of the family justice system to reduce tensions between former partners, the child support system actually exacerbated problems between them. At present, this is not a part of the English legal system that is currently fit for purpose. It will be interesting to see whether the new scheme will make any significant difference; past experience is not encouraging.

Domestic violence

Another way in which the family justice system has been transformed over the last 25 years has been the recognition of the problem of domestic violence and the need for the law and legal procedures to deal with cases swiftly and effectively. There are now three principal items of legislation relevant in this context:

- Part IV of the Family Law Act 1996;
- the Protection from Harassment Act 1997; and
- the Forced Marriage (Civil Protection) Act 2007.

Part IV of the Family Law Act 1996

This Act provides a set of remedies in domestic violence cases, which can be sought either in the county court or the magistrates' court or (rarely) in the High Court. Two types of order may be made:

- a *non-molestation order* to prohibit a person from behaving in a particular way towards another or which may seek to prohibit molestation in general; and

- an *occupation order*, which can define or regulate the rights of a person to occupy a home (irrespective of his ownership rights in that home).

Occupation orders are available not only to married couples, but also to cohabiting couples, others who live or have lived in the same household as the person seeking the order (though not tenants, boarders, or lodgers), certain relatives (such as parents, or brothers or sisters), and those who have agreed to marry. From July 2007, it has been a criminal offence to breach a non-molestation order.

If the court thinks that the respondent has used or has threatened violence against either the applicant or any child of the applicant, then the court must attach a power of arrest to the order, unless satisfied that the applicant or child will be adequately protected without such a power being attached.

In addition, the court may at the same time add an *exclusion requirement* to an *emergency protection order* or *interim care order* made under the Children Act 1989 (*see Orders*), so that the suspected abuser (rather than the abused child) may be removed from the dwelling.

There is a substantial case-load arising from these provisions. In 2011, over 18,000 non-molestation orders and over 3,000 occupation orders were made.

Protection from Harassment Act 1997

This Act was initially introduced to combat the problem of stalking, but it applies more generally to the victims of harassment. Section 3 allows civil proceedings to be taken against anyone pursuing a course of harassment. The remedies available are an injunction—an order to prevent such behaviour in the future—and/or damages. Since September 1998, the courts have had power to make breach of an injunction enforceable by warrant of arrest. No information is available on the use of these provisions.

Forced Marriage (Civil Protection) Act 2007

This Act came into force on 25 November 2008. It enables 15 designated county courts to make forced marriage protection orders to prevent forced marriages from occurring and to offer protection to victims who might have already been forced into a marriage. Data on the use of these provisions is also not available.

The practitioners

Lawyers

Given the fact that so many aspects of family life are regulated by law, in particular the issues relating to children, relationship breakdown, and other financial matters, it is inevitable that legal practitioners should be deeply involved in family law issues. This is a major area for legal specialism, with large numbers of lawyers offering family law services. A considerable part of the legal aid budget is devoted to family law issues.

Practitioners have given considerable thought to their proper role in assisting the resolution of family disputes. For example, should they engage in heavily adversarial forms of litigation designed to advance their clients' interests, irrespective of the interests of the other party to the marriage or relationship and the children? Or should they adopt a more conciliatory approach?

The perception that lawyers often added to the problems of separating couples rather than helping their resolution led, some years ago, to the formation of the Solicitors' Family Law Association—now called Resolution. (There is an equivalent for barristers—the Family Law Bar Association.) It aims to bring a less hostile atmosphere to the resolution of family disputes.

Research suggests that, in general, solicitors have been rather successful at not exacerbating the conflicts between couples. This is not to say that lawyers are above criticism in the area of family disputes. For example, they are criticized for:

- a desultory approach to negotiation;
- large case-loads but with little activity on each individual case;
- high costs; and
- high levels of pressure to reach final settlements, as cases approach court.

Nevertheless, client demand for legal services to assist in the resolution of family disputes has remained high. Surveys of clients' responses to the legal services provided have, in general, been positive.

One of the ways in which practitioners have sought to develop the nature of their work with clients in the family law area has been through schemes of specialist training. For a number of years, the Law Society has run a *Childrens' Panel*, aimed particularly at solicitors who act for children in public law cases. Admission to the panel involves the lawyers demonstrating appropriate levels of qualifications and experience.

In addition, during 1999, the Law Society announced that it would establish a Family Law Panel. The Solicitors' Family Law Association also established its own Family Law Panel and, in 1999, it launched a scheme for the accreditation of those lawyers who sought to join the panel.

Those who practise family law have recognized the particular character of the work they have to undertake, dealing not only with the very considerable complexities of the law but also the strong emotional context within which such work has to be carried out. As the need for special training of the judiciary has been accepted, so too the importance of special training for practitioners has been acknowledged.

Mediation and mediators

Notwithstanding the efforts of professional lawyers to shape the nature of family law practice to the needs of clients, successive governments have made changes to the ways in which family disputes are resolved, particularly cases paid for by the state. This has led to the view that a preferable way of resolving family disputes should be through *mediation* outside the courts, rather than *litigation* in the courts.

Mediation is a form of assisted negotiation. However, instead of a negotiation taking place just between the parties to the dispute and/or their representatives, mediation involves the intervention of an impartial third party, the mediator. The mediator's function is to try to help the parties to a dispute reach an agreement acceptable to both sides. While the mediator cannot impose a solution on the parties, the presence of the mediator can contribute to the pressure to settle disputes.

Mediation has been used to resolve family disputes for many years. Experience suggests that it is often successful in bringing the parties to an agreement. There is also evidence that it is liked by those who have gone through the process. Nevertheless, despite the enthusiasm of those who offer mediation services, only a small number of parties to family disputes voluntarily ask for their disputes to be mediated.

Notwithstanding the lack of consumer demand, official policy is that the use of mediation in the context of family disputes should be encouraged. At least one of the reasons in the government's mind is that use of mediation may save costs.

Part III of the Family Law Act 1996 amended the Legal Aid Act 1988 by providing that legal aid money could be used to pay for mediation services. These provisions were to apply in the context of all 'family matters', defined broadly to cover most of the issues considered in this chapter, not just divorce proceedings. The key test in the legislation was whether or not mediation might be suitable in any particular case. A code of practice provided that mediation would clearly not be suitable if there was any fear of violence; nor, more generally, if either of the parties was not willing to use mediation.

The teeth in the new provisions were in section 29, which provided that, before legal aid for representation of a party before a court could be granted, the party to a family dispute who was seeking legal aid (usually the woman) had to attend a mediation meeting to determine whether or not mediation would be suitable. These provisions were introduced in September 1998, in six pilot areas.

The impact of these provisions on costs and outcomes was researched on behalf of the Legal Aid Board. The researchers found that the number of cases deemed not suitable for mediation rose substantially, and that relatively few cases got beyond the intake appointment stage. A number of more specific problems were also identified:

- solicitors remained reluctant to use mediation, and were critical of the delays inherent in the process, particularly where mediation would clearly not be suitable;

- very little could be done at present to engage the second party, if he would not attend the intake appointment. Even a case deemed suitable for mediation cannot go to mediation if the second party was not willing to contemplate mediation; and

- a lot of resource was being expended on the intake appointment where no actual mediation resulted.

Notwithstanding all these difficulties, the government decided that family mediation should remain an important form of dispute resolution for family disputes. It is a central feature of the review of family justice (*see Box 7.3*). Reforms to legal aid, coming into effect in April 2013, make mediation even more central to the family dispute resolution process (*see Reform of legal aid*).

Funding family law cases

For decades, family law matters were subject to special rules for the purpose of legal aid funding. These were retained when the former legal aid scheme became the Community Legal Service (*see Chapter 10, Community Legal Service: civil legal aid*). Under the Community Legal Service's *Funding Code* family proceedings are defined to include all proceedings which arise out of family relationships, including cases involving the welfare of children. Special priority is given to domestic violence cases.

Following amendments to the funding code in 2007, five levels of service are available in family cases. *Legal Help* covers the initial meeting and any follow-up advice. Cases not resolved at this stage may be referred to *Family Mediation*. Where this is not appropriate, *Family Help (Lower)* exists to provide more substantial advice, assistance, and negotiation to resolve disputes. This can also be used to support families through Family Mediation. *Family Help (Higher)* is used where is it necessary to issue proceedings with a view to securing the early resolution of a family dispute; it does not cover preparation for or representation at any final hearing. Where needed *Legal Representation* is available.

Children Act proceedings

Funding is automatically available for a child in respect of whom an application for a care or supervision order, a child assessment order, an emergency protection order, or the extension or discharge of an emergency protection order has been made. In addition funding is available for any parent of or person with parental responsibility for such a child. A child against whom a secure accommodation order might be made restricting the child's liberty will also obtain legal services funding. This applies only to first instance proceedings. However, funding for any appeal is subject to a merits test—assessing the merits of the case. A limited merits test also operates in the case of adoption proceedings.

In the case of private law children disputes, legal representation may be refused unless reasonable attempts to resolve the dispute through negotiation or in other ways without recourse to proceedings have been made. A similar principle applies in cases relating to financial provision and other proceedings, such as contested divorce proceedings or nullity proceedings. Special rules apply to child abduction cases.

Reform of legal aid

Total expenditure on family cases is substantial, currently over two-thirds of the Community Legal Service budget. For many years, practitioners have reported that achieving profitability in legal aid practice is increasingly difficult; there were signs that the Legal Services Commission had begun to share that concern. However, these arguments have not found favour with the Coalition government. Under the Legal Aid, Sentencing and Punishment of Offenders Act 2012, major changes to legal aid come into effect in April 2013. In short, instead of legal aid potentially covering any matter of law, in future only defined categories of work will be regarded as within the scope of the legal aid scheme and therefore eligible for legal aid funding.

In the case of family matters, only the following matters will be within the scope of the legal aid scheme:

- public family law cases regarding protection of children;
- private family cases where there is evidence of domestic violence;
- private law children cases where there is evidence of child abuse;
- child abduction matters;
- representation for child parties in private family cases;
- legal advice in support of mediation;
- domestic violence injunction cases;
- forced marriage protection order cases.

Anything else will not be fundable by legal aid. This is likely to hurt women particularly badly, as they tended to be funded by legal aid more often than men.

Conclusion

Family law disputes involve extremely difficult issues which must be handled with particular care—especially where children are involved. This is an area both of substantive law and of legal practice which has evolved considerably in recent years, and will continue to do so. It is also an area in which the impact of research on the development of law and practice has been significant.

Looking to the future, many of the issues likely to come onto the agenda for the reform of family law will be very controversial. Although governments may claim that they are happy for individuals to make their own choices about how they should structure their lives and relationships, a desire to get 'back to basics' and to promote 'family values' is one that successive Prime Ministers seem to find hard to resist.

Questions

Use the self-test questions on the Online Resource Centre to test your understanding of the topics covered in this chapter and receive tailored feedback:

www.oxfordtextbooks.co.uk/orc/partington13_14/

Weblinks

Check the Online Resource Centre for a selection of annotated weblinks allowing you to easily research topics of particular interest:

www.oxfordtextbooks.co.uk/orc/partington13_14/

Blog items

See www.martinpartington.com (access via the Online Resource Centre)

Issues discussed include: the reform of family justice; the Family Proceedings Rules; the use of mediation; the importance of empirical research to shape policy development; domestic violence.

Further reading

BARLOW, A., DUNCAN, S., GRACE, J., and Park, A., *Cohabitation, Marriage and the Law: Social Change and Legal Reform in the 20th Century* (Oxford, Hart Publishing, 2005)

BROPHY, J., and Smart, C., *Women-in-law: Explorations in Law, Family and Sexuality* (London, Routledge & Kegan Paul, 1985)

CRETNEY, S., *Law, Law Reform and the Family* (Oxford, Clarendon Press, 1998)

—— *Same-sex Relationships: From Odious Crime to Gay Marriage* (Oxford, Oxford University Press, 2006)

—— MASSON, J. M., BAILEY-HARRIS, R., and PROBERT, R., *Principles of Family Law* (8th edn, London, Sweet & Maxwell, 2008)

DAVIES, G., *Partisans and Mediators: The Resolution of Divorce Disputes* (Oxford, Clarendon Press, 1998)

—— CRETNEY, S., and COLLINS, J., *Simple Quarrels: Negotiations and Adjudication in Divorce* (Oxford, Clarendon Press, 1994)

—— EEKELAAR, J., and MACLEAN, M. (eds), *Family Law* (Oxford, Oxford University Press, 1994)

FREEMAN, M. D. A., *Understanding Family Law* (London, Sweet & Maxwell, 2007)

LIND, C., KEATING, H., and BRIDGEMAN, J., *Taking Responsibility, Law and the Changing Family* (Aldershot, Ashgate, 2010)

PARKINSON, L., *Family Mediation* (2nd revised edn, Bristol, Family Law, 2011)

ROBERTS, M., *Mediation in Family Disputes: Principles of Practice* (3rd edn, Aldershot, Ashgate Publishing, 2008)

STRANG, H., and BRAITHEWAITE, J., *Restorative Justice and Family Violence* (Cambridge, Cambridge University Press, 2004)

WIKELEY, N., *Child Support: Law and Policy* (Oxford, Hart Publishing, 2006)

8

The civil and commercial justice system

Introduction: civil and commercial justice

The scope of the civil and commercial justice system is huge, embracing a wide range of issues relating to legal obligations and entitlements. It is in this context that many of the relationships between law and society considered in *Chapter 2* are seen to operate—particularly those relating to law and economic order. This is the part of the English legal system where the protection of property and other rights may be asserted, and where questions of the ownership of land, or intellectual property, or other forms of personal property are determined. So too are the consequences of breaches of contract and acts of negligence.

Much of the conceptual framework of the civil law has been shaped by the common law. The fundamental principles of contract, negligence, trusts, and property, and the principles of the law of equity have all been created by judges. These days, in response to considerable social pressures, most common law principles have either been supplemented or in many cases replaced by legislation. Parliament has enacted measures, usually designed to protect the weaker party, which the common law was unable adequately to establish. Obvious examples are measures relating to the protection of consumers or tenants or employees. A great deal of the work of the civil justice courts is taken up with the application of fundamental common law principles, as moderated by modern protective legislation.

There are constant pressures to add to the scope of civil justice. For example:

- as commercial interests become ever more complex and as the economy becomes more global, new demands for the protection of globalized interests arise;

- new forms of financial instrument have been created to take advantage of the internationalization of banks and other players in the capital markets, which need protection not only within English domestic law but also taking European and other foreign legal regimes into account;

- new technologies present major challenges. For example, there is much current debate about the legal implications of the use of the internet for commercial activity on principles of the law of contract. How are consumers and suppliers of goods and services provided through the internet to be protected? Issues are emerging as to how to regulate use of the internet to spread defamatory statements, or pornography; and

- the legal implications of the new bio-technologies must be addressed. What can be patented? Which legal system should provide protection of the intellectual and other property rights involved? What are the legal implications of the human genome project?

While these issues may not routinely trouble the minds of district judges dealing with a list of possession cases, they emphasize the point that the civil and commercial branches of the English legal system cannot be divorced from their social and economic context. The legal system always needs to change in response to external social and economic pressures. Apart from any other consideration, if the English legal system does not respond, other legal systems will. The globalization of economic activity implies increased globalization of legal activity. If those who seek the law's protection cannot find it in England, they will take their work elsewhere.

Notwithstanding these broader considerations, the bulk of the work of the courts is devoted to more mundane matters: dealing with the consequences of people getting into debt, or breaking their contracts, or suffering personal injury (negligence). There are also more specialist areas of activity—for example relating to bankruptcy and the winding up of companies, or trade mark protection. The civil and commercial justice system plays a significant role, both in economic life and in the regulation of other social relationships, by seeking to ensure that bargains are kept, other rights are protected, and that compensation for the adverse consequences of legally unacceptable behaviour is awarded to those who have been affected.

The importance of these propositions is reinforced when one considers what happens in those countries where the rule of law to regulate social and economic behaviour is not accepted. It is extremely hard to attract investment into a country where there can be no guarantee that contracts will be enforced or property rights upheld.

Litigation and society: a compensation culture?

One complaint that is often heard is that modern society has become too litigious. It is asserted that people are too willing to rush to court when something has gone wrong. It is argued we have created a 'compensation culture'. This needs thinking about carefully.

It could be argued that, with better education, more people can now use the procedures and facilities that in the past were open only to the rich and powerful. Thus rather than being a bad thing, an increase in the use of litigation may indicate that ordinary people are no longer willing to accept things without question, as they might have done before. On that basis an increase in litigation to assert rights may not only be expected, but to a degree welcomed.

Against this, it may be argued that there comes a point where the level of litigation suggests that something rather different has happened. People have acquired a willingness to complain and to seek to put the blame on others in situations where they should be taking responsibility themselves. This in turn may lead to unacceptable levels of resource—both cash and manpower—being expended on taking or defending cases in court which could be better spent in more socially productive activity. It may also lead to the view that the ability of the citizen to take sensible risks is being undermined.

In recent years, a number of developments have encouraged the view that a 'compensation culture' is developing in the United Kingdom. Particularly noteworthy are the television advertisements or the mobile phone messages encouraging those who have suffered personal injury or the mis-selling of insurance policies to claim. There have also been locations, particularly hospitals, where advertisements have appeared that seem designed to encourage people to think about taking proceedings against the hospital. The government is anxious to ensure that advertisements do not appear in inappropriate locations, and—more importantly—do not create false hopes amongst those who respond to them. But a blanket ban on such advertisements seems impractical.

Indeed, there is compelling empirical evidence that one of the key problems which continues to confront the civil justice system is that too many people still do not know how to assert their legal entitlements through the legal system, either through ignorance or through fear of the costs that may be involved.[1] Thus the view that *any* rise in levels of litigation is by definition a symptom of a society ill at ease with itself, as is sometimes suggested, should not be accepted uncritically. What is important is to support those with genuine and proper claims, while deterring those making claims that are wholly without foundation or merit. Achieving this goal is extremely difficult. One contribution to this would be the provision of more and better quality information about civil rights and obligations; but, if taken seriously, this would be a huge and expensive task. An alternative approach, which has been adopted elsewhere, is to limit the extent of liability, particularly for personal injury, so that claims would be admitted only where a defined percentage of injury has occurred; however, this is not currently on the agenda in England.

The provision of a civil justice system

One fundamental question that needs asking is: should the state provide a system of civil justice at all? Since the disputes arising in this context are, by and large, private disputes between private parties, why should they not make arrangements for resolving those disputes themselves? There are many answers to this provocative question, which go back to the important constitutional role of the legal system in the overall system of government:

(1) As discussed in *Chapter 3*, our common law system requires a mechanism for the development of the principles of the common law. Fundamental legal concepts cannot develop without the existence of the courts and the authority that our

---

[1] See Pleasance, P. and others, *Causes of Action: Civil Law and Social Justice* (Norwich, The Stationery Office, 2006).

constitutional arrangements give to the judges that sit in them. Although the law-making functions of Parliament and other institutions are now far more predominant than they were 100 years ago, modern statute law is still set in the common law context that has been developed by the senior courts.

(2) The very fact that statute law is now a much more significant source of law means that there is a constitutional need for a body—the court system—to provide independent interpretations of the meaning of statutory provisions. All legislation has social and political objectives. Much modern legislation is designed to reduce imbalances in power, for example between landlords and tenants, employers and employees, or manufacturers and consumers. If the courts did not exist, much of this protective legislation—designed to achieve a wide range of policy objectives, including altering the nature of the relationships between parties—would be rendered even less effective than is often the case in any event.

(3) A third reason is more legalistic. Article 6 of the European Convention on Human Rights, incorporated into English law by the Human Rights Act 1998, provides that people should have a right to a fair trial for the determination of civil as well as criminal matters. A court system is necessary to satisfy this international obligation.

(4) A fourth reason for the continued existence of a civil justice system is that there would be a danger that resort to private dispute resolution procedures would, in practice, be likely to benefit more those who could afford to establish them and take advantage of them than those who could not afford them. At least the rhetoric and ambition of the courts is that all those who appear before them should be treated equally, even if this does not always happen in practice.

Problems with the civil justice system

In recent years, there has been wide recognition that the civil justice system has not been operating effectively. The main criticisms were that:

- it costs too much to bring cases to court;
- the system is too slow;
- court procedures are unnecessarily complex; and
- even if an issue is decided by a court, it may be impossible to enforce the decision.

These are not new problems. For over 100 years, there have been numerous reviews of and attempts to change the civil justice system. (Indeed, these problems are not unique to England; they are found in most other countries with well-developed economies and justice systems.) 26 April 1999 saw the launch of a new set of principles as well as new rules for the operation of the civil justice system.

Access to Justice: reform of the civil justice system

The process began in 1994 when Lord Woolf was asked to undertake a review of the civil justice system. His report, *Access to Justice*, was published in 1996. His vision was that those who wanted to bring cases to court should be able to do so efficiently, and at a cost proportionate to the amount in dispute. At the same time, the court should be the forum of last resort; every encouragement should be given to parties to settle their own disputes. At its most ambitious, Lord Woolf sought to change the culture of litigation by creating a framework within which both professional lawyers and those who wished to take their own cases to court (litigants in person) could do so with their eyes focused on the issues which needed determination by a judge and setting aside those matters that were not essential to the determination of the issue.

Following a further review, the government accepted that a programme of change to the civil justice system should be introduced. This led to the enactment of the Civil Procedure Act 1997, which provided the statutory authority for the production of the Civil Procedure Rules (CPR).

Civil Procedure Rules 1999

Before 1999, civil litigation was subject to two distinct codes of procedure:

- the *Rules of the Supreme Court* for cases dealt with in the High Court; and
- the *County Court Rules* for cases heard in county courts.

These two bodies of procedural law had broadly the same purpose, but there were myriad differences between them that added to the complexity of proceedings. These two codes were replaced by a single code of procedural law, the *Civil Procedure Rules 1999*, made by the Civil Procedure Rule Committee.

Practice directions

The procedural rules are supplemented by *practice directions*, which contain directions about how the rules are to be used in practice. This has the very practical consequence that both practitioners and other potential users of the civil justice system must be as aware of the directions and the requirements they impose as of the rules themselves. The mix of rules and practice directions, and the frequency with which they were being amended following commencement of the new scheme, led to fears that it might result in the reintroduction of some of the complexity it was hoped the new system would eliminate. However, the pace of change has slackened and, in general, the new rules and directions have been widely welcomed.

Pre-action protocols

One of the most significant innovations of the post-Woolf era is that of *pre-action protocols*. These are in effect guides to good litigation practice, setting standards and timetables for the conduct of cases before court proceedings are started. They are negotiated and agreed by experienced practitioners, and approved by the Deputy Head of Civil Justice, a senior judge in the Court of Appeal. They are designed to ensure more exchange of information and fuller investigation of claims at an earlier stage so that potential litigants may be able better to assess the merits of a case and to ensure that proper steps are taken to resolve as many of the issues in dispute as possible, prior to the parties getting anywhere near a courtroom.

There are currently 12 protocols relating to defined classes of case: personal injury, clinical disputes, disease and illness claims, construction and engineering disputes, defamation, professional negligence, judicial review, housing disrepair, claims for possession based on rent arrears, possession claims based on mortgage or home purchase plan arrears in respect of residential property, dilapidations claims relating to commercial property, and low value personal injury claims arising from road traffic accidents. There is also a practice direction that sets out guidance as to pre-action steps in cases where there is no relevant protocol. The protocols are set out in the CPR.

Key features

The CPR have, at their heart, two key features: track allocation and case management.

Track allocation depends on the size and complexity of the case. There are three tracks:

- 'small claims track' for simpler, low value cases—currently up to £5,000 (£1,000 for personal injuries and housing);
- 'fast track' for moderately valued cases (usually between £5,000 and £25,000); and
- 'multi-track' for the most complex.

See Box 8.3 for proposals to change the boundaries between the tracks.

Following allocation, the progress of the case is determined by judges managing the timetable for the case. Each county court circuit has a *designated judge* who has responsibility for ensuring that cases are actively managed.

Both these principles—track allocation and case management—are directed to tackling delay, and trying to ensure that the process (and its cost) is proportionate to the value and complexity of what is in dispute.

Other reforms

Many other related reforms were introduced, including:

- *Legal language.* The language of the rules was changed to make it more easily understandable. For example, those who bring cases to court became 'claimants' rather than 'plaintiffs'; they swear or affirm 'statements of truth' instead of 'affidavits'; claimants now seek 'specified damages' instead of 'liquidated damages' or 'unspecified damages' instead of 'unliquidated damages'. The essential features of the case are set out in a 'statement of case' instead of 'pleadings'. There are numerous other examples. In short, the Rules seek to eliminate the Latin phrases and other old terminology that were thought to make legal proceedings less comprehensible than they should be.[2]

- *Forms.* A related development was that much work was done on the forms used to start and progress potential cases. Again this is designed to make it easier for the ordinary individual to use the courts, and to reduce professional costs by ensuring that particular documents do not always have to be specially drafted by professional advisers. The forms are available for download on the website of Her Majesty's Courts and Tribunals Service (HMCTS).

- *Use of experts.* Lord Woolf wanted to limit the use of experts to one, who would be there to assist the court, rather than to represent the interests of either side. This was felt to be too draconian a step to take. Nevertheless, the CPR provide that experts have a duty to help the court on matters within their expertise, and this duty overrides any obligation to the person by whom they have been instructed or by whom they are paid. Experts give evidence only if the court gives permission. Instructions to experts are no longer privileged, and thus their substance must be disclosed in their report. In practice, a single jointly appointed expert is becoming a common feature of civil litigation, save where the complexity of the issues warrants both sides having their own expert.

The purpose of the civil justice system: the forum of last resort

It might be thought that the primary purpose of the civil justice system was the resolution of disputes by a judge. While it would be overstating it to say that nothing could be further from the truth, the situation is much more complicated than that. The courts have long been used as a last resort in situations where the parties to a dispute cannot themselves resolve their differences. Even before the Woolf reforms were introduced, the 'typical' dispute was resolved by negotiation and settlement, not by a trial in court. The Woolf reforms reinforced the view that the courts must be the forum of last resort.

Latest available figures show that 1,553,983 civil cases started in 2011, a fall of four per cent compared to 2010. This continues the general downward trend seen since 2006. There were 52,660 trials and small claims hearings in 2011, a fall of 13 per cent from the previous year and lower than in any year from 2006. Thus, typical civil

---

[2] Of course, law students will still have to be aware of the old language, as an understanding of reported decisions made before the changes came into effect still depends on that knowledge. But for the future, things should be clearer.

proceedings are resolved outside the courtroom, not in it. The civil justice system is much more frequently used *indirectly* as part of the process of resolution, rather than *directly* with a case being tried before a judge.

There are huge incentives on parties to settle. Three may be particularly noted:

- *Costs.* The cost of litigation increases dramatically as the parties get closer to the courtroom door. It is at this point that the numbers of lawyers involved in a case tend to increase. Where barristers are used, their fees are significantly higher when they appear in court than when they are sitting in chambers providing written advice to clients;

- *The indemnity principle.* This provides that, in the usual case, the loser of the case pays a large proportion of the costs of the winner. Given that clear-cut cases should not be coming to court at all, and that therefore there is always some uncertainty about the outcome of a trial (described by one legal academic as a 'forensic lottery') this rule also helps to concentrate the minds of litigants;[3] and

- *Payments into court and offers to settle.* The CPR also provide that parties to proceedings may offer to settle a case or pay a sum of money into court. The formalities for making an offer or payment are set out in Part 36 of the CPR. If the offer or payment is not accepted, and the party who did not accept fails to do better at the end of any trial than the offer or payment in, then that party will be ordered to pay any costs incurred by the other side after the latest date on which such offer or payment could have been accepted without needing the permission of the court. The court has a discretion to depart from this principle where application of the rule would, in its view, be unjust.

The pre-Woolf system did little to prevent delay. Although there were incentives to settle, they did not really bite until a trial date was getting near. The speed at which a trial date approached was on the whole determined by the parties to the dispute and their advisers. By giving the judges clear powers of case management to set the timetable for the litigation process, the Woolf reforms were intended to ensure that settlements are reached much more speedily.

Alternative dispute resolution

The Woolf reforms embraced another development that has occurred over recent years—*alternative dispute resolution* (ADR) (*see Box 8.1*) or, as it is perhaps better labelled, appropriate dispute resolution. This is an umbrella term describing a range of practices designed to assist parties achieve a resolution of their dispute without the necessity of going to court for a full trial in a courtroom. Many of these techniques

---

[3] The indemnity principle is now under attack and may well be restricted (*see Chapter 10*).

were developed in the United States where they are widely used. Their use in England has been less marked,[4] but is growing slowly.

Box 8.1   Legal system explained

Forms of alternative dispute resolution

ADR comes in a variety of forms. The principal ones are:

- arbitration;
- mediation; and
- early neutral evaluation.

Arbitration is a process whereby the parties to a dispute choose an arbitrator to determine their dispute. It is a private process. The arbitrator is often an expert in the matter which is the subject of the dispute, say a building contract. The parties are usually bound, contractually, to accept the decision of the arbitrator. It is thus like a court decision, an imposed decision, though, unlike with the court, the whole process takes place in private, out of sight of the general public. Indeed, confidentiality is one of arbitration's perceived advantages for many disputants.

Mediation is a technique whereby a third party—mediator—who is neutral so far as the parties to the dispute are concerned, attempts to explore the possibilities for the parties reaching an outcome which satisfies both of them. This is sometimes known as 'win–win', to contrast it with a court process which may be characterized as 'win–lose'. This outcome will not necessarily be one which a court would have reached (or would have had power to reach), for example because the particular remedy—e.g. saying sorry—is not a remedy available in court. It has the advantage that the decision will be one at which the parties have themselves arrived, albeit with the advice and assistance of the mediator.

Early neutral evaluation is a process where someone with legal or other relevant expertise is given a preliminary view of the case and is asked to provide a frank appraisal of the likely outcome, should the case go as far as court. This may be used as a stage in attempting to reach a settlement by negotiation, rather than going to a full trial in court.

In the case of small claims, the court system itself has long used a form of ADR, as the district judges who determine these cases do so not in a formal trial but by an informal procedure, with only the parties to the dispute present and—usually—lawyers excluded. They used to be called small claims arbitrations, although, since the introduction of the small claims track, such cases are now known as small claims hearings. Nevertheless, the same procedural informality applies.

An ADR scheme has been available in the Commercial Court (see later) since 1993. An ADR scheme is also available in the Court of Appeal. The largest-scale experiment

---

[4] The use of mediation in the family justice system is discussed in *Chapter 7, Mediation and mediators*.

in the use of court-centred ADR has been in the Central London County Court, started in May 1996. A number of other courts have also developed ADR schemes. These were the subject of detailed evaluation by Professor Dame Hazel Genn.[5] The common feature of all these experiments is that, to date, their use has been modest. There is evidence that those who take advantage of ADR in general find it a helpful way of resolving their disputes. But the use of ADR is not as widespread as in other countries, particularly the United States, and certainly not as widespread as those who provide ADR services would like.

The importance of ADR to the success of the Woolf reforms is not yet clear. Some initially argued that the civil procedure changes, combined with changes in the rules on the funding of litigation (*see Chapter 10*), would result in a substantial increase in litigation and the potential use of the courts. As this would lead to a need to divert cases from the courts, ADR would become an important means of achieving such diversion. In fact, levels of civil litigation fell quite sharply after the new rules were introduced, and the trend is still downward. The pressures that might have resulted from increased case loads have not materialized.

A different set of arguments is based on the suggestion that the new procedural rules are changing 'litigation culture'. As the nature of litigation changes so both clients and their professional advisers will, it is argued, want to move away from the adversarial procedures of the litigation process towards less confrontational forms of ADR to resolve disputes. There is some evidence that this is happening, particularly in large commercial disputes. But, as already noted, take-up in other classes of litigation is still limited. Much depends on the extent to which lawyers and other ADR providers are able to receive payments for this form of dispute resolution, particularly from the Community Legal Services Fund (*see Chapter 10*).

The post-Woolf civil justice system does give power to the judge, as part of the case management strategy, to stay a case for up to 28 days to give the parties a chance to use ADR where this seems to be appropriate. These powers have not been extensively used. However, the Court of Appeal has on a number of occasions stressed the importance of parties using ADR where they can. It has also indicated that unreasonable failure to do so may result in adverse rulings on the recovery of costs, though they have been reluctant to push too far in this direction (see *Halsey v Milton Keynes General NHS Trust, Steel v Joy and another* [2004] EWCA Civ 576, CA).

After a slow start, the Ministry of Justice now actively promotes the use of ADR. It sponsors an online directory of accredited mediators, who provide mediation services for people in dispute on a civil law matter. Mediation is provided for a fixed fee, which varies according to the amount of money in dispute. The fees are set out on the first page of the website. It makes the process of finding a mediator very easy and is clearly designed to encourage use of mediation in the dispute resolution process.

---

[5] Genn, H. and others, *Twisting Arms: Court Referred and Court Linked Mediation under Judicial Pressure* (London, Ministry of Justice, 2007).

There is also a Small Claims Mediation Service. This is a telephone-based mediation service which has mediated over 15,000 cases in each of the last two years. The government intends to ensure that all cases in the small claims track are referred to the mediation service.

There are a number of difficult issues relating to the development of ADR that are currently unresolved. Among these issues are:

- *Compulsion.* At present no court can *require* the use of ADR.[6] Experience in the United States suggests that use of ADR does not take off until at least an element of compulsion is introduced. But is it right for the courts to require parties to a dispute to pay for something that may not resolve the matter but only add to costs and delay? Certainly, the consensus in England and Wales is that, while ADR may be encouraged, it should not be compulsory;

- *Standards.* Secondly, there is a question of how proper standards for those who offer ADR services are to be set and monitored. This is being addressed by the Civil Mediation Council, which has devised principles for the accreditation of ADR providers;

- *Costs.* Currently, government does not fund the provision of ADR services save for limited provision through the Community Legal Service (*see Chapter 10*). But ADR services must be paid for. If the costs are too high and nevertheless parties are required by the courts to use a process of ADR, may this not add to the cost of dispute resolution—something the Woolf reforms were attempting to reduce?

- *Outcome.* Will the fact that the parties may well be happier at the end of the ADR process than they might have been at the end of a trial compensate them for the expense of using ADR? It may well do. One of the most powerful claims for ADR is *not* that it is cheaper, but that it enables parties to disputes to retain control of the dispute resolution process, which may in turn enable them to move on with their lives more amicably than they might be able to do after a court hearing. But this will not always be the case. Indeed there will always be those who, on principle, want to litigate and refuse to use any form of ADR.

The court structure: preliminary issues

Having considered the context within which the civil and commercial justice system has developed in recent years and noted the considerable changes that have occurred, the structure of the courts is now considered. Four preliminary issues will be mentioned.

---

[6] The position in the family justice system is discussed in *Chapter 7, Funding family law cases.*

Generalist v specialist

One of the claims made for the courts in the civil justice system is that they are, and should be, generalist rather than specialist in nature. Certainly, any type of case that does not fall into any other of the jurisdictional categories considered in this book (criminal, administrative, and family) must be disposed of in the civil courts. While the claim that the courts are generalist in nature is still to a large extent true, it should be treated with caution. There is now an increasing number of specialist courts that have been created, primarily because of the technicalities of the law and issues to be determined by those courts. This has happened particularly in areas of commercial and business law. This raises the obvious further question whether there should be more specialist courts. In recent years arguments have been made, for example, for the creation of a specialist housing court and for a specialist environment court.

There are many arguments in favour of greater specialization. Specialist judges dealing with a specific range of issues should be better informed about the relevant law; thus the quality and consistency of decision making might be enhanced. (This is one of the arguments in favour of tribunals.) Procedures could be better adapted to suit the users of the specialist courts and the types of issues to be dealt with in those courts. For example, special facilities might be available to deal with the particular types of emergency cases that might arise out of ordinary court hours. The practitioners who specialize in the areas of law concerned might be able to operate more efficiently by concentrating their resources in more specialized courts.

Against, it is argued that judges might become too narrowly focused and thus become bored with the tasks they were required to perform. Judicial manpower in specialist courts could not be used efficiently if the case-loads in those courts were insufficient to keep the relevant judges busy. However, this problem can be avoided by the flexible deployment of judges. Given recent trends, it seems likely that there will be more rather than less specialization in the years ahead.

Court fees

A second preliminary issue that needs to be borne in mind is the decision by government that the civil justice system should be—broadly—self-financing. A consequence of this is that HMCTS sets court fees (which claimants must pay before they can get their cases started and allocated to the appropriate track) at levels that achieve this financial target. This has led to considerable controversy. One particular criticism is that the policy was introduced, in the early 1990s, without any parliamentary announcement or debate.

Some argue that, on principle, 'justice' should be regarded as a 'free good', not subject to the principle of self-financing at all. Access to the courts for the determination of legal rights and entitlements is a constitutional right to which there should be no barriers—certainly not financial ones. Against that, others argue that the well-heeled, who may be fighting over financial matters worth thousands, perhaps millions, of pounds, should make—through the payment of fees—a contribution towards the running of the civil justice system.

Following complaints from judges, lawyers, and consumer groups that the combination of the fee for issuing the claim together with the fee that had to be paid when a case was allocated to a particular track was having a disproportionately adverse impact on those bringing small claims, the government decided to abolish the £80 allocation fee for defended civil actions worth £1,000 or less.[7] Apart from this concession, there has been no other relaxation in the civil justice fees regime; indeed other court fees have been regularly adjusted upwards. This issue is a source of significant conflict between the judiciary and the government.

Enforcement of judgments

A third issue that the civil justice system must address is enforcement of judgments. There is nothing more frustrating than taking a case to court, winning it, but then finding that it is well-nigh impossible to obtain satisfaction of the judgment. In situations where the loser has the backing of an insurance company, or (either private individual or company or other legal body) is extremely resource-rich, this is not usually a problem. But where the person against whom proceedings are brought is of moderate means or is a company with only limited resources, enforcement can be a major problem.

The government acknowledges this and has reviewed the procedures available to the courts for the enforcement of judgments. The Tribunals, Courts and Enforcement Act 2007 gives further powers to the courts to enforce judgments. In particular, courts now find it easier to discover what the financial position of a debtor is and to track debtors if they change employment.

Enforcement is an exceptionally difficult issue, particularly distinguishing between those who could pay but will not, and those who simply cannot pay. There would be considerable political opposition to a return to the Dickensian days of throwing debtors into jail.[8] Yet there is no doubt that, if the civil justice system cannot force to pay up those against whom judgments, in particular awards of damages, are made, this is seen by users of the system as a serious weakness. In turn, this may encourage others not to pay.

Delivering the Court Service: local initiatives and centralized justice

The courts are managed by HMCTS, the executive agency set up in April 2005, expanded to include tribunals in 2011. The day-to-day running of the courts is carried

---

[7] This decision was effective from April 2000. New fees were introduced in April 2003. Research published by the Ministry of Justice suggests that the level of court fees is relatively unimportant in determining whether a person will start proceedings in court: see *What's cost got to do with it? The impact of charging court fees on users* (London, Ministry of Justice, 2007).

[8] Even under present law, failure to pay certain taxes—a particular form of debt—can result in the imposition of a prison sentence.

out on a regional basis through six *circuits*.[9] Supervision of the judicial work of each circuit is the responsibility of the *presiding judges*. These are judges of the High Court appointed—two for each circuit—by the Lord Chief Justice. They operate under a Senior Presiding Judge.

When Lord Woolf was preparing his *Access to Justice* report, he found that many courts had developed their own particular procedures for dealing with specific types of matter. This did not imply that the outcomes of cases would differ, but the ways in which the courts worked certainly did. Lord Woolf felt that it was important that someone appearing for trial in one town should be dealt with in essentially the same way as in any other. One of his hopes for the CPR was that this would encourage greater uniformity of process. Given the not inconsiderable discretion that is given to judges to manage cases, Lord Woolf's hopes in this respect have not been fully realized.

Indeed, a degree of procedural experiment should be encouraged to see whether the work of the courts can be made more efficient. However, this should be as part of a controlled programme of pilot projects that can be properly evaluated by HMCTS, rather than the result of individual courts going their own way. It is also important that when new procedures are tested and found helpful, the results of good practice should be spread throughout the court system as a whole, not kept as a 'private custom' in a particular court or circuit. This will happen only if innovations are managed by HMCTS.

The county court

The county court deals with the largest numbers of civil cases. Founded in 1846 it was designed to provide a forum for the resolution of what would these days be regarded as relatively modest consumer complaints. Over the years, its jurisdiction has expanded.

Today all civil actions can be started in the county court (*see Box 8.2*), save for a small number of cases where there are special statutory rules that require proceedings to be started in the High Court. There used to be 216 county courts throughout England and Wales, but this number is being reduced by 49—just under 25 per cent. Each court is assigned at least one district judge, and some have at least one circuit judge. (Although circuit judges are full-time appointments, most do not spend all their time on civil matters, but sit as trial judges in criminal cases in the Crown Court.) District judges work full-time on civil issues (including some family justice matters). On 1 April 2012, there were 665 circuit judges in England and Wales, and 447 district judges. They are assisted by deputy district judges who are judges in training and who sit part-time (*see Chapter 4, Diagram 4.1*). An outline of proposals to reform county courts is discussed in *Box 8.3*.

---

[9] Midland and Oxford, run from Birmingham; North Eastern from Leeds; Northern from Manchester; South Eastern from London; Wales and Chester from Cardiff; and Western from Bristol.

Box 8.2 System in action

Work of the county courts

County courts deal with all contract and tort cases, and all proceedings for the recovery of land, irrespective of value. In addition, some county courts deal with bankruptcy and insolvency matters, certain equity and contested probate actions (e.g. arising from alleged breaches of trust obligations or questions about the administration of a will) where the value of the trust fund or the estate does not exceed £30,000, plus any case which the parties agree can be heard in the county court. Straightforward money and possession claims can now be issued online.

In 2011, 1,553,983 cases were started in the county court. A very large percentage of these cases were undefended; defences were issued in only 275,920. In total, there were 52,660 trials and small claim hearings, 13 per cent less than in 2010 and lower than in any year from 2006 onwards. Thus while the number of proceedings started is huge, the number of trials is tiny. (This is true generally in the civil justice system.) Of the total, there were:

- 995,895 claims for specified sums, mostly to recover debts; 38 per cent of these were claims for less than £500;
- 178,234 claims for unspecified sums, mostly for personal injuries;
- 215,000 possession claims for recovery of land (largely for failure to pay rent or mortgage payments);
- 49,724 insolvency petitions; and
- 114,866 non-money claims including for return of goods (not mortgage and landlord repossession).

The vast majority of money claims resulted in a 'default judgment'—where the defendant did not defend the proceedings; or a judgment 'by acceptance and determination' where the defendant made an offer which was accepted by the claimant.

In addition, the courts have power to order injunctions—orders for people to stop doing something such as harassment or anti-social behaviour.

The county court also does a great deal of work relating to the enforcement of its judgments. These include:

- attachment of earnings—where an employer is ordered to pay a defined part of the defendant's wages direct to the court, which pays it to the creditor; 51,737 applications for these orders were made in 2011;
- third party debt orders—where money owed by a third party to the defendant is seized and ordered to be paid to the judgment creditor (4,137 sought orders in 2011);
- charging orders, which are imposed on property and give security for the payment of a court order (90,286 orders sought in 2011); and
- administration orders, imposed where a person has got into serious debt, which enable regular payments to be made to the court, which then distributes the monies to the creditor(s).

Source: Adapted from *Judicial and Court Statistics, 2011* (London, Ministry of Justice 2012), Chapter 1.

Since the introduction of the CPR, overall there has been a downward trend in the activity levels of the county court (which arguably challenges the view that we are becoming an increasingly litigious society).

In those (rare) cases which actually go to trial, the average waiting time between the issue of the claim and the start of the trial is 56 weeks. Small claims take an average of 30 weeks to come to trial.

Box 8.3   Reform in progress

Reform of the county court

Early in 2011, the government launched a consultation paper on the work of the county court. The government's proposals were based around the following principles:

- *Proportionality*: disputes resolved in the most appropriate forum, with processes and costs commensurate with the complexity of the issues involved;
- *Personal responsibility*: citizens should take more responsibility for resolving their own disputes, with courts only adjudicating particularly complex issues;
- *Streamlined procedures*: procedures should be citizen- and business-friendly, and timely;
- *Transparency*: clear information on the dispute resolution options open to citizens.

To achieve these objectives, the paper proposed:

- a simplified claims procedure on a fixed-costs basis, similar to that for road traffic accidents under £10,000, for more types of personal injury claim; exploring the possibility of extending the framework of such a scheme to cover low value clinical negligence claims; and examining the option of extending the upper limit of those simplified claims procedures to £25,000 or £50,000;
- introducing a dispute management process and fixed recoverable costs by specific case types up to £100,000;
- increasing the upper jurisdiction threshold for small claims (excluding personal injury and housing disrepair) from £5,000 to £10,000, £15,000, or £25,000;
- requiring all cases below the small claims limit to have attempted settlement by mediation before being considered for a hearing;
- introducing mediation information/assessment sessions for claims above the small claims limit;
- encouraging greater use of online dispute-resolution services;
- providing a simpler and more effective enforcement regime; and testing the public appetite for further enforcement reforms and jurisdictional changes;
- introducing a number of jurisdictional changes in the civil courts, including the introduction of a single county court jurisdiction for England and Wales.

In February 2012, the Coalition government announced the following:

(1) Expanding mediation for those who have small claims.

Box 8.3 *Continued*

(2) Expanding the small claims track, initially to £10,000. The government may consider a further increase to £15,000 in due course. The current lower limits for housing and personal injury cases will be unchanged.

(3) Judges will have power to transfer suitable business to business cases with a dispute value over £10,000 to the small claims track without requiring the consent of the parties. The judiciary will also have the option of referring more complex cases with a case value below £10,000 to the fast track if that is considered appropriate.

(4) Introducing a fixed-cost simplified claims procedure for more types of personal injury claims, similar to that which was introduced in 2010 for road traffic accidents under £10,000.

(5) Going ahead, as soon as is feasible with proposals for streamlining enforcement processes, implementing some of the Tribunals, Courts and Enforcement Act 2007 provisions and to introduce a minimum threshold for Orders for Sale.

(6) Introducing a single county court jurisdiction for England and Wales to facilitate greater flexibility in the use of courts around the country and enable more proceedings to be issued from centralized processing centres.

(7) A number of specialist areas of work will be removed from the county court and transferred to the High Court. The government will increase the financial limit below which equity claims may be commenced in the county courts from £30,000 to £350,000. And the financial limit below which non-personal injury claims may not be commenced in the High Court will be increased from £25,000 to £100,000.

Item 6 is being dealt with in a provision in the Crime and Courts Bill 2012 currently before Parliament. The other measures do not require legislation; but the government has not announced an implementation timetable.

The High Court

The High Court consists of three divisions. The Family Division is considered in *Chapter 7.* The other two divisions are:

- the Queen's Bench Division; and
- the Chancery Division.

These two divisions handle different types of civil and commercial work.

The courts in these divisions handle cases both arising at first instance (i.e. cases being determined for the first time) and on appeal from courts lower in the hierarchical structure—the county court and a number of administrative tribunals. When sitting as an appeal court and when dealing with analogous matters such as judicial review, the High Court is known as the *Divisional Court.* Each division has a divisional court.

The Queen's Bench Division[10]

The Queen's Bench Division is headed by the President of the Queen's Bench Division (a post created by the Constitutional Reform Act 2005). He is supported by 73 full-time High Court judges, assisted by part-time deputy High Court judges, and circuit judges sitting as High Court judges. (High Court judges also go round the country 'on circuit' in order to hear the most serious criminal cases in the Crown Court.) The part-time judges deal with nearly 50 per cent of all trials.

The court deals primarily with common law business—actions relating to contract and tort. Torts (civil wrongs) embrace not only negligence and nuisance, but also other wrongs against the person, such as libel, or wrongs against property, such as trespass. Contract cases involve, for example, failure to pay for goods or services, or other alleged breaches of contract. Some fact situations give rise to actions both in tort and contract.

It is central to the philosophy of the post-Woolf era that only the most important cases should be dealt with in the High Court. As a result only personal injury claims with a value of £50,000 or more may be started there. In other cases the claim must be for £25,000 or more. The High Court also has powers to enforce its judgments (*see Box 8.4*).

Box 8.4   Legal system explained

Enforcement powers of the High Court

Judgments may be enforced in many ways, including:

- writ of *fieri facias* (fi-fa) (now called a writ of control) directing the sheriff (the equivalent of the bailiff in the county courts) to seize and if necessary sell the debtor's goods to raise money to pay off the debt;
- writ of possession of land (with eviction if necessary to ensure that possession of property or land is recovered);
- writ of delivery of goods, an order to hand over specific goods;
- a charging order on land (this has the same effect as a mortgage, so that if the property is sold the amount of the charge (debt) must be paid out of the proceeds of the sale);
- a third party debt (formerly garnishee) order, which orders that a third party, normally a bank, holding money for the judgment debtor pay it to the judgment creditor direct;
- appointment of a receiver who will manage the judgment debtor's property or part of it in such a way as to protect the judgment creditor's interest in it.

---

[10] The work of the Administrative Court, also part of the Queen's Bench Division, is considered in *Chapter 6*.

Box 8.4 *Continued*

An order to attend court for questioning (formerly an oral examination) is a procedure used in connection with enforcement. The debtor is required to attend court to give details of his earnings, expenses, savings, etc., so that the creditor can decide how best to enforce the judgment. In 2011, 46,564 enforcement proceedings were issued in the High Court—the majority for the writ of control.

Source: Adapted from Ministry of Justice, *Judicial and Court Statistics 2011* (London, Ministry of Justice, 2012), Chapter 6.

In addition, four specialist jurisdictions come within the scope of the Queen's Bench Division:

- the Admiralty Court;
- the Commercial Court;
- the Mercantile Court; and
- the Technology and Construction Court.

Cases to be tried in these courts are required to be started in the High Court, irrespective of financial amount (though in practice they are often substantial). There are also a number of other types of proceedings which, by statute, must be started in the High Court.

Jury trial

There is a right to trial by jury in civil proceedings for fraud, libel, slander, malicious prosecution, or false imprisonment. In other cases, a judge may in her discretion allow trial by jury; but this rarely happens. Where there is a jury, the jury will decide not only liability (e.g. were the words used libellous or not) but also the amount of any damages.

Work-load

In 2011, 13,928 claims and originating summonses were issued in the Queen's Bench Division, down 16 per cent from the previous year. Of these, 4,726 were issued in London, the rest in High Court District Registries around the country. Fewer than 200 were disposed of after a full trial. As in other parts of the legal system, a full trial is the exceptional, not the typical, mode of disposal.

Divisional Court

Judges in the Queen's Bench Division usually sit alone; when they sit with others they are known as a Divisional Court. The Divisional Court of the Queen's Bench Division deals with judicial review cases,[11] appeals by way of 'case stated',[12] *habeas corpus*,[13] committal for contempt of court committed in an inferior court, or appeals and applications under a variety of statutory provisions.[14] The bulk of the work is judicial review (*see Chapter 6*).

The Chancery Division

The Chancery Division of the High Court is presided over by the Chancellor of the High Court, supported by 18 other High Court judges. They are assisted, as needed, by deputy High Court judges, who are either practitioners approved to act as such by the Lord Chancellor, or retired High Court or circuit judges. The extent of their use depends on the level of business before the courts.

The principal categories of business dealt with by the division relate to corporate and personal insolvency disputes; disputes relating to business, trade, and industry; the enforcement of mortgages; intellectual property matters including copyright and patents; disputes relating to trust property; and disputes arising from wills and the administration of deceased people's estates (probate matters) (*see Box 8.5* for uncontested probate matters). The bulk of the work is handled in the Royal Courts of Justice in London, together with eight provincial centres that have High Court Chancery jurisdiction.[15]

Box 8.5 Legal system explained

Uncontested probate matters: the Family Division

Uncontested probate matters are dealt with in the Principal Registry of the Family Division of the High Court, in any of the 11 district probate registries or 18 probate sub-registries in England and Wales. Grants of probate are made in cases where there was a will; letters of administration where there was not. There is a heavy work-load. 261,352 grants/letters were issued in 2011.

A review of probate work in 2004 led to the creation of a new Probate Service website (see <www.justice.gov.uk/guidance/courts-and-tribunals/courts/probate/index. htm>); a telephone helpline (run as part of HMRC's Inheritance Tax Advice Service); and the ability to download forms online.

---

[11] Powers of judicial review are exercisable both over inferior courts and tribunals—e.g. where it is alleged that there has been a breach of proper fair procedure or an incorrect interpretation of the law—and against public bodies or government ministers or others carrying out public acts or duties.

[12] A process used, e.g. by the Crown Court or a magistrates' court to obtain a ruling on a particular provision of criminal law.

[13] Where unlawful detention is alleged.

[14] E.g. under the town and country planning legislation.

[15] Birmingham, Bristol, Cardiff, Leeds, Liverpool, Manchester, Newcastle upon Tyne, and Preston.

In 2011 a total of just under 7,500 claims and other originating proceedings were started in the Chancery Division; during the year, only 183 cases were disposed of following a trial. In addition, 8,269 bankruptcy petitions were issued in the High Court in London, together with 3,852 other originating applications. (This figure supplements the insolvency work of the county courts: *see Work of the County Courts in Box 8.2.*) The Divisional Court of the Chancery Division also disposed of a small number of appeals from the county court. In addition to the general work of the Chancery Division, there are two specialist jurisdictions: the Companies Court and the Patent Court.

Once again we can see that, as with other parts of the civil justice system, the court is very much the place of last resort for the resolution of disputes.

The commercial justice system

Notwithstanding the reluctance of the judiciary to specialize, the fact is that within both the High Court and the county court systems, there now exists a range of specialist courts, established to deal with a range of (primarily) commercial and company law matters. These developments reflect the position of London in the global economy, and the need for the courts to provide appropriate levels of expertise in specialist areas. They have spread to provincial centres where there is also significant commercial activity. The specialist courts may be listed as follows.

The Companies Court

This court is part of the Chancery Division of the High Court. It deals primarily with the compulsory liquidation of companies and other matters arising under the Insolvency Act 1986 and the Companies Acts. For example, a registered company that seeks to reduce its capital may do so only with the approval of the court. The bulk of this work is done in London, but the eight provincial district registries have the same powers.[16] Over 16,000 applications were filed in the Companies Court in 2011.

The Patents Court

This is another specialist part of the Chancery Division, dealing not only with patents, but other forms of intellectual property, including registered designs. It also hears appeals against decisions of the Comptroller General of Patents. Cases suitable for determination by a county court are heard in a specially designated county court—the Central London County Court. The work-load of this court is not high—during 2011, 53 actions were listed for hearing, 19 of which were withdrawn. However, the trials that went ahead were heavy duty affairs, dealing with major commercial disputes, for example over the design of mobile phones.

[16] See n. 15.

The Admiralty Court

This is part of the Queen's Bench Division of the High Court, dealing—as the name suggests—with shipping matters, principally the consequences of collisions at sea and damage to cargos. As with patents, most cases are dealt with in London, but there is power to refer suitable cases to specially designated county courts. In 2011, 115 actions were started; only five were disposed of by trial.

The Commercial Court

This is also part of the Queen's Bench Division of the High Court. A cadre of 15 specialist judges deals with a wide range of commercial matters, for example, banking, international credit, and the purchase and sale of commodities. It also deals with shipping matters not handled by the Admiralty Court—contracts relating to ships, carriage of cargo, insurance, as well as the construction and performance of mercantile contracts more generally. The Commercial Court also deals with questions that may arise from commercial arbitrations. 1,331 claims were issued in 2011.

The Mercantile Court

This deals with business disputes which require specialist judges but fall outside the remit of the Commercial Court or the Chancery Division. It provides a regional court service to national and international businesses in a similar way to the Commercial Court in London. The Mercantile Court only deals with claims that:

- relate to a commercial or business matter in a broad sense;
- are not required to proceed in the Chancery Division or in another specialist court;
- would benefit from the expertise of a mercantile judge.

The majority of Mercantile Courts deal with cases that relate to commercial or professional disputes over contracts or torts, or to issues arising from arbitration claims and awards. There are no maximum or minimum financial limits upon claims.

The Technology and Construction Court

This is another section of the Queen's Bench Division. It usually sits in London with five full-time *circuit* judges, and two High Court judges, though hearings are possible outside London before specially designated or nominated judges. The court deals primarily with building and engineering disputes and also computer litigation. It can also deal with other matters such as valuation disputes and landlord and tenant matters involving dilapidations. And it handles questions arising from arbitrations in building and engineering disputes. During 2011, 483 proceedings were received; 49 trials were held in London. (Figures for cases dealt with outside London are not available.)

Other courts and offices

In addition to the courts so far identified, there are also a number of other offices that form part of the Senior Court. These include:

- *The Office of the Official Solicitor and Public Trustee.* The Official Solicitor operates under the authority of section 90 of the Senior Courts Act 1981. His primary duties are to protect the interests of children and mental patients, i.e. those who do not have full legal capacity to look after their own affairs. His department has a substantial work-load. Among his responsibilities are child abduction cases. In 2001, the Official Solicitor took over responsibility for the *Public Trust Office.* The Public Trustee acts as executor or administrator of deceased persons' estates or trustees of wills or settlements where he has been named and has accepted the nomination. On 1 April 2007, the Court Funds Office merged with the Offices of the Official Solicitor and Public Trustee to become the Offices of Court Funds, Official Solicitor, and Public Trustee.

- *The Court of Protection.* The Mental Incapacity Act 2005 provides for the creation of the Court of Protection. It is a superior court of record, able to sit anywhere in England and Wales. Welfare matters previously referred to the High Court may be referred to this court. It has a central office and registry in Archway in London; but cases are also dealt with in Birmingham, Preston, Bristol, and Cardiff. The court has powers to call for reports to assist in determining a case. Such reports can be commissioned from the Public Guardian (a statutory official), local authorities, National Health Service (NHS) bodies, or Court of Protection Visitors (replacing the former Lord Chancellor's Visitors). Local authority staff or NHS staff may already be providing services to the person concerned and be able to report to the court on the basis of their existing involvement. The Public Guardian or Court of Protection Visitor who is reporting to the court has access to health, social services, or care records relating to the person and may interview him in private. Where a Court of Protection Visitor is a Special Visitor (e.g. a registered medical practitioner or someone with other suitable qualifications or training), he or she may, on the directions of the court, carry out medical, psychiatric, or psychological examinations.

The reform of civil justice: new developments

Despite the large number of changes that have taken place within the civil justice system over the last few years, many important issues remain. In addition to proposed changes to the county court (*see Box 8.3*), there is a range of fundamental questions that, despite the Woolf reforms, still need addressing:

- How can procedures for dispute resolution be made more efficient?
- How will the courts cope with larger numbers of litigants in person?

- Can the adversarial model of litigation continue to be the predominant model of dispute resolution in the context of civil disputes?
- What realistic alternatives should be developed?
- How can the cost of those proceedings be made more proportionate to the issues subject to dispute?

We return to the question of the cost of funding litigation in *Chapter 10*. As regards litigants in person in the courts, this was recently the subject of an important study by the Civil Justice Council (*see Box 8.6*).

Box 8.6   Reform in progress

Litigants in person

With cuts in legal aid, the judiciary has become increasingly concerned about the 'problem' of litigants in person—people who want to take a case to court, but who cannot afford a professionally qualified lawyer to represent them. With no realistic prospect that the cuts in legal aid will be reversed, it is important to get people in the system thinking about how civil justice might be delivered differently. In 2011, a working group set up by the Civil Justice Council, chaired by Robin Knowles QC, was asked:

(1) To consider what steps could be taken to improve access to justice for litigants in person.
(2) To consider what steps could be taken to prepare for the possibility that the number of litigants in person will increase materially.
(3) To focus on steps that would not require material additional financial resources.
(4) To consider the possibilities for further development of pro bono advice and assistance for litigants in person.

In its report, published in November 2011, the working group did not welcome the proposed cuts to legal aid; far from it. But it argued that there will be an increase in the numbers of the self-represented, and that much more should be done to make it easier for them to use the courts. Adopting the language of the Leggatt Review of Tribunals, the working group observed that users of the court system—by which it meant members of the public, not lawyers or judges—should be taken into account much more consciously than has been the case in the past. (There are areas of the legal system where parties routinely represent themselves; social security tribunals—which hear hundreds of thousands of cases a year, rarely with representation—is the prime example.)

   To achieve this, the working group made a substantial number of recommendations, both short-term and longer-term. It focused on the importance of making processes simpler; making information easier to understand; giving advice to judges and court staff on how to assist the self-representing litigant; devising a code of practice to prevent professional advocates taking advantage of the self-represented litigant.

Box 8.6 *Continued*

The working group also gave strong backing to the promotion of public legal education designed to make information about rights and entitlements, and also about court
procedures more readily available.

Many of the proposals are sensible and with the appropriate leadership and cham-
pionning might offer some assistance to those with legal rights to assert but who cannot afford lawyers to assert those rights. But underlying the report, unacknowledged,
is the fundamental question: can the current model of adversarial justice ever deliver
proportionate justice to the ordinary person who wants to use the law to assert his or
her legal rights?

It is not yet clear how the government is going to respond to the report; but it merits
much more public attention than has so far been paid to it.

Alternatives to courts

Although the current squeeze on public expenditure is regarded by many as a major
threat to the provision of legal services, in particular, dispute resolution services,
there are others who see it as an opportunity to explore alternatives to the courts,
which would be both less costly to the state, and less costly for the individual to access.
Indeed, there are already many alternatives available in specific contexts. To give just
a few examples:

- The Financial Services Ombudsman now deals with nearly all claims against
  financial institutions up to a value of £150,000.

- Tenancy deposit disputes are resolved by private arbitration, underpinned by
  legislation.

- Many consumer disputes are resolved by trading standards officers, not through
  the courts.

- The Coalition government is currently promoting the Groceries Adjudicator Bill,
  which will create a new scheme for adjudicating disputes between suppliers and
  the 'big name retailers'. Indeed, there are over 60 industry adjudication schemes
  already in existence in the United Kingdom, many of them not well understood,
  but resolving disputes that otherwise might have gone to the courts.

- With prompting from the European Union, schemes are being developed for
  the increased use of ADR and online dispute resolution of consumer issues on a
  pan-European basis.

- Many law firms and other companies are developing alternative resolution
  processes for resolving particular categories of case, for example employment
  disputes.

There is no doubt that alternatives can be developed in different contexts. What is interesting is that many of these initiatives are being driven by the private sector or by parts of government other than the Ministry of Justice. It seems likely that in many contexts the use of courts to resolve civil disputes will, save in the most complex cases, become increasingly rare.

Appeals and the appeal courts

We have already noted in passing that many courts have power to hear appeals in defined circumstances. Many appeals are satisfactorily disposed of in that context.

However, a number of courts deal exclusively with appeals. They are particularly important in the English legal system, not just because they have greater authority within the hierarchical court structure, but also because it is through their reported judgments that the primary source of authority for the development of the common law and the interpretation of statutes is to be found (*see Chapter 3*). It can be argued that these appeal courts are the only truly generalist courts, in that they have the responsibility for dealing with whatever is presented to them by way of appeal.

Policy issues

In recent years, it has been suggested that there were too many avenues of appeal; and that the level of court at which an appeal is determined was not always the right one. Important changes were introduced by the Access to Justice Act 1999.

Permission to appeal

It was always the case that, in order to bring an appeal in the Court of Appeal, it was necessary for the appellant to seek the permission (formerly called the 'leave') of the court to bring an appeal. Under section 54 of the Access to Justice Act 1999 rules of court have been made that require permission to appeal to be obtained for all appeals to the county courts, the High Court, or the Court of Appeal (Civil Division). There are limited exceptions; for example appeals relating to court orders that affect the liberty of the individual. There is no appeal against a decision either to give or refuse permission. Where permission is refused, there remains the possibility of making a further application for permission, either in the same or another court.

Second appeals

Once a county court or the High Court has decided a matter on appeal, section 55 of the Access to Justice Act 1999 provides that there is no possibility of a further appeal unless either the appeal would raise an important point of principle or practice, or there is some other compelling reason for the appeal to be heard. All applications for permission to bring a further appeal are dealt with by the Court of Appeal, irrespective of the court that determined the first appeal. If permission is granted, the Court of Appeal also hears the appeal.

Destination of appeals

Section 56 of the Access to Justice Act 1999 gave the Lord Chancellor power to vary, by order, the avenues of appeal to and within the county court, the High Court, and the Court of Appeal. Thus:

(1) for fast track cases heard by a district judge appeals lie to a circuit judge;

(2) for fast track cases heard by a circuit judge appeals lie to a High Court judge;

(3) in multi-track cases, appeals against interlocutory decisions by a district judge are to a circuit judge; by a master[17] or circuit judge to a High Court judge; and by a High Court judge to the Court of Appeal;

(4) in multi-track cases, appeals against final orders will be direct to the Court of Appeal, irrespective of the court making the initial decision.

The appeal courts

The courts of appeal considered here are:

- the Supreme Court, which has taken over the judicial functions of the House of Lords;
- the Judicial Committee of the Privy Council; and
- the Court of Appeal.

The Supreme Court

On 1 October 2009, the Supreme Court took over the judicial functions of the House of Lords. There are currently 11 Supreme Court Justices. The President of the Supreme Court is Lord Neuberger. The Constitutional Reform Act 2005 provides that new members of the Court are to be selected by a selection committee procedure. Membership is open not only to existing judges but also to those with long experience in practice. The first such appointment, of Jonathan Sumption QC, was announced in 2011. The Court can, with permission, hear appeals from any orders or judgments of the Court of Appeal in England, the Court of Session in Scotland, or the Court of Appeal in Northern Ireland.[18] In addition, appeals may be taken, with permission, from the High Court when it has been sitting as a Divisional Court (i.e. as a court of appeal or

---

[17] Masters are judicial officers of the High Court who determine interlocutory matters.

[18] Save, in the case of Northern Ireland or Scotland, where this is prevented by statute.

when dealing with cases such as judicial review). In limited circumstances, an appeal may be brought direct from the High Court or the High Court in Northern Ireland, when sitting as a trial court. This is known as 'leapfrogging' and can occur where is it clear that the law in question needs clarification at the highest level, perhaps because there are inconsistent decisions from the Court of Appeal.

Permission may be granted either by the relevant Court of Appeal or, if that is not forthcoming, by the Supreme Court. (If a lower court grants permission, the Supreme Court cannot overturn that decision.) In practice, permission is granted by the lower courts very infrequently.[19] The right of the citizen to 'take her case to the highest court in the land' is in reality highly contingent, subject to considerable procedural constraint. The Supreme Court is a judicial resource that is sparingly used.

Most appeals are heard by courts of five Justices. Very significant cases may go to seven or even nine judge panels. Hearings are tightly time-controlled, lasting usually only two days. In 2011, 208 petitions for permission to appeal were presented. 202 were disposed of, of which 143 were refused outright. In the same year, 77 appeals were presented to the court; the majority of these came from the Court of Appeal Civil Division. They related to a wide variety of different issues.

Section 41 of the Constitutional Reform Act 2005 made specific provision as to the effect of decisions of the Supreme Court as judicial precedents. In essence, a decision made by the Supreme Court is to have the same effect as decisions of the House of Lords or the Judicial Committee of the Privy Council. So in the case of jurisdiction transferred from the House of Lords, a decision of the Supreme Court on an appeal from one jurisdiction within the United Kingdom will not have effect as a binding precedent in any other such jurisdiction, or in a subsequent appeal before the Supreme Court from another such jurisdiction. In the case of the devolution jurisdiction transferred from the Judicial Committee of the Privy Council, a decision of the Supreme Court is binding in all legal proceedings except for subsequent proceedings before the Supreme Court itself.

The Judicial Committee of the Privy Council

This remains the final court of appeal from those British Commonwealth Territories and four independent republics within the Commonwealth that have retained this right of appeal. It also determines constitutional issues arising from those independent territories that have a written constitution. The Judicial Committee also has jurisdiction over a number of domestic matters[20] and 'pastoral' matters (which relate to the Church of England). The statutory powers of the Committee derive from the Judicial

---

[19] It is not uncommon for the Criminal Division of the Court of Appeal to certify that a point of law of general public importance is involved in a case, but still to refuse permission to appeal to the Supreme Court.

[20] Hearing appeals from a number of professional bodies, in particular under the Medical Act 1983 and the Dentists Act 1984. The Judicial Committee's powers to deal with devolution issues arising out of the passing of the Wales Act and the Scotland Act 1998 have been transferred to the Supreme Court.

Committee Act 1833, though the history of the Committee can be traced back to mediaeval times. The judges who sit in the Judicial Committee are (broadly) the same as those who sit in the Supreme Court, though they are on occasion joined by a senior member of the judiciary from the country whence an appeal has come.

Many find the jurisdiction of the Judicial Committee highly anachronistic—a throw-back to a British imperial past that is long gone. Nevertheless, the Judicial Committee has a steady stream of work. In 2011, 37 appeals were entered and 37 petitions for special leave to appeal were dealt with. (These special petitions relate to appeals in criminal cases where the Judicial Committee will not hear an appeal unless satisfied that the case raises a matter of great general importance or where there appears to be the danger of a grave miscarriage of justice.) The issues it deals with are, by definition, of very considerable legal and social importance, not just for the country in question but for the common law world in general.

The Court of Appeal: civil appeals[21]

The Court of Appeal is divided into two divisions: the criminal and the civil. The Lord Chief Justice (who is also head of the judiciary) heads the Criminal Division; the Master of the Rolls heads the Civil Division. They are assisted by 37 Lords Justice of Appeal. Other High Court judges assist, as required and as available, in the Criminal Division. Both the President of the Family Division and the Chancellor of the High Court sit in the Court of Appeal for part of their time. By comparison with the Supreme Court and the Privy Council, the Court of Appeal has a substantial case-load.

The Civil Division

The number of appeals coming to the Civil Division rose steadily during the early 1990s. They began to fall in 1996, and are now holding steady. During 2011, 1,269 appeals were filed, 1,263 were disposed of, of which 520 were allowed. In addition there were 3,758 applications for permission. During the same period 34 interlocutory appeals—on matters that are related to the proceedings, but not finally determinative of the issues in question—were were disposed of. Only 10 were allowed.

Comment on the civil justice system

(1) While popular rhetoric suggests that it is the right of every English person to have his or her day in court, in practice access to the courts is surrounded by barriers. There are substantial procedural and financial pressures on litigants to settle their differences outside the courts; and appealing against the decision of a court is subject to even more restrictions.

---

[21] Information on criminal appeals is in *Chapter 5, Criminal appeals.*

(2) Judicial manpower is an expensive resource to be used only where really needed, particularly at the most senior levels. Much of the simpler case work is dealt with by part-time judges. There are also many occasions in which judges sit in a court of a higher level than the one to which they have been appointed—circuit judges in the High Court; High Court judges in the Court of Appeal, for example. There is thus considerable flexibility in how the available resource is used, though this begs the question—given the policy on court fees[22] —whether the public is actually getting the judicial service it thinks it is paying for.

(3) Delay and cost were the principal issues identified as in need of reform by Lord Woolf. The CPR have seen reductions in the time taken for a case to get to court. However, there are still serious complaints about the costs of taking proceedings.[23]

(4) There is also considerable frustration at the slow pace of investment in information technology in the civil justice system, promised when the Woolf reforms were introduced but which has still not yet been fully delivered. The historic failure to invest in IT may prove a hindrance to the development of more efficient court procedures since much more civil work could be conducted electronically if the resources were available.

(5) Increasingly, disputes affecting ordinary people are being dealt with outside the court system.

Questions

Use the self-test questions on the Online Resource Centre to test your understanding of the topics covered in this chapter and receive tailored feedback:

www.oxfordtextbooks.co.uk/orc/partington13_14/

Weblinks

Check the Online Resource Centre for a selection of annotated weblinks allowing you to easily research topics of particular interest:

www.oxfordtextbooks.co.uk/orc/partington13_14/

---

[22] *See Court fees.*
[23] See Goriely, T., Moorhead, R., and Abrams, P., *More Civil Justice? The Impact of the Woolf Reforms on Pre-action Behaviour* (Research Study 43) (London, The Law Society and Civil Justice Council, 2002).

Blog items

See www.martinpartington.com (access via the Online Resource Centre)

Issues discussed are: reforming the county court; introducing online mediation; the work of the new Supreme Court (including interview with Lady Hale); the development of mediation (including interviews with Karl Mackie and Jeremy Tagg); the work of the Civil Justice Council (interview with former Chief Executive); Jackson review of costs of civil litigation; dealing with litigants in person.

Further reading

ABEL, R. L., *The Politics of Informal Justice* (London and New York, NY, Academic Press, 1982), 2 vols

BALDWIN, J., *Lay and Judicial Perspectives on the Expansion of the Small Claims Regime* (LCD Research Paper 8/2002) (London, Lord Chancellor's Department, 2002)

——*Small Claims in the County Court* (Oxford, Clarendon Press, 1996)

BLOM-COOPER, L., QC., Dickson, B., and Drewry, G. (eds), *The Judicial House of Lords: 1876–2009* (Oxford, Oxford University Press, 2011)

BOULLE, L., and NESIC, M., *Mediation: Principles, Process, Practice* (London, Butterworths, 2001)

BROWN, H., and Marriott, A., *ADR: Principles and Practice* (3rd edn, London, Sweet & Maxwell, 2011)

CRANSTON, R., *How Law Works: The Machinery and Impact of Civil Justice* (Oxford, Oxford University Press, 2006)

DREWRY, G., BLOM-COOPER, L., and BLAKE, C., *The Court of Appeal* (Oxford, Hart Publishing, 2007)

GENN, H., *Judging Civil Justice* (Cambridge, Cambridge University Press, 2009)

—— *Mediation in Action—Resolving Court Disputes Without Trial* (London, Calouste Gulbenkian Foundation, 1999)

——and others, *Twisting Arms: Court Referred and Court Linked Mediation under Judicial Pressure* (London, Ministry of Justice, 2007)

ISON, T., *The Forensic Lottery: A Critique of Tort Liability as a System of Personal Injury Compensation* (London, Staples Press, 1967)

JACOB, J., *Civil Litigation: Practice and Procedure in a Shifting Culture* (Welwyn Garden City, Emis Professional Publishing, 2001)

JACOB, SIR JACK, *The Fabric of English Civil Justice* (London, Stevens, 1987)

MOORHEAD, R., and SEFTON, M., *Litigants in Person: Unrepresented litigants in First Instance Proceedings* (DCA Research Series) (London, Department for Constitutional Affairs, 2005)

PALMER, M., and ROBERTS, S., *Dispute Processes: ADR and the Primary Forms of Decision-Making* (London, Butterworths, 1998)

PEYSNER, J., and SENEVIRATNE, M., *The Management of Civil Cases: the Courts and the post-Woolf Landscape* (DCA Research Series) (London, Department for Constitutional Affairs, 2005)

PLOTNIKOFF, J., and WOOLFSON, R., *Evaluation of Appellate Work in the High Court and the County Courts* (DCA Research Series) (London, Department for Constitutional Affairs, 2005)

POLDEN, P., *A History of the County Court, 1846–1971* (Cambridge, Cambridge University Press, 1999)

SHAPLAND, J., SORSBY, A., and HIBBERT, J., *A Civil Justice Audit* (LCD Research Paper 2/2002) (London, Lord Chancellor's Department, 2002)

WOOLF, LORD, *Access to Justice: Final Report to the Lord Chancellor on the Civil Justice System in England and Wales* (London, The Stationery Office, 1996)

PART III

THE DELIVERY AND FUNDING OF LEGAL SERVICES

9

Delivering legal services: practitioners, adjudicators, and legal scholars

Introduction

Discussions about the delivery of legal services tend to focus on the role of the legal profession and its two branches: *solicitors*, and *barristers*. Here a broader approach is adopted. In the same way that we have argued that the institutional framework of the English legal system can only be understood by referring to a wide range of institutions, not simply the courts, so too thinking about the full range of those who deliver services about legal rights and entitlements involves consideration of a much greater range of actors. The purpose of this chapter is to provide an introductory account of the principal groups that provide legal services. It considers not only the professionally qualified, but also those who provide legal services without necessarily having legal professional qualifications. This is important, not least because there is a steadily growing body of opinion that the present model for the delivery of legal services, predominantly by lawyers working in private practice, is not sustainable. The legal services market is also undergoing rapid change. Thus many of those now starting to study law must—if they wish to do law-related work—consider a much wider range of career options.

While the bulk of the chapter focuses on those who deliver legal services directly or indirectly to clients, the chapter also includes consideration of those who provide legal services by adjudicating disputes. Lastly, the role of the legal scholar is considered.

The practitioners

Three groups are considered in this part of the chapter:

- those professionally qualified as lawyers;
- those in professional groups allied to law; and
- lay advisers.

Professionally qualified lawyers: solicitors and barristers

There are currently well over 127,000 solicitors practising in England and Wales. In addition there are over 12,000 barristers in private practice, with a further 2,900 plus employed barristers working 'in-house' for a wide variety of companies, government departments, and agencies. All these totals have increased sharply over the last quarter of a century. They reflect increased demands for legal services resulting from economic growth, structural changes affecting the commercial world such as globalization and involvement in Europe, and numerous other social changes with greater emphasis on citizens' rights.

These global figures mask two important developments. First, there is a significantly improved gender balance of those entering the legal profession than there was 25 years ago. For a number of years now, more women than men have become solicitors. About a third of those in private practice at the bar are women. Secondly, the ethnic balance of entrants, though far from satisfactory, has improved. While the legal profession may still be a predominantly middle-class one, it is significantly less white and male than it used to be. However, these changes are not yet reflected in the number of women and members of ethnic minority groups who have reached the highest positions in the law, for example judicial appointments, QCs, or partners in solicitors' firms.

What lawyers do

It is impossible to summarize the enormous variety of work that lawyers undertake. A long list would not be particularly enlightening. Much of the work of the large city firms relates to the commercial transactions of their clients, for example the headline-grabbing financial deals or takeover bids that shape economic and commercial life. Others offer services focused on the individual client, for example defending people accused of crime, dealing with the consequences of personal injuries particularly arising from road traffic accidents, buying and selling property, handling divorces, or winding up estates after death.

The focus of this chapter is on lawyers who work in private practice. However, the work of other significant groups of qualified lawyers should also be noted. Three specific examples may be given.

Lawyers in industry. Considerable numbers of lawyers work in industry, not indirectly through the services provided for companies by those in private practice, but directly through their employment by the firms concerned. Most major companies have legal departments, staffed by professionally qualified lawyers, able to advise them on those legal issues that directly affect the company and its operations, for example matters relating to employment law, or health and safety legislation, or real estate.

Lawyers in the Civil Service and local government. There are—broadly—two ways in which those professionally qualified as lawyers may be employed in central government. First, they may be specifically employed for their technical legal expertise: to draft legislation (Parliamentary Counsel), or to deal with the wide range of legal issues that arise in departments (the Government Legal Service). In addition, there are many with law degrees and other legal qualifications who are not employed as lawyers, but who form part of the general Civil Service.

In local government, lawyers often hold senior positions in local authority administrations and play a very important role in ensuring that local authorities act within the scope of the powers given to them by Act of Parliament.

Lawyers in court administration. Qualified lawyers also play a very important part in the work of those courts and other dispute resolution bodies that do not use legally qualified adjudicators, for example justices' clerks in the magistrates' courts.

One of the great attractions of law is the enormous range of employment opportunities that the law provides for those who wish to practise or work in the legal system. There are also increasing opportunities to work in international agencies of various kinds, particularly in Europe.

Preliminary issues

When thinking about what lawyers do, two preliminary distinctions should be drawn, between: (1) litigious and non-litigious matters; and (2) lawyers' services and legal services.

Litigious and non-litigious matters. It is essential to bear in mind from the outset the fundamental distinction between litigious and non-litigious matters. A great deal of the work of lawyers is directed to non-litigious work—work designed to *prevent* litigation. This includes, for example, the provision of advice or the drafting of documents designed to ensure that people's affairs run smoothly. By contrast, litigious work arises where things have gone wrong, where there are disputes that need to be resolved either between individuals or companies or between the citizen and the state. Rights to conduct litigation and to be heard in a court are subject to special statutory rules.

Legal services and lawyers' services. A second important distinction is between *lawyers' services*, services that can *only* be provided by professionally qualified lawyers, and *legal services*, which may, though do not have to, be provided by professional lawyers. One feature of the English legal system is that many people, other than those professionally qualified as lawyers, provide legal services, which are required by members of the public, and which deal with legal issues, for example advice about legal entitlements or the completion of legal transactions. The role of para-legal staff and lay advisers is discussed later in this chapter. (*See Box 9.1* for examples.)

Box 9.1   Legal system explained

Legal services and lawyers' services

Some examples of the distinction in practice are:

- The first source of legal advice for many people faced with problems about their employment ('have I been unfairly dismissed by my employer?') is a *Citizens' Advice*

Box 9.1 *Continued*

Bureau or a *trade union*. The person they see is trained to give the appropriate advice; the adviser may indeed recommend that the person should see a qualified lawyer. But the initial *legal service* does not usually come from a lawyer, but from a trained lay adviser.

- Similar points may be made in relation to advice sought by a tenant in a dispute with her landlord; or to advice sought by a consumer where something has gone wrong with the provision of goods or services.
- Many people anxious to obtain advice regarding their legal entitlements to social security benefits are more likely to turn to the services of a *welfare rights officer*—- again a lay person, albeit specially trained, rather than to professionally qualified lawyers.
- Those who buy or sell houses may use the services of a *licensed conveyancer* rather than a solicitor to complete their transaction. Many who want to make a will use will-writers who are not professionally qualified as lawyers.

Some legal services are provided by other professional groups. The most obvious example is that matters relating to individuals' legal liability to pay tax are typically dealt with, not by lawyers, but by *accountants*. In short, *legal services* are not provided exclusively by qualified lawyers.

Lawyers' services may be seen as a special sub-set of the total provision of legal services: they are services which either have to be provided by those qualified as lawyers (such as the provision of advocacy services in court—which are restricted to those who have achieved particular professional qualifications) or which, as a matter of practice, are provided by those qualified as lawyers. For example, it is inconceivable that large corporations would turn to lay advisers—however well trained—for advice on questions relating to a corporate takeover. Such clients want the expertise that professional lawyers hold themselves out as offering, and, should anything go wrong, the comfort of the insurance protection that is a part of professional responsibility.

Part 3 of the Legal Services Act 2007 enshrines this distinction in legislation. It sets out a number of 'reserved legal activities' (rights of audience, conduct of litigation, probate activities, notarial activities, the administration of oaths, and 'reserved instrument activities') that may only be performed by lawyers or others authorised to undertake such work. It is a criminal offence to undertake such work without authorisation.

One example of the distinction between legal services and lawyers' services that has attracted considerable public attention is claims management. Claims-management companies advertise their willingness to take on the cases of people who have suffered harm as the result of accident on a 'no win, no fee' basis. A regulatory regime was introduced in 2006, designed to ensure that non-lawyers who offered such services were authorized to do this work, and adhered to specified rules of conduct (*see Box 9.2*).

Box 9.2   Legal system explained

Regulation of claims management

Under the Compensation Act 2006, persons providing a regulated claims-management service need to be authorized. The regulation applies to claims made for compensation in relation to personal injury, criminal injuries compensation, industrial injuries disablement benefit, employment matters, housing disrepair, and financial products and services.

Those who are already regulated (e.g. by being a solicitor, or under financial services legislation) are exempt from these requirements, as are certain other categories of persons or organizations including charities, not-for-profit advice agencies, and some trade unions. The Act makes it an offence to operate without authorization, unless exempted.

The following services are covered: (1) advertising for, or otherwise seeking out (e.g. by canvassing or direct marketing), persons who may have a cause of action; (2) advising a claimant or potential claimant in relation to his claim or cause of action; (3) referring details of a claim or claimant, or a cause of action or potential claimant, to another person, including a person having the right to conduct litigation (but not if it is not undertaken for or in expectation of a fee, gain, or reward); (4) investigating, or commissioning the investigation of, the circumstances, merits, or foundation of a claim, with a view to the use of the results in pursuing the claim; (5) representation of a claimant (whether in writing or orally, and regardless of the tribunal, body, or person to or before which or whom the representation is made).

Among the requirements of the rules of conduct are: (1) cold calling in person is prohibited; other cold calling must be in accordance with industry codes; (2) referral fees paid must be disclosed; (3) certain information must be given to clients before they sign a contract; (4) there is a 14-day cooling-off period after a contract has been signed; (5) where a contract is cancelled any cancellation fee must be reasonable in the circumstances and reflect work done; (6) there must be an internal complaints procedure; and (7) where client money is held it must be held in client accounts that meet stipulated standards.

A team within the Ministry of Justice is responsible for regulating claims-management companies. It issues annual reports on its work and other industry bulletins.

Source: See generally <www.justice.gov.uk/claims-regulation>.

Regulation of the legal profession

Professional bodies like to be allowed to regulate themselves. There are many arguments in favour of self-regulation, in particular that only those within the profession can set and monitor proper professional standards. Against this, it is argued that self-regulation can result in the creation of restrictive practices that work against the public interest. Over the last 60 years, there has been enormous change to the ways in which the English legal profession is regulated. Government has become increasingly involved.

The attack on restrictive practices and the encouragement of competition

The attack on the restrictive practices of the legal profession began with a study by the Monopolies Commission, published in 1968. In evidence to the Commission, Michael Zander provided a devastating critique of professional practices which he argued were not in the public interest. Many others joined the attack. For example, during the early 1970s, Austen Mitchell, MP, led a sustained attack on the conveyancing monopoly then enjoyed by solicitors. This attack was supported by some solicitors including Mr Joseph (*see Further reading*).

A Royal Commission on Legal Services, which reported in 1979,[1] concluded that, while a large number of detailed changes to professional practice needed to be made, many of the restrictive practices of the legal profession were in the public interest. Nevertheless, when the Thatcher government came to power in the same year, Mrs Thatcher was determined to make the British economy generally much more competitive. The legal profession became caught up in a general attack on monopolistic power.[2]

Abolition of the conveyancing monopoly

The first, and most symbolically significant, change to lawyers' restrictive practices occurred in 1987, when the conveyancing monopoly was broken. Until then, only solicitors were entitled to charge for the work required to convey the title in real estate from a vendor to a purchaser. Part II of the Administration of Justice Act 1985 allowed a system of licensed conveyancers, regulated by the Council for Licensed Conveyancers, to be established. The first licences under the scheme were granted in 1987. In addition, the practice of using fixed-scale fees for conveyancing was stopped. There is no doubt that many solicitors had benefited very substantially from the original arrangements, though there is also evidence that there was at least some indirect social benefit, in that many solicitors used profits from conveyancing to subsidize other less profitable areas of practice.

Right to litigate and right of audience

Fundamental changes were also made to the rights to conduct litigation and rights of audience. Before 1990, only solicitors could prepare cases for trial; only barristers had rights to be heard arguing cases in court. Under the Courts and Legal Services Act 1990,

---

[1] (Cmnd 7648) (London, Her Majesty's Stationery Office, 1979).
[2] There is a tendency for all professional groups to feel that they alone are being picked on. In fact all professional groups have been subject to similar pressures.

the government began to put these rights on a statutory footing. Instead of the professional bodies simply prescribing rules relating to advocacy and litigation, as they had done in the past, the Act established a framework for authorized bodies (the Bar Council and the Law Society together with the Institute of Legal Executives) to set the rules.

The Access to Justice Act 1999 changed the rules again. It made the following provisions:

- all barristers and solicitors were to have the right of audience before every court in all proceedings. This is not an unqualified right; those wishing to exercise it must obey the rules of conduct of the professional bodies and meet prescribed training requirements (section 36) (see, e.g. the Solicitors' Higher Rights of Audience Regulations 2010);

- Crown prosecutors and other employed advocates (whether solicitors or barristers) were to have the same right of audience as if they were in private practice (section 37);

- advocates and litigators employed by the Legal Services Commission or by bodies established by the Legal Services Commission were enabled to provide services directly to the public, without the need to receive instructions through a solicitor or other person acting for the client (section 38);

- where a person, a barrister, had been granted the right of audience by one professional body (e.g. the Bar Council), she became entitled to retain that right if she became a solicitor, and thus a member of the Law Society (section 39);

- barristers employed by firms of solicitors were able to act on the same basis as solicitors; Bar Council rules that treated barristers employed by solicitors as 'non-practising' and thus able to offer only a limited range of services were disapplied (section 44);

- the General Council of the Bar and the Institute of Legal Executives were given power to grant their members the right to conduct litigation (section 40); and

- procedures for authorizing (and in extreme cases revoking authorizations to) new bodies to grant the right of audience and the right to conduct litigation, and for approving alterations to or the adoption of new regulations or rules of conduct were streamlined (section 41).

The overriding duties of advocates and litigators to the court to act with independence in the interests of justice and to comply with their professional bodies' rules of conduct were put on a statutory footing (section 42). All authorized advocates and litigators must refuse to do anything required, either by a client or an employer, that is not in the interests of justice (e.g. the suppression of evidence).

Other changes

Numerous other changes also occurred. In particular, rules on advertising were significantly relaxed so that, within boundaries set by the Law Society's *Guide to Professional*

Behaviour, firms of solicitors became entitled to advertise their services. While legal advertising in the England and Wales may not have the flamboyance of lawyers' advertisements in the United States, nevertheless this development was also a significant break with past tradition. All significant legal practices, both solicitors' and barristers', now engage in a wide range of promotional 'practice development' activity.

Further developments

The changes of the 1980s and 1990s, far from being the end of a process, were merely a foretaste of what was to come. In March 2001, the Office of Fair Trading produced a report, *Competition in Professions*, that recommended that unjustified restrictions on competition should be removed. The government responded with a consultation paper and report into competition and regulation in the legal services market. It concluded that 'the current framework is out-dated, inflexible, over-complex and insufficiently accountable or transparent ... Government has therefore decided that a thorough and independent investigation without reservation is needed'.

In July 2003, Sir David Clementi was appointed to carry out an independent review of the regulatory framework for legal services in England and Wales. His terms of reference were: to consider what regulatory framework would best promote competition, innovation, and the public and consumer interest in an efficient, effective, and independent legal sector; and to recommend a framework that would be independent in representing the public and consumer interest, comprehensive, accountable, consistent, flexible, transparent, and no more restrictive or burdensome than is clearly justified.

In December 2004, Sir David published his report. The main recommendations, which the government broadly accepted, were:

- to establish a new legal services regulator, the Legal Services Board, to provide oversight regulation of frontline bodies such as the Law Society and the Bar Council;
- to set statutory objectives for the Legal Services Board, including promotion of the public and consumer interest;
- to prescribe regulatory powers that would be vested in the Legal Services Board, but with powers to devolve regulatory functions to frontline bodies (i.e. professional bodies), subject to their competence and governance arrangements;
- to ensure that the frontline bodies made new governance arrangements that would separate their regulatory and representative functions;
- to create a new Office for Legal Complaints—a single independent body to handle consumer complaints in respect of all members of frontline bodies, subject to oversight by the Legal Services Board;
- to establish alternative business structures that could see different types of lawyers and non-lawyers managing and owning legal practices.

Details of the government's response were set out in the white paper, *The Future of Legal Services: Putting the Consumer First*, published in October 2005. This, in turn, led to the Legal Services Act, which passed through Parliament in October 2007. It created the regulatory framework envisaged by Clementi.

Legal Services Act 2007

The potential impact of this legislation on the legal profession is enormous.

Representation and regulation

First, both the Bar Council (responsible for barristers) and the Law Society (responsible for solicitors) reorganized themselves so that their representative functions (sometimes referred to as their 'trade union' functions), designed to promote their members' interests to the wider public, have been separated from their regulatory functions. While the Law Society and the Bar Council still retain some regulatory functions, primary responsibility for regulating solicitors now rests with the Solicitors' Regulation Authority (SRA), established in 2007 as the independent regulatory body of the Law Society; similarly barristers are now regulated by the Bar Standards Board, the independent regulatory body of the Bar Council. Other bodies, such as the one representing legal executives, have similarly divided their representational and regulatory functions.

Establishment of Legal Services Board

Secondly, the Legal Services Board was established. It became fully operational in January 2010. It has a number of tasks in addition to overseeing the regulatory activities of the professional bodies. For example it is required to increase public understanding of law and support the rule of law, tasks that had never before been set out in legislation (*see Box 9.3*).

Box 9.3   Reform in progress

Legal Services Board: the regulatory objectives

The Legal Services Board is the body responsible both for overseeing approved legal regulators in England and Wales (which include the Law Society, the Solicitors' Regulatory Authority, the Bar Council, and the Bar Standards Board) and the newly established Office for Legal Complaints, the new organization being established to handle consumer complaints about lawyers.

The Board must deliver eight regulatory objectives, set out in the Legal Services Act 2007:

- protecting and promoting the public interest;
- supporting the constitutional principle of the rule of law;
- improving access to justice;
- protecting and promoting the interests of consumers;

Box 9.3 *Continued*

- promoting competition in the provision of services in the legal sector;
- encouraging an independent, strong, diverse, and effective legal profession;
- increasing public understanding of citizens' legal rights and duties;
- promoting and maintaining adherence to the professional principles of independence and integrity; proper standards of work; observing the best interests of the client and the duty to the court; and maintaining client confidentiality.

The Board has published its own commentary on these regulatory objectives. See <www.legalservicesboard.org.uk/news_publications/publications/pdf/regulatory_objectives.pdf>.

In the Board's early years, it developed the institutional infrastructure required to enable it to work. It has put in place the arrangements for the licensing by the Approved Regulators of Alternative Business Structures. It tested the governance arrangements of the Approved Regulators to ensure their independence. It started to develop a research strategy designed to help the Board assess the extent to which it is meeting its statutory functions. Among its first reports is one on the problems facing women and members of ethnic minority groups reaching senior positions in the law.

The Board also started an important piece of work on the extent to which there should be consumer protection, including access to the Office for Legal Complaints for legal work—such as will-writing, or the giving of legal advice—that is not undertaken by professionally qualified lawyers.

Dealing with complaints

Thirdly, the Office for Legal Complaints was established and the Legal Ombudsman appointed. This is the latest stage in a long process of trying to ensure that users of legal services had an effective way of resolving complaints and disputes.

The situation before 1990 was—very broadly—that while the courts were able to deal with the most serious cases of professional negligence, and while the professional bodies were able to control other forms of *gross* misconduct, the more mundane complaints—rudeness, slowness in responding to letters, general inefficiency—were not being dealt with seriously. Yet these were precisely the sorts of issues that the ordinary client, who felt she was not getting good value for the money she was being asked to pay, wanted to complain about. Both the Law Society and the Bar Council took steps to try to address these concerns.

During the 1990s, there were significant statutory developments. The Courts and Legal Services Act 1990 established the office of Legal Services Ombudsman. The Access to Justice Act 1999 extended the power of the Ombudsman; and made provision for the appointment of a Legal Services Complaints Commissioner. Under the Legal Services Act 2007, both these posts were abolished and replaced by the Office for Legal Complaints and the Legal Ombudsman.

The approved regulators such as the SRA and the Bar Standards Board still have responsibility for ensuring that their members have proper complaints-handling procedures in place. However, from 6 October 2010, all complaints about lawyers must be referred to the new Office. Building on operational principles developed over the previous 20 years, the Legal Ombudsman is clear that initial responsibility for dealing with complaints lies with the firms or chambers of those professionals against whom complaints are made. If resolution is not possible at that stage, complaints must be taken to the Office for Legal Complaints. From April 2013, the Ombudsman will deal with complaints about claims-management companies.

The Ombudsman wants most complaints to be resolved informally by the law firm or other authorized entity involved. If this fails, the Ombudsman determines what further investigation is to be undertaken. The details of the Ombudsman's procedural rules are published on his website. In the first full year of operation (2011–12), the Office received over 75,000 applications, of which around 8,400 were taken forward for further investigation. Of these, around 35 per cent were dealt with by a decision of the Ombudsman.

Alternative business structures

The fourth, and potentially most far-reaching, change effected by the Legal Services Act 2007 relates to creating new forms of business structure for those providing legal services (*see Alternative business structures*).

The promotion of good practice and ethical standards

This is another issue that has received considerable attention in recent years, not just in relation to the work of lawyers, but in all areas of professional activity. This is not the place to enter a detailed consideration of the need for the legal profession to adopt good practice and employ an ethical approach to its work, nor of the role of the professional bodies in promoting these ends. However, it is important to be aware of some of the key issues that relate to the promotion of good practice and ethical standards.

It is perhaps true that, until relatively recently, the provision of legal services was seen by members of the legal profession themselves as a public service to which, in some rather mysterious way, commercial pressures somehow did not apply. The adoption of good practice and an ethical approach were, on this view, inherent in the provision of the service.

Whether there was ever any real justification for this belief, there can be no doubt that in the modern world the provision of legal services is quite clearly a business. If lawyers do not make a profit at the end of the year, they go bust. Legal practice must be subject to the disciplines of financial control, quality control, and efficiency that characterize all business activity. The concern with good practice and ethical standards may have arisen from a perception that focusing exclusively on the financial and commercial imperatives of legal practice might encourage lawyers to take short cuts and to forget the ethical principles that should also underpin their work.

Over the years, the professional regulatory bodies have developed guidance on professional conduct, which includes a statement of the ethical framework needed for professional activity (*see Box 9.4*). Understanding these principles is a crucial part of professional legal education, not least because failure to follow the guidance can result, in extreme cases, in loss of the right to practise as a barrister or solicitor.

Box 9.4   Reform in progress

The new SRA Handbook

In October 2011, the SRA brought into effect a new handbook on good practice and ethical practice. It adopts what is described as outcomes-focused regulation, which concentrates on the high-level principles and outcomes that should underpin the provision of legal services for consumers. The new handbook replaces a much more detailed and prescriptive rulebook. The intention is to establish a targeted, risk-based approach concentrating on standards of service that those regulated by the SRA should provide to consumers. However, the new approach allows greater flexibility to firms in how they achieve their outcomes (standards of service) for clients. The aim of the SRA is to set out a unified approach with the same standards applying to both traditional law firms and alternative business structures.

At the heart of the new approach are ten mandatory principles that apply to all. Those regulated by the SRA must:

- uphold the rule of law and the proper administration of justice;
- act with integrity;
- not allow their independence to be compromised;
- act in the best interests of each client;
- provide a proper standard of service to their clients;
- behave in a way that maintains the trust the public places in them and in the provision of legal services;
- comply with their legal and regulatory obligations and deal with their regulators and ombudsmen in an open, timely, and co-operative manner;
- run their business or carry out their role in the business effectively and in accordance with proper governance and sound financial and risk-management principles;
- run their business or carry out their role in the business in a way that encourages equality of opportunity and respect for diversity; and
- protect client money and assets.

These principles are supported by more detailed notes indicating how they should work in practice. For further details, see <www.sra.org.uk/solicitors/handbook/handbookprinciples/content.page>.

Whatever the cynical view of lawyers may be, there are two particular respects in which the legal profession is able at least in part to demonstrate its ethical commitment: pro bono work; and test case litigation.

For free (pro bono) work

There has long been a tradition that lawyers offer free legal services to the poor. Before there was legal aid, there was a history of such provision in London and other major conurbations. In recent years, there has been a renewed emphasis on pro bono work. Because the large commercial firms in the City of London and other commercial centres have been so obviously financially successful, there has been a renewed interest in the provision of free legal services by their staff in citizens' advice bureaux and other agencies. Some may regard this as little more than a token gesture. But, given the precarious funding position that many such agencies are in, it is work that makes a significant contribution to local legal service delivery. It is also true that the majority of those who offer pro bono services derive a great deal of professional interest and pleasure from the work they do.

The professional bodies have taken a great deal of trouble to promote pro bono work over the last decade. Many important new initiatives have been taken, including an annual 'pro bono' week, with events being held around the country. There are 'pro bono' awards to lawyers who have developed outstanding examples of pro bono practice, both in the United Kingdom and in some cases overseas. This is an aspect of modern legal practice that should be much better understood.

Test case litigation

Test case litigation, sometimes called 'cause lawyering', is also often associated with lawyers being willing to take up broad general issues, particularly on behalf of more disadvantaged groups in the community. Historically, test case litigation in the United Kingdom has not had the same impact as, for example, in the United States, where legal provisions or policies were able to be tested for their constitutionality against the provisions of the Constitution of the United States. However, with ever greater involvement in Europe, both through the European Union and, in relation to human rights, through the Council of Europe, many challenges to English law have been mounted, in some cases with dramatic success. The Human Rights Act 1998 has generated more test case legislation, as provisions of English law are tested for their compatibility with the European Convention on Human Rights.

Independence of the legal profession

Independence is a key attribute claimed for the legal profession. This is, constitutionally, extremely important. It involves lawyers asserting their right to give advice independently of the views of the government of the day, and being protected if they do so. It also involves a professional obligation to take on cases that may be widely regarded as disagreeable or distasteful. The proposition that a person is innocent until proved guilty depends on lawyers being willing to develop and advance arguments on behalf of their clients no matter how unpleasant those clients may be. The 'cab-rank' principle that applies to the Bar, whereby barristers are professionally obliged to take on whatever case comes to them next, is perhaps the clearest example of the operation of this principle.

The assertion of independence may also imply that the professions should be free to regulate themselves in accordance with their own rules of professional conduct, without interference from government. As we have seen, there has been significant erosion of the ability of the legal profession to regulate itself. The abolition of restrictive practices, changes to legal aid, and to modes of dealing with complaints about the quality of work have all resulted from increased government intervention. The Legal Services Act 2007 takes this process further.

Each example of government involvement may be justified, particularly in contexts where the legal profession has not been willing to reform itself in the public interest. However, the question how far government should go in regulating the legal profession is one needing constant attention if the role of the legal profession in assisting the individual, often against agencies of the state or other powerful bodies, is not to be compromised.

Trends in legal practice

As a consequence of these and other developments, the legal profession has in recent years undergone profound change. These changes continue. A number of trends affecting the profession are noted here.

The blurring of the distinction between solicitors and barristers

The organization of the practising legal profession in England and Wales differs markedly from that in many other countries. There is still an important distinction in professional identity between 'solicitor' and 'barrister'. However, the practical implications of the distinction are far less today than they were 35 years ago. Many of the services that used to be the exclusive preserve of one branch of the profession are now open to all.

There has also been concern that there should be no unnecessary restrictions on the tasks that people may perform within the legal system. The most important change in this context has been the adoption by statute of the principle that the highest judicial offices should be open to solicitors as well as to barristers (who formerly had a monopoly in relation to these appointments).[3]

---

[3] The appointment of Mr Laurence Collins, QC, a very distinguished commercial solicitor, to the High Court was the first such appointment, made in 1999. The possibility of distinguished legal scholars being appointed to the highest levels of the judiciary just on the strength of their academic record has not been formally accepted. However, the appointment of Dame Brenda Hale (who prior to her appointment as a Law Commissioner had a distinguished academic career at the University of Manchester) first to the High Court bench, then to the Court of Appeal, and now to the Supreme Court is, perhaps, the start of a development in the direction of acknowledging the contribution legal scholars can make to the judiciary. The appointment of Professor Jack Beatson, QC, from the University of Cambridge to the High Court is another example. This certainly happens in the European courts and the United States. Academics have long been appointed judges to the International Court of Justice.

Fusion? The obvious question that these developments pose is whether the time has come for the two branches of the legal profession to fuse into a single profession, as happens in most other countries. Should the historic distinction between solicitors and barristers continue to be defended? This has been debated on many occasions, though surprisingly not seriously in the last few years, despite the developments that have occurred and that are sketched out earlier. The arguments asserted by the Bar for its independence, in delivering both advocacy and other forms of legal advice, are actually very powerful, more powerful than some of the advocates for fusion allow. But in other countries with fused professions, the independence of the advocate is still strongly asserted. Other ways could be found to protect professional independence without the retention of a divided profession. It seems inconceivable that at some point in the not too distant future this issue should not again become the subject of public debate.

Growth and globalization

A second trend to be noted is the growth in the size of law firms and the increasingly global scope of their practices. These have resulted from the context within which lawyers practise, which cannot be divorced from other changes in the economy at large. In the United Kingdom, the last 35 years have seen a major shift from an economy based on manufacturing to one based on services. Increased globalization of the world economy has led to a growth in the demand for lawyers able to advise corporations about all the national contexts within which they are required to operate. The globalization of the economy has been accompanied by globalization in the provision of legal services. British lawyers have responded in a variety of ways:

- many of the large law firms in the City of London have gone through substantial programmes of merger and expansion;

- significant groupings of leading firms in provincial commercial centres—for example Leeds, Birmingham, Bristol—have also developed, either through mergers and takeovers or the creation of networks of legal practices;

- many of these firms have established presences in other key centres of economic activity, in Europe, the Middle East, the Far East, and the Americas;

- mergers of English law firms with firms in other countries in Europe and the United States have resulted in the creation of new forms of international partnership;

- there has been a significant increase in the presence of overseas law firms, in particular US law firms, in London, which has added to the competitive pressures on British-based firms; and

- there have been moves towards the creation of professional groupings that cut across traditional disciplinary boundaries—in particular, lawyers and accountants.

There is every likelihood of further developments of these kinds in the years ahead.

Specialization and niche practices

A third trend has been the increasing development of specialist/niche practices. In part this is a response to the trend towards 'mega-lawyering' noted in the previous section. Increasingly, small firms of solicitors and sets of barristers' chambers have come to specialize in particular areas—family law, criminal law, employment law, housing law, to give some examples. These developments have been supported in part by the legal professional bodies themselves. For example, the Law Society has established a number of specialist panels, including the Children's Panel, the Mental Health Panel, and the Medical Negligence Panel.

In addition, members of the profession themselves have taken the lead in establishing specialist groups, many of which cross over traditional solicitor/barrister boundaries. There are now well over 40 such groups. They act in a variety of ways:

- they may be able to act collaboratively (within the competitive market) to promote the specialist services that they offer (thereby seeking to exclude non-specialists from their work);
- some, such as the Solicitors' Family Law Association, have promoted new modes of legal practice, designed to provide a different form of lawyering for their clients—in the context of family law, a less confrontational approach designed to assist those whose relationships have broken down (*see Chapter 7, The practitioners*);
- others, such as the Patent Lawyers' Association, have developed specialist programmes of advanced legal education and training designed to give their members special expertise and, thus, it is hoped, a competitive edge in the legal services market place; and
- the specialist lawyer groups have also developed a very important influence in government. They can offer advice on how particular areas of legal practice may be affected by proposed policy changes in ways in which the general professional bodies such as the Law Society or Bar Council may be unable to achieve.

Legal services to the poor

A fourth noteworthy trend in the shape of the legal profession has been the transformation of the legal aid scheme. The details of the scheme and the process of contraction it is currently experiencing are considered in *Chapter 10*. Here the principal point to note is that, whereas ten years ago in effect any firm of solicitors that wished to do legal aid work could do so, now only those firms with a contract to provide legal aid services can undertake publicly funded legal aid work. Many practitioners who used to do modest amounts of legal aid work as part of a portfolio of general legal services provided to mainly private clients have been affected by these changes. One response to these changes has been an increased emphasis on the legal profession providing services pro bono (*see For free (pro bono) work*).

High street practice

A consequence of these last two developments is that generalist high street practices, found in smaller towns, suburban areas and other locations, which have in the past provided a general service to private clients, have come under increasing commercial pressure and face considerable uncertainty. The ability to make a living from a mixed practice of some criminal work, some property transactions (such as conveyancing or probate), a little bit of family and divorce work, and some personal injuries work, which even ten years ago was quite common, is now increasingly difficult. Many of the remaining sole practitioners and small firms fall into this category. The future of high street practice is under considerable threat, unless those who remain in this sector of the legal services market are prepared to rethink their commercial strategies.

A graduate profession

A significant change over the last 30 years is that the legal profession has become a largely graduate one. The old days when professional qualifications could be obtained simply by apprenticeship in a solicitor's office or a barrister's chambers (and the passing of some not very demanding professional exams) are now long gone. Despite this, many of the graduates who enter the legal profession come with degrees other than in law. They obtain their legal qualifications through conversion courses undertaken following the obtaining of a first degree in another discipline. This has been the subject of fierce argument between the legal professional bodies and the legal academics, the latter asserting that only the grounding of a good law degree gives potential entrants to the legal profession a real understanding of how law is made and fundamental legal principles.

Information technology

In common with everyone else, the legal profession has been increasingly affected by the development of new information technologies. Use of IT has transformed professional practice management. And as legal information from government and the legal publishers and other sources becomes increasingly available in electronic form, and as court procedures become increasingly technology-driven, the impact of IT on legal practice has intensified. Lack of IT investment, particularly in the civil courts, still limits the use of IT in civil litigation. But legal practice, including litigation, will continue to change enormously in the next decade, reflecting both increased investment and further rapid technological change. These developments are likely to have a significant impact not only on how those who deliver legal services interact with the courts and other agencies, such as the Land Registry (which has made it possible to register transfers of land online), but also on the organization of legal services, with much routine work being outsourced to other countries where labour costs are lower.

Pay and conditions

The expectations of those entering the profession about the pay and conditions they should receive have also changed considerably in the last quarter of a century. A real problem in this context is that the financial rewards for those in some parts of legal practice, particularly the corporate sector, are hugely different from those in many specialist or niche areas, particularly those offering services to the less well-off groups in society. Much of the problem is the result of a type of macho legal journalism that has developed over the last 15 years, but that arguably is not wholly in the interest of the legal profession (*see Box 9.5*).

Box 9.5   Legal system explained

Legal journalism

One consequence of the changed context of legal practice, particularly the relaxation of restrictions on advertising, is that a significant branch of journalism has developed, devoted to the telling of stories about individuals and firms in the law and their doings. Some of the broadsheet newspapers have a weekly law section, much of which is concerned with what is in effect legal gossip. In addition there are specialist papers for the profession that focus in particular on the activities of law firms and sets of chambers. The 'free' paper, the *Lawyer*—which appears weekly—is supplemented by the expensive and glossy *Legal Business*, which focuses in particular on firms operating in the City and overseas.

One consequence of this new journalism is that public information about lawyers is to a large extent dominated by the stories which the PR departments of the large firms are able to place in this press. Stories about the impact and importance of the small high street firms find little place beside dramatic tales of takeovers, mergers, and other commercial/corporate activity. This creates at least three distortions:

- those thinking of entering the law as a profession are denied the opportunity to consider the full range of legal careers open to them;
- they come to assume that the only type of lawyering worth undertaking is that which pays enormous salaries; and
- the public assume that all lawyers act—and most significantly are paid—in ways suggested by the stories that appear in this press.

Much of the public hostility towards lawyers is, it may be surmised, the result of assumptions that legal services are very expensive and thus affordable only by the very rich. A more balanced picture would indicate that there are still many lawyers providing valuable services to the public for extremely modest fees.

Future trends

Alternative business structures

Historically, solicitors in private practice usually came together to form partnerships, though a substantial minority practise on their own as 'sole practitioners'.

A recent development is that firms of solicitors have been able to form limited lia-bility partnerships. Barristers in private practice work in 'chambers' but they are all self-employed within those chambers. Barristers were not permitted to form partnerships.

In his review of the legal services market, Clementi thought competition and effi-ciency would not be fully realized without alternative business structures allowing different combinations of lawyers and non-lawyers to own and manage legal practices. He envisaged outside investors being brought into the market as well as the possibil-ity of lawyers establishing multi-disciplinary partnerships (with other professional groups such as accountants). Independent research published by the Department for Constitutional Affairs in 2005 suggested that new forms of practice would not under-mine the independence of the legal profession and would not reduce access to justice. Despite his proposals being strongly contested by the leaders of the professions, the government stood firm. The Legal Services Act 2007 makes it possible for these devel-opments to occur.

After much consultation, in 2011 the Legal Services Board agreed how approved regulators would be able to licence alternative business structures. The first licence was issued by the Council of Licensed Conveyancers in October 2011. The SRA received approval to issue licences in January 2012. Since then over 35 licences have been granted. Perhaps the most high profile one was that granted to the Co-op to deliver legal services. For developments, keep an eye on my blog, www.martinpartington. com.

New marketing and legal service developments

In parallel with the development of alternative business structures, practitioners are finding innovative ways to provide services. To give just some examples:

- *'virtual' legal services*: here, practitioners work largely from home. They may come into an office for meetings or to meet clients, but office space is kept to a mini-mum. Practitioners do not have their own rooms but hot-desk as needed. This enables practices to operate with greatly reduced overhead costs. One example is Virtual Law, offering business legal services. Another, offering principally legal services to individual clients is Scott-Moncrieff & Associates. A third is Road Traffic Representation, an internet and phone-based service offering advice to those charged with motoring offences.

- *franchises*: new forms of legal franchise are emerging, enabling individual law firms to continue to operate in their own right, but under the umbrella of the franchise operator which seeks to guarantee standards of service, control of fees payable by clients, and so on. An example is Quality Solicitors, whose mem-bers offer legal services in over 400 locations in England and Wales. They have established legal access points in around 150 branches of WH Smith, the high street stationery retailer.

- *direct public access*: in 2004, rules preventing direct access to barristers by members of the public were significantly relaxed. A number of examples of barristers offering legal services direct to the public, not from traditional chambers, have emerged over the years. One of the most long-standing is Clerksroom, originally based in Taunton, but now with a presence in a number of cities including London, Manchester, Birmingham, and Leeds. A more recent development is Stobarts Barristers. Created by a firm known primarily for its road haulage business, Stobarts Barristers offers the public access to a network of barristers throughout the country.

The internet: DIY law

There are also major developments taking place to enable ordinary members of the public effectively to undertake their own legal work, for example in drawing up wills, preparing divorce papers or drafting standard commercial documents. At present, these initiatives are more developed in the United States. But companies such as Legalzoom are exploring how their services might develop for the UK market. Research into the potential for IT and the internet to deliver legal services in new ways is the subject of academic research in the ReInvent Law Laboratory in Michigan State University.

New professional groupings

The changing face of legal service delivery is likely to mean significant changes in the work undertaken in law firms. Professor Richard Susskind, who has thought about this more than anyone in the United Kingdom, writes:

The emerging consensus is that traditional lawyers will still be needed for complex legal work in tomorrow's legal world but that routine, repetitive, process-based, and administrative work will be conducted through a variety of alternative sources – for example, by legal process outsourcing, near-shoring, off-shoring, sub-contracting to lower cost law firms, and so forth. When work is packaged and tackled in this way, new roles for legal professionals people will emerge – the legal knowledge engineer, the legal process analyst, the legal project manager, and the legal risk manager, for instance.[4]

---

[4] Extract from Susskind, R., *Provocations and Perspectives*, a working paper submitted to the UK CLE Research Consortium (Legal Education and Training Review), October 2012, available at <http://letr.org.uk/wp-content/uploads/2012/10/Susskind-LETR-final-Oct-2012.pdf>.

Professional groups allied to the legal profession

This last point is a good link to a brief consideration of the currently existing professional groups allied to the legal profession. These groups cannot be forgotten. It is they who provide many of the legal services that are not delivered by professionally qualified members of the legal profession. It should be noted that the Legal Services Board already has oversight of a number of these groups. In 2011, it started a consultation exercise on the extent to which other providers of legal services should be brought within the scope of the regulatory system, not least to ensure adequate consumer protection for those who use such services.

Legal executives

Many of the staff employed in solicitors' offices are not formally qualified as solicitors, but nonetheless provide a great deal of legal service to the public. These are known collectively as 'legal executives'. Many of these are members and fellows of their own professional representative body, the *Chartered Institute of Legal Executives* (CILEX). CILEX organizes its own training programmes and examinations, which must be passed before a legal executive can call him- or herself a fellow of the Institute. Legal executives play a central role in many legal practices, often being more expert in their areas of expertise than their fully professionally qualified colleagues. Legal executives who are fellows of CILEX are able, by taking additional courses and sitting additional examinations, to qualify as solicitors, and a number do so each year.

CILEX has a Code of Professional Conduct, which is applied by the CILEX Professional Standards Board, an independent body created in October 2008 on a similar basis to the SRA, to ensure that CILEX members comply with their code. CILEX and the CILEX Professional Standards Board are both authorized regulators under the Legal Services Board.

Intellectual property attorneys

There are two specialist groups that operate in the intellectual property area: patent attorneys and trade mark attorneys. Each has a professional representative body, respectively the Chartered Institute of Patent Attorneys, and the Institute of Trade Mark Attorneys. Recently, they have established the Intellectual Property Regulation Board, to regulate both groups. All three bodies have become approved regulators under the Legal Services Board.

Licensed conveyancers

Licensed conveyancers came into existence following the ending of the solicitors' conveyancing monopoly. Their activities are regulated by the Council of Licensed Conveyancers, another approved regulator under the Legal Services Board.

Costs draftsmen

This group offers specialist legal services, drafting statements of lawyers' costs. They have a regulatory body—the Association of Law Costs Draftsmen—which is an approved regulator under the Legal Services Board.

Insolvency practitioners

Insolvency practitioners advise on, and undertake appointments in, all formal insolvency procedures—both personal (bankruptcies, sequestrations, individual voluntary arrangements, and trust deeds) and companies and partnerships (liquidations, company and partnership voluntary arrangements, administrations and administrative receiverships). They also advise on, and act in, informal rescheduling of debts, reconstructions and reorganizations for individuals and businesses facing financial difficulties. They belong to the Insolvency Practitioners' Association (IPA), a membership body recognized for the purposes of authorizing (licensing) insolvency practitioners under the Insolvency Act 1986. They are subject to oversight and inspection, not by the Legal Services Board, but by the Insolvency Service acting for the Secretary of State.

Tax advisers

This last group is not subject to the same forms of regulation as the other groups mentioned. It may, however, be noted that the Association of Chartered Certified Accountants is an approved regulator under the Legal Services Board in relation to reserved probate activities.

Lay advisers and other providers of legal services

Lay advisers/advocates

In addition to the formally qualified, there are substantial numbers of people who have not obtained legal qualifications, but who nevertheless deliver legal services. These include: the lay advisers who work in advice agencies, such as the Citizens' Advice Bureaux; welfare rights workers, often employed in local authority sponsored welfare rights offices; housing-aid workers working in housing advice centres; and many other lay advice workers working in a vast range of social, environmental, and other agencies.

Law Centres

One particular context in which the professionally qualified lawyer and the lay adviser come together is the Law Centre. The Law Centre movement started in the 1970s with the specific objective of targeting legal services to those who lived in deprived areas, principally towns and cities. Historically, they have had a somewhat hand-to-mouth existence. Some have been funded by local authorities; others by private charities; one or two by central government. Agencies that satisfy standards set by the Legal Services Commission are also able to obtain legal aid funding for defined categories of work (*see Chapter 10*).

Membership services

A number of membership organizations also provide legal services to their members. These services may either be general or related to the matters that arise from membership. Examples at the more general end of provision are the legal services provided as the result of membership of trade unions or other professional groups (e.g. the Medical Defence Union); more specific legal services are provided to members of, for example the Automobile Association or the Royal Automobile Club.

Specialist agencies

In addition to the foregoing, a number of pressure groups also provide legal services. One motivation for this is to find appropriate test cases that might be brought to test the boundaries of statutory provisions. Examples include the Citizens' Rights Office, which is attached to the Child Poverty Action Group; the Public Law Project; Liberty (formerly the National Council for Civil Liberties); Shelter; and a number of environmental groups, such as Greenpeace. These agencies have been particularly successful in expanding the range of groups entitled to make representations to the courts in judicial review cases.

Adjudicators and dispute resolvers

Much has been written about judges in the English legal system. As with other topics in this book, most accounts focus on a rather narrow body of the judiciary, namely those who sit in the High Court, Court of Appeal, and the Supreme Court. There can be no doubting the influence of the judges who sit in these higher courts in shaping English law. But the chances of any member of the public appearing before one of these judges is remote in the extreme. Far more likely is an encounter with a district judge, a lay magistrate, a tribunal judge, a circuit judge, or one of the army of other dispute resolvers and complaints handlers that now exist. It is these adjudicators or dispute resolvers who are, in practice, the face of the judiciary, as seen by the public at large.

Definition

For the purposes of this book, adjudicators and dispute resolvers are all those who are empowered[5] to resolve disputes that have been brought to them. This definition includes all the senior judicial figures who sit in the High Court and other higher courts just mentioned. But it also includes:

(1) *circuit judges*, who determine civil cases in the county court, and criminal cases in the Crown Court;

(2) *district judges*, who determine civil cases, including small claims hearings, in the county court;

(3) *recorders*, who are, in effect, circuit judges in training;

(4) *magistrates*, both lay and professionally qualified,[6] who determine the vast majority of criminal cases that are dealt with in magistrates' courts;

(5) *arbitrators*, who determine a wide range of disputes referred to them under specially agreed arbitration agreements. Arbitrators are particularly used to resolve commercial disputes, both national and international;

(6) *tribunal members and judges*, who deal with specific issues arising in defined legislative contexts: for example, disputes about entitlement to social security benefit, or disputes about employment matters;

(7) *ombudsmen*, as they appear in their various guises; and

(8) *mediators, conciliators, complaints handlers*, and others who offer alternative forms of appropriate dispute resolution (ADR).

Numbers

It is not possible to give a complete picture of the total number of people holding various kinds of adjudicative office. The Ministry of Justice issues statistics of the numbers of judicial office-holders. In addition to the principal judicial office-holders—the Lord Chief Justice of England, the Master of the Rolls, the President of the Queen's Bench Division, the President of the Family Division, and the Chancellor, the number of full-time judicial office-holders at 1 April 2012 is set out in *Diagram 4.1*.

In addition to the appointments there listed, there are some 29,000 lay magistrates. Information about numbers of office-holders in other dispute resolution contexts is harder to establish. Figures are not easily available. There may be around 20,000 full- and part-time tribunal judges and members.

---

[5] This definition could include those who determine disputes under purely private contractual arrangements, for example internal employment dispute resolution procedures or student disciplinary procedures, but they are not considered here.

[6] They are called *district judges (magistrates' courts) (see Box 5.10)*.

Judicial independence and impartiality

The importance of judicial independence was considered earlier (*see Box 3.11*). An equally important practical consideration is the importance of judges and adjudicators being impartial. There have been cases where it is suggested that there may be judicial bias, in the sense that a judge may have some direct personal interest in the outcome of a particular case (*see Box 9.6*). However, in general, the impartiality of the judiciary in England and Wales is largely taken for granted. Instances of judicial corruption familiar in some jurisdictions do not seem to be a significant problem here.

Literature on the judiciary

With few exceptions, books about the judiciary have not in any strict sense been socially scientific works. Drawing inferences about how judges think and thus come to decisions simply from the skewed sample of their work represented by reported decisions in the law reports is a wholly inadequate basis for serious analysis of how judges approach the judicial task.[7] Further, it is all too easy to assume that because someone is white, male, middle-aged, and probably public school and Oxbridge educated, he (less frequently she) brings attitudes to his (or her) judicial work that affect his (or her) decisions. Such links are not provable without detailed empirical study that has only rarely been taken into the judiciary.[8]

There has, of course, been a problem, in that researchers who have sought access to the judiciary in order to conduct research into it have often found such access difficult to obtain. The stereotype of judges as white, male, of middle to late age, and from the (upper) middle class may, broadly though by no means exclusively, apply to the higher judiciary. It is far less accurate as a descriptor of the totality of judges/adjudicators/dispute resolvers in the vast array of fora that determine the disputes brought to them by ordinary members of the public.

Box 9.6   Legal system explained

Case study: judicial bias

The issue of judicial bias became the subject of much public discussion in 1999 following the revelation that Lord Hoffmann, one of the members of the House of Lords who sat in judgment in the case involving General Pinochet (the former dictator from Chile), was a member of Amnesty, one of the parties in the proceedings involving the General.

---

[7] Griffith, J. A. G., *The Politics of the Judiciary* (5th edn, London, Fontana, 1997); cf. Hodder-Williams, R., *Judges and Politics in the Contemporary Age* (London, Bowerdean, 1996).
[8] See Paterson, A., *The Law Lords* (London, Macmillan, 1982).

Box 9.6 *Continued*

The issue having been raised, the House of Lords decided that the decision in which Lord Hoffmann had taken part could not be allowed to stand. In an unprecedented move, the original decision of the Lords was set aside, and referred for determination by another Appeal Committee from the House of Lords (*R v Bow Street Metropolitan Magistrates, ex p Pinochet Ungarte* [1999] 2 WLR 272, HL).

Shortly thereafter a number of other cases were heard by the Court of Appeal which, though not as dramatic as that involving Pinochet, raised similar issues for consideration. In reviewing the position, the Court of Appeal laid down the following propositions (*Locabail (UK) v Bayfield* [2000] 1 All ER 65, CA):

- in general, membership of professional, political, or other organizations would not give grounds for an allegation of bias;
- neither would racial or ethnic origin, class, extra-judicial activities, sexual orientation, or previous judicial references to parties or witnesses, even if forthright;
- personal acquaintance with or antagonism towards any individuals involved in a case, especially if their credibility might be an issue, would give rise to a real danger of bias;
- the independent status of barristers when sitting judicially absolved them from responsibility for the interests of other members of chambers; and
- solicitors maintained responsibility for acts of their partners and owed a duty to their firms' clients, even if they had not acted for them personally.

Comment on adjudicators

A number of general points about those who perform dispute resolution functions in the legal system may be made:

- they are not all professionally qualified as lawyers. Some have other professional qualifications, such as accountants, surveyors, or doctors. Many have no specific professional qualification at all. In the same way that many legal services are provided by persons other than professionally qualified lawyers, so too many dispute resolution services are provided by those without legal qualifications;
- many academic lawyers are embraced by this broader definition. The notion that somehow those with an academic background have no capacity to determine disputes in a fair and proper manner is simply not borne out by the evidence;
- the total number of dispute resolvers is considerably larger than traditional definitions of the judiciary suggest;
- many appointments are full-time, but many more are part-time;
- only the highest judiciary hold office 'on good behaviour'—a concept designed to enhance the fundamental independence of the judiciary by guaranteeing their

right to remain a judge until the statutory retiring age, so long as they are of good behaviour. Most other groups, particularly part-timers, hold office on terms that can result in their being required to step down before the official retirement age;

- only a limited number are able to take advantage of the attractive (non-contributory) pensions that are provided by government to full-time members of the judiciary;

- many judges sit in more than one jurisdiction. For example a tribunal judge may also sit as a part-time district judge, thereby enabling him or her to acquire wider judicial experience. The Tribunals, Courts and Enforcement Act 2007 is encouraging even greater flexibility and enabling the Judicial Appointments Commission to develop the notion of a judicial career (*see Chapter 4, Judicial appointments*);

- many judges now start to sit in their early forties, some even in their thirties. They are much younger than popular images of judges may suggest;

- there are more women holding judicial office than is often appreciated, though the numbers at the highest levels are still far too low. The numbers from the ethnic minorities are significantly less impressive;

- most judicial appointees now receive at least some training for the job through the Judicial College (*see Chapter 4, Judicial College*), though the amount of training decreases with the seniority of the post;

- there is still only a limited amount of monitoring of judicial performance. Such monitoring as does take place tends to be limited to the performance by part-timers, and is often undertaken by those in full-time office. While too heavy monitoring could compromise judicial independence, certain factors, for example the ability to be civil to those appearing before them or to deliver written decisions within agreed timescales, would not seem impossible targets for assessment;

- there is a huge amount of procedural variation as between each of the adjudicative systems. The formal courts operate within a very detailed procedural framework, with a large number of rules of practice supplemented by yet more practice directions and protocols. Many other bodies have only the barest procedural outline prescribed by law, and instead operate with considerable discretion as regards procedural matters;

- not all tribunals operate on the basis that their 'typical' adjudication will involve a formal hearing of the parties. Many reach determinations on the basis of information presented in written form alone;

- while it is usual for tribunals that hold hearings to sit in public, in the sense that members of the public are entitled to attend hearings should they so wish, many do not, particularly where sensitive personal or financial information is being discussed;

- the dress of the judiciary is also much more varied than is often realized. The highly formalized process of the High Court, with impressive uniforms, dark wooden panelling, and advocates in wigs and gowns—the image of the television or film drama—is a statistical rarity. The vast majority of dispute resolvers operate with none of these formal trappings; and

- dispute resolvers work in a wide variety of locations. Many sit in court buildings or other specially dedicated accommodation. But there are many examples of adjudicative bodies sitting in local authority accommodation, or in hotels, or even on occasion in people's homes.

If one takes this broader view, it is seen that there is considerably more variety and flexibility of approach to dispute resolution than is often realized. Different procedures and practices have been developed to meet the specific needs of particular bodies.

The legal scholars

Law claims to be a learned profession. Thus, a third group, delivering a rather different kind of legal service and one not usually given adequate recognition, should be noted, namely the work of the law teachers and jurists. Law teachers in the university law departments and in other locations where legal education is provided have a variety of functions. It is they who are responsible for the foundational stages in the professional formation of those qualified to deliver legal services.

First, law teachers provide basic education in law and legal principles, which provides new generations of lawyers with the fundamental intellectual tools to enable them to become lawyers. The leading university law schools also offer, through their law degrees, a traditional liberal university education, giving students the capacity to think critically about law and its impact on society.

Secondly, law teachers deliver a wide range of professionally focused courses that transform the recent graduate from the preliminary academic stage to a person with the skills required to enter the world of practice. Some of these courses are offered within university law departments, but other providers, including the University of Law, and other private companies play a significant part in this market as well.

Thirdly, the law schools together with the private providers offer much of the further education and advanced training in new developments in the law that are needed by legal practitioners to enable them to keep abreast of developments in the law and to break into new areas of law.

Lastly, law teachers—particularly those who work in the leading research universities—assist in the development of law and the legal system through the research they undertake, the books and articles they write, and the advice they give to governments and other agencies. The scope of legal scholarship has expanded enormously in recent years, again reflecting the growing complexity of the law, not only domestic law but also law coming from Europe and elsewhere. The impact of legal scholarship on practitioners is hard to gauge. Certainly the old rule that only dead authors could be cited in court has long been abandoned. Advocates now often refer to academic articles and books in their submissions, and in many reported cases the judgments adopt (or reject) the analyses of legal scholars. But this is the tip of the iceberg. Many practitioners developing a legal argument, or simply struggling to understand a particular legal doctrine, turn to the textbook writers for assistance. The importance of the work of the jurists in helping to shape legal argument should not be underestimated. Their work is also central to the work of the law reform agencies, particularly the Law Commission.

A number of areas of practice that have developed in recent years have been the result of a combination of the work of legal scholars who helped to shape the areas and the practitioners who took them into practice. Examples include: the development of administrative law that arose from analysis of the principles of judicial review; development of family law is another; the law of restitution is a third. A number of more specialist areas including private and public international law, housing law, and social welfare law have similarly been shaped by important academic contributions.

Notwithstanding these observations, there has been a surprising reluctance by the jurists to get involved in the scholarly analysis of legal practice and procedure. Thus while endless books and articles are published offering systematic expositions and analyses of substantive law, it has been left to a very small number of legal scholars to focus on the questions of practice and procedure that are the lifeblood of most legal practice, an understanding of which is essential to understanding law and the legal system.

In addition, alongside what is sometimes described as 'black-letter' legal research, focusing on the detailed analysis of legal doctrine, there has emerged over the last 25 years an increasingly rich body of 'socio-legal' scholarship, in which the law is analysed in an inter-disciplinary context, employing insights and methodologies from other social sciences, such as economics, social psychology, politics, and sociology. Much of this research is empirical in nature, and much has involved research into the practice of law. A number of areas of government legal policy have been significantly influenced by the outcomes of socio-legal research.[9]

Access to the legal profession

One of the key functions that the university and professional law schools have played over the last 20 years has been to open up access to the legal profession to people from a wider range of backgrounds (a trend noted at the outset of this chapter). This has been

---

[9] The importance of investing in empirical research in law was reasserted in the Nuffield Foundation report, Genn, H., Partington, M., and Wheeler, S., *Law in the Real World: Improving Our Understanding of How Law Works* (London, Nuffield Foundation, 2006).

of particular benefit to women, who now comprise the majority of those studying law at university and in the professional law schools.

Despite these trends, the extent to which people from different *class* backgrounds have been able to take advantage of these developments may not have been as great as many would wish. There have been a number of initiatives designed to encourage potential students from less privileged areas to contemplate university in general and the study of law in particular. For example:

- The Sutton Trust, founded in 1997 by Sir Peter Lampl, has for many years offered children from non-privileged backgrounds places on summer schools, designed to introduce them to university study.

- In 2006, the College of Law joined with the Sutton Trust to create the *Pathways to Law* programme, run in partnership with seven Russell Group universities. Some 400 places a year are on offer.

- The Social Mobility Foundation has, since 2005, been developing ways to support Year 12 school students in their university and professional choices. The Foundation works with law firms to provide internships. It also provides mentoring in association with the Diversity and Community Relations Judges, a group of volunteer judges from different parts of the country who work with schools and community groups to provide insight into the legal system and its workings.

- More generally, the judiciary have for a number of years encouraged school students to visit courts and have offered to visit schools.

- The Bar Council has taken a number of steps to promote the message that the Bar is open to anyone with the right aptitude and talent to become a barrister.

- The former Labour government commissioned a report—the Milburn Report—on fair access to the professions.

- The Law Society runs two access schemes offering assistance with legal practice course fees: the bursary scheme and the diversity access scheme.

Despite all these initiatives, there are concerns that, in practice, the legal professions are not as open to all-comers as they might like to be—a concern shared by the Legal Services Board (*see Legal Services Board: the regulatory objectives in Box 9.3*). Recent decisions on the funding of higher education make many fear that opportunities to enter the legal profession may be reducing rather than expanding, with those from better-off backgrounds finding it easier to get started in the legal professions. And with evidence beginning to emerge that there are starting to be downturns in the level of recruitment to the legal professions, there is no doubt that entry to the legal professions will become even harder than it has been in the past.

It is in this context that the law teachers bear a particular responsibility both to understand what is currently happening to the legal professions and to increase their awareness of the other career options—of which there are many—that should be considered by their students.

Questions

Use the self-test questions on the Online Resource Centre to test your understanding of the topics covered in this chapter and receive tailored feedback:

www.oxfordtextbooks.co.uk/orc/partington13_14/

Weblinks

Check the Online Resource Centre for a selection of annotated weblinks allowing you to easily research topics of particular interest:

www.oxfordtextbooks.co.uk/orc/partington13_14/

Blog items

 See www.martinpartington.com (access via the Online Resource Centre)

Issues discussed include: alternative business structures; new judicial career opportunities; the work of the Legal Ombudsman (podcast); pro bono lawyering; the media treatment of lawyers (interview with Joshua Rozenberg); researching the judiciary; the promotion of ADR; review of legal education.

Further reading

ABEL, R. L., *English Lawyers Between Market and State: The Politics of Professionalism* (Oxford, Oxford University Press, 2003)

ABEL-SMITH, B., and STEVENS, R., with the assistance of Brooke, R., *Lawyers and the Courts: A Sociological Study of the English Legal System 1750–1965* (London, Heinemann, 1967)

—— ZANDER, M., and BROOKE, R., *Legal Problems and the Citizen: A Study in Three London Boroughs* (London, Heinemann Educational, 1973)

BLACKSELL, M., ECONOMIDES, K., and WATKINS, C., *Justice Outside the City: Access to Legal Services in Rural Britain* (Harlow, Longman Scientific and Technical, 1991)

BLOM-COOPER, L., and DREWRY, G., *Final Appeal: A Study of the House of Lords in its Judicial Capacity* (Oxford, Clarendon Press, 1972)

—— DICKSON, B., and DREWRY, G. (eds), *The Judicial House of Lords 1876–2009* (Oxford, Oxford University Press, 2009)

COCKS, R., and COWNIE, F. A., *Great and Noble Occupation: The History of the Society of Legal Scholars* (Oxford, Hart Publishing, 2009)

Committee on Legal Education, *Report* (Cmnd 4595) (London, Her Majesty's Stationery Office, 1971)

DEVLIN, BARON P., *The Judge* (Oxford, Oxford University Press, 1979)

DWORKIN, R., *Political Judges and the Rule of Law* (Oxford, Oxford University Press, 1980)

ECONOMIDES, K. (ed.), *Ethical Challenges to Legal Education and Conduct* (Oxford, Hart Publishing, 1998)

GALANTER, M., and PULAY, T., *Tournament of Lawyers: The Transformation of the Big Law Firm* (Chicago, IL, Chicago University Press, 1991)

GENN, H., *Hard Bargaining: Out of Court Settlement in Personal Injury Actions* (Oxford, Clarendon Press, 1987)

GREEN, S., and LEACHAM, K., *Tax Advice in the UK: Why Things Go Wrong and the Implications for the Tax Adviser's Profession* (London, Chartered Institute of Taxation, 1997)

GRIFFITHS, J. A. G., *The Politics of the Judiciary* (5th edn, London, Fontana, 1997)

HARLOW, C., and RAWLINGS, R., *Pressure Through Law* (London, Routledge, 1992)

HODDER-WILLIAMS, R., *Judges and Politics in the Contemporary Age* (London, Bowerdean, 1996)

JOSEPH, M., *The Conveyancing Fraud* (Harmondsworth, Penguin, 1975)

Justice, *The Judiciary: The Report of a Justice Sub-committee* (Chairman of Subcommittee, Peter Webster) (London, Stevens, 1972)

—— *The Judiciary in England and Wales: A Report by Justice* (Chairman of Committee, Robert Stevens) (London, JUSTICE, 1992)

LEE, S., *Judging Judges* (London, Faber, 1989)

LEWIS, P. S. C., *Assumptions about Lawyers in Policy Statements: A Survey of Relevant Research* (London, Lord Chancellor's Department, 2000)

MALLESON, K., *The New Judiciary: The Effects of Expansion and Activism* (Aldershot, Dartmouth, 1999)

MANSFIELD, M., *Memoirs of a Radical Lawyer* (London, Bloomsbury, 2010)

MAUGHAN, C., and WEBB, J., *Lawyering Skills and the Legal Process* (2nd edn, Cambridge, Cambridge University Press, 2005)

PANNICK, D., *Judges* (Oxford, Oxford University Press, 1987)

PATERSON, A., *Lawyers and the Public Good: Democracy in Action?* (Cambridge, Cambridge University Press, 2011)

—— *The Law Lords* (London, Macmillan, 1982)

ROBERTSON, D., *Judicial Discretion in the House of Lords* (Oxford, Clarendon Press, 1998)

SARAT, A., and SCHEINGOLD, S., *Cause Lawyering and Professional Responsibilities* (New York, NY, Oxford University Press, 1998)

SACHS, A., *The Strange Alchemy of Life and Law* (Oxford, Oxford University Press 2009; paperback edn, 2011)

SHETREET, S., *Judges on Trial: A Study of the Appointment and Accountability of the English Judiciary* (Amsterdam and Oxford, North-Holland, 1976)

STEVENS, R., *Law and Politics: The House of Lords as a Judicial Body, 1800–1976* (London, Weidenfeld & Nicolson, 1979)

—— *Law School: Legal Education in America from the 1850s to the 1980s* (Chapel Hill, NC, University of North Carolina Press, c. 1983)

—— *The English Judges: Their Role in the Changing Constitution* (Oxford, Hart Publishing, 2002)

—— *The Independence of the Judiciary: The View from the Lord Chancellor's Office* (Oxford, Clarendon Press, 1997)

SUSSKIND, R., *The End of Lawyers? Rethinking the nature of legal services* (2nd edn, Oxford, Oxford University Press, 2010)

—— *Transforming the Law: Essays on Technology, Justice and the Legal Marketplace* (Oxford, Oxford University Press, 2003)

TWINING, W., *Blackstone's Tower: The English Law School* (London, Stevens & Son/Sweet & Maxwell, 1994)

—— *Law in Context: Enlarging a Discipline* (Oxford, Oxford University Press, 1997)

WILSON, G. P. (ed.), *Frontiers of Legal Scholarship: Twenty-five Years of Warwick Law School* (Chichester and New York, NY, Wiley, 1995)

ZANDER, M., *Lawyers and the Public Interest: A Study of Restrictive Practices* (London, published for the London School of Economics and Political Science by Weidenfeld & Nicolson, 1967)

10

Funding legal services

Underpinning this book is the claim that law plays a central role in the functioning of our society (*see Chapter* 2). This role will, however, be limited if the people potentially affected by law are not able to take advantage of the rights and protections it affords. Thus the final issue considered in this book is how legal services provided to the public can be paid for. The overall effectiveness of the English legal system depends on services required by the public actually being available.

Implicit in *Chapter 9*, where the distinction between lawyers' services and legal services was drawn, is the fact that funding legal services in the broad sense is done in a variety of ways. Some services are paid for by clients themselves; other services are provided free or at low cost from grants paid by central or local government; some services are provided free (pro bono) by the legal profession; other services are paid for through membership of organizations such as trade unions or other professional organizations. Yet other services are funded by insurance companies out of premiums paid by their customers. There is a complex mosaic of funding streams for legal services in the broad sense used in *Chapter 9*.

This chapter takes a closer look at one particular form of legal service provision, namely litigation—the resolution of disputes in a court or other dispute resolution forum. It is in this specific context that there is currently great upheaval and uncertainty. There is much agreement that going to court is too expensive; much less agreement on how policy on the funding of litigation should develop and whether there should be greater use of alternatives to litigation.

This chapter does not consider the funding of dispute resolution services for the corporate sector or for wealthy individuals. For present purposes it is assumed that they can afford the services they require. This chapter concentrates on how legal services, in particular litigation, to the less well-off and the poor are paid for.

This aspect of the English legal system is undergoing profound change at the moment. The legal aid scheme and the bases on which civil litigation is funded are both experiencing major reform. So extensive are these changes that, when combined with the changes that are happening to the courts system (*see Chapter 8*) and the legal profession (*see Chapter 9*), it is not possible at present to offer a definitive account of them. What this chapter seeks to do is to make the reader aware of what is on the agenda, and identify the issues which will continue to develop in the future.

The discussion is in two unequal sections: the first, and longer, looks at the changing shape of *publicly* funded legal services; the second considers more briefly developments relating to the control of cost and the *private* funding of litigation and other legal services. It also asks whether there are alternatives to litigation which would be more appropriate.

Publicly funded legal services

The changing face of legal aid

When the Welfare State emerged in legislative form after the Second World War, one measure introduced by the then Labour government was the Legal Aid Act 1949. There are many accounts of the history of this fundamentally important development; only an outline is given here. Initially, the scope of the legal aid scheme was limited to *civil legal aid*—the provision of legal representation in proceedings taken in the civil courts. It subsequently developed to embrace:

- *criminal legal aid*—funding representation in criminal cases, eventually including a scheme for the provision of legal advice in police stations;

- a '*green form scheme*' designed to permit the provision by lawyers of legal advice and assistance on any matter of English law; and

- '*assistance by way of representation*' (ABWOR) which permitted in a limited number of circumstances the lawyer to extend assistance under the green form scheme to the provision of some representation.

Despite these developments, policy on legal aid was the subject of fierce debate:

- Notwithstanding its potentially wide coverage, in practice civil legal aid was used primarily to fund litigation on matrimonial matters and on personal injuries/accidents. Other areas of social law, for example housing or social welfare provision, were largely ignored by legal aid practitioners.

- The provision of legal aid was subject to means-testing—it went only to those falling below certain income and capital limits. When the first Legal Aid Act was passed it was estimated that nearly 70 per cent of the population was potentially entitled to legal aid. However, as the costs of legal aid increased, one of the mechanisms used by government to restrain levels of public spending was to make the means tests meaner; the percentage of the population covered was severely reduced.

- New forms of legal service delivery—in particular through law centres, which began to develop in the late 1960s—were excluded from funding by the legal aid schemes, save where such centres took on individual cases that qualified for legal aid.

- There were many fora in which legal aid was just not available at all. In particular, there was no legal aid for proceedings before the majority of the tribunals established to deal with disputes between the citizen and the state. (*see Chapter 6*).

- From the government's point of view it was hard to control public expenditure on legal aid. It was a 'demand-led' service—the government was committed to paying for all those cases in which the individual established an entitlement to legal aid.

- There were also worries about the quality of some of the work undertaken. Any legal practice could offer to do legal aid work, irrespective of the level of expertise on the issue in question in the firm.

Successive governments tried to reform the legal aid scheme in ways that would deliver a wider range of services to the public, without public expenditure on legal aid reaching unacceptable levels.

The first change followed the Legal Aid Act 1988. This transferred responsibility for the administration of the scheme from the Law Society to a new government agency, the Legal Aid Board. The Board tried to address the problem of providing a quality service by establishing a franchising scheme. Firms of solicitors could obtain a franchise only if they passed a special quality audit process. Under the scheme, solicitors were able to obtain a franchise in one or more of ten franchise categories.[1] Some 2,900 firms of solicitors obtained at least one of the available franchises.

In addition, the Legal Aid Board began a series of pilot studies to test the viability of franchises being awarded to agencies other than solicitors' firms, such as advice agencies, which might provide legal advice and assistance to the same standards as solicitors' firms.

In 1997, the Legal Aid Board started to award contracts to franchised firms for the provision of defined categories of legal services. Firms with contracts were able to deliver legal services with reduced bureaucracy. Instead of having to submit claims for each item of legally aided work, they were able to deliver their services (and get paid for so doing) within the framework of the contract. A number of legal aid services had to be offered on the basis of a fixed fee, rather than the traditional method of charging by the hour.

However, these measures were felt still to be inadequate to address the paradox of ever rising costs, without any significant expansion in the range of services that were funded by the legal aid scheme.[2]

---

[1] These included: criminal, family, personal injury, housing, and social welfare. A clinical negligence franchise was developed in February 1999.

[2] Although costs rose by 48 per cent in a six-year period, the numbers of people assisted rose by only seven per cent. Indeed expenditure on civil and family legal aid rose by 42 per cent while the numbers of people assisted fell by 30 per cent.

The Access to Justice Act 1999, which came into effect in 2000, made further changes. The Legal Aid Board was replaced by a new body—the Legal Services Commission. Legal aid was 'rebranded' as two new services: the *Community Legal Service* (CLS) and the *Criminal Defence Service* (CDS).

Notwithstanding all these changes, expenditure on legal aid continued to rise during the first decade of the 21st century, even though, in recent years, the legal aid budget has not been 'demand-led' but has been capped. Current annual expenditure is over £2.1 billion, a *per capita* level of expenditure well above that in other advanced countries.[3] In practice, the majority of legal aid, around £1.2 billion, is spent on criminal legal aid; the rest goes on civil legal aid—principally family legal aid.

The present Coalition government, seeking to make considerable savings in public expenditure, has targeted legal aid for very significant cuts. These changes are provided for in the Legal Aid, Sentencing and Punishment of Offenders Act (LASPO) 2012. As usual, the Act only sets out the broad framework of the new scheme. The detail will emerge as regulations made under the new law are published.

One important decision is known. When the legal aid provisions of LASPO come into force in April 2013, the Legal Services Commission is abolished. Administration of legal aid is transferred to a new agency within the Ministry of Justice, headed by a specially designated Director of Legal Aid Casework. The details of exactly how the new agency will operate are not at the time of writing known. For present purposes it is assumed that the broad administrative structure created by the Legal Services Commission remains in place.

The other crucial decision is that, the *scope* of the legal aid scheme, particularly civil legal aid, is seriously narrowed.

Community Legal Service: civil legal aid

Many people obtain advice on legal problems, not by going to see a solicitor, but by visiting one of the over 1,500 Citizens' Advice Bureaux, law centres, and other independent advice agencies that it is estimated exist in England and Wales.

These services often have lawyers or other professionally qualified staff attached to them. Around 6,000 people with a variety of qualifications work in these agencies, supported by nearly 30,000 unpaid volunteers. They deal with over ten million inquiries each year and receive around £250 million from a wide variety of sources of public funding, from both central and local government.

The services that these agencies offer have developed haphazardly, often in response to specific local initiatives. Coverage throughout England and Wales is patchy. In some areas, there is under-provision, with no effective service at all. In others, there may be a number of agencies offering very similar services, with a consequent waste of scarce resources—both cash and manpower. The aim of the Community Legal Service was to rationalize existing provision and to create a network of services for the whole country.

---

[3] See <www.justice.gov.uk/downloads/statistics/mojstats/international-legal-aid-comparisons.pdf>.

Funding Code

Funding for the Community Legal Service is provided under the terms of a *Funding Code*. This sets out the detailed framework within which publicly funded legal services are delivered. It was last revised in October 2007. Originally, funding was 'demand-led'. Now the Community Legal Service operates within fixed budgets; a sum is fixed at the start of the financial year, which must be rationed throughout the year.

In 2011–12, the Commission held 1,711 (previous year: 2,039) contracts to undertake civil work, covering 2,557 (2,903) solicitors' offices. In addition, there were 265 (296) contracts with not-for-profit agencies, covering 431 (491) offices.

Priorities

In shaping the detail of the scheme, the Legal Services Commission took into account priorities set by the Lord Chancellor (section 6(1) of the Access to Justice Act 1999). They include:

- proceedings under the Children Act 1989 for which legal aid was formerly available without either a means or a merits test;
- civil proceedings where the life or liberty of the client is at risk;[4]
- housing and other social welfare cases that enable people to avoid or to climb out of social exclusion;
- domestic violence cases;
- cases concerning the welfare of children; and
- cases alleging serious wrongdoing, breaches of human rights, or abuse of position or power by a public body or servant.

Exclusions

Only legal services for individuals may be funded under the scheme. Services for firms or other types of non-individual legal persona (e.g. partnerships or clubs) cannot be provided under the scheme. In addition, certain types of legal service were excluded from the scheme altogether. These include:

- services relating to allegations of *negligently*[5] caused injury or death, though not allegations of clinical negligence (the reason for this is that it is assumed that personal injury cases are suitable for conditional fee agreements (CFAs) (*see Conditional fee agreements*));
- cases relating to injuries caused by negligence, even where the legal claim is not cast in terms of the law of negligence (e.g. tripping cases, where the local authority is alleged to be in breach of a statutory duty to maintain the highway);

---

[4] This was the principle that led to the extension of legal aid to hearings before the Asylum and Immigration Tribunal.

[5] The exclusion does not extend to cases of injury arising from an alleged assault or deliberate abuse.

- other areas excluded because they have been judged not to have sufficient priority to justify public funding. These include allegations of negligent damage to property;[6] conveyancing; boundary disputes; matters of trust law or the making of wills; and matters arising from company or partnership law or the running of a business, where risks should be covered by insurance;
- representation in cases involving defamation and malicious falsehood.

Notwithstanding the general exclusions, help relating to making a will may be available to a person over 70, or a disabled person or a parent or guardian of such a person who wishes to provide for that person, and in certain cases involving those under the age of 16.

More generally funding of matters otherwise excluded might nonetheless be possible:

- where the matter is only incidental to an issue for which funding is permitted, or where the issue is brought into the proceedings by someone who is not being assisted by the scheme; or
- where there are two distinct claims, one of which is an excluded matter, but where it is impossible or impracticable to deal with them separately and the Commission thinks they cannot be funded by a conditional fee agreement or in some other way;
- where issues relating to boundaries, trusts, or company or partnership law arise in funded housing proceedings or funded family disputes or proceedings they may be funded even though they are more than incidental to the principal proceedings;
- conveyancing services where they arise in the course of other funded proceedings, or to give effect to a court order or agreement to settle;
- furthermore, and notwithstanding the general exclusion of personal injury negligence claims, some help may be made available in such cases if the costs of the claim are exceptionally high (and thus likely to deter insurers or those offering CFAs);
- cases that involve a wider public interest may also exceptionally be included even though they would otherwise fall in the excluded categories;
- the broad exclusion of funding services for representation before coroners' courts and tribunals is retained.

Exclusions following the Legal Aid, Sentencing and Punishment of Offenders Act 2012

The principle of excluding categories of work from civil legal aid is taken much further by the LASPO. From April 2013, civil legal aid is still routinely available in

---

[6] Housing disrepair cases brought by a tenant against a landlord are not excluded, as the property is not owned by the claimant.

civil and family cases where people's life or liberty is at stake, or where they are at risk of serious physical harm, or immediate loss of their home. For example, legal aid is retained for asylum cases, for debt and housing matters where someone's home is at immediate risk, and for mental health cases. It is retained for cases involving domestic violence or forced marriage. And it is retained for cases where people seek judicial review, for some cases involving discrimination that are currently in scope, and for legal assistance to bereaved families in inquests, including deaths of active service personnel. The extremely complex details are set out in Part 1 of Schedule 1 to LASPO.

But the original aim of the legal aid scheme—that it should be possible to get legal aid and advice on any matter of English law—is abandoned. Instead, taking further the exclusions already introduced to the scope of legal aid, there is a much narrower scheme that directs reduced resources only to those issues that are regarded as having sufficient priority to justify the use of public funds, subject to people's means and the merits of the case. Many types of case no longer routinely qualify for legal aid funding. The details are set out in Part 2 of Schedule 1 to LASPO. (For the impact in family law cases, see *Chapter 7, Reform of legal aid*.)

Legal aid funding may still exceptionally be provided for individual cases through a new funding scheme for excluded cases, but generally only where it is necessary to meet wider domestic and international legal obligations.

Objectives of the Community Legal Service

Under section 4(2) of the Access to Justice Act 1999, the Community Legal Service had five broad objectives. These are the provision of:

(1) general information about the law and legal system (e.g. leaflets in supermarkets or the creation of legal websites);

(2) help by giving advice about how the law applies in particular circumstances (e.g. initial advice at a Community Advice Centre or Citizens' Advice Bureau);

(3) help in preventing or settling or otherwise resolving disputes about legal rights and duties (e.g. the provision of more detailed assistance, such as telephone calls or letter writing or even some representation by a solicitor);

(4) help in enforcing decisions by which such disputes are resolved; and

(5) help in relation to legal proceedings not relating to disputes.

To ensure quality, all service providers must obtain a quality mark relevant to the type and level of service they are offering.[7]

---

[7] For details, see, <www.legalservices.gov.uk/civil/how/quality_mark.asp>. A quality mark scheme for barristers was launched in September 2002. A quality mark standard for mediation in family law was launched in January 2003.

Service levels

There are currently eight service levels:[8]

- legal help;
- help at court;
- family help (lower);
- family help (higher) (*see Chapter 7*);
- legal representation (investigative help);[9]
- legal representation (full representation);
- family mediation; and
- such other services as are authorized by the Lord Chancellor.

The Legal Services Commission and the government have sought to direct funding away from the provision of representation in court, towards the provision of legal advice services that do not require the use of lawyers in court.

Means test

Clients entitled to funded services must demonstrate that they are financially eligible—in other words they are subject to a means test.[10] Where applicants fall below a lower threshold, they pay nothing. If they fall between a lower financial threshold and a higher one, the provision of a funded service is subject to the funded client making a financial contribution towards the cost.[11] In addition, where the proceedings are designed to obtain an award of damages or other financial provision, any award of damages is subject to a 'charge' in favour of the Community Legal Service fund.

Under LASPO, further changes are envisaged. All civil legal aid applicants will undergo an assessment of their available capital, including those on welfare benefits. Greater account will also be taken of the equity in people's homes when assessing their capital means. A minimum £100 contribution to their legal costs will be introduced for all successful applicants with £1,000 or more disposable capital, and higher contributions will be expected from those who currently contribute to their legal fees.

Merits test

The general approach is that funding should be available only where a reasonable private paying client would be prepared to fund the case. Thus account must be taken of

---

[8] The details are set out in the Funding Code, see <www.legalservices.gov.uk/civil/guidance/funding_code.asp>.

[9] This is available where the size of the claim is likely to exceed £5,000 or where the strength of a case needs to be assessed; it may lead to full representation.

[10] The provision of information and the provision of services to proceedings under the Children Act 1989 are outside this rule. Funding in family cases is discussed in *Chapter 7, Funding family law cases*.

[11] Legal Help, Help at Court, and Family Mediation are not subject to the making of a contribution.

whether the proceedings would be cost-effective;[12] and there must be an assessment of the prospects of success.[13] Cost–benefit ratios are to be determined by relating the likely costs to the percentage prospect of success.[14] Funding is refused in cases where a conditional fee agreement should be obtained. There are special rules for cases against public bodies that raise human rights issues. Where a court has given permission for a judicial review case to proceed to a hearing, there is a presumption that legal services funding will be granted, so long as the client is within the financial threshold.

Very expensive cases

To prevent a large proportion of the Community Legal Services fund being expended on a relatively small number of very expensive cases, a Special Cases Unit controls the costs of such cases. Cases likely to exceed £25,000 in costs are referred to the Unit. Special arrangements also apply to multi-party actions, where a large number of claimants are claiming loss from a single event or cause.

Alternative dispute resolution

Alternative dispute resolution is funded where this may be more effective than court proceedings. Where complaints procedures or ombudsman schemes are available that might be appropriate to resolve the problem in question, funding is not considered until these have been exhausted.

Criminal Defence Service: criminal legal aid

The Criminal Defence Service (CDS) is the other legal service introduced by the Access to Justice Act 1999. The Legal Services Commission had to secure the provision of legal advice, assistance, and representation for those suspected of committing a criminal offence and thus under investigation, or actually facing criminal proceedings[15] in court.

There are four principal components of the CDS:

(1) the provision of criminal defence services in police stations and magistrates' courts through contracts with private-practice solicitors' firms;

---

[12] In framing the Funding Code's provisions on these matters, the Legal Services Commission is required to take into account the *statutory factors* which are set out in s. 8(2) of the Act.

[13] This criterion does not apply to many housing cases or cases with a wider public interest. The Legal Services Commission is advised on the public interest by a Public Interest Advisory Panel.

[14] E.g. where prospects of success are 80 per cent or better, the likely damages must exceed the likely costs; where the prospects of success are 60–80 per cent, the likely damages must exceed likely costs by 2:1; where prospects of success are 50–60 per cent, likely damages must exceed likely costs by 4:1.

[15] 'Criminal proceedings' are defined to include not only criminal trials, appeals, and sentencing hearings, but also extradition hearings, binding-over proceedings, appeals on behalf of a convicted person who has died, and proceedings for contempt in the face of any court: Access to Justice Act 1999, s. 12. The Lord Chancellor has power to add to this.

(2) the provision of a national network of police station and magistrates' court duty solicitor schemes. This includes a national telephone advice service, CDS direct;

(3) the management of individual case contracts with defence teams for very high cost criminal cases; and

(4) the provision of services directly to the public through the Public Defender Service (PDS).

A key difference from the Community Legal Service is that the CDS remains a demand-led, rather than a cash-limited, service.[16]

The bulk of legal services provided under the CDS are provided by solicitors in private practice. All such firms have to have a contract to provide such services with the Legal Services Commission. At 31 March 2011 there were 1,640 (1,733 at 31 March 2010) criminal contracts covering 2,309 (2,418) solicitors' offices.

Launched in 2001–02, the salaried PDS was designed to:

- provide independent, value-for-money criminal defence services to the public;

- provide examples of excellence in the provision of criminal defence services nationally and locally;

- provide the Commission with benchmarking information to be used to improve the performance of the contracting regime for private practice suppliers;

- raise the level of understanding within government, including the Lord Chancellor's Department and all levels and areas of the Commission, of the issues facing criminal defence lawyers in providing high quality services to the public;

- provide the Commission with an additional option for ensuring the provision of quality criminal defence services in geographical areas where existing provision is low or of a poor standard;

- recruit, train, and develop people to provide high quality criminal defence services, in accordance with the PDS's own business needs, which will add to the body of such people available to provide criminal defence services generally; and

- share with private-practice suppliers best practice in terms of forms, systems, etc., developed within the PDS to assist in the overall improvement of CDS provision.

Originally, eight offices were opened, which in 2004–05 dealt with 4,500 cases. Clients are not compelled to use the PDS in areas where it exists; they can choose between the PDS and solicitors with contracts from the Legal Services Commission. Thus PDS offices must compete with private suppliers. The PDS was reviewed in the light of experience, and from 2007, the number of offices was reduced to four. In 2011–12 it opened 3,197 files.

---

[16] Access to Justice Act 1999, s. 18. It is this principle that leads to loss of resources for the Community Legal Service while the costs of the CDS rise substantially.

The creation of the CDS was the subject of fierce debate in Parliament. Critics argued that:

(1) it meant that the better off, who do not rely on publicly funded legal aid, had complete freedom of choice over who should represent them, leading to an unacceptable distinction between services for the better off and the less well off. However, there was an opposing argument, that those providing legal services paid for out of public funds should be able to demonstrate basic levels of professional competence—which limiting provision to those with contracts is designed to achieve—so that there will be some guarantee that public money is not wasted on the incompetent or inexperienced; and

(2) there was some evidence from the United States[17] that public defender schemes do not work as well as they should in defending the interests of the accused or suspect. There were worries that if the predominant form of provision in England were to become the public defender system, this would lead to a less competent mode of delivering criminal legal services. While this might be a problem were the publicly funded service to become the sole mode of delivering this form of legal service, this is certainly not currently the situation.

The current arrangements are more streamlined than the former, often highly fragmented, provision in which a person might get advice in the police station under one funding scheme, advice in the solicitor's office or in prison under another, and representation in court under yet a third. The new criminal law contracts provide for a single service from arrest until completion of the case. Nevertheless, the CDS has continued to attract criticism.

First, it is criticized by the legal profession, who argue that it does not offer a sufficient level of remuneration to enable practitioners to remain in business. However, a review of the procurement of legal services in 2006, under the chairmanship of Lord Carter of Coles, recommended substantial changes to the procurement system for criminal legal services to achieve maximum value for money and control over spending, whilst ensuring quality and fairness in the criminal justice system, primarily by greater use of fixed fees. The Commission also developed a preferred supplier scheme, designed to offer benefits to providers who provide significant amounts of high quality legal services.

Secondly, there was criticism that criminal defence services were being provided without a means test. There were a number of high-profile cases where apparently very wealthy individuals received substantial aid from the scheme. Means-testing had been used before but had led to two problems. It was wasteful of money; means-testing is an expensive process. And it added to delay, in that a trial could not proceed until the issue of representation had been sorted out. Notwithstanding these criticisms, the

---

[17] See McConville, M., and Mirsky, C. L., 'Criminal Defence of the Poor in New York City' (1986–87) 15 *New York University Review of Law and Social Change* 581–964.

government decided to reintroduce means-testing. The Criminal Defence Service Act 2006 provided for this, which it was hoped would save about £35 million a year.

Thirdly, decisions on funding criminal defence in magistrates' courts were taken by magistrates, not the CDS. It was felt this hampered the ability of the Legal Services Commission to control the costs of the CDS. The Criminal Defence Service Act 2006 also provided for these decisions to come under the control of the CDS.

Criminal legal aid: impact of LASPO

By comparison with civil legal aid, criminal legal aid emerges from LASPO *relatively* unscathed. Criminal legal aid is retained for those criminal cases where it is currently available, in order to ensure that those accused of more serious criminal offences can access the representation required to provide a fair trial.

However, changes will be made to the way that lawyers are paid. The original intention was to move towards a competitive market to replace the current system of administratively set fee rates. This was fiercely contested by criminal legal aid lawyers, and the Lord Chancellor announced that any plans to move to the competitive tendering of criminal legal services are to be put on hold. Nevertheless, a series of proposals has been designed to achieve savings. These include proposals to pay the same fee in respect of a guilty plea in the Crown Court regardless of the stage at which the plea is entered. In Crown Court cases that could realistically have been dealt with in the magistrates' court, it is proposed to pay a single fixed fee for a guilty plea based on fee rates in the magistrates' court. This complements other reforms to the justice system designed to encourage cases to be brought quickly and efficiently to justice, so sparing the justice system significant but avoidable costs.

To contain the growth in costs of Very High Cost Criminal Cases (VHCCCs) it is proposed to bring the arrangements for solicitors in VHCCCs into line with those the previous government introduced for advocates. This will mean that more of these cases will be paid within a graduated fee scheme where costs are more easily controlled.

Future prospects: from Commission to Agency

Since its creation, the Legal Services Commission has, notwithstanding the criticism directed at it, been responsible for developing a network of legal services in partnership with other funders such as local authorities and central government. It has also been innovative. The Commission introduced a number of important changes:

- First, it enabled appropriately qualified 'lay advice and assistance agencies' (not-for-profit agencies) to receive public funding for the provision of certain types of legal services, in addition to lawyers working in private practice.

- Secondly, it introduced a new unified contract so that all service providers operate on the same terms. (These have been replaced by 'standard' crime and civil contracts.)

- Thirdly, the Legal Services Commission developed new models for the delivery of legal services. It makes considerable use of information technologies to provide advice on legal problems through its CLS and CDS Direct services, which have both a website and a call centre phone advice line. It is also possible to use an interactive digital TV facility.

- The Commission also piloted new models for the delivery of legal assistance through Community Legal Advice Centres (CLACS) and Community Legal Advice Networks (CLANS). The first CLAC opened in Gateshead in 2007; four other CLACS have opened, in Derby, Hull, Portsmouth, and Leicester. The first CLAN opened in the East Riding of Yorkshire in March 2010. Research had shown that many people do not have single problems, but clusters of problems. The intention is that those requiring advice should be able to obtain it as far as possible from a single point of contact, rather than being referred to a number of different advice agencies.

- In all this, the Commission was seeking to shift from a historic emphasis on funding litigation to a greater emphasis on funding advice and assistance to prevent cases coming to court in the first place. (Of course, this is less easy to achieve in the context of criminal cases than civil cases.)

- The search for value for money led, following Lord Carter of Coles' review of the ways in which the Commission procured its legal services, to much greater use of services being provided on a fixed or graduated fee basis, rather than charging on the basis of hourly rates. Fixed fees for most categories of civil legal aid work were introduced in October 2007.

- Many areas of work have been subject to competitive tendering procedures.

What is not currently clear is the extent to which the new agency will be able to promote new ways for delivering legal advice and assistance. It is already clear that telephone services will be extended to help people find ways to resolve their problems. It is quite unclear whether the new models for the delivery of legal services, promoted by the Legal Services Commission, will be sustained by the new agency.

Predictably, the government's proposals were strongly criticized by both solicitors and barristers. They condemned the measures for undermining the principle that a just society demands that there should be access to justice for all.

It can be anticipated that, particularly on the civil legal aid side, the proposed changes are going to make a significant difference to the provision of legal advice and assistance. Despite the emphasis on the provision of advice, many advice agencies that currently have contracts with the Legal Services Commission risk loss of funds and thus the ability to deliver legal advice services.

Yet there is little doubt that, in England and Wales, expenditure on legal aid is higher than that in other countries. Given the fact that cuts look inevitable, questions must be asked as to whether the ways in which legal advice and assistance has been delivered in the past have been as economically efficient as they could be. Why cannot modern communication technologies be used to give basic advice to those who need it? Does advice always have to be given in law offices? Are the procedures currently used for determining particular types of dispute the best that can be devised? Are courts needed for all the processes that they currently undertake? Are there ways in which members of the public can be assisted to help themselves?

It should not be assumed that there are any easy answers to these and other questions that may be raised about the potential impact of cuts in legal aid expenditure. What may be asserted, however, is that the proposed cuts provide a stimulus to thinking about new ways of delivering legal services to ordinary people. It is in this context that the future becomes very hard to predict. Re-engineering the ways in which the courts operate (*see Chapter 8*) and in which the legal (and related) professions organize themselves, following the Legal Services Act 2007 (*see Chapter 9*), are likely to combine with new rules relating to the funding of legal work, in particular litigation, to lead to types of legal service delivery quite different from current experience. The next section outlines some of the other ideas that have been considered in recent years to control the costs of going to court as well as ideas relating to new ways of funding legal advice and court proceedings.

Making litigation (more) affordable: other approaches

Changes to legal aid cannot be seen in isolation. Other means to reduce the cost of taking legal proceedings and other ideas for providing funding for taking legal proceedings have also been introduced or considered in recent years. Behind all these developments has been a desire to increase access to justice, while maintaining control of public expenditure. The challenge has been and remains to devise ways of enabling those who might want or need to litigate to do so without incurring disproportionate costs.

A number of developments are considered here:

- controlling costs;
- fixed fees;
- CFAs;
- litigation funding agreements;
- alternative procedures;
- the response of the legal profession; and
- other ideas—report from the Civil Justice Council.

Controlling costs

As noted in *Chapter 8*, Lord Woolf saw reduction in the costs of taking a case to court as a key objective in the reforms that he was proposing. There were two principal ways in which he envisaged that this objective might be achieved: making costs proportionate, and active case management.

Making costs proportionate

Before the Woolf reforms were introduced, the basic principle used to determine disputes about costs was that those charging the costs had to demonstrate that the costs they incurred were reasonable. Following the introduction of the Civil Procedure Rules (CPR), this principle was amended. The costs must be both reasonable *and* proportionate to the issue in dispute.[18] In cases where relatively small sums of money are involved, it might well be reasonable for a number of legal steps to be taken in preparing the case, but if the cost of taking those steps was substantial, the total costs, while reasonable, might still not be proportionate. A judge would therefore be required to disallow costs that, though reasonable, were not proportionate. The difficulties with this principle are obvious: What is reasonable? And what is proportionate?

Active case management

A second principle advanced by Lord Woolf and contained in the CPR is active judicial case management. This was designed to ensure that cases were dealt with more quickly. By preventing proceedings from dragging on, it was thought that the cost of litigation could be reduced. The problem here is that this objective is, to a significant extent, in conflict with other changes introduced in the CPR. Since the CPR also stresses the need for parties to put their cards on the negotiating table earlier than they used to, this means that cases which, prior to the introduction of the Woolf reforms, would have settled well before any trial was likely to take place, now require more work to be done at an early stage. This leads to a 'front-loading' of expense, which increases the costs of such cases.

While there has been generally broad support for the Woolf reforms, there was considerable evidence that the goal of cost reduction has yet to be achieved. In 2009, a new inquiry, led by the Court of Appeal Judge Sir Rupert Jackson, was launched. It had the wide remit of examining the whole question of taking civil proceedings in the courts. His final report was published in January 2010. It is extremely long and detailed. For some of the main findings, *see The Jackson Review and plans for reform.*

Fixed fees

A second strategy for controlling costs is greater use of fixed costs for bringing cases to court. This is in effect a variation of the principle of proportionate costs. In this context, the Civil Justice Council, which advises the government on issues relating to the civil justice system, led a series of discussions with practitioners and the insurance industry to try to make some of the costs of litigation more predictable. It was accepted, at least initially, that a fixed costs regime would not work in every litigation

---

[18] The details are set out in CPR Part 44—general rules about costs.

context. Nonetheless, the Council thought it right to explore whether there were situations in which fixed costs would be reasonable.

In 2003, this approach resulted in the creation of a scheme for the use of fixed fees in relation to claims arising out of road traffic accidents for less than £10,000. These apply where liability for the accident is admitted, and where the only issue is the exact amount to be paid to settle the claim. The principle of predictable costs has been extended to the success fees to be applied in employers' liability cases and industrial disease cases. It is one of the issues that was taken further by Lord Justice Jackson.

Conditional fee agreements

A third way of facilitating the bringing of litigation was the development of the CFA. This has been around for over 20 years, long before Lord Woolf started his work, having been introduced by the Conservative government in 1990. A CFA is defined in section 58 of the Courts and Legal Services Act 1990, as amended by section 27(1) of the Access to Justice Act 1999, as 'an agreement ... which provides for ... fees and expenses, or any part of them, to be payable only in specified circumstances'—in effect 'no-win, no-fee'.

The importance of CFAs was significantly increased by the Access to Justice Act 1999. It became a principle that Community Legal Service funding should not be provided in cases where alternative funding (including CFAs) is available.[19] (CFAs cannot be entered into in relation to criminal and most family proceedings.)

CFAs allow solicitors to take a case on the understanding that, if the case is lost, they will not charge their clients for all or any of the work undertaken. But the client also agrees that if the case is successful, the solicitor can charge a *success fee* on top of the normal fees, to compensate for the risk the solicitor has run of not being paid all or some of her fees in cases that are not successful. The success fee is calculated as a percentage of the normal fees and the level at which the success fee is set reflects the risk involved. Regulations provide that the 'uplift' of the success fee should be no more than 100 per cent of the normal fee.

Until 1999, the success fee was paid out of damages recovered. Since 1999, the law was amended so that the success fee had to be paid by the party against whom a costs order has been made (in essence the losing party) in addition to any damages that may have been awarded. The same party also has to pay the costs of any after the event insurance (ATE) premium.

The party who loses an action now faces the prospect of considerable costs. Since most of those represented under CFA agreements do not have the resources to pay those costs, ATE insurance is designed to cover them. This change to the funding of litigation meant that where a person covered by insurance lost, the insurance

---

[19] See the *statutory factors* in the Access to Justice Act 1999, s. 8(2). This criterion did not apply in all cases, e.g. housing cases.

company was liable not only to meet the costs of the other side, but also the 'success' fee and the ATE premium.

While CFAs arguably provided a means for enabling people to go to court who might not otherwise have been able to contemplate such a step (and in this sense increased access to justice), they are open to a number of forms of abuse, which were identified by the late Lord Bingham in his judgment in *Callery v Gray* [2002] 1 WLR 2000 at [5], HL:

(1) Lawyers may charge excessive costs knowing that their own client will not have to pay them; the costs burden thus falls quite disproportionately on the losing party. Where that party is an insurance company, this has the effect of forcing up insurance premiums.

(2) Lawyers may set the success fee at a level that is grossly disproportionate to any fair assessment of the risk involved in the case.

(3) Insurers may charge premiums grossly disproportionate to the risk being underwritten.

All these problems were acknowledged by Lord Justice Jackson who recommended that success fees and after the event insurance premiums should no longer be recoverable from the losing party. He saw them as being the greatest contributor to disproportionate costs.

Litigation funding agreements

Section 28 of the Access to Justice Act 1999 introduced a new concept, the *litigation funding agreement*. This allows a party to be funded by a third party (rather than the solicitor), for example a trade union or other prescribed group. In these cases the funder pays the solicitor's normal fees. However, where the case is won, the funder was entitled to be paid the success fee by the losing side and was able to retain that element of the fee to cover losses on cases that are not won.

Alternative procedures

Although not usually considered in this context, there have been a number of important policy initiatives that have effectively taken the potential for litigation away from the courts and provided a completely alternative procedure for the resolution of disputes. The most notable example is the role of the Financial Services Ombudsman, which now resolves the vast bulk of disputes concerning the private customers of financial institutions, up to a value of £150,000—considerably more than many of the cases that come before the courts (*see Chapter 8, The reform of civil justice: new developments*). In a different context, the scheme for tenancy deposit protection established by the Housing Act 2004 offers a free dispute resolution service where landlords and tenants are in dispute about how a tenancy deposit should be divided at the end of a tenancy.

Large numbers of consumer disputes are resolved either by the complaints departments of large companies or through the work of different trade associations representing various providers of goods and services. Some of these bodies are entirely
self-regulated; others are underpinned by statute. Similarly, mediation as an alternative form of dispute resolution (*see Chapter 8, Alternative dispute resolution*) has
been promoted at least in part on the basis that it offers a less costly way of resolving
disputes.

The lesson here is that effective ways of avoiding much of the expense of going to
court can be achieved by the creation of procedures that take place outside the court
context. The common feature of all these alternatives is that they are provided either
free or at very low cost for those who seek to use them.

The response of the legal profession

There is also evidence that the legal profession is having to respond to the challenge
of the cost of dispute resolution. In addition to the used of fixed fees in the context of
legal aid and certain classes of relatively modest claim, the profession is moving away
from its traditional reliance on hourly charge out rates to offer legal services on a more
pre-determined basis. There is market pressure to deliver more for less.

In addition, the pro bono activities of the legal profession should also be mentioned (*see Chapter 9, For free (pro bono) work*). This has been driven by the recognition that many lawyers have done extremely well out of the way in which legal
services are currently delivered. There is a good moral case for them to give something back to the community; this has been recognized by the leaders of the legal
profession.

In the same context, it is worth noting that many law-teaching institutions have
developed different forms of clinical legal education, which offer legal advice and
assistance to members of the public. One of the most long-standing is the Free
Representation Unit promoted by young barristers and student barristers. The main
professional law course providers, such as the University of Law and BPP, now offer
pro bono options, which large numbers of law students participate in. A number of
university law schools—for example, Warwick, Kent, and York—run law clinics that
take in cases from members of the public. In addition, Street Law is a project developed
in the United States, but now brought to the United Kingdom, in which law students
in a large number of universities offer information about legal rights to community
groups and members of the public.

Other ideas: Civil Justice Council

While the developments listed earlier might be welcome, they did not really represent
a coherent package of changes to the funding and delivery of legal services. In 2009,
the Civil Justice Council published an important advisory paper urging that consideration be given to a number of ideas for additional funding.

Firstly, it recommended a *Supplementary Legal Aid Scheme*, based on a model developed in Hong Kong, which provides legal aid to a wider group of people than the current scheme. This requires those who have received assistance from legal aid to pay a levy into the scheme either from the damages they recover or the costs they recover, which can then be used to fund further activity. A somewhat similar idea has been developed by the Bar Council for a Contingent Legal Aid Fund, under which funds would be provided for advancing a case, and where—if the case was successful—a percentage of damages secured would be returned to the Fund.

Secondly, and anticipating Jackson, the Council argued that there should be a move from conditional fees to *contingency fees*. This is the principle used not only in the United States, but also every Canadian province save Ontario. The key feature of contingency fees is that lawyers get their fees by taking a percentage out of the damages recovered by their own clients. The Civil Justice Council argued that initially this should only be used in multi-party claims arising out of a single set of events. Experience might lead to consideration of extending contingency fees to other classes of case.

The third idea advanced by the Council is *third party funding*. Here an investor buys the right to conduct litigation on behalf of a claimant or, more usually, a group of claimants. The funder recovers the cost of the investment by taking a percentage of damages or costs recovered, as agreed at the outset. This process, sometimes called 'claim-farming', has been developing in a number of other jurisdictions notably in Australia.

The Jackson Review and plans for reform

Against this background of concern about the cost of taking court proceedings and worries that this was reducing access to justice rather than enhancing it, Lord Justice Jackson undertook his review of civil litigation costs. It is worth noting that the review was sponsored by the senior judiciary, not the government. It was the judges who were particularly concerned about the impact of costs on access to justice.

Jackson's final report was published in January 2010. The report itself is extremely detailed and hard to summarize; the response of the government has been equally complex. Here a summary of the principal issues is offered:

(1) Jackson reasserted the importance of the principle of proportionality; the costs system should be based on legal expenses that reflect the nature/complexity of the case. Of course, the challenge remains of how proportionality is to be decided in particular cases.

(2) Jackson wanted much greater use of fixed costs. He proposed that the current regime of fixed fees should be considerably extended so that fixed costs should be

set for all 'fast track' cases (those with a claim up to £25,000) to provide greater certainty of legal costs.

(3) He argued for the establishment of a Costs Council to review annually fixed costs and lawyers' hourly rates, to ensure that they are fair to both lawyers and clients.

(4) He made detailed recommendations for changes to the CFA regime.

(5) To offset the effects of this for claimants, general damages awards for personal injuries and other civil wrongs should be increased by ten per cent.

(6) Jackson further proposed what is called 'qualified one way costs shifting'. This would create an exception to the normal rule that the loser of an action pays the costs of the winner. Under his proposals, claimants, whose claims are unsuccessful, would only make a small contribution to defendant costs (as long as they had behaved reasonably). This would remove the need for them to purchase after the event insurance.

(7) He recommended that referral fees should be scrapped—these are fees paid by lawyers to organizations that 'sell' damages claims to them but offer no real value to the process (apart from making the referrer better off).

(8) Jackson wanted lawyers to be able to enter into contingency fee agreements (as opposed to CFAs), under which if a claim is successful lawyers are paid a percentage of actual damages won, rather than a sum based on the cost of the work undertaken.

(9) Jackson also argued for much greater promotion of 'before the event' legal insurance, encouraging people to take out legal expenses insurance, either on a 'stand-alone' basis or as part of another insurance purchase, such as household insurance.

Jackson argued that his proposed reforms should be seen as a whole and not 'cherry-picked', asserting that they provided a coherent framework whereby parties could enter into litigation with greater certainty about the costs involved. He argued that they would also assist in allowing for some claims to be resolved earlier with greater use of mediation.

His suggestions provoked considerable controversy, particularly among legal practitioners. The Coalition government has not been persuaded to adopt his recommendations wholesale. However, important changes have been made, and further changes are in the pipeline. LASPO implements a number of Jackson's recommendations. These include:

- abolition of referral fees;
- abolition of the principle of recoverability of success fees and ATE insurance from the losing party (this applies to litigation funding agreements as well as contingency fee agreements);

- allowing damages-based agreements (also known as contingency fees) in litigation before the courts.

However, the government has not reached a final view on other issues. It is consulting further on some of Lord Justice Jackson's other recommendations, including the proposed ten per cent increase in general damages, and the introduction of a mechanism to protect the vast majority of personal injury claimants from paying a winning defendant's costs through qualified one-way costs shifting.

The government has also announced that there will be proposals to further encourage parties to make and accept reasonable offers (by amendment to CPR Part 36; *see Chapter 8, Payments into court and offers to settle*), as well as introducing a new test to ensure that overall costs are proportionate. It is also proposed to increase the costs that can be recovered by people who win their cases without representation by lawyers.

The government has not directly responded to the recommendation for the greater promotion of before the event insurance. The proposed reductions in publicly funded legal aid may, to an extent, prove the incentive for more people to cover possible legal expenses through private insurance. The obvious problem with this outcome is that the very poorest cannot afford such insurance.

Nor has the government yet come to a view on whether there should be a Supplementary Legal Aid Scheme or a Contingent Legal Aid Fund, though Jackson has continued to argue for this reform.

The legal services industry itself has taken forward proposals for the third party funding of litigation. An industry group—the Association of Litigation Funders—has devised a code of conduct to which litigation funders must adhere. The concerns Jackson identified in relation to third party funding were: would funders have an adequate capital base to provide their funding; funders should not be entitled to withdraw funding during the proceedings; the ability of funders to influence litigation and settlement of proceedings should be restricted and defined with clarity. The code of practice deals, adequately in Jackson's view, with all these matters.

The question of whether the cost of proceedings can be made more reasonable by changes in the courts is currently the subject of a separate consultation on the role of the county court in civil proceedings, outlined in *Chapter 8*.

Conclusion: the challenge of funding legal services

Access to justice is essential if the claim to have an efficient legal system is to be sustained. We have seen in this chapter that the availability of legal aid, particularly in civil matters, is currently being seriously cut back.

Debate on legal aid was, in the past, dominated to a large extent by the legal profession. The legal aid scheme was largely designed and developed by the Law Society.

While there should be no doubt that those who undertook this work were determined to create a scheme that delivered a needed service to the public, it is also the case that the legal profession was the principal beneficiary of it. The injection of over £2 billion of public money into the legal profession is not trivial. The rate of growth of public expenditure in this area—despite rhetorical claims that 'justice is without price'—could not be sustained.

Put another way, if policy-makers had started the legal aid scheme from scratch with a budget of over £2 billion, would they have devised the legal aid scheme that eventually developed? Those who accept that the answer to this question must be 'no' must then think what the shape of any alternative might be.

At present, it looks as though criminal legal aid, which during the last decade had been criticized for taking the lion's share of the available resources, has emerged from the current reform proposals *relatively* unscathed. (I am sure many practitioners would disagree with this view.) But civil legal aid, which in my view had been the most innovative area for the development of legal services, is badly hit. This has already led to a number of suggestions for different ways of delivering legal services on civil legal matters. It looks inevitable that the balance between funding by the state and other private sources of funds will alter. How newly emerging business entities offering legal services will respond to the new environment is, at present, impossible to foretell. However, it is worth noting that there have been many occasions in the past in which lawyers, having failed to preserve some then current practice (e.g. the conveyancing monopoly), have, once they realize that they have lost the argument, responded in imaginative and unexpected ways to regain ground that would otherwise be lost to other providers.

My hunch is that the delivery of legal services for civil matters will also develop more positively than many critics of the current changes presently fear. In particular, it is likely that there will be much greater use of different forms of insurance to spread the risk of litigation whilst ensuring that there are income streams available to fund litigation.

At the same time, and although this will be resisted fiercely by legal practitioners and the judiciary, there is likely to be much greater emphasis on the individual undertaking dispute resolution without the benefit of professional legal assistance. In turn, this could lead to a sharp debate about the continuing viability of the adversarial litigation process which is currently at the heart of the English legal system.

Questions

Use the self-test questions on the Online Resource Centre to test your understanding of the topics covered in this chapter and receive tailored feedback:

www.oxfordtextbooks.co.uk/orc/partington13_14/

Weblinks

Check the Online Resource Centre for a selection of annotated weblinks allowing you to easily research topics of particular interest:

www.oxfordtextbooks.co.uk/orc/partington13_14/

Blog items

 See www.martinpartington.com (access via the Online Resource Centre)

Items considered include: a summary of the Legal Aid, Sentencing and Punishment of Offenders Bill 2011 and LASPO; the Jackson report and government responses to it; public legal education; pro bono lawyering; mediation; the reform of legal aid; new ways to fund litigation; handling litigants in person in the courts.

Further reading

Davis, G., Donkor, K., and Morgan, R., *Ethnic Minorities' Legal Needs and Perceptions of Legal Services: Report of a Pilot Investigation for the Law Society* (London, The Law Society, 1993)

Department for Constitutional Affairs and the Law Centres Federation, *Legal and Advice Services: A Pathway to Regeneration* (London, Department for Constitutional Affairs, 2004)

Genn, H., *Paths to Justice* (Oxford, Hart Publishing, 1999)

Goriely, T., and Das Gupta, P. (with Bowles, R.), *Breaking the Code: The Impact of Legal Aid Reforms on General Civil Litigation* (London, Institute of Advanced Legal Studies, 2001)

—— Moorhead, R., and Abrams, P., *More Civil Justice? The Impact of the Woolf Reforms on Pre-action Behaviour* (Research Study 43) (London, Law Society (and the Civil Justice Council), 2002)

Kempson, E., *Legal Advice and Assistance* (London, Policy Studies Institute, 1989)

Legal Action Group, *A Strategy for Justice: Publicly Funded Legal Services in the 1990s* (London, Legal Action Group, 1992)

Legal Services Commission, *Making Legal Rights a Reality* (London, Legal Services Commission, 2005)

Legal Services Research Centre, *Causes of Action: civil law and social justice. The final report of the first LSRC survey of justiciable problems* (2nd edn, London, Legal Services Commission, 2006)

Ling, V., and Pugh, S., *Making Legal Aid Work: A Handbook for Practitioners* (London, Legal Action Group, 2009)

Lord Chancellor's Advisory Committee on Legal Education and Conduct, *Setting Standards for Community Legal Services* (London, Lord Chancellor's Department, 1999)

Regan, F., and others, *The Transformation of Legal Aid: Comparative and Historical Studies* (Oxford, Clarendon Press, 1999)

Steele, J., and Seargeant, J., *Access to Legal Services: The Contribution of Alternative Approaches* (London, Policy Studies Institute, 1999)

CONCLUSION

11

Is the English legal system
fit for purpose?

Introduction

At the start of this book, the question was posed: is the English legal system currently fit to meet the demands placed upon it? In subsequent pages, many issues have been considered: What are law's functions? How is law made? What are the contexts in which it is practised? Who are the different actors in the legal system? How are legal services funded? The book has raised a number of specific issues about the fitness of the legal system to achieve its apparent purposes.[1] In my blog,[2] I also posit a number of images of law that those coming new to the study of law may have about, law, lawyers, and the legal system. In this last chapter I want to reflect a little further on some of these questions. This chapter does not provide definitive answers but raises matters not specifically considered earlier. It is designed to encourage readers to think critically about the issues that have been raised.

As we have noted, law plays a variety of functions, not necessarily consistent with each other, in the organization of modern society. Countries where the rule of law is less well established than in the United Kingdom may be seen to be at a disadvantage. In the globalized economy, countries able to demonstrate commitment to the rule of law are at a distinct advantage over countries that cannot. However, the world is going through a period of rapid and considerable change. Is the English legal system able adequately to respond to this changing world?

Images of law

The images of law offered in my blog suggest that those without direct experience of law or lawyers can come to the study of law with preconceptions about the legal system that are at best limited, at worst seriously distorted. The chapters in the book

---

[1] Just by way of example, *see Chapter 7, Child support*, for comments on child support.
[2] www.martinpartington.com.

have demonstrated that there is much more to the legal system than crime; that those providing legal services are far more varied in character than the fat-cat lawyers sometimes portrayed in the press; that both the institutions of the legal system and those who deliver legal services are undergoing profound change; that problems of inefficiency and delay, particularly in the litigation process, are increasingly acknowledged and are being addressed.

In recent years, institutional innovation was driven at least in part by the former government's modernization agenda, and its response to social pressures—such as antisocial behaviour. The new Coalition government has different priorities and is currently very concerned with controlling public expenditure. This will have significant impacts on the institutions of the legal system. But innovation is also a response to the needs of an increasingly global economy, which contribute substantially to the pressure for institutional change. In the past, leaders of the legal profession have, on occasion, appeared resistant to change as they sought to defend the interests of practitioners who feared an uncertain future and were unwilling to embrace change. Today, they are more open to the need for change and to respond to the consumers of legal services. Indeed, many individual practitioners and firms of lawyers have shown considerable dynamism and imagination in reshaping their practices to meet clients' needs and wider pressures.

Many other indicators suggest that negative images of law and the legal system are unfair. There is still a great desire on the part both of professionally qualified lawyers and other legal advisers to deliver legal services to all sections of the public, not just the well-heeled and powerful. Standards of education and training of lawyers and other advisers have increased greatly in recent years. There is widespread commitment to high ethical standards. The judiciary is notably free of corruption.

But to stop at this point would risk the complacent conclusion that the English legal system is the best in the world, requiring at most only modest further adjustment. The fact is that there are many other issues on which one can be more critical. It is important that those coming to the legal system for the first time think about those features that can be criticized. The future development of robust legal institutions lies at least in part in the hands of those now entering the legal system.

One key problem is the treatment of legal issues in the mass media. Apart from the drama of the big criminal trial or a scandal involving a miscarriage of justice, discussion about law in the mass media is not well-rounded. With notable exceptions such as the BBC radio programme, *Law in Action*, or the weekly law pages in some of the broadsheet newspapers, and related online blogs, together with a number of consumer programmes that touch on aspects of the law, there is little rounded discussion about law-making, the practice of law, or the impact of law on the citizen. Unlike other aspects of our intellectual life, such as history, science or medicine, law is not regularly the subject of mainstream media programming.

Yet the centrality of law to different social orders suggests that the media neglect of law and legal issues is unsatisfactory. Programme makers may feel that law is too complex a subject to make it attractive for mass programming. But this failure simply contributes to the mystique of law and enhances the power of the lawyer in society, at a time when arguably opportunities for greater general understanding of and access to law should be growing. There are signs that this may change a little. In 2010 there were two excellent TV programmes on the new Supreme Court. Sky News offers live coverage of Supreme Court proceedings. And the Coalition government has announced plans for more widespread televising of some forms of court proceedings.

However, there are no plans to televise criminal trials. This happens a great deal in the United States. There was a notable experiment in the United Kingdom when a number of trials in Scotland were shown in edited form on television. However, while such a step might give the appearance of greater openness of the legal system to the public, it should be remembered that televising trials may merely serve to exacerbate current images of law—that the typical legal process is a criminal one, in which there is a lengthy trial of the case for and against the accused. We know from *Chapter 5* how *untypical* such cases are. There is no discussion about televising cases in the administrative justice, family justice, or civil justice arenas; or programmes dealing with the vast majority of cases that are resolved without a full-scale trial.

Part of the reason public discussion of legal issues is so limited may be that those who operate within the legal system themselves have shown only limited interest in presenting their work to a wider audience. Much professional legal activity is conducted on the basis of secrecy and confidentiality, which may result in a lack of individual enthusiasm to enter the public eye. Furthermore, there are those in the legal profession who think that it goes against the professional grain to seek publicity for their work. However, a consequence of such attitudes is that the law and its practitioners tend to hit the headlines only when things have gone wrong.

Considerable effort is these days spent placing stories in the media which form part of the public relations activity of individual legal firms or practices. Lawyers and other practitioners should also be willing to shape a more educational public information agenda, and to work with the media to develop opportunities for a fuller understanding of law and the legal system in all our lives. The difficulties of making a wider range of programmes about law may be substantial; nevertheless, the challenge remains to provide a new, more informed, treatment of legal issues in the mass media. This could play an important part in the shaping of public perceptions about the legal system and those who work in it, which could in turn contribute to making the legal system function more effectively. The fact that the Legal Services Board has public legal education on its statutory list of tasks is a welcome recognition of the importance of this issue.

In addition to the treatment of law in the media, there are important questions still to be resolved about patterns of recruitment to and career development in the legal profession. Although there are now greater opportunities for women to become lawyers than was the case some years ago, they have not yet achieved their full potential to rise to the most senior positions. In addition, the improvement in the opportunities for women to enter law has not been matched by comparable increases in the opportunities for those coming from working-class or ethnic minority backgrounds.[3]

---

[3] The issue was considered in Chapter 3 of Alan Milburn's Report (2012), see <www.cabinetoffice.gov.uk/sites/default/files/resources/IR_FairAccess_acc2.pdf>.

Given the importance of equality of treatment in the delivery of legal services, it is important that those running the profession and the institutions of the law take issues of recruitment and advancement seriously. The Legal Services Board has this issue on its agenda.

Law's functions

A wide range of issues about the social functions of law were considered in *Chapter 2*. In relation to many of these, readers have their own views, not all of which can be canvassed in an introductory work. The tension between the use of law to control and regulate behaviour and the use of law to protect people by giving them rights and entitlements was particularly emphasized.

The issue that arises out of that discussion, which bears most fundamentally on the question whether the English legal system is fit for purpose, is whether there is now too ready a recourse to the use of law to try to deal with the issues facing modern society. There are occasions on which politicians and others pay lip-service to the proposition that law should not be used to regulate human activity more than absolutely necessary. But there are few incentives *not* to make law. Politicians' and civil servants' reputations are based on the laws they create, not those that they prevent. And the reputation of practitioners is enhanced by their pushing at the boundaries of law, as they try to establish new areas of legal liability, not by seeking to limit the scope of law. The Human Rights Act 1998 has added to these pressures. Certainly the amount and complexity of the law that emerges from government and the courts are constantly increasing.

In this context, the proposition that ordinary citizens can in any real sense be assumed to know the law that governs their lives is just not tenable. While it may not be realistic to complain that there is too much law, the implications for law-makers and others involved in working the legal system in providing better information about law are clear. The Legal Services Commission started to invest in the provision of useful information about the law and its procedures on the internet. Other agencies are also increasingly using this as a source of information. But lack of usable information remains a weakness in the current institutional arrangements of the legal system. As with the challenge of providing better general information about law through the mass media, there is still a considerable challenge to be faced, particularly within government, about the use of new information and communication technologies to make information about citizens' rights available to a much wider public than is presently the case. Initiatives around public legal education, much better developed in some other countries (e.g. Canada), should also be welcomed and strongly supported in the United Kingdom.[4]

---

[4] <www.lawforlife.org.uk/>. Also noteworthy is the fantastic 'democracy live' website, part of the BBC News website; it is an amazing source of information about developments in all four UK governments and the European Union.

Law-making: legitimacy and authority

The primary law-making bodies today are the legislative institutions of the United Kingdom and the European Union. Both claim to derive legitimacy for the exercise of legislative powers from political theories of democracy. However, the extent to which ordinary people understand the nature of such assertions of legitimacy must be open to doubt. The processes of Parliament are poorly understood; those of the institutions of the European Union are shrouded in even greater mystery. There is great ignorance about the links between institutional assertions of legitimacy and the democratic will of the people. Even less clear is the relationship between majority opinion and the protection of minorities—a key issue in modern pluralist societies.

There is evidence that this is beginning to be taken seriously. Many of the institutional and constitutional reforms, both in the United Kingdom and in Europe, are influenced by an increasing acknowledgement that voter apathy is not a satisfactory basis on which to claim legitimacy for the exercise of law-making power. At some point, unless more is done to encourage people to understand that, for example, elections are important, there is a danger that those theoretically governed on the basis of consent may come to deny the legitimacy of their governors to govern. The decision to introduce instruction on citizenship into the school curriculum (in England, but not Wales) is a recognition of the importance of this issue.

A likely trend in the next decade is much greater effort by government institutions to explain what they are doing and to encourage input into the law-making process.[5] Many of the recent procedural innovations to the law-making machinery in the United Kingdom—considered in *Chapter 3*—reflect this need. Questions remain, though: do these changes go far enough? Should recent procedural changes in both the UK and European Parliaments be taken further? Should there be further changes to the electoral system? To what extent is there a 'democratic deficit'? If there is such a deficit, what measures are needed to reduce it? Should there be greater opportunities for lobbyists and other groups to influence the shape and content of legislation?

The law-making functions of the judges are also under intense scrutiny, particularly since the coming into force of the Human Rights Act 1998. So far, English judges have been very restrained and have not used the 1998 Act to usurp the essentially political functions of Parliament and the executive to deliver its legislative agenda. Some voices are being heard that the judges have been too timid; others argue quite the opposite. It is impossible to predict how the judges will respond to such pressure, though they are likely to continue to take a cautious line for some time yet.

In any event, most governments would claim that they already operate within both the spirit and the letter of the European Convention on Human Rights. But a moment's reflection indicates that, in difficult cases, there is potential for considerable

---

[5] In fact, a vast amount of consultation already goes on between government and groups in society; indeed, some complain of 'consultation fatigue' as yet another consultation exercise arrives in the post or email. But it is important that, whatever the problems, governments continue this trend.

tension to develop between the legislative and executive branches of government and the judicial branch. If a significant political/legislative objective is declared incompatible with the European Convention on Human Rights by the courts, whether in the United Kingdom or in Strasbourg, this may at best result in embarrassment for the government, at worst in considerable frustration. There is a powerful argument that adherence to human rights standards by government should be in general a political responsibility, not a judicial one.

Experience in the United States, where the Supreme Court has long asserted a power to review legislation in the context of the Constitution of the United States and the Bill of Rights, may suggest that the impact of the UK courts on the legislative process has been limited. Experience in other countries—for example Canada—suggests that such a view may be too sanguine. Whichever way the British judiciary goes, it seems inevitable that the constitutional role of the judiciary will become the focus of sharp debate in the years ahead.

This leads to a broader question: has the time come for the creation of a written constitution, which seeks to provide specific legitimacy for the different branches of government, and the systems of checks and balances that should operate to preserve the rule of law and prevent abuse of power?

Notwithstanding all the procedural changes, there remain many practical questions about the law-making process that still need addressing. For example, where there is agreement that a particular rule of law needs changing, the problem of parliamentary time means that this cannot be achieved as easily as it should be. A significant number of Law Commission reports remain unimplemented. Where the common law lacks clarity or certainty, the ability of the judiciary to develop legal principle is dependent on the right case being brought before it. Should special procedures, either in Parliament or before the courts, be made more readily available to change law that is clearly unsatisfactory?

A different issue relates to styles of legislative drafting. One of the reasons legislation, in particular, is so hard to understand is that legislative draftsmen seek to define everything in legislation—whether primary, secondary, or tertiary—with a very high degree of linguistic precision. This leads to very considerable complexity. In turn this raises the question whether a more 'plain English' approach to the drafting of statutes might be appropriate. Certainly, the Civil Procedure Rules were drafted on the basis that they should be easier to read and understand. And there are lawyers who have signed up to the Plain English Campaign's[6] initiative for clearer drafting of legal documents. The question of the extent to which such initiatives should spread more widely into legislative drafting practice is being considered.

In fact, legislative drafting styles change. An Act or a bill drafted today is very different from one drafted 25, 50, or 100 years ago. Currently, the focus is on getting the architecture of an Act right so that the reader can acquire more easily a sense of what the legislation is seeking to achieve. This is supported by the new practice of publishing

---

[6] See <www.plainenglish.co.uk/>.

explanatory notes. A particular difficulty is to know whether new drafting practices would lead to more or less legislative uncertainty. It is likely that, to be fully effective, radically new legislative drafting practices would have to be supported by the senior judiciary.

Justice and efficiency

The chapters in *Part II* reveal a number of common themes. Most prominent is the pressure in all justice systems to deal with cases as expeditiously and as economically as possible. These are perfectly proper aims, but nevertheless raise the question of the extent to which the shaping of the legal system should be driven by demands for efficiency and value for money, as opposed to other demands, such as the need for the justice system to be just. While unnecessary delay and expense must be deplored, it should still be asked whether current trends to dispose of cases rapidly or even to divert them completely from courts and other dispute-resolution fora always operate in the interests of justice.

These issues cannot be addressed by vague assertions that 'justice has no price'. Justice clearly does have a price, which has to be paid for either by the citizen or by the state (whose resources come from the taxpayer). At the same time important principles relating to the need for fairness of the trial process must be borne in mind. There must be some doubt, especially in the context of criminal justice, whether the apparently increasing focus on the 'crime control' model of criminal justice is compatible with a 'due process' model. If taken too far, the question will arise whether the system will be compliant with the human rights standards set down in the European Convention on Human Rights.

Another set of issues relates to avenues of appeal. In the context of the criminal justice system, for example, some of the recent serious cases of miscarriage of justice seem to have been exacerbated, at least in part, by the rather restrictive bases on which the Court of Criminal Appeal may determine criminal appeals. The creation of the Criminal Cases Review Commission was designed in part to assist. Will this be enough to prevent further serious miscarriages of justice? What other mechanisms are needed to ensure both that the innocent are not convicted and sentenced, and that those who have committed offences are brought to trial?

In relation to administrative justice and civil justice, the question was raised whether there were too many avenues of appeal and complaint for the individual to pursue. Changes to appeal routes in the civil justice system have reduced the number of appeals that can be brought in that context. The reform of the tribunal system may be the first step in a more fundamental review of the administrative justice system. It may be asked whether the current sharp distinctions between courts and tribunals will exist in ten years' time.

One issue that affects the whole of the institutional framework of the English legal system is whether all citizens, and particularly members of ethnic minorities, feel that they are dealt with fairly. Following the Stephen Lawrence case,[7] a major programme of research on the experience of those from the minority groups in all parts of the legal system was undertaken. On the whole, little overt discrimination was found. But the issue must be kept under review. If the legal system is revealed as being unable to deliver equal treatment to all those who come into contact with it, this will be a concern of the utmost importance which will have to be dealt with urgently.

One pressure for change not considered in the main text is a set of ideas currently being developed within the policy-making bodies in Europe that might lead towards the development of a more European-wide court system. There could be some merit in these ideas. If the European Union encourages greater freedom of movement of its citizens around the different countries of Europe, should it not also enable those citizens to enforce their rights in the country of their choice? However, for many the very idea of such integration would be anathema. This is not an idea that is currently well-developed and has certainly not been widely discussed. It is not pursued further here. But it is an issue to which attention needs to be drawn. Were such moves to be seriously contemplated, the major distinctions between the British common law approach to law and the Continental European civil law approach would be likely to prove a major hurdle to the integration of judicial systems. It is in this context that the suggestion of the need for closer legal integration between the common law countries of Europe, principally the United Kingdom and Ireland, might gain more significance.

Professional organization

Chapter 9 considered a number of questions relating to professional organization. It considered the increasing part played by government in seeking to regulate standards of professional activity. It was suggested that this could prove a worrying trend. Although there is no suggestion that government is seeking to limit the independence of the professionally qualified lawyer to take up controversial or unpopular cases, this does not mean that this could not happen at some future time if the trend towards greater government intervention accelerates further.

What is also not clear is the extent to which the new opportunities created by the Legal Services Act 2007 to set up new forms of partnership between legal and other professionals, or to develop alternative business structures, with capital investment coming from outside the legal profession, will lead to change in the professional organization of the legal profession. What is clear is that there will be change in the

---

[7] See <www.guardian.co.uk/uk/1999/feb/23/lawrence.ukcrime9>.

ways lawyers do their work. The profession that new students of law will face will be quite different from that of their parents' generation.

Funding legal services

The final issue addressed in the book is whether arrangements for funding legal services will—in some general sense—'work'. Here there is considerable uncertainty. The new arrangements for legal aid and related ideas for alternative ways of funding litigation are too recent for any definitive conclusion to be reached.

Those who in recent years have predicted a complete breakdown in the provision of quality legal services to the public have so far been confounded. Practitioners who have faced up to cuts in legal aid budgets are developing new service delivery models. Such changes are having a big impact on the legal profession, particularly small firms or sole practitioners in small towns or rural areas, where it is hard for them to generate the levels of business needed to stay afloat financially. There will have to be more mergers and consolidations to increase business efficiency that have already taken place at the more commercial end of the legal professional market.

It also seems inevitable that the line between legal services and lawyers' services will become even more blurred, with more legal services being delivered by those without formal professional legal qualifications. There are likely to be more profound challenges to the assumption that the adversarial model of litigation is best.

Conclusion: fitness for purpose

Much of the English legal system is pretty fit for purpose, but it is by no means perfect. There is always room for change and improvement. Those coming new to law should seek to support what is good, but not seek to defend the indefensible. The discussion in these pages is designed to encourage the thought and action needed to bring about necessary change while preventing undesirable change.

Blog items

See www.martinpartington.com (access via the Online Resource Centre)

Items considered include: the Protections of Freedoms Act 2012; public legal education; reporting of legal issues in the media; resources for teachers; young people and the legal system; court dress.

INDEX